# AMERICAN APPEASEMENT

ARNOLD A. OFFNER

# American
# Appeasement

UNITED STATES FOREIGN
POLICY AND GERMANY,
1933-1938

The Belknap Press of

Harvard University Press

CAMBRIDGE, MASSACHUSETTS

1969

*80161*

FOR ELLEN

# PREFACE

Crisis at home and abroad seems to be the prevalent state of modern society, and this condition was especially characteristic of the 1930's. The administration of Franklin D. Roosevelt, from the moment of its inauguration, confronted the consequences of the Great Depression and the challenges that Germany and Japan posed to international stability. Historians of the era have tended to focus first on the domestic reform of 1933–1938, and only later have they turned full attention to foreign affairs, especially the events in Asia that precipitated United States entry into the Second World War.

Germany under Adolf Hitler, however, did not wait for other nations to alleviate their domestic problems, and during 1933–1938 the Roosevelt government had to deal with successive crises that undermined European and ultimately American security and contributed significantly to the tragedies that soon engulfed the world. For the United States, the "German problem" was difficult and ironic. In the 1920's Americans had used diplomacy and dollars energetically to reintegrate Germany into the Western political and economic community, and German diplomats had emphasized good relations with the United States as one means of revising the Treaty of Versailles and altering the balance of power in Europe.

From the historical record—and the luxury of retrospect—we see that Hitler's accession to power and the dynamics of National Socialism quickly made inappropriate or irrelevant many traditional assumptions about problems old and new. At the time, honest men could and did differ about the nature of the problems they faced and the solutions that were needed. The record also makes clear that some men were more prescient than others, and that American and European diplomats for a variety of reasons missed opportunities to shape events to the benefit of their own and later generations. The following book is a history of America's role in the appeasement of Germany during the European crises of 1933–1938.

I am happy to acknowledge the many people and institutions that have helped me with my research and writing. The staff at the Franklin D. Roosevelt Library at Hyde Park facilitated research in the President's papers, as well as those of R. Walton Moore; quotations from the latter are by permission of Mrs. Fairfax S. McCandlish. The staff at the National Archives assisted me with the records of the Department of State, and the staff at the Manuscript Division of the Library of Congress aided in the use of numerous collections. Martha Dodd has generously allowed me to quote from the papers of her father William E. Dodd, and quotations from the papers of Jay Pierrepont Moffat and William Phillips are by permission of the Harvard College Library. I am grateful to the University of Delaware Library for permission to cite from the George S. Messersmith papers; to the Cornell University Library for permission to quote from the papers of Jacob Gould Schurman; and to the Columbia University Library for permission to use the Theodore J. Marriner papers and the Oral History Collection Memoirs of Claude Bowers, William Phillips, and John C. White. The Tamiment Library of New York University Libraries put the Baruch Charney Vladeck papers at my disposal, and citations from the papers of the Joint Boycott Council are courtesy of the Manuscript Division, The New York Public Library, Astor, Lenox and Tilden Foundations. Permission has been granted by Barry Bingham, Sr., to quote Robert W. Bingham; by Patricia Bowers to quote Claude Bowers; by Jack I. Straus to quote Jesse Straus; and by Hugh R. Wilson, Jr., to quote Hugh R. Wilson. The staff at the Cornell University Library provided a neighbor with many books sometimes hard to come by, and the Syracuse University Library purchased numerous reels of microfilm to serve my special interest.

The American Council of Learned Societies helped support my research with a summer grant-in-aid, which was supplemented by the Maxwell Graduate School and the Paul H. Appleby Research Fund of Syracuse University. Syracuse University also generously afforded a semester's leave of absence to allow me to conclude my writing.

Ernest R. May of Harvard University gave me a thoughtful and challenging critique of the manuscript, and Max Hall, Editor for the Social Sciences at Harvard University Press, has provided decisive criticism, encouragement, and patience over several years.

My debt to Robert H. Ferrell of Indiana University is incalculable.

It has been my privilege to join the increasing number of historians who have derived so many precious advantages from his knowledge and his facility with language. He has read and improved more drafts than I care to admit I have had to make his burden, and enlightened in a spirit of scholarship and friendship that I cherish.

I must acknowledge my daughter Deborah, whose arrival made conclusion of this work more difficult than I had anticipated but all the more rewarding. I cannot imagine having proceeded without my wife Ellen, whose editorial skill and unfailing humor have sustained and shaped every aspect of this book.

Errors of fact or judgment are my responsibility.

A.A.O.

*Boston, Massachusetts*
*September 1968*

# CONTENTS

# CONTENTS

# AMERICAN APPEASEMENT

## ABBREVIATIONS IN THE NOTES

*DBFP*    E. L. Woodward and Rohan Butler, eds., *Documents on British Foreign Policy, 1919–1939*

*DDF*    Ministère des Affaires Etrangères, *Documents Diplomatiques Français, 1932–1939*

*DGFP*    U.S. Department of State, *Documents on German Foreign Policy, 1918–1945*

DS    U.S. Department of State files, National Archives, Washington, D.C.

*FDRL*    Elliott Roosevelt, ed., *F.D.R.: His Personal Letters, 1928–1945*

*FR*    U.S. Department of State, *Foreign Relations of the United States*

GFM    Microfilm records of the German Foreign Ministry, National Archives, Washington, D.C.

*PPFDR*    Samuel I. Rosenman, comp., *The Public Papers and Addresses of Franklin D. Roosevelt*

PSF    President's Secretary's File, Franklin D. Roosevelt papers, Franklin D. Roosevelt Library, Hyde Park, N.Y.

For full descriptions, see Bibliographical Essay.

# 1. GOOD YEARS TO BAD

The letter was difficult to write, especially for a man who had spent a quarter-century in his country's foreign service. There was no turning back, though. Friedrich W. von Prittwitz und Gaffron had been German ambassador to the United States for more than five years, representing the German cause, as he explained to his superiors, to the best of his ability and conscience. By March 1933 the world was on the threshold of a new era. Prittwitz sensed vaguely the changes that were to come, and recognized that he no longer had a role to play. He informed Germany's foreign minister, Konstantin von Neurath, that he could no longer function successfully in America and asked relief from his post. He reminded Neurath that a man "does not write such lines with a light heart."[1] Privately, he hoped that his ambassadorial colleagues in London and Paris, Leopold von Hoesch and Roland Köster, would follow his example as a rebuke to the Nazi regime.[2]

The diplomatic world scarcely noted Prittwitz' departure. The *New York Times* on March 20 devoted a few bland paragraphs to the resignation; the editors were delighted that the new ambassador, Hans Luther, a former German chancellor and recently resigned Reichsbank

1. Prittwitz to Neurath, Mar. 11, 1933, U.S. Department of State, *Documents on German Foreign Policy, 1918–1945*, series C, *The Third Reich: First Phase*, 5 vols. (Washington, D.C., 1957——), I, 147–148; hereafter cited as *DGFP*.
2. Friedrich von Prittwitz und Gaffron, *Zwischen Petersburg und Washington —ein Diplomatenleben* (Munich, 1952), 228.

president, stood for sound currency backed by gold. Appointment of such a man, they said, "argues strongly that the new regime in Germany is not contemplating anything startling or wild in foreign policy."

In some respects Adolf Hitler's appointment of Luther did portend more change than immediately evident. Nine years after the event, Hitler, in one of his bombastic conversations, declared that shortly after becoming chancellor he had talked with Luther and had been stunned by how little money the then president of the Reichsbank had been willing to make available to speed up German rearmament. He warned Luther that as they obviously could not collaborate, he would brook no opposition and, if necessary, "break" him. Shortly thereafter, Hitler recalled, at the suggestion of the state secretary in the Reich Chancellery, Otto Meissner, Luther was offered the ambassadorial post, which he accepted along with a bonus in his pension.[3] Luther himself later said that in 1933 he had recognized he could wield no influence at home and hoped to achieve more in Washington. Meissner recalled that Luther gave up his powerful and prestigious job at the Reichsbank "very much against his will."[4] In any event, the way was now clear for Hitler to appoint as Reichsbank president a financial wizard who was far more sympathetic to German rearmament expenditure, Hjalmar Horace Greeley Schacht.[5]

Americans found it difficult to believe that the changes of early 1933, even including Hitler's accession to power, could mean much. Relations between the United States and Germany throughout the 1920's had been cordial and frequently fruitful in finding solutions to difficult international problems. The anti-German hysteria in America touched off by the World War had subsided soon after the fighting. The debate

3. Entry for April 22, 1942, in *Hitler's Secret Conversations* (New York, 1953), 349–350.

4. Hans Luther, *Politiker Ohne Partei: Errinerungen* (Stuttgart, 1960), 420–421; Otto Meissner, *Staatssekretär unter Ebert-Hindenburg-Hitler: Der Schicksalsweg des deutschen Volkes von 1918–1945, wie ich ihn erlebte* (Hamburg, 1950), 270.

5. Actually American officials were not surprised by the change. Three days after Hitler's accession, Alfred Kliefoth, chargé ad interim in Berlin, reported that Schacht had told him that he wanted to be president of the Reichsbank and that Luther would be forced out. Kliefoth to Hull, Feb. 2, 1933, Department of State files, number 862.00/2894, National Archives, Washington, D.C.; hereafter Department of State unpublished records cited as DS, followed by file number.

over the Treaty of Versailles had hardly ended when Americans began to doubt German responsibility for causing the war. There soon appeared such works as Albert Jay Nock's *Myth of a Guilty Nation* (1922), which placed major responsibility for the war on France and Russia, and John Kenneth Turner's *Shall It Be Again?* (1922), which argued that President Woodrow Wilson had led America to war to preserve Wall Street. In December 1923 a liberal Democrat, Senator Robert Owen of Oklahoma, gave a forty-thousand-word speech which, like Nock's work, blamed France and Russia for causing the catastrophe of 1914.[6] Harry Elmer Barnes's *The Genesis of the World War* (1926) capped this kind of writing, insisting that prewar Germany was not as nationalist or imperial as was the Triple Entente—England, France, Russia. Sidney B. Fay's two-volume *The Origins of the World War* (1928) restored some balance, but was generally favorable to Germany.[7] By the end of the 1920's Germany's reputation in the United States was sound.

During all this discrediting of war and the Paris Peace Conference, many German-Americans made the most of their opportunity. Subjected to harsh treatment during the war, the largest foreign-born nationality in the country now formed such organizations as the Steuben Society of America, which grew rapidly, emphasized the contribution of German emigrants to American institutions, and distributed literature. The society republished Albert Bernhardt Faust's *The German Element in the United States: With Special Reference to Its Political, Moral, Social, and Educational Influence* (1927), a two-volume work of over twelve hundred pages extolling the German contribution to such American causes as abolition, civil service reform, sound money, peace congresses, and personal liberty.

Diplomatic reports from Germany during this era were highly encouraging. As early as January 1919 the head of a special State Department mission to Berlin reported that the Germans earnestly wanted

6. *Congressional Record*, 68th Cong., 1st sess., LXV, Part 1, pp. 355–399, as cited in Selig Adler, "The War-Guilt Question and American Disillusionment, 1918–1928," *Journal of Modern History*, XXIII (Mar. 1951), 9n61, 15.

7. Fay's book rested heavily on the German diplomatic record, *Die grosse Politik der europäischen Kabinette*, 40 vols. (Berlin, 1922–27). The British and French had not published anything comparable at the time; in the preface to his revised edition (1930) Fay said that their recent publications did not alter essentially his narrative or conclusions.

to resume prewar relations and hoped Americans would overlook the war and afford Germany sufficient financial aid for reconstruction.[8] The appointment of Alanson B. Houghton as ambassador to Germany in February 1922 (after the United States and Germany had negotiated the Treaty of Berlin of August 21, 1921, which gave Americans all of the benefits of the Treaty of Versailles but none of the liabilities) signified a revived interest in Germany. The chairman of the board of Corning Glass Works and a prominent contributor to Republican campaign coffers who had done graduate work in Göttingen, Houghton was sympathetic to the German point of view and interested in reviving trade.[9] In fact, the British ambassador in Berlin at this time noted in his diary that American businessmen in Germany were "pro-German," doubted German responsibility for the war, and virtually denied Germany's need to pay even reduced reparations.[10] About six months after his arrival Houghton did worry that radical groups had so fired up the populace against reparations and the Western powers that the nation was moving toward dictatorship and the "people seem to me to be slowly going mad."[11] But by the time he left Berlin in 1925 to take up a new post in London, he was convinced that militarism was dead in Germany and that the nation sought only economic rehabilitation in order to be a bulwark against Bolshevism.[12]

Houghton's successor, Jacob Gould Schurman, ambassador from 1925 through 1929, sent back glowing reports of a transformation from autocracy to democracy. Schurman had been president of Cornell University for nearly thirty years and took great interest in German academic affairs. Most recently he had served as minister to China, then

8. Reports by Ellis Loring Dresel in U.S. Department of State, *Papers Relating to the Foreign Relations of the United States, 1919: The Paris Peace Conference*, 13 vols. (Washington, D.C., 1942–47), II, 132–170.

9. Robert Gottwald, *Die deutsch-amerikanischen Beziehungen in der Ära Stresemann* (Berlin-Dahlem, 1965), 12–13; see also Dexter Perkins, "The Department of State and American Public Opinion," in Gordon A. Craig and Felix Gilbert, eds., *The Diplomats, 1919–1939* (Princeton, 1953), 305.

10. Viscount D'Abernon, *The Diary of an Ambassador: Rapallo to Dawes*, 3 vols. (Garden City, N.Y., 1929–31), II, 75.

11. Houghton to Charles Evans Hughes, Nov. 21, 1922, quoted in Merlo J. Pusey, *Charles Evans Hughes*, 2 vols. (New York, 1951), II, 580–581.

12. Selig Adler, *The Isolationist Impulse: Its Twentieth Century Reaction* (New York, 1957), 176.

torn by civil war. In contrast the Weimar Republic—among whose political and industrial leaders he moved easily—was attractive. President Paul von Hindenburg and other important officials, so Schurman wrote a friend in September 1925, had received him cordially; relations were "most intimate and friendly. I feel very great sympathy with the Germans and great admiration for their achievements."[13] Germany was doing "wonderfully well." Officials and citizens were working to meet their obligations and "the whole land today looks like a garden."[14] The foreign minister, Gustav Stresemann, Schurman reported to President Calvin Coolidge in March 1926, was "not only a statesman, but also a sagacious politican and an aggressive party leader."[15] Schurman spared no effort to reunite American scholars with German universities and persuade American financiers to invest in German business. He told the New York Chamber of Commerce in November 1928 that advocates of a socialized Germany or restoration of the old empire were destined to remain "solitary voices in the wilderness." Radicalism, he insisted, would never amount to anything.[16]

Throughout the 1920's the Germans sought American friendship, doubtless in part as a means to blunt French efforts at retribution. As early as spring 1921 the German government proposed that the United States determine reparation payments, but Secretary of State Charles Evans Hughes declined, although he did make a brief if unsuccessful effort at finding a basis for negotiations between Germany and the European powers.[17] The appointment of Otto Wiedfeldt, a member of the board of directors of Krupp Works, as ambassador in 1922 indicated a German desire to have a representative who could get along well with American businessmen. Wiedfeldt soon reminded his superiors that although the press and public opinion in America were generally favor-

13. Schurman to Reverend Luis Muirhead, Sept. 16, 1925, Jacob Gould Schurman papers, Regional History Collection, Cornell University Library, Ithaca, N.Y.

14. Schurman to Frank Thilly, Sept. 16, 1925, *ibid.*

15. Schurman to Coolidge (copy), Mar. 9, 1926, *ibid.*; see also Gottwald, *Ära Stresemann,* 105.

16. Text of speech, Nov. 1, 1928, Schurman papers; see also Adler, *Isolationist Impulse,* 177–179.

17. Perkins, "Department of State," in Craig and Gilbert, eds., *The Diplomats,* 304; Gottwald, *Ära Stresemann,* 12.

able, if the government in Berlin did not actively seek American good will the United States could quickly become less inclined to intervene in European politics in Germany's behalf.[18]

Germany needed and desired American intervention in Europe, especially when in January 1923 French and Belgian troops occupied the Ruhr after the Reparation Commission created at the Paris Peace Conference, on which the United States was not represented because it had not ratified the Treaty of Versailles, declared Germany in default of payment on its reparations assessment of $33 billion.

The Ruhr occupation provided American diplomats with opportunity to oppose the French policy of force by extending the peaceful influence of the dollar. Secretary Hughes for some time had been sounding European diplomats on forming a new committee to revise German financial liabilities, and in an address before the American Historical Association in December 1922 he had promised that distinguished Americans in private capacity would serve on it.[19] As soon as he learned of the French action on the Ruhr he announced that the few remaining American occupation troops would be withdrawn from Germany, and within three weeks the last of the soldiers were gone. The British too refused to support the Franco-Belgian maneuver. The Germans made the most of their opportunity and through passive resistance and reckless inflation thwarted the effort to collect. Finally, in November 1923, the Reparation Commission proposed two new committees—the first to handle budget and currency, the second to seek means of returning capital to Germany. Wiedfeldt told Hughes that progress was possible only if Americans served on the committees, whereupon Hughes suggested an invitation to Brigadier General Charles G. Dawes.[20] In the winter of 1923–24 the colorful Dawes, a now-forgotten conservative banker with a slapstick sense of humor, who symbolized the platitudes and prosperity of his decade, and Owen D. Young, president of the General Electric Company, went to Europe.

In a few months the negotiators in London hammered out the Dawes

---

18. Gottwald, *Ära Stresemann*, 13.

19. U.S. Department of State, *Foreign Relations of the United States, 1922*, 2 vols. (Washington, D.C., 1938), II, 199–202; hereafter cited as *FR*, followed by year, volume, page. See also Pusey, *Hughes*, II, 581–582.

20. Wiedfeldt to Hughes, Dec. 7, and Hughes to Herrick, Dec. 11, 1923, *FR 1923*, II, 104–105.

Plan, which the European powers agreed to carry out.[21] The Dawes Plan was not a final reparations solution but a five-year initial program which put reparations on a sliding scale based on German ability to pay. Included was a loan to Germany of $200 million, slightly more than half of which the United States was to provide. Although some bankers hesitated, Hughes assured them that political conditions in Germany were good and in a short while the rush to subscribe to the loan exceeded by ten times the required amount and banks had to allot subscriptions among eager applicants.[22] The diplomacy of the dollar worked well enough during the next few years. There seemed no end to the money Americans would pour into Germany, no end to Germany's ability to recover, organize, and produce.[23]

Economic prosperity seemed to bring political stability after 1925, and while Ambassador Schurman sent glowing reports from Berlin, German diplomats did all they could to ensure a favorable American view. In February 1925 the first president of the Weimar Republic, Friedrich Ebert, died. When Field Marshal Paul von Hindenburg succeeded him there was some worry in the United States about future German foreign policy. Under instruction, Ambassador Ago von Maltzan undertook a campaign to reassure Americans, and soon he reported to Berlin that people in Washington were speaking affectionately of "dear old Hindy."[24]

The Locarno treaties in October 1925 guaranteed the Franco-German and Belgo-German frontiers; established arbitration treaties between Germany and Poland and Germany and Czechoslovakia, and

21. Text of Dawes Plan, and brief report of the committee concerned with recovery of German capital, are in Harold G. Moulton, *The Reparation Plan* (New York, 1924), 139–308.

22. Herbert Feis, *The Diplomacy of the Dollar: First Era, 1919–1932* (Baltimore, 1950), 40–42.

23. Total American investment in Germany from 1924 through July 1, 1931, cannot be given precisely, but it was not less than $2.6 billion. John D. Hicks, *Republican Ascendancy, 1921–1933,* in Henry Steele Commager and Richard B. Morris, eds., *The New American Nation Series* (New York, 1960), 143. The State Department did not adopt an official policy about American investment in Germany, although occasionally it questioned some short-term loans and the usefulness of other investments. See, e.g., *FR 1926*, II, 205–210, and *FR 1927*, II, 728–730.

24. Gottwald, *Ära Stresemann*, 40–45.

Franco-Polish and Franco-Czech treaties for mutual assistance in case of German aggression; and provided for German entry into the League of Nations. American diplomats were delighted with these developments; Ambassador Houghton even thought that the resulting political security would provide France with conditions necessary for financial stability.[25] The "spirit of Locarno," illusory though it was, permeated the Western world right down to the just as illusory Kellogg-Briand Pact of August 1928, which grandly provided for renunciation of war as an instrument of national policy. Then, in February 1929, with the Dawes Plan soon to expire, Owen D. Young went to Europe again, gathered the experts, and prepared a final solution to reparations: payment of $8 billion over fifty-nine years at 5½ per cent interest. The Reichstag passed the laws necessary to implement the plan in March 1930, and in June the last French occupation troops left the Rhineland.[26]

Germany had reaped dividends from cooperation with the United States, and diplomats like Ambassador von Prittwitz, for example, wished to continue the policy. Typically, at the end of 1930 he warned his government not to deviate from the Weimar course of the last years or else foreign policy would suffer.[27] In February 1932 Consul General Otto Kiep extolled not only the American credit that had helped rebuild Germany but also what he considered to be such pioneering efforts in international arbitration as the establishment of the Mixed Claims Commission to determine war damages recoverable by American citizens.[28] And at the end of that year Consul General Otto Vollbehr reminded his Foreign Ministry that the United States was "not

25. *Ibid.*, 48–49, 59, 106; Houghton to Schurman, Aug. 24, 1925, Schurman papers.

26. Andreas Dorpalen, *Hindenburg and the Weimar Republic* (Princeton, 1964), 156–161. See also Harold G. Moulton and Leo Pasvolsky, *War Debts and World Prosperity* (New York, 1932), 71–108, and Edward W. Bennett, *Germany and the Diplomacy of the Financial Crisis, 1931* (Cambridge, Mass., 1962), 6–8.

27. Prittwitz to Bernhard von Bülow, Dec. [n.d.], 1930, in Prittwitz, *Zwischen Petersburg und Washington*, 219–221.

28. Text of Kiep speech at a dinner in honor of Sir Norman Angell, Feb. 18, 1932, microfilm records of the German Foreign Ministry, serial 5747/frames HO33841–HO33845, National Archives; hereafter cited as GFM, followed by serial/frame numbers.

only the best friend, but actually the only friend which the Reich has in international society."[29]

Nevertheless, in 1930–1933 American relations with Germany faltered. In October 1929 German Foreign Minister Stresemann died and Americans experienced the crash on Wall Street. The ensuing Great Depression made diplomacy almost unworkable. For Germany the stock market collapse meant the drying up of foreign, chiefly American, loans. In March 1930 Heinrich Brüning, a conservative nationalist of the Catholic Center, became chancellor. His government, a minority regime, faced an extraordinarily difficult task amidst the spiraling depression and the increasing allure of the tunes of even the most bizarre Pied Pipers. Nor is it clear that Brüning, however honorable his intentions, pursued the wisest domestic or foreign policies. In mid-July he dissolved the Reichstag after a no-confidence vote on his effort to implement new tax measures through decrees, powers granted by President von Hindenburg. To everyone's astonishment, in the voting on September 4 for the new Reichstag Hitler's National Socialist German Workers' party (NSDAP) gained nearly 6½ million votes and increased its deputies from 12 to 107, making it second only to the Social Democrats. As the American chargé in Berlin, George A. Gordon, reported, there was now loose in Germany a "dangerous mentality" which had dealt a "body blow" to the Republic. Germany's decline could not "be lightly overlooked or explained away as some elements —including certain official circles—seem to be evincing a not unnatural tendency to do." A short while later, Gordon wrote, political parties between extremes of Right and Left seemed to have learned nothing from the elections: they proceeded as before, "jockeying, bickering, and bargaining."[30]

To a large and perhaps disastrous extent Brüning sought to exploit the dangerous situation at home to persuade other nations to eliminate Germany's reparation payments. He hoped that this success in foreign

29. Vollbehr to Foreign Ministry, Dec. 30, 1932, serial 330, quoted in Josef Engelbert Heindl, *Die diplomatischen Beziehungen zwischen Deutschland und den Vereinigten Staaten von Amerika, von 1933 bis 1939* (Ph.D. dissertation, University of Wurzburg, 1963 [privately printed, 1964?]), 41.

30. Gordon to Stimson, Sept. 15 and Sept. 30, 1930, *FR 1930*, III, 77–79, 85–86.

policy would ameliorate people's economic miseries, which he unwittingly was compounding by pursuit of a traditional deflationary policy. In the recent September 1930 elections, instead of justifying the Young settlement and cheering the Rhineland evacuation, the German government demanded such further revisions of the Versailles Treaty as return of the Saar and Polish Corridor. Brüning clearly sought an end to reparations, although he had acknowledged the Young obligation and his foreign minister, Julius Curtius, had been its chief advocate in the Reichstag.[31] Doubtless reparations added to Germany's financial plight, but the government's emphasis on the reparations problem only aided its fiercest opponents, especially the Nazis, in their effort to destroy the Weimar democracy.[32]

Brüning singlemindedly pursued his policy. In December 1930 he suggested to Ambassador Frederic M. Sackett, Schurman's successor, a world conference to consider the whole war debt-reparations problem. Sackett, a wealthy businessman and former Republican senator whom Brüning cultivated, agreed to put the matter before President Herbert Hoover after the New Year. Hoover ignored the proposal.[33] The Germans kept up pressure on the British and made no effort to stop the flight of capital from Germany, while the ever suspicious French blocked a proposed German-Austrian Customs Union in March 1931. In May the Germans indicated to American diplomats that they intended to cease some reparations payments, and on the eve of Brüning's departure for talks with the British at Chequers, on June 5, his cabinet published a manifesto, planned for a month, which declared that Germany had suffered all the imposed privation it could bear and that the presuppositions of the Young Plan no longer existed. The statement could only have an adverse effect on international credit, and it angered American officials.[34] President Hoover on the week end of June 20-21 called for a one-year moratorium on intergovernment and relief debts and reparations. Within a week everyone agreed to Hoo-

31. Wolfgang S. Helbich, "Between Stresemann and Hitler: The Foreign Policy of the Brüning Government," *World Politics,* XII (Oct. 1959), 27, 32–33; Dorpalen, *Hindenburg,* 214; cf. Bennett, *German Diplomacy,* 9–11, 123, 331.

32. Wolfgang S. Helbich, *Die Reparationen in der Ära Brüning: Zur Bedeutung des Young-Plans für die deutsche Politik, 1930 bis 1932* (Berlin-Dahlem, 1962), 92–93.

33. Bennett, *German Diplomacy,* 33, 39.

34. *Ibid.,* 118, 128–130.

ver's proposal—except the French. But American pressure prevailed and the French gave in on July 6, causing Under Secretary of the Treasury Odgen Mills to remark that the United States now had made the world safe for Germany.[35]

Hoover's moratorium afforded Germany only temporary relief, and Brüning wanted a permanent end to reparations. He got Germany's creditors to agree to a conference in Lausanne in January 1932 to reconsider German obligations, but when word of his ultimate purpose leaked to the press the French forced postponement of the meeting.[36] Eventually the Lausanne Conference met in June–July 1932 and cut German reparations to virtually nothing contingent on similar American reduction of war debts, which never came about.[37] The Germans repudiated reparations and every country except Finland defaulted permanently on its war debts in 1934, causing an angry Congress to pass a debt default act sponsored by Senator Hiram Johnson of California which forbade purchase of securities or bonds or making loans to nations in default. In some respects time had borne out Brüning's risky reparations policy, but the rush of ominous events had overtaken it and increased economic unrest and political intrigue had caused his resignation in May 1932.

Affairs in Germany were running rapidly downhill and American diplomats began to wonder about the future of democracy in Germany and about whether Hitler and his Nazis might gain control. Ambassador Sackett thought not. At the start of the year he insisted that despite depression, growing unemployment, and "phenomenal gain" in local elections, Nazi triumphs would be limited. He thought Hitler would not want to seize a government confronting "explosive international questions, shrinking national receipts, and shaky finances." Sackett grew more convinced and was gratified when in the German presidential election of March 1932 the incumbent Hindenburg won more votes than his major opponent Hitler. Sackett wrote that Hitler had demon-

35. Mills to Robert McKay, July 7, 1931, cited in Robert H. Ferrell, *American Diplomacy in the Great Depression: Hoover-Stimson Foreign Policy, 1929–1933* (New Haven, 1957), 115n14.

36. Helbich, *Reparationen*, 89–90; Dorpalen, *Hindenburg*, 252.

37. For details, see Arthur M. Schlesinger, Jr., *The Age of Roosevelt: The Crisis of the Old Order, 1919–1933* (Boston, 1957), 442–443; cf. Ferrell, *American Diplomacy*, 232–233, 236, 238–246.

strated "unwisdom" in running.[38] Nonetheless, Hindenburg's failure to get an absolute majority forced him to win only in a run-off in April, when Hitler reduced the margin between them.

As the German government became more unstable, American officials became more uncertain, especially when the crafty Franz von Papen succeeded Brüning as chancellor. As military attaché in Washington before American entrance into the World War, Papen had been expelled for plotting to blow up bridges and railroads. Sackett classified him as an "unruly" man whose government—which included Neurath as foreign minister and General Kurt von Schleicher as defense minister—was "strongly indicative of a military dictatorship." The secretary of state, Henry L. Stimson, told the ambassador that the new government would not last and that he should deal "politely" but "somewhat distantly" with Papen. The chief of the State Department's Division of Western Affairs, Pierre De L. Boal, warned that Germany awaited the "favorable opportunity and moment to repudiate the military clauses and perhaps all of the Versailles Treaty."[39] Papen dissolved the Reichstag in June 1932 and set new elections for the end of July, while lifting the ban on parades by the Nazi storm troopers which led to demonstrations in the cities. He deposed the Socialist provincial government of Prussia. And in July 1932 the National Socialist party won a smashing electoral victory, its 230 seats now making it the largest party in the Reichstag. Sackett hoped the Nazis had reached their maximum strength.[40]

Few Americans were interested in all this political flux in Germany. They too were having elections in 1932. No one said much about foreign affairs in the presidential campaign. The Democratic platform advocated a "firm" foreign policy, noninterference in internal affairs of other countries, international agreement for arms reduction, and collection of war debts; the Republican platform praised Hoover's efforts in the Far East and blamed "a train of events . . . in Central Europe" for spoiling a business upturn in the spring of 1931.

While Hoover's administration prepared in late 1932 to give way to

38. Sackett to Stimson, Jan. 5, Feb. 1, and Mar. 16, 1932, *FR 1932*, II, 277–281, DS, 862.00/2670, and *FR 1932*, II, 287–288.

39. Sackett to Stimson and Stimson to Sackett, June 1, and Boal to Stimson, June 4, 1932, *FR 1932*, II, 293–296.

40. Sackett to Stimson, Aug. 1, 1932, *ibid.*, 302–303.

that of Franklin D. Roosevelt, there occurred perhaps the most important event in all German history, from the time of the first gatherings of the barbarian tribes in the ancient teutonic forests down to and including all the developments in the medieval and modern eras. Hitler, on January 30, 1933, became chancellor. The German people made that day an occasion of pageantry. In the evening twenty-five thousand storm troopers strutted in parade dress past the Chancellery, torches and swastika banners aloft, while the eighty-four-year-old Hindenburg looked on, now and then attempting to tap his crooked stick in time to the military marches. A short distance away Hitler leapt with joy, unable to contain himself in his hour of triumph.

The sinister pattern of future events in Germany now began to reveal itself. After Hitler dissolved the Reichstag and called for new elections, there occurred the famous Reichstag fire on February 27, and the next day old Hindenburg signed a decree that curtailed civil liberties and gave Hitler a pretext to suppress political opposition. The March 5 election gave the Nazis 43.9 per cent of the electorate and 288 deputies; Alfred Hugenberg's Nationalists turned over their 8 per cent of the vote and 52 deputies to give Hitler a governing majority. On March 23 the Reichstag voted the Enabling Law, which turned legislative power over to the cabinet and gave Hitler authority to carry out his larger designs. Preparing to return to America, Sackett had concluded that the "much heralded Third Reich" had become a reality but what form it would finally take was "not yet clear."[41]

What did Germany's new leader think of the Americans? In retrospect German career diplomats, former members of Hitler's inner circle, and historians have believed that Hitler's assessment of the United States over the long run was highly negative and grossly distorted by his racial and political views—his grudging admiration of American economic power in the mid-1920's notwithstanding. In his earliest political commentary, in 1919, Hitler took little note of the United States except to observe that two million Jews controlled New York's banks, industry, and press, and this fact caused American entrance into the World War in 1917 solely for financial gain.[42] These same Jews, he

41. Sackett to Stimson, Mar. 3 and Mar. 9, 1933, *FR 1933*, II, 201–204, 204–209.
42. Günter Schubert, *Anfänge nationalsozialistischer Aussenpolitik* (Cologne, 1963), 65.

contended in *Mein Kampf*, had become regents of the stock exchange, which was the source of American power, and only "one great man, Ford," stood between them and their gaining control of the souls of 120 million laborers.[43] Ernst "Putzi" Hanfstaengl, Hitler's confidant and tutor of sorts, tried to get him in 1925 to broaden his horizon through a trip to the United States, but Hitler, who imagined the country as nothing other than "millionaires, beauty queens, stupid records, and Hollywood," brushed the idea aside: Americans could play no role in European or Asian conflicts because "you would only have to blow up the Panama Canal and they would not be able to exert pressure either way." When Ambassador von Prittwitz returned from his mission in the spring of 1933, Hitler asked him only a few questions about American domestic affairs. About a month later Hitler told the leader of the Nazis in Danzig, Hermann Rauschning, that America's chance for greatness had vanished when the South lost the Civil War, despite later "spurious" prosperity brought about by a "corrupt caste of tradesmen." America was in the throes of "the last death-rattle of a corrupt and outworn system" and could be liberated only by a "real *Herrenclass*," the "German component of the American people." The inferiority and decadence of this new world was evident in its military inefficiency.[44]

Hitler's views showed no apparent change during 1933–1938. In the spring of 1938, not without good reason, he replied to a reminder about American influence in the Far East by remarking that the United States was incapable of military leadership and would restrict its intervention in the war between China and Japan to empty warnings.[45] Hitler in 1939 would deride American appeals for peace and apparently never consider American aid to his opponents as of any possible importance. Although he would try to avoid provocative incidents during 1939–1941, he did not consider war with the United States a serious matter, even if he did seek an alliance with Japan to discourage American entry into the war.[46] Insofar as he followed anyone's advice,

43. Adolf Hitler, *Mein Kampf*, 2 vols. in 1 (New York, 1939), 930.

44. Quoted in Ernst Hanfstaengl, *Unheard Witness* (Philadelphia, 1957), 234, 141; Prittwitz, *Zwischen Petersburg und Washington*, 228; quoted in Hermann Rauschning, *The Voice of Destruction* (New York, 1940), 68–71.

45. Erich Kordt, *Wahn und Wirklichkeit: Die Aussenpolitik des Dritten Reiches, Versuch einer Darstellung* (Stuttgart, 1948), 142.

46. Saul Friedländer, *Hitler et les Etats-Unis (1939–1941)* (Geneva, 1963),

Hitler tended to accept only the views of those writers and military analysts, especially his military attaché in Washington during 1933–1941, General Friedrich von Boetticher, who saw America as too racially and politically corrupt to disturb Germany.[47]

During the Second World War, Hitler was given to denouncing America for a variety of reasons, the more so as events refused to conform to his plans or will. He said in 1942 that he felt "hatred and deep repugnance" toward Americans whose country—"half Judaised and the other half Negrified"—was doomed by its mercenary qualities and racial and social impurities. In 1945 he insisted that the war between America and Germany was a tragedy, "illogical and devoid of any reality," brought about by Jews, the failure of the New Deal, and "this Jew-ridden Roosevelt" whom Americans had failed to recognize as an "idol with feet of clay."[48] "That madman, Roosevelt," had tricked the British and "this Jew-ridden, half-American drunkard," Churchill, into fighting.[49] No longer could the *Herren*-class of German émigrés save America: "Transplant a German to Kiev and he remains a perfect German. But transplant him to Miami, and you make a degenerate of him—in other words, an American."[50]

Hitler also drew favorable conclusions about the United States. In *Mein Kampf* he referred to this "gigantic American State Colossus, with its enormous wealth of virgin soil" which challenged Great Britain for world dominance.[51] In fact, America's enormous *Lebensraum* accounted for its "unheard-of internal strength" and demonstrated why Germany had to acquire new territory in Europe proper.[52]

Hitler elaborated this view of America in 1928 in his second, and

273–276; James V. Compton, *The Swastika and the Eagle: Hitler, the United States, and the Origins of World War II* (Boston, 1967), 31–34, 128, 136, 186–201; Gerhard L. Weinberg, "Hitler's Image of the United States," *American Historical Review*, LXIX (July 1964), 1013–1015, 1020.

47. Compton, *Swastika and Eagle*, 11–14, 53–54, 105–124; Weinberg, "Hitler's Image," *American Historical Review*, 1012–1013.

48. Entry for Jan. 7, 1942, *Hitler's Secret Conversations*, 155; entry for Feb. 24, 1945, François Genoud, ed., *The Testament of Adolf Hitler: The Hitler-Bormann Documents, February–April 1945* (London, 1961), 87–90.

49. Entry for Feb. 4, 1945, Genoud, ed., *Testament of Hitler*, 29, 32, 35.

50. Entry for Jan. 7, 1945, *ibid.*, 46.

51. *Mein Kampf*, 929.

52. *Ibid.*, 180–181.

unpublished, book. Americans were a "young, racially select" people comprised of the best of Europe's emigrants who produced the boldest inventions, and whose government wisely ensured the future of the United States by restrictive immigration standards.[53] By entering the World War the United States had become a decisive power in international politics.[54] America's mass productive and consumptive capacities could defeat Europe in a struggle for markets, as witness the invasion of the automobile even into Germany.[55] America presented "a model living standard" which Germany could match only by greatly enlarging its continental territory, coming to a political orientation that no longer threatened British sea or trade interests, and then leading "a new association of nations" opposed to American world domination.[56] Hitler repeated his theses in speeches in 1930 about American racial selectivity, economic advance, and the need to mobilize Europe against the American onslaught.[57] And in the summer of 1933, when someone accused him of underestimating the United States, Hitler replied that on the contrary he was certain that "at the right moment a new America will exist as our strongest supporter when we are ready to stride into overseas space. We have the means of awaking this nation in good time. There will be no new Wilson arising to stir up America against us."[58] Events developed differently, of course, and Hitler in 1945 would complain bitterly that "at a time when the whole of Europe—their own mother—is fighting desperately to ward off the bolshevist peril, the United States . . . can think of nothing better to do than to place their fabulous material resources at the disposal of these Asiatic barbarians."[59]

As career diplomat Erich Kordt has pointed out, Hitler was probably

53. *Hitler's Secret Book,* trans. Salvator Attanasio (New York, 1961), 11, 102–103. The original version of the manuscript was first published by Gerhard Weinberg, ed., as *Hitlers Zweites Buch: Ein Dokument aus dem Jahr 1928* (Stuttgart, 1961).

54. *Hitler's Secret Book,* 117–118.

55. *Ibid.,* 98.

56. *Ibid.,* 95–96, 156–158, 209.

57. Konrad Heiden, *Der Fuehrer: Hitler's Rise to Power,* trans. Ralph Manheim (Boston, 1944), 322–325.

58. Quoted in Rauschning, *Voice of Destruction,* 71–72.

59. Entry for Feb. 7, 1945, Genoud, ed., *Testament of Hitler,* 45.

more misguided about America than about any other country.[60] By rational standards his image of America was inconsistent if not chaotic. Nevertheless, Hitler had extraordinary understanding of the uses of power, and the traditional as well as totalitarian diplomatic means to achieve his goals.[61] His response to American efforts would depend not only on his view of the United States but on how its diplomats and foreign policy responded to Germany and the impending European crises.

60. Kordt, *Wahn und Wirklichkeit*, 141.

61. Gordon A. Craig, "Totalitarian Approaches to Diplomatic Negotiation," in A. O. Sarkissian, ed., *Studies in Diplomatic History and Historiography in Honour of G. P. Gooch, C.H.* (London, 1961), 113–115; E. M. Robertson, *Hitler's Pre-War Policy and Military Plans, 1933–1939* (London, 1963), 7–8. On Foreign Ministry personnel changes see Paul Seabury, *The Wilhelmstrasse: A Study of German Diplomacy Under the Nazi Regime* (Berkeley, 1954), 26–30; and D. C. Watt, "The German Diplomats and the Nazi Leaders, 1933–1939," *Journal of Central European Affairs*, XV (July 1955), 154.

# 2.     THE END OF DISARMAMENT

The President said little about foreign policy. Probably few among the crowd of almost 100,000 people gathered before the Capitol, or among the millions listening to their radios, cared. Diplomacy seemed of limited importance on that overcast March 4, 1933. Most Americans were concerned above all with what Franklin D. Roosevelt proposed to do about the crisis at home. Accordingly, he spoke only briefly of foreign relations, dedicating the United States to the inexactly defined policy of the good neighbor.[1]

Roosevelt's background militated against passiveness in world responsibilities, however. His patrician tradition was international, from schoolday visits in the 1890's to Bad Nauheim and bicycle trips in the Black Forest, to his cousin Theodore's example as *arbiter mundi*. After Groton, Harvard, and Columbia Law School, and a turn at New York politics, Roosevelt had seen much of Wilsonian principles during his eight-year tenure as Assistant Secretary of the Navy. As nominee for vice-president in 1920, he campaigned for entry into the League of Nations, although during the 1920's he tucked his sails on that issue,[2] and in 1932, to placate the William Randolph Hearst faction in the Democratic party, he opposed entry. But two months before assuming the

---

1. Samuel I. Rosenman, comp., *The Public Papers and Addresses of Franklin D. Roosevelt*, 13 vols. (New York, 1938–50), II, 14; hereafter cited as *PPFDR*.

2. In "Our Foreign Policy—A Democratic View," *Foreign Affairs*, VI (July 1928), 573–586, Roosevelt said it was beside the point to talk about America's joining the League and proposed instead wholehearted cooperation with it.

presidency he appeared to support the doctrine of nonrecognition which Hoover and Stimson had applied in January 1932 to Japan's assault on Manchuria, and by the time of his inauguration Roosevelt seemed a "cautious advocate of collective security."[3] There was room for hope that this man who had enormous confidence in himself and his nation, and possessed an extraordinarily alert mind that grasped ideas and opportunities, might seize the moment to lead the world as well as his country.

The new secretary of state, Cordell Hull, sixty-one years of age, distinguished looking, with whitening hair, and speaking in firm tones marked by a soft southern drawl, had achieved national stature after emerging from Olympus, Tennessee, in the foothills of the Cumberlands. After state legislative and judicial service, he won a seat in Congress in 1906, which he held for all but one term until 1930 when he entered the Senate. Hull had gained prominence championing the income tax, the League of Nations, and, above all, a low tariff. He chaired the Democratic National Committee from 1921 through 1924, and in 1932 wrote much of the Democratic platform and helped secure Roosevelt the California delegation's vote at the Chicago convention. Hull's provinciality contrasted with Roosevelt's urbanity, and the two never were intimates. Undoubtedly, need to ensure southern support of New Deal legislation was an important consideration in Roosevelt's selection of Hull. The new secretary of state was a bit old-fashioned, believed too much, perhaps, in phrases and in increased trade as means to international peace. For all their differences, the two men shared important perspectives stemming from their common Wilsonian heritage. Thus, when Raymond Moley, a member of Roosevelt's "brain trust" and shortly to be assistant secretary of state, reported that some politicians objected to Hull's appointment because of overidealistic tariff views, the President retorted: "You tell the Senators I'll be glad to have some fine idealism in the State Department."[4]

The world sorely lacked international idealism in 1933. Even as Roosevelt and his cabinet took office, Japanese troops occupied Jehol City in Manchuria, Bolivia and Paraguay argued over the valuable

---

3. Robert A. Divine, *The Illusion of Neutrality* (Chicago, 1962), 42.
4. Quoted in Raymond Moley, *After Seven Years* (New York, 1939), 114.

Gran Chaco, and Colombia and Peru struggled over the tiny village of Leticia, seen by some as a key to the Amazon River. In Geneva, talks the delegates managed between adjournments of the World Disarmament Conference that opened in February 1932 proceeded unsatisfactorily. The United States had sponsored a nine-point program in February 1932, and in June of that year President Hoover had proposed that all nations reduce armaments by a third. These proposals brought little progress. The head of the German delegation, Rudolf Nadolny, a career diplomat who had been chief of the Reich Chancellery under President Ebert and later ambassador to Turkey, found the American delegation more sympathetic than any other toward German aspirations, but unable to narrow the widening breach between French demands for security and German demands for equality in military armament.[5] Shortly after the Hoover proposal, Germany announced that it would not meet with the conference when it reconvened in September. In November the French offered their plan for disarmament and the British followed with a long statement of policy. The Germans refused to rejoin the meetings, however, until on December 11 England, France, and Italy jointly promised Germany and all other nations disarmed by treaty "equality in a system which would provide security for all other nations."[6]

Nothing was accomplished in disarmament negotiations during early 1933. In March Hugh Gibson, the acting head of the American delegation, warned Hull that the Germans would likely reject any treaty, except one arrived at soon which granted full equality by abolishing the military restrictions of the Treaty of Versailles. France would not consider such revision until given political guarantees. Finding a way out of that Franco-German difficulty, Gibson wrote, would be the deciding factor in a treaty. One week later he reported that the Disarmament Conference was in a "precarious state," and adjournment meant a "definite breakdown." Germany would then feel free to rearm, with unforeseeable consequences. At the very least rearmament would aggravate Europe's tensions; "at the worst the possibility of armed conflict

5. Rudolf Nadolny, *Mein Beitrag* (Wiesbaden, 1955), 117–119.
6. Texts of the French plan, British statement, and joint statement are in John W. Wheeler-Bennett, ed., *Documents on International Affairs, 1932* (London, 1933), 217–234.

in the near future cannot be ignored." The problem at Geneva was "the entire relations of the European states to one another."[7] Nadolny confirmed these fears. When Gibson and Hugh Wilson, America's minister to Switzerland, visited him on March 12, Nadolny said Germany would work "indefinitely" to achieve equality through a treaty. But if a treaty did not grant equality, Germany "could take it for herself."[8]

The British were distressed when the statesmanlike German ambassador to England, Leopold von Hoesch, told their foreign secretary, Sir John Simon, that contrary to British hopes Germany had no plans to send a ranking official to Geneva. Simon was upset, not only because the regime in Germany seemed increasingly uninterested in disarmament proposals, but also because both French Premier Edouard Daladier and British Prime Minister Ramsay MacDonald were to travel to Geneva shortly. Such a meeting without a German representative, Simon said, might give more the appearance of an Anglo-French accord than the British wished to commit themselves to presently.[9]

MacDonald and Simon arrived in Geneva the second week in March. For several days they consulted the delegations, indicating they were about to present a disarmament program they had designed independently. In Washington, State Department officials fretted. Roosevelt had just appointed Norman Davis, a member of the American delegation, its chairman with the rank of ambassador. Davis, like Hull, came from Tennessee, was a close friend of Hull (he could walk in on most State Department meetings unannounced), and had been a contender for secretary of state in 1933. After a business career in Cuba, Davis had joined the Treasury Department in 1917 and served as Wilson's chief financial adviser at the Paris Peace Conference. He became assistant secretary of state in 1919, and under secretary in 1920. During the twenties he was an unofficial Democratic spokesman on foreign policy. Labeled "the king of optimists" by the current under secretary, William Phillips, and a "horse trader" by Hugh Wilson, Davis knew many European diplomats and enjoyed a good reputation, although the chief adviser to the British delegation in Geneva, Alexander Ca-

7. Gibson to Hull, Mar. 5 and Mar. 12, 1933, *FR 1933*, I, 24–25, 31–32.
8. Gibson to Hull, Mar. 12, 1933, *ibid.*, 34–37. The German account of the meeting is in Nadolny to Foreign Ministry, Mar. 13, 1933, *DGFP*, C, I, 152–154.
9. Hoesch to Foreign Ministry, Mar. 7, 1933, *DGFP*, C, I, 121.

dogan, did refer to him once as "the direct spiritual descendant of the Duke of Plaza Toro."[10]

Davis and Hull worried that without preparation a new disarmament plan would fail. They preferred to have Gibson secure postponement of meetings for five or six weeks, allowing the new administration time for strategy. Both men believed disarmament might best come through close British and American collaboration, and wanted Davis to meet with MacDonald in London before the British presented their plan. By the time Gibson got to explain the American position to MacDonald and Simon, the British had decided to go ahead on their own. All the United States could do, Gibson said, was deny any charges that the proposed British plan was an Anglo-American effort, and wait for the French to "destroy it in detail."[11]

MacDonald made an impassioned hour-and-twenty-minute speech to the Disarmament Conference on March 16, 1933. He pleaded, coaxed, and cajoled, insisting the delegates could prevent destruction of the conference, halt the arms race, avoid war, and save the evolution of man. The disarmament figures his nation was about to offer were imperfect; they were not intended to be the figures of the laws of the Medes and Persians. He taunted that to refuse to negotiate in the name of national honor was to display "feminine foibles." He hoped the children of the delegates would remember them not by their difficulties but for the success of their efforts and the glory that would rightfully belong to the conference. Polite applause followed.[12]

Taking as its starting point the Kellogg-Briand Pact, the MacDonald plan in Part I allowed any signatory of it and the Kellogg Pact to call for a conference in event of a breach, or threatened breach, of the latter agreement.[13] The consulting powers—in whose decisions the

10. Entry for Nov. 14, 1933, William Phillips Diary, I, 33, Phillips papers, Houghton Library, Harvard University, Cambridge, Mass.; Hugh Wilson, *Diplomat Between Wars* (New York, 1941), 270; Cadogan is quoted in *The Memoirs of Anthony Eden, Earl of Avon: Facing the Dictators* (Boston, 1962), 31–32. In *The Mist Procession: The Autobiography of Lord Vansittart* (London, 1958), 404, the permanent under secretary of the Foreign Office said the British referred to Davis as a "peripatetic bore."

11. Davis to Gibson and Hull to Gibson, Mar. 14, and Gibson to Hull, Mar. 15, 1933, *FR 1933*, I, 40–42.

12. *New York Times,* Mar. 17, 1933.

13. Text of the plan, including later revisions, is in John W. Wheeler-Bennett, ed., *Documents on International Affairs, 1933* (London, 1934), 151–194.

United States, the United Kingdom, France, Germany, Italy, Japan, and the Soviet Union had to concur—were to try to prevent a breach, or determine responsibility if one occurred. Part II defined troops, a critical point because the French insisted that the German *Schutzstaffel* (S.S.) and *Sturmabteilung* (S.A.) forces be considered regular troops, and limited the number of effectives allowed each European country. Germany, having no colonies, could have 200,000 troops on its own soil; France could maintain 200,000 troops at home and 200,000 overseas. Continental soldiers could serve for eight months only, thus converting the Reichswehr into a short-term army and allowing France the advantage of building a long-term overseas force. Most important, troop reduction would take place over five years. Meanwhile France would be stronger than Germany, and the rest of the world would learn whether the Hitler government intended to behave. Part III dealt with exchange of information; Part IV dealt with prohibitions on chemical, incendiary, and bacterial warfare; and Part V established a Permanent Disarmament Commission, which was to submit at least one report a year and investigate by request, or on its own, alleged treaty infractions. The League Council would review the commission's reports.

The MacDonald plan contained little that the negotiators had not previously talked about, but the idea of consultation in event of breach of the Kellogg Pact, and setting down figures on armies and armaments, were outstanding features. Never since disarmament discussions began under League of Nations auspices had such concrete proposals been made.[14] The French were delighted at the prospect of armies standardized on a militia basis, but felt the political guarantees of the proposal too vague and disliked the idea of making the German army—even on a short-term basis—twice its current size. The Germans, too, felt the draft treaty needed modification, but seemed willing to accept it as a basis for negotiation, even if only because their secret rearmament plans did not go much beyond the figures it set.[15] Further, Ambassador von Prittwitz, still in Washington awaiting Luther's arrival, conferred with Roosevelt after MacDonald's speech.

14. Arnold J. Toynbee, ed., *Survey of International Affairs, 1933* (London, 1934), 257.
15. Robertson, *Hitler's Pre-War Policy*, 121; Gerhard Meinck, *Hitler und die deutsche Aufrüstung, 1933–1937* (Wiesbaden, 1959), 86–87.

He reported that Roosevelt fully understood the German point of view, and that although he appreciated French requests for security, he could not give them further guarantee.[16]

The American government, occupied with domestic problems, was not ready to support the MacDonald plan. Hull instructed Gibson to couch his remarks in "friendly but very general terms." He worried that Part I of the plan appeared to go further than mere consultation, and under no circumstances could the United States agree in advance to determine which party had breached the peace. That would make America not an associate but "an active member of a peace-enforcing machinery."[17] Adjournment of the conference gave the State Department a month to plan.

Davis sailed for Europe on March 22, going first to London and then to Paris to confer about disarmament and the World Economic Conference. Whether he should accept Foreign Minister von Neurath's invitation to come to Berlin to discuss disarmament perplexed American diplomats. Under Secretary Phillips opposed the visit. He conceded that Germany held the key to disarmament, but thought a visit at that time by a representative of the President might appear an effort to press the German government to moderate its increasing assaults on the Jewish people, a matter in which the State Department was extremely reluctant to involve itself. Further, there was now doubt that Neurath was going to retain his position.[18]

Davis wanted to go to Berlin, insisting to Hull that it was impossible to "size up" the disarmament situation without learning at "first hand" the attitude of the German government. The talks might prove helpful, he said, in determining policy for the World Economic Conference. Hull consulted Roosevelt, who gave Davis permission to go to Berlin, provided he restricted his talks to disarmament and economic matters. Hull so informed Davis, then in Paris talking with Daladier. Daladier approved the American decision, feeling Davis' visit endorsed

16. Prittwitz to Foreign Ministry, Mar. 16, 1933, *DGFP*, C, I, 173–175, and Köpke to Delegation in Geneva, Mar. 17, 1933, GFM, K1868/K471929. Gerhard Köpke was director of Department II, Foreign Ministry.

17. Hull to Gibson, Mar. 20, 1933, *FR 1933*, I, 66.

18. Phillips Memorandum, Apr. 4, 1933, *ibid.*, 80–81. Neurath originally invited Davis to come to Germany in December 1932, and Davis replied that he would like to come but was not sure when it would be convenient. Davis to Neurath, Jan. 4, 1932, GFM, K1868/K471927-K471928.

disarmament, not Hitler. Further, he agreed with Davis' estimate that if the Germans would "calm down and be intelligent for six months," France would find itself hard put to justify its great armaments. The French, Davis said, had too long relied on "German stupidity" to obtain friends in time of need.[19]

Davis met with Hitler on April 8. Years later Hitler would mock him as a "petty profiteer."[20] On this day the chancellor was cordial enough, but firm. After the usual introductory remarks, he launched his standard assault on the Treaty of Versailles. The conversation ranged to other wars and other peace treaties, with both men fumbling for facts to fit their theories. When they returned to present problems, Davis tried to convince Hitler that France was more conciliatory than at any other time in the last fifteen years, that the Treaty of Versailles could be revised peacefully if everyone spoke softly. Hitler returned to his theme: Germany was defenseless, France had no reason to fear Germany, and Germany must have equality at once. Having seen the terrors of one war, the chancellor said, he had no desire to precipitate another, but Germany would not alter its fundamental demand for equality.[21] As Davis reported to his friend Theodore Marriner, the chargé at the Paris embassy, Hitler's moderate attitude was somewhat encouraging.[22]

By mid-April, nonetheless, the Disarmament Conference clearly needed diplomatic assistance. The European delegations, particularly the British, wanted to know what the United States would do if, under Part I of the MacDonald plan, the European states invoked sanctions against one or more states violating the Kellogg Pact. Would the United States refrain from interfering with the sanctions or, as in the case of the First World War, demand neutral trade rights?

For some time Wilson, Gibson, and Ferdinand L. Mayer, the counselor of the American legation in Geneva, had been discussing

19. Atherton to Hull (containing message from Davis to Hull), Roosevelt Memorandum, Hull to Marriner (for Davis), Apr. 4, and Davis Memorandum, Apr. 5, 1933, *FR 1933*, I, 79–83.

20. Entry for May 17, 1942, in Henry Picker, ed., *Hitlers Tischgespräche im Führerhauptquartier, 1941–42* (Bonn, 1951), 87.

21. Memorandum Davis-Hitler Conversation, Apr. 8, 1933, *FR 1933*, I, 85–89.

22. Entry for Apr. 10, 1933, Theodore J. Marriner Diary, Marriner papers, Manuscript Division, Columbia University Library, New York, N.Y.

this complex and crucial question with Arthur Henderson, president of the Disarmament Conference. Acting largely on Henderson's suggestion, they told Hull that the United States should declare that if the European states decided on collective action against a Continental aggressor, and if the United States concurred, it would refrain from obstructing collective security measures. Hull responded that it was inadvisable for the United States to go "so far so fast."[23] Shortly after Davis reached Geneva he became a supporter of this plan and sent Hull two cables insisting that such an announcement would contribute to disarmament. He knew that the proposed declaration was "a new form of undertaking" for the United States, but America's former neutrality rights were "becoming somewhat obsolete."[24]

Immersed in domestic problems, Roosevelt delayed while the State Department studied this matter. By the time MacDonald reached Washington on April 23 to discuss the World Economic Conference, Roosevelt had made his decision. He assured MacDonald that he sympathized with Part I of his plan, but that American public opinion did not favor a multilateral treaty that would limit American neutral rights. He added that a declaration or unilateral note, which unlike a treaty did not need Senate ratification, might accomplish the same purpose. The statement Roosevelt outlined to the prime minister resembled the Davis-Wilson-Mayer plan. The President said he would declare that if the United States concurred in the decision of the European states to designate one or more countries as aggressors for breaching the Kellogg Pact, it would refrain from any act that might defeat collective security measures, including not protecting citizens whose activities undermined the collective effort. The proposed statement, the President told MacDonald, would be as valid as the Monroe Doctrine.[25]

23. Gibson to Hull, Mar. 8, and Hull to Gibson, Mar. 10, 1933, *FR 1933*, I, 25–27, 29–30; in *Diplomat Between Wars*, 285–286, Wilson omitted mention, probably through oversight, of Henderson's contribution, but clearly, judging from Gibson's telegram of Mar. 8, 1933, Henderson played a key role. See also Julius W. Pratt, *Cordell Hull, 1933–1945*, vols. XII and XIII in Robert H. Ferrell and Samuel Flagg Bemis, eds., *The American Secretaries of State and Their Diplomacy*, 2 vols. (New York, 1964), I, 22, 402–403n3.

24. Davis to Hull, Apr. 10, 1933, *FR 1933*, I, 89–97.

25. Memorandum Roosevelt–MacDonald Conversation, Apr. 23, 1933, *ibid.*, 103–104.

Hull informed Davis of this decision, explaining that America could not sign Part I of the MacDonald plan because that would involve joining in conference action to determine an aggressor and the remedy to be applied against an aggressor. As a requisite to Roosevelt's making the declaration offered to MacDonald, there would have to be a "substantial" agreement on disarmament. Hull also gave Davis permission to state that the United States regarded the MacDonald plan as an excellent first step. At a later conference America would demand additional limits on offensive and surprise attack weapons in "answer to any German effort to increase armaments now, for in effect we ask them to stay as they are," with other nations reducing to their level by steps.[26] A few days later Roosevelt met with the leader of the French opposition Radical Socialist party, Edouard Herriot, who was in Washington to discuss the Economic Conference, and told him of the confidential instructions to Davis. Herriot approved but said he felt disarmament agreement was likely to be held up by Germany's demand to build prototypes of large guns and tanks which the Treaty of Versailles prohibited but which the MacDonald plan did not mention. Roosevelt promised that America would support France's position on this matter in Geneva.[27] The United States, France, and England appeared to agree on procedure for disarmament. American diplomats had to find the appropriate time to make public the administration's new policy.

Disarmament negotiations resumed on April 26, and Davis announced that the United States was not yet ready to approve categorically Part I of the MacDonald plan, but perhaps discussions could shift to other sections. Nadolny promptly presented stringent new German amendments to Part II to minimize France's advantage in being allowed to build an overseas army, especially in North Africa. The Germans insisted on including trained reserves and forces stationed in colonies near the home country in the total forces allowed each country. They said that S.A. and S.S. troops should not be regular effectives and that Continental armies should not be standardized until a second disarmament conference met four or five years

26. Hull to Davis, Apr. 25, 1933, *ibid.*, 106–107.
27. Memorandum Roosevelt–Herriot Conversation, Apr. 26, 1933, *ibid.*, 109–111.

later. In the interim, Nadolny concluded, Germany must have any defensive weapons other nations had.[28]

The MacDonald plan and the Disarmament Conference were in danger. Davis had counseled against "unqualified support" to the French, for fear they might use it to prevent disarmament by making demands the Germans would never accept.[29] Now the French found the German demands unacceptable, and said that if the Germans persisted it would be senseless to proceed. The young British under secretary for foreign affairs, Anthony Eden, seeking to bridge the Franco-German gap, prevailed upon Nadolny to say, if in equivocal fashion, that Germany's demands were not its final word on the subject. Still, Davis found the situation in Geneva "ominous."[30] Eden found the Germans "exasperating." Proceedings, he recalled, reminded him of a 1917 campaign in Flanders: progress could be made only in the mud between pill boxes, and strong points attacked only at the last—"and as in Flanders, the pill boxes are again occupied by Germans."[31]

Hitler declined an invitation to Washington and instead sent Hjalmar Schacht, the volatile president of the Reichsbank.[32] Roosevelt did not like Schacht, and privately enjoyed mocking him by putting his hands on his forehead and crying, "Ach, you must help my poor guntry."[33] Nonetheless, the President greeted him on May 6 with appropriate ceremony, a Marine band playing "Deutschland über Alles" and a toast (with water, as Prohibition was still in effect) to Hitler's health. A week of talks with Roosevelt and various State Department officials accomplished nothing.[34] In their initial meeting Roosevelt supported the MacDonald plan in principle, agreed that other nations had to scale their offensive weapons downward, but said that Germany's in-

28. Toynbee, ed., *Survey 1933,* 262.

29. Davis to Hull, Apr. 28, 1933, *FR 1933,* I, 117.

30. Davis to Hull, Apr. 28, 1933, *ibid.,* 121–122.

31. *Facing the Dictators,* 42–43.

32. Prittwitz to Foreign Ministry, Apr. 7, and Neurath to Prittwitz, Apr. 25, 1933, *DGFP,* C, I, 263–264, 344.

33. Henry Morgenthau, Jr., "The Morgenthau Diaries—III—How FDR Fought the Axis," *Colliers,* CXX (Oct. 11, 1947), 72.

34. For a general assessment of the trip see Gerhard Weinberg, "Schachts Besuch in den USA im Jahre 1933," *Vierteljahrshefte für Zeitgeschichte,* XI (Apr. 1963), 166–180.

sistence on rearmament was the real barrier to agreement at Geneva. Schacht replied that he had no knowledge of political or military matters, but, he protested, his nation was still at the mercy of Poland— a reference to Poland's reinforcement in March of its small garrison at the Westerplatte peninsula in Danzig harbor and rumors in the spring of 1933 that Marshal Joseph Pilsudski was planning a preventive war against Germany.[35] In a second conversation, on May 8, Schacht took a stronger position: Germany had lived with continuous disappointment for fifteen years, he said, and it now seemed the negotiators were putting another dictate before it in their demands for limits on the German army as provided for in Part II of the MacDonald plan.[36] Ambassador Luther stated the German case more mildly in a meeting with Hull and Phillips three days later. For domestic political reasons, he said, his government needed to be allowed a "small increase" in offensive armament, and he hoped the Americans would explain this to the British and French.[37] But in his farewell talk on May 12, Schacht had one of his familiar tantrums. He paced the floor, turned red in the face, accused the Americans of supporting exorbitant French demands while ignoring the wishes of 65,000,000 Germans, and warned that unless Germany were left alone to solve its problems with France there would be a "smash."[38]

Tension heightened in Europe meanwhile. Hitler's assumption of power had caused consternation, but many diplomats hoped that retention of Neurath as foreign minister—at Hindenburg's wish—would

35. Schacht to Foreign Ministry, May 6, 1933, *DGFP*, C, I, 390–393; Hull to Bingham, May 8, 1933, *FR 1933*, I, 131. Robert W. Bingham was ambassador to Great Britain. On the matter of Pilsudski's preventive war, see Wacław Jędrzejewicz, "The Polish Plan for a 'Preventive War' Against Germany in 1933," *Polish Review*, XI (Winter 1966), 62–91. See also Zygmunt J. Gasiorowski, "Did Pilsudski Attempt to Initiate a Preventive War in 1933?" *Journal of Modern History*, XXVII (June 1955), 135–151, and Alexander Bregmann, "German Fears of Preventive War in 1933," *Poland and Germany*, II (Mar. 1958), 5–14.
36. Bülow to Delegation in Geneva, May 9, 1933 (copy of Luther to Foreign Ministry, May 8, 1933), GFM, K1868/K471941-K471942.
37. Hull Memorandum, May 11, 1933 (copy enclosed in Hull to Davis, May 20, 1933), Norman H. Davis papers, Box 21, Manuscript Division, Library of Congress, Washington, D.C.
38. Diary entry for May 12, 1933, Nancy Harvison Hooker, ed., *The Moffat Papers: Selections from the Diplomatic Journals of Jay Pierrepont Moffat, 1919–1943* (Cambridge, Mass., 1956), 96.

act as a restraining influence. Neurath had entered diplomatic service in 1901 and served as ambassador to Italy from 1922 to 1930 and to Great Britain from 1930 to 1932 before becoming foreign minister under Papen in June 1932.[39] Neurath was not a Nazi but a fervent Nationalist, self-serving and rarely given to initiative. Even those members in the German diplomatic corps who liked him found it hard to praise him for anything other than functionary qualities.[40] Papen claimed that he "never does anything," and the future American ambassador would note in 1937 that although Neurath might personally oppose Hitler's ways, "he always surrenders."[41] Hitler found him "unimaginative," "shrewd as a peasant, but with no ideas," and in 1933 even liked having him around because of "his benevolent appearance that is of most use to me. You can't imagine a man like that going in for a revolutionary policy."[42] In April Davis had reported to the State Department that even Daladier agreed that Neurath was a "reasonable character" who would try to bring about a reasonable frame of mind in Berlin.[43]

There was, then, surprise and apprehension when the May 11 *Leipziger Illustrierte Zeitung* carried an article by Neurath declaring that regardless of the Geneva talks Germany had to rearm on equal footing with other nations. Neurath's statement, intended to force the British and French to yield to German demands, had the opposite effect.[44] The British secretary for war, Lord Douglas Hailsham, threatened military sanctions if Germany rearmed in violation of the Treaty of Versailles, and the French foreign minister, Joseph Paul-Boncour,

39. When Brüning's government fell, he approached Nadolny about becoming Foreign Minister under Papen, but Hindenburg chose Neurath. Nadolny, *Mein Beitrag,* 121.

40. See, for example, *Memoirs of Ernst von Weizsäcker,* trans. John Andrews (Chicago, 1951), 109–110.

41. Papen quoted in entry for July 15, 1934, and Dodd's entry for July 14, 1937, in William E. Dodd, Jr., and Martha Dodd, eds., *Ambassador Dodd's Diary, 1933–1938* (New York, 1941), 129, 424. Ambassador William E. Dodd's daughter Martha recalled that at social functions Neurath "stood still usually, like a gigantic owl in face, like a penguin in shape," and when he moved did so "with such dignity and self-importance it was almost like the Sphinx itself deciding to shake its head!" *Through Embassy Eyes* (New York, 1939), 248.

42. Hitler quoted in Rauschning, *Voice of Destruction,* 275.

43. Davis Memorandum, Apr. 5, 1933, Davis papers, Box 9.

44. Meinck, *Hitler und die deutsche Aufrüstung,* 27.

supported the British stand.[45] Hitler used the opportunity to tell his ministers on May 12 that further disarmament negotiations could lead only to destruction of the German army or blame for Germany if the conference failed. Both Neurath and General Werner von Blomberg, the minister of war, supported the contention that negotiations no longer would serve any purpose, and the cabinet thereupon announced that the chancellor would respond to recent statements and developments before a special session of the Reichstag on May 17.[46] In Geneva, Nadolny was so distressed anticipating a truculent address that he rushed to see Hitler and asked him to meet the British halfway by accepting the MacDonald plan as a basis for negotiation. But Hitler only banged his fists on the table, denounced the French, and ended the interview even while Nadolny persisted in his advice.[47]

American diplomats believed the time to act had come. In response to Hull's inquiry, the chargé in Berlin, George A. Gordon, surmised that Hitler was going to declare that the failure of the powers to grant Germany military equality had vitiated the MacDonald plan. At the same time Davis sent two frantic cables, one urging that Roosevelt speak out before Hitler, and the other proposing that Roosevelt summon Luther to the White House to ask him to urge his country to align itself with the United States, England, and Italy by supporting the MacDonald plan.[48] Roosevelt meanwhile summoned his advisers—Hull, Phillips, William C. Bullitt, special assistant to Hull, and Louis Howe, Roosevelt's omnipresent secretary—and they drafted a message to the heads of the fifty-four states represented in Geneva. Then they turned the draft over to Assistant Secretary Moley with instructions, as he recalled, to "pretty up the language," and "put the old organ roll into it."[49]

The President's May 16 message emphasized the economic burden that heavy arms placed upon nations. The overwhelming majority of

45. *New York Times,* May 12 and May 13, 1933. See also John W. Wheeler-Bennett, *The Pipe Dream of Peace: The Story of the Collapse of Disarmament* (New York, 1935), 115–117.

46. Minutes of the Conference of Ministers on May 12, 1933, *DGFP,* C, I, 409–412; *New York Times,* May 14, 1933.

47. Nadolny, *Mein Beitrag,* 133–134.

48. Hull to Gordon, May 14, and Gordon to Hull and Davis to Hull, May 15, 1933, *FR 1933,* I, 139–142.

49. *After Seven Years,* 214.

peoples, he said, retained excessive armaments because they feared aggression in an age when modern offensive weapons were vastly stronger than defensive ones. To escape this tragic dilemma by eliminating offensive weapons Roosevelt proposed a four-step program: acceptance of the MacDonald plan, agreement on time and procedure for steps following it, maintenance of armaments at present levels while carrying out the first and following steps, and a nonaggression pact. He warned that if any strong nation refused to cooperate in the efforts for political and economic peace the world would know whom to blame.[50] Major newspapers lauded the President's words. Typically, the *New York Times* of May 17 praised them as even more bold than any proposal made by Woodrow Wilson and noted that the world eagerly awaited the German response. Neurath at once advised Hitler that he could not avoid a careful response to Roosevelt's message in his scheduled address, but that it would be possible to concur with American principles yet skirt the demand that Germany not begin to rearm. He sent him a draft of such a reply on the morning of May 17.[51]

Hitler, in full Nazi uniform, as were the majority of the audience, addressed an excited overflow session of the Reichstag. He spoke softly and swiftly, opening with the usual attack on national passions that clouded judgment and wisdom in 1919 and explaining the Nazi revolution as a response to economic conditions and a bulwark against "threatened Communist revolution." The Treaty of Versailles, Hitler insisted, granted rights to the conquered as well as the conqueror; Germany's demand for equality was therefore one of "morality, right and reason." What contribution was the Third Reich willing to make to the present disarmament tangle? Germany would disband its entire military establishment, destroy its few remaining weapons if neighboring countries did the same, and accept the MacDonald plan. Germany would have to maintain defense forces as long as other nations did, and not

50. *PPFDR*, II, 185–188. Davis had thought Roosevelt should confine his remarks to Europe primarily, or Germany specifically, but Roosevelt preferred to make them applicable to the world. See Hull to Davis, May 16, 1933, *FR 1933*, I, 145–146.

51. Neurath to Hitler, May 16, and Unsigned Memorandum, May 17, 1933, *DGFP*, C, I, 447, 451. Hitler's speech did follow Neurath's advice, and diplomats generally acknowledged the speech had been prepared for Hitler. See Gordon to Hull, May 17, and Atherton to Hull, May 18, 1933, *FR 1933*, I, 149–151.

include S.S. and S.A. men as part of the total effectives permitted. Finally, Hitler in behalf of his country thanked Roosevelt for his message and, for the first and only time during the decade, welcomed the "magnanimous proposal of bringing the United States into European relations as a guarantor of peace."[52] The German Consul in Chicago, Hugo Simon, reported that Hitler's speech had made an extraordinary impression on everyone, and two days afterward Nadolny stated that his government accepted the MacDonald plan not only as a starting point for discussion but also as a basis for the future agreement, and he withdrew German amendments to the sections on standardization of Continental armies.[53]

The French were suspicious and perturbed. According to Chargé Marriner in Paris, the brilliant secretary general of the French Foreign Office, Alexis Saint-Léger Léger, thought Roosevelt's message an English-inspired trick to make France's position at Geneva difficult, and Marriner had to work hard allaying his fears.[54] The popular political journalist, Andre Géraud (*Pertinax*), writing in *l'Echo de Paris* on May 27, considered Roosevelt's ideas naïve and argued that wars resulted from not defending treaties rather than from defending them. In England the "official mind," in Chargé Ray Atherton's words, would not accept Hitler's speech as a declaration of policy unless Germany without further delay standardized its army. In Berlin Chargé Gordon, recognizing that Hitler had taken a statesmanlike and conciliatory position, suspected it might well be a ruse to gain time to secure control at home, and then the world might see what Nazis privately had described to Gordon as "the real Hitler—the advocate of the doctrine of force, as laid down in his book *My Struggle*."[55]

52. Norman H. Baynes, ed., *Hitler's Speeches, April 1922–August 1939*, 2 vols. (London, 1942), II, 1041–1058. Hitler apparently was unhappy with the conciliatory position he had to assume. When Nadolny went up to congratulate him after the speech, Hitler only muttered "thanks" and turned away. Nadolny, *Mein Beitrag*, 134. Roosevelt listened to the speech on the radio with Moley and secretaries Stephen J. Early and Marvin H. McIntyre. *New York Times*, May 18, 1933.
53. Simon to Foreign Ministry, May 20, 1933, GFM, 5747/HO34698-HO34700; Wheeler-Bennett, *Pipe Dream of Peace*, 120.
54. Entries for May 16 and May 17, 1933, Marriner Diary, Marriner papers; Marriner to Hull, May 18, 1933, *FR 1933*, I, 148.
55. Atherton to Hull, May 18, and Gordon to Hull, May 20, 1933, *FR 1933*, I, 151, 159–164.

Davis did not share his colleagues' skepticism or fear. He thought Hitler and Germany more conciliatory than ever and believed the "profound effect" of Roosevelt's speech had induced Germany to retreat "from an almost impossible position." It was now time, he said, for the United States to make "some move," perhaps a meeting of the heads of state of Europe's major powers. Roosevelt and Hull agreed, and instructed Davis to expand upon Roosevelt's May 16 message by way of a public response to the proposals Henderson had been discussing with American diplomats in Geneva since March.[56]

Davis told the Disarmament Conference on May 22 that although his government opposed rearmament it was neither just nor wise for some nations to be permanently subjected to special arms limitation. Other nations were obligated to reduce armaments to defense levels. The United States was willing to do this, and support the MacDonald plan. Then Davis caught Europe's diplomatic attention. He said that if the European nations reached a general agreement on disarmament the United States would be willing to consult other states in case of a threat to peace. If the consulting states determined that a nation had violated its international obligations, and proposed measures against the aggressor, the United States, if it concurred in the judgment, would not do anything that might interfere with the collective effort to restore peace.[57]

As Hull would recall, Davis' proposal marked a "radical change" in the traditional American attitude toward neutrality and freedom of the seas.[58] Despite the requisite agreement on disarmament, and independent concurrence, the promise not to interfere with possible sanctions under Article XVI of the League Covenant meant cooperation with collective security (and removed British opportunity to refuse to cooperate on the excuse that American neutral rights destroyed sanctions) and indicated a greater American willingness to assume responsibility for international peace than at any time since 1920.[59] Significantly, two

---

56. Davis to Hull, May 21, and Hull to Davis, May 22, 1933, *ibid.*, 165–166; see also entry for May 18, 1933, Marriner Diary, Marriner papers, and *The Memoirs of Cordell Hull*, 2 vols. (New York, 1948), I, 227–228.

57. U.S. Department of State, *Peace and War: United States Foreign Policy, 1931–1941* (Washington, D.C., 1943), 186–191.

58. *Memoirs*, I, 228.

59. Divine, *Illusion of Neutrality*, 51. In an exaggerated response, John Bassett Moore, a professor at Columbia University and a leading authority on inter-

days after Davis' speech, the British amended Part I of the MacDonald plan to establish, on a basis acceptable to the United States, the right of any signatory nation to call for consultation in event of a threatened or actual breach of the Kellogg-Briand Pact.[60] Disarmament seemed nearer than ever.

Then came the first of the tragic events that would ruin the American effort at assisting collective security and contribute to the failure at Geneva. Shortly after Roosevelt had taken office, Hull and Davis prevailed upon him to support a congressional resolution, which was originally requested by Secretary Stimson and supported by Hoover but which Congress had never acted upon, that would allow the chief executive to embargo arms and ammunition to any nation that threatened or committed aggression. Representative Samuel D. McReynolds of Tennessee, chairman of the House Foreign Affairs Committee, introduced the resolution in the House on March 16, 1933, and it passed by a large majority on April 17 after Hull, McReynolds, and their supporters exerted pressure on congressional and State Department opponents of it.[61] Hull in a long statement to the Senate Committee on Foreign Relations on May 17 pleaded for the resolution. He insisted that the chief executive would exercise his new power only to maintain world peace, and with necessary regard for American policies and interests. The executive departments of a majority of major nations, including Great Britain, France, and Germany, had similar authority, he pointed out, and the United States had to keep pace in the effort to prevent or end conflict. It was impossible to foresee all circumstances under which the President would invoke the embargo, Hull admitted, whether it would be against one, some, or every nation in a controversy, or whether it would be invoked at all. The important point was that the resolution was "a peace measure and it would be used to promote peace."[62]

One week later the old isolationist from California, Senator Hiram

---

national law, called the proposed commitment "the gravest danger to which the country has ever been exposed, a danger involving our very independence." "An Appeal to Reason," *Foreign Affairs*, XI (July 1933), 571.

60. *New York Times*, May 25, 1933.

61. *Ibid.*, Apr. 18, 1933. See also Divine, *Illusion of Neutrality*, 32–33, 43–47.

62. Hull to Senate Committee on Foreign Relations, May 17, 1933, *FR 1933*, I, 369–378.

Johnson, challenged the administration's effort to reorient American foreign policy. He insisted that the proposed embargo apply to all parties in a dispute, not only the aggressor.[63] At this juncture a worried Key Pittman, the chairman of the Senate Foreign Relations Committee, who drank heavily and inveterately, swore constantly, and carried a silver pistol to his favorite bars, hastened to see Roosevelt.[64] Lacking strong views on foreign policy and preferring conciliation—almost to a fault—to fighting, Pittman told the President the committee would not pass the embargo measure without Johnson's amendment. Perhaps not grasping the major change in course that Johnson was demanding, Roosevelt said not a word to Hull and agreed to the proposed amended embargo.[65] As soon as Hull learned of this conversation from Pittman he sent a note pointing out that the amendment conflicted with the position Davis had taken at Geneva and hinting strongly that Roosevelt should do something about "certain extremists among the Senators" who were trying to block peace legislation.[66] Roosevelt would not intervene, and the Senate committee reported favorably on the amended resolution on May 27.[67] Only then was Hull able to make headway with the President. Unwilling to reverse himself, Roosevelt agreed to drop the embargo issue, and action on the legislation remained suspended.[68] The Johnson amendment had its negating effects. Hull ad-

63. *New York Times,* May 25, 1933.

64. For a critical appraisal of Pittman's work, see Fred L. Israel, *Nevada's Key Pittman* (Lincoln, Neb., 1963), esp. 131–133; more favorable is Wayne S. Cole, "Senator Key Pittman and American Neutrality Policies, 1933–1940," *Mississippi Valley Historical Review,* XLVI (Mar. 1960), 644–662.

65. Entry for Jan. 2, 1934, Jay Pierrepont Moffat Diary, Moffat papers, Houghton Library, Harvard University. Moffat, then chief of the Division of Western European Affairs, in explaining this matter to Davis, related that Pittman had "gone behind Hull's back," and that Roosevelt gave "reluctant consent" to the Johnson amendment without fully grasping the effect it would have on Davis' efforts at Geneva. Robert A. Divine, "Franklin D. Roosevelt and Collective Security, 1933," *Mississippi Valley Historical Review,* XLVIII (June 1961), 57–58, adds that Roosevelt did not want to jeopardize passage of the National Recovery Act and the Glass-Steagall banking reform by a debate on foreign policy. Further, Roosevelt was expressing his own isolationist convictions, which he did not abandon until several years later.

66. Hull Memorandum for Roosevelt, May 27, 1933, Cordell Hull papers, Box 34, Manuscript Division, Library of Congress. See also Hull, *Memoirs,* I, 229–230.

67. *New York Times,* May 28, 1933.

68. Hull, *Memoirs,* I, 230; Divine, *Illusion of Neutrality,* 54.

mitted at a news conference on May 29 that the administration's effort to work collectively against aggressors had been defeated.[69] The Disarmament Conference now was in trouble.

Attention shifted in June 1933 from Geneva to London, where representatives of sixty-six nations were to take part in the World Economic Conference. American negotiations with Germany prior to the conference were friendly, routinely formal, and superficial. Hull and Ambassador von Prittwitz agreed in March that there could be no substantial reduction of European protective tariffs on agriculture, and in April the Germans indicated to Davis that Hull's proposal to cut tariffs generally by 10 per cent was insufficient.[70] Schacht's conversations in May with Roosevelt, and then with key State and Agriculture Department officials and private bankers, made no headway toward international stabilization of currency, which Schacht favored (although not necessarily on a gold standard), and which Roosevelt called for in a fireside chat on May 7.[71] German officials, in fact, regarded stabilization as only of "secondary importance" and were more concerned with slashing interest rates on their foreign indebtedness, a policy American officials opposed. Hence, Roosevelt and Schacht's joint statement on May 12 expressed good will and nothing else.[72] The day before Hull sailed for London Roosevelt told him that neither he nor any member of the delegation he headed was to discuss war debts or disarmament, thus freezing these two major problems.[73] Most important to Hull was the copy he carried of an attractive legislative proposal to establish reciprocal trade agreements with willing nations. But before Hull landed Roosevelt wired that he was not going to submit the proposal to Congress, which he hoped would adjourn before paper money inflationists and bonus enthusiasts carried the day. As Hull would recall, doubtless

69. *New York Times*, May 30, 1933.

70. Prittwitz to Foreign Ministry, Mar. 8, and Ritter Minute, Apr. 13, 1933, *DGFP*, C, I, 125–126, 273–276. Karl Ritter was director of the Economic Department of the Foreign Ministry.

71. Schacht's views are stated in Minutes of the Economic Policy Committee of the Reich Government, Apr. 24, 1933, *DGFP*, C, I, 334–342; fireside chat in *PPFDR*, II, 165–167.

72. Unsigned Memorandum (prepared for Neurath conversation with Davis), Apr. 7, 1933, *DGFP*, C, I, 264–266; joint statement in *PPFDR*, II, 174–175.

73. Roosevelt to Hull, May 30, 1933, *FR 1933*, I, 620–621.

with exaggeration, he had gone to Europe "with the highest of hopes, but arrived with empty hands."[74]

The World Economic Conference opened formally on June 12. After King George V welcomed the delegates, MacDonald upset the Americans by declaring that war debts had to be discussed without delay, violating a preconference arrangement that this subject would not be discussed.[75] Hull's first address, scheduled for the next day, had to be put off twenty-four hours when Roosevelt, finding the text too long and categorical, delayed wiring approved revisions. The British misinterpreted the delay as peevishness over MacDonald's comments. When Hull did speak, he could only describe economic nationalism as a "discredited policy" and call for international reduction of tariffs as the way to prosperity and peace.[76] Because the United States had been as responsible as any other nation for the economic nationalism that had characterized the previous fifteen years, and because Hull had no specific proposals, the speech generated little enthusiasm.

The possibility that interested the British and French above all was international stabilization of the gold exchange rate of the dollar, pound, and franc. In his conferences with MacDonald and Herriot in the spring, Roosevelt apparently had led them to believe that he too favored stabilization, as he had indicated in his May 7 fireside chat and May 16 message to the nations represented at the Geneva Disarmament Conference. But Roosevelt was becoming more nationalist daily and wary that his chances of raising domestic commodity prices might be hurt if stabilization pegged the dollar at too high a ratio to the pound. His resistance to stabilization probably increased too when in mid-June the French defaulted on their debt payment to the United States and England made only a token payment.[77] On June 15 Roosevelt expressed displeasure at the "wild reports" he heard out of London about stabilization; nonetheless, a day later he received word from two American financial advisers there that they supported a proposed stabilization agreement.[78] The President vetoed the proposal, and although he

74. *Memoirs*, I, 250–251, 255; cf. Herbert Feis, *1933: Characters in Crisis* (Boston, 1966), 174–175.

75. *New York Times*, June 13, 1933; Hull, *Memoirs*, I, 256.

76. Moley, *After Seven Years*, 226–227; text of Hull speech in *FR 1933*, I, 636–640.

77. Feis, *1933*, 182.

78. Roosevelt to Hull, June 15, and Sprague to Roosevelt and Warburg to

left the door open to future agreement, he warned that too much emphasis was being put on existing and temporary monetary fluctuations
and not enough on balanced budgets and permanent national curren-
cies.[79] He also decided to send Assistant Secretary Moley to Europe,
soon.[80]

Precisely what Roosevelt intended to accomplish by sending Moley,
who was no friend of Hull, to London remains a question to this day.
But there is no doubt that the drama which surrounded Moley's mission—his race from Washington by navy plane and then destroyer to
consult Roosevelt on his schooner *Amberjack* off Nantucket, departure
next day for Europe on the *Manhattan*, and the special plane (which
he did not take) sent to speed his journey from Cobh to London—mes-
merized Europe's diplomats. Moley arrived on June 27 and conferred
for several days with important delegates. Then he asked Roosevelt to
support a joint declaration that pointed to future stabilization when
each nation deemed the time appropriate. To Moley's chagrin, Roosevelt rejected the proposal outright.[81] In this message of rejection, sent
to Hull, Roosevelt pointed out that the British had been off the gold
standard for almost two years, the French for more than three, that the
conference had been scheduled before America went off gold, and that
its purpose was to discuss solutions to world economic problems, not
American domestic policy only. Nor would he agree to any arrangement that would obligate the government to export gold.[82] As Herbert
Feis, at the time economic adviser to the State Department and present
at the London meetings, has pointed out, the President's reply was
"guarded and anticipatory," and the proposed stabilization probably
would not have interfered much with his efforts to raise domestic prices,
although he could not have pursued his policy of devaluing the dollar.
Significantly though, the drain on American gold reserves probably
would have led to the very inflation and speculation against the dollar

---

Roosevelt, June 16, 1933, *FR 1933*, I, 641–645. Professor O. M. W. Sprague of
Harvard University was adviser to the Treasury Department; James P. Warburg,
a young New York banker and friend of Moley, was financial adviser to the
delegation.

79. Roosevelt to Hull, June 17, 1933, *ibid.*, 645–646; Feis, *1933*, 185–186.

80. Moley, *After Seven Years*, 231.

81. *Ibid.*, 255–256; text of proposed joint statement is in *FR 1933*, I, 670–
671.

82. Roosevelt to Hull, June 30, 1933, *FR 1933*, I, 699–700.

conservative bankers and businessmen claimed they feared; thus Roosevelt, even if he did not believe in the outmoded gold standard, was using America's gold to protect it against fortune and other nations' maneuvers.[83]

Moley, at Hull's advice, let other delegates know only that the President had rejected the proposed stabilization measure in its present form, and he awaited further word.[84] There followed, of course, Roosevelt's famous "bombshell" message, wired to Hull on the evening of July 2 and released next day, which declared that for the conference to lull itself by the "specious fallacy" of stabilization, a temporary and probably artificial measure, would be a "catastrophe amounting to a world tragedy." Roosevelt also derided the "old fetishes" of international bankers who failed to understand the need to establish a dollar with constant purchasing power.[85] Seen in this light, the President's message was perhaps slightly less excessive than historians have judged it, although for all practical purposes it destroyed the conference, whose adjournment the American delegation held off until July 27.[86] In the London *Daily Mail* of July 4 John Maynard Keynes, under a headline terming Roosevelt "magnificently right," exhorted statesmen to begin to think about managed currency, while scores of economists and politicians in the United States and Europe applauded Roosevelt's position.[87] Nevertheless, as one member of the American delegation noted, MacDonald was in a "complete state of depression" and inconsolable, while England's chancellor of the Exchequer, Neville Chamberlain, in his own words, went fishing "to forget the behavior of the American

83. Feis, *1933*, 223–225. A short while later Roosevelt told Moley that he had "pretty good word" to the effect that there would have been a drain of half a billion dollars. *Ibid.*, 245.

84. *Ibid.*, 228.

85. Roosevelt to Hull, July 2, 1933, *FR 1933*, I, 673–674.

86. For evaluation of Roosevelt's response, see Arthur M. Schlesinger, Jr., *The Age of Roosevelt: The Coming of the New Deal* (Boston, 1959), 222–223; Ferrell, *American Diplomacy in the Great Depression*, 273–277; William E. Leuchtenburg, *FDR and the New Deal, 1932–40*, in Commager and Morris, eds., *New American Nation Series* (New York, 1963), 202–203; Pratt, *Hull*, I, 59; Feis, *1933*, 232–233. For details of the conference see William Kamman, "The United States and the London Economic Conference of 1933" (Master's thesis, Indiana University, 1956).

87. Schlesinger, *Coming of the New Deal*, 223–224; Kamman, "United States and London Economic Conference," 87–88.

President and the French delegation," which was furiously but vainly trying to get other delegations to denounce the American action.[88]

German diplomats delighted in Anglo-French-American discord. The German delegation, which included Neurath, Schacht, Minister of Economics Alfred Hugenberg, and various Nazi as well as Foreign Ministry officials, was torn by its own bickering. Hugenberg, who had led the campaign in his government to reject Hull's efforts at tariff reductions, had also been at odds with cabinet officers and Foreign Ministry officials over his unsuccessful effort during April and May to have Germany attempt to organize a European bloc to place a special import levy on goods from the United States, France, and the Soviet Union.[89] At the conference Hugenberg intended to deliver a contentious address on June 14 virtually demanding a "correct debt settlement," a German colonial empire in Africa, and population and economic expansion into the Soviet Union, and, in contrast to Hull's efforts, emphasizing German autarchy. The German delegation did what little it could to soften Hugenberg's impact by altering some paragraphs and handing out a doctored version as a press release.[90] Nevertheless, Hugenberg's tactlessness led, expectedly, to scores of Soviet protests, and to his resignation a couple of weeks later.[91]

Neurath too had his difficulties. When he returned to Germany he complained bitterly—and Schacht supported his view—that even the most pessimistic expectations of the German delegation had been "outdistanced by far," that Germany could expect no success in the economic realm, and that the attitude of other nations "could hardly be

88. The comment about MacDonald is from the unpublished diary of James P. Warburg, entry for July 3, 1933, as cited in Feis, *1933*, 235; Chamberlain is quoted in Keith Feiling, *The Life of Neville Chamberlain* (London, 1946), 224.

89. Hugenberg's views on American tariff proposals are stated in Extract from the Minutes of the Cabinet Sessions of May 5 and May 12, 1933, *DGFP*, C, I, 380–381, 406–408; for details of Hugenberg's proposal see Hugenberg to Hitler, Apr. 16, and Bülow Memorandum, May 13, 1933, *ibid.*, 293–297, 411–412.

90. Unsigned Memorandum, June 14, 1933, *DGFP*, C, I, 562–567; see also Paul Schmidt, *Statist auf diplomatischer Bühne, 1923–1945: Erlebnisse des Chefdolmetschers im Auswärtigen Amt mit den Staatsmännern Europas*, 2d ed. (Frankfurt-am-Main–Bonn, 1964), 266–267.

91. Extract from the Minutes of the Conference of Ministers and Cabinet Session, June 27, 1933, *DGFP*, C, I, 607–608; on the Soviet protests see *ibid.*, 581–582, 584–585, 590–592, 603–604, 640–642.

worse."[92] Germany was not interested in the struggle over gold stabilization and took no part.[93] But given their own failure to convince anyone of Germany's plight or correctness of course, and smarting at their own embarrassments, German officials had to look with glee upon the failure of the other powers to reach economic accord and the subsequent collapse of the conference. Hence, after the final adjournment, Carl Krogmann, deputy chief of the German delegation, smugly reported that the Foreign Ministry's prediction that the conference would achieve "no positive result . . . has been fully borne out." There was good hope, he added, that Germany might now increase trade with the United States, since that nation and its President evidently were seeking to "emancipate" themselves from "British tutelage and are apparently looking about for friends."[94]

What, in the meantime, of the disarmament tangle? Early in June, Davis had gone to Paris for private conversations with Eden, Daladier, and Paul-Boncour. The French insisted the MacDonald plan was insufficient; they said disarmament could begin only after a trial period, of perhaps three years, during which time the effect of supervision and good faith of the Hitler government could be tested. Davis and Eden pressed Daladier, insisting that Germany could not be expected to sign a treaty unless France undertook some immediate disarmament. Daladier conceded France might agree to halt construction of various heavy guns and tanks, reduce armed forces in stages, and then gradually destroy war matériel. No binding agreement emerged from the talks, but a week later Davis cabled that he was "more hopeful than ever" about disarmament.[95]

Shortly thereafter Arthur Henderson, president of the conference,

92. Extract from the Minutes of the Conference of Ministers, June 23, 1933, *ibid.*, 598–603. Neurath in fact was so unpopular that British crowds booed him and his aides when they departed. See *New York Times*, June 22, 1933, and Seabury, *Wilhelmstrasse*, 27.

93. Schmidt, *Statist auf diplomatischer Bühne*, 274.

94. Krogmann to Neurath, Aug. 1, 1933, *DGFP*, C, I, 712–714.

95. Davis to Hull, June 8 and June 15, 1933, *FR 1933*, I, 190–192; British version of talks in Record of a Conversation at the Quai d'Orsay, June 8, 1933, in E. L. Woodward and Rohan Butler, eds., *Documents on British Foreign Policy, 1919–1939*, three series, 32 vols. (London, 1946———), 2d series, V, 336–348; hereafter cited as *DBFP*. See also Eden, *Facing the Dictators*, 47.

gamely returned to London hoping to further progress toward disarmament while negotiations took place during the World Economic Conference. But delegates virtually ignored him, and as one observer noted, there have been few more "pathetic figures" than that of Henderson "gazing enviously at the milling groups of representatives who surged up and down the floor and cast not a glance at the lonely, rubicund, kindly figure in the corner." In mid-July he left London to tour the European capitals for several weeks like "Diogenes looking for an honest man."[96] On July 22 Hitler told him that Germany absolutely rejected a trial supervision period to precede French disarmament.[97]

While Henderson toured, Davis returned to the United States where he talked with Ambassador Luther, who reported to Berlin that Davis' attitude was not unsympathetic to Germany and that he fully understood Germany's demand for equality of rights. But when Davis brought up the question of a trial period, adding that France could not be pushed further, Luther too insisted upon immediate French disarmament.[98] Still, the Americans persisted in efforts at a disarmament agreement, although by September Roosevelt believed, as he told his ambassador in Rome, Breckinridge Long, that the man who could do most for disarmament was Italy's Benito Mussolini, who was suggesting a conference of foreign ministers at Stresa—a proposal that the Germans were mulling over.[99] Nevertheless, while humorously promising Davis burial in Arlington Cemetery if he could "pull off" disarmament, the President thought the "crux of the problem" lay between Germany and France and that perhaps Davis could arrange a meeting between Hitler, Daladier, MacDonald, and Mussolini which would hasten progress toward the "only answer": controlled disarmament and international supervision. At the same time Roosevelt wrote MacDonald that he felt "concerned by events in Germany," and worried that Europe was engaged in an "insane rush" to further armaments.[100]

Davis remained optimistic in early September. On his way to Ge-

---

96. Wheeler-Bennett, *Pipe Dream of Peace*, 164–165.
97. Neurath Memorandum, July 22, 1933, *DGFP*, C, I, 686–687.
98. Luther to Foreign Ministry, Aug. 26, 1933, GFM, K1868/K471950.
99. Roosevelt to Long, Sept. 11, 1933, Breckinridge Long papers, Box 105, Manuscript Division, Library of Congress.
100. Roosevelt to Davis (two letters), and Roosevelt to MacDonald, Aug. 30, 1933, *FR 1933*, I, 208–210.

neva he told Simon that he feared only that current apprehension over the Hitler regime would make the British side too closely with the traditionally suspicious French and thus lose their ability to pressure them. Simon assured him that British pressure would be "vigorous and continuous."[101] Simon, Eden, and Davis then proceeded to Paris, where on September 22 they reached tentative accord with the French, who now insisted on a four-year trial period before significantly reducing their army and armaments. But, in addition to agreeing to a doubling of the size of the Reichswehr from 100,000 to 200,000 men, they conceded to allow Germany some intermediary weapons currently prohibited under the Treaty of Versailles. Details concerning supervision and possible guarantees in case of violation of a future agreement also had to be worked out.[102] Two days later, however, Neurath, who had gone to Geneva, told Simon that Germany would not accept a trial period, unless the French agreed at once and "very precisely" to the dates on which it would destroy specified types and amounts of weapons; more cynically, Neurath added in his report to Berlin, he did not think anyone would agree to allow Germany's demand for "samples" of weapons other nations now possessed "and the negotiations here presumably will collapse over this point."[103] In further discussions Neurath insisted on the German right to acquire weapons currently prohibited by treaty, especially aircraft, despite diplomatic pleadings that France had already made major concessions by agreeing to an enlarged Reichswehr and to destroying French armaments in a few years.[104] Nevertheless, Davis remained "guardedly hopeful" that agreement could be reached.[105]

Neurath returned to Berlin on September 30, evidently highly dissatisfied at the refusal of the other powers to give in to German demands, and he immediately raised the question of whether negotiations should be broken off or delayed. Hitler responded that an agreement

101. Davis Memorandum, Sept. 6, 1933, Davis papers, Box 9.
102. Davis to Hull, Sept. 23, 1933, *FR 1933*, I, 224–226. British version in Record of a Meeting at the Quai d'Orsay, Sept. 22, 1933, *DBFP*, 2d ser., V, 621–624.
103. Neurath to Foreign Ministry, Sept. 24, 1933, *DGFP*, C, I, 836–838; British version in Simon to Foreign Office, Sept. 27, 1933, *DBFP*, 2d ser., V, 632–635.
104. Neurath Memoranda, Sept. 26, Sept. 28, and Sept. 29, 1933, *DGFP*, C, I, 844–849, 871–872, 874–875.
105. Davis to Hull, Sept. 28, 1933, *FR 1933*, I, 232–235.

would be desirable "even if not all our wishes were fulfilled by it," and further, with regard to equality of rights in matériel, asking for more than Germany was technically, financially, and politically able to produce in the next few years would be wrong. He wished this view to be maintained in further negotiations.[106]

Why Hitler now appeared more conciliatory than his foreign minister and various of his diplomats cannot be determined positively, but there are important clues. To begin, as noted earlier, the MacDonald plan as originally proposed nearly matched Germany's contemplated secret rearmament program and capacity. Then, Ambassador Ulrich von Hassell had just reported from Rome that in a long interview Mussolini had evidenced his desire to achieve a treaty, expressed great sympathy for the German position, and thought French fears "utterly unfounded." But he still urgently suggested that Germany give him exact figures for all categories of weapons it demanded so that perhaps the trial period could be reduced to two years.[107] Further, for some time the German chargé in Washington, Rudolf Leitner, had been sending lengthy reports of an aroused American public opinion highly critical of German policy. Leitner was an extremely able career diplomat who had good relations with American newsmen and was known to compile exact and reliable reports for the Foreign Ministry.[108] In August he noted that American newspapers were emphasizing Germany's diplomatic isolation. In September he reported that correspondents always commented on German foreign policy in a manner of "outspoken unfriendliness, which borders on odiousness," and that they encouraged European nations to align themselves so as to isolate Germans. Again on September 25 Leitner reported that newspapers in America had created the impression "that an iron ring had been forged around Germany," and there was even word from some Paris correspondents that preventive war was a possibility.[109] Hitler, of course, paid scant attention to traditional diplomatic assessments, but he was astute enough to recognize the implications of various evidence. Hence his remarks to Neurath on September 30 may probably be taken at face value as a

106. Neurath Memorandum, Sept. 30, 1933, *DGFP*, C, I, 882.
107. Hassell to Foreign Ministry, Sept. 30, 1933, *ibid.*, 879–882.
108. Prittwitz, *Zwischen Petersburg und Washington*, 177.
109. Leitner to Foreign Ministry, Aug. 14, Sept. 8, and Sept. 25, 1933, GFM, 5747/HO34969-HO34971, 5741/HO35022-HO35025, 5747/HO35039-HO35045.

realistic assessment of the current possibilities and limits of German diplomatic achievement.

Nevertheless, Hitler was not about to allow himself to be bound by anyone else's diplomatic initiative and was disturbed when on October 4 the German chargé in London, Otto von Bismarck, reported that the British and Americans were preparing a revised draft convention that would stipulate the types and amounts of weapons Germany could have. Hitler, supported by Neurath, War Minister von Blomberg, and the state secretary in the Foreign Ministry, Bernhard von Bülow, promptly had communicated to Simon in London and Davis in Geneva an *aide-mémoire* on October 6 which accepted the MacDonald plan as a basis for negotiation but rejected a trial period and insisted no limits be placed on weapons allowed Germany where other countries were not similarly bound.[110]

Diplomats everywhere received Germany's message badly. Hull told Luther that America would never be party to an agreement that provided for rearmament, which was what the Germans were demanding. Luther, seemingly bewildered by the adverse response, then went to see Jay Pierrepont Moffat, the chief of the Division of Western European Affairs. Moffat too emphasized that the United States would not sanction German rearmament "in no matter how modified a form" and insisted France had made more concessions than ever, but Luther "brushed these aside as mere words."[111] In England the Germans made no more headway. Simon told Hoesch that it was unthinkable that Germany's neighbors would disarm without assurances of security and that no one would consent to immediate increases in German armaments. In Geneva, Nadolny talked individually with Henderson, Davis, and later Simon; no one would give ground.[112] Yet Davis remained surprisingly confident. Nadolny, he remarked, was clearly upset and had come to see him "as a father confessor" for advice; the Germans,

---

110. Bismarck to Foreign Ministry, Bülow Memorandum, and Bülow to Weizsäcker, Oct. 4, 1933, *DGFP*, C, I, 885–899. Ernst von Weizsäcker was minister to Switzerland. Text of *aide-mémoire* in Wheeler-Bennett, ed. *Documents 1933*, 279–281.

111. Hull, *Memoirs*, I, 230; Moffat Memorandum, Oct. 9, 1933, *FR 1933*, I, 243–245; see also diary entry for Oct. 9, 1933, Hooker, ed., *Moffat Papers*, 100–104.

112. Hoesch to Foreign Ministry, Oct. 10, and Nadolny to Foreign Ministry, Oct. 12, 1933, *DGFP*, C, I, 898–900, 912–913.

he concluded, would "take what they can get," and minor changes would make an agreement palatable to them.[113]

Time was running out, however, and perhaps no one sensed it better than Nadolny, who obviously sought accommodation and agreement even while maintaining his country's position according to instruction. On October 7 he received a cable informing him he was being transferred to Moscow, indicative of the forthcoming end of disarmament negotiations.[114] Five days later he received word from Neurath that Hitler was ordering him back to Berlin. Nadolny replied that he had good information Davis was trying to arrange a compromise agreement and he pleaded to be allowed to remain, but Neurath insisted on his return.[115]

Meanwhile Hitler pursued his policy. He took Neurath and Papen to see President von Hindenburg, and persuaded him to support their intention to quit both the Geneva discussions and the League of Nations—overcoming his doubts about leaving the League by insisting it was merely an extension of the Treaty of Versailles and that German withdrawal would not take place finally for two years, allowing time for every country to consider a new accord with Germany. Neurath admitted at Nuremberg in 1945 that after his return from Geneva in September 1933 he had encouraged Hitler in this step because he felt no disarmament agreement was possible and that without the United States, the Soviet Union, and departed Japan, "there was no League of Nations anymore." According to Hindenburg's secretary, Meissner, Papen too supported Hitler's contentions, although he later insisted that he had opposed leaving the League with "utmost vehemence" but could get no help on this point from Neurath.[116]

Thus supported, Hitler confronted his cabinet in the early evening of October 13 and declared that the time had come to "torpedo the

---

113. Davis to Moffat, Oct. 10, 1933, Davis papers, Box 41.
114. Nadolny, *Mein Beitrag*, 138.
115. Neurath to Nadolny (2 cables), and Nadolny to Neurath, Oct. 12, 1933, *DGFP*, C, I, 915–916, 915n1, 915n3.
116. Meissner, *Staatssekretär*, 347–348; Neurath's testimony in U.S. Department of State, *Nazi Conspiracy and Aggression*, 8 vols. plus supplements A and B (Washington, D.C., 1946–48), supp. B, 1504; Franz von Papen, *Memoirs*, trans. Brian Connell (New York, 1953), 297–298. Papen rationalized his public support for Hitler's policy on the ground that Hindenburg's consent left no choice, and he still hoped to neutralize Nazi radicals.

Disarmament Conference . . . The path of negotiation is now closed."
The chancellor announced his intention to dissolve the Reichstag, set
new elections, and asked the German people through a plebiscite to affirm their faith in the "peace policy of the Reich Government." With
regard to possible sanctions against Germany, "it was only a matter of
keeping cool and remaining true to one's principles." Everyone approved, according to the official record of the meeting.[117] But apparently Nadolny had reached Berlin by then, walked in on the meeting,
and raised questions about Neurath's interpretation of the British terms
for a trial period—for which assertion Neurath and the Reich air minister, Hermann Göring, bitterly attacked him. Nevertheless, Blomberg,
who had been on Nadolny's staff at Geneva before becoming war minister in February 1933, wondered if the situation might not be different
than assumed, apparently causing Hitler to adjourn the meeting and
put off the final decision until the next day.[118]

Hitler and Neurath knew they would have their way, for that evening
they informed their ambassadors that because of unacceptable demands
put forward by the British and French, and supported by the Americans, Germany was going to withdraw from the Disarmament Conference.[119] Next morning Nadolny, who apparently did not know of these
telegrams, called on Hindenburg to explain what had happened at the
cabinet meeting and to seek support. But, according to his recollection,
he received only sarcastic pleasantries—and according to Hitler's later
gleeful recall, Hindenburg virtually threw Nadolny out, brusquely ordering him to get to his new post in Moscow.[120] Whatever the case, by
the time Nadolny returned from his interview he discovered to his dismay that the cabinet had already met without him to confirm the previously proposed action, leaving him little to do but lament to Papen.[121]
In mid-afternoon of October 14 Henderson received a telegram from
Neurath informing the conference of Germany's action while the gov-

117. Minutes of the Conference of Ministers on October 13 and October 14,
1933, *DGFP, C,* I, 922–926.
118. Nadolny, *Mein Beitrag,* 140.
119. Neurath to Embassies in Italy, Great Britain, France, and the United
States, Oct. 13, 1933, *DGFP, C,* I, 921.
120. Nadolny, *Mein Beitrag,* 140; entry for May 21, 1942, *Hitler's Secret
Conversations,* 406.
121. Nadolny, *Mein Beitrag,* 140–141.

ernment formally proclaimed its decision and Hitler put the finishing touches on the day's activities in an evening broadcast assailing the "deliberate degradation" of Germany and calling upon his people to make a "historic declaration" in the forthcoming November 12 election and referendum.[122]

Amid the wreckage Davis remained composed. Talking on the telephone to Roosevelt and Hull, he said he was "disturbed" but not without hope; information led him to believe that "Hitler is the best one of the lot and this election is going to get rid of some of the worst in his group. He certainly wants to make peace with France." Two days later Davis wrote that Hitler had withdrawn his country from the conference and the League only for "interior political reasons"; in a couple of days he added that Germany's action might well have a "sobering effect" on later and more determined disarmament negotiation.[123] Roosevelt held to the instructions he had given Davis on the telephone: Davis was to declare publicly that the United States was in Geneva for disarmament purposes only and not interested "in the political element or any purely European aspect of the picture," and the European nations had to determine whether disarmament talks would continue.[124]

Europe's response to Germany's action was resigned if not feeble. Henderson replied to Neurath's telegram only that he could not accept the reasons offered in it as justifying Germany's grave decision.[125] The British regretted the failure of their efforts and hoped, as Simon put it to Ambassador Sir Eric Phipps in Berlin, that thereafter the Germans would avoid a rigid attitude and learn to "promote neighbourly relations." The French response, Marriner noted after a talk with Léger, was "very temperate."[126] And Mussolini, who had urged Hitler to be moderate in the broadcast of October 14 to avoid antagonizing the

122. Text of telegram in *FR 1933*, I, 265; text of proclamation in *DGFP*, C, II, 1–2; text of speech in Baynes, ed., *Hitler's Speeches*, II, 1092–1104.

123. Memorandum Roosevelt-Hull-Davis Conversation, Oct. 16, 1933, *FR 1933*, I, 273–276; Davis to Moffat, Oct. 18 and Oct. 20, 1933, Davis papers, Box 41.

124. Davis to Hull, Oct. 16, 1933, *FR 1933*, I, 277; Hull, *Memoirs*, I, 230–231.

125. Henderson to Neurath, Oct. 16, 1933, Wheeler-Bennett, ed., *Documents 1933*, 286.

126. Simon to Phipps, Oct. 23, 1933, *DBFP*, 2d ser., V, 706; entry for Oct. 15, 1933, Marriner Diary, Marriner papers.

Americans, thought everyone ought to stay calm while the Germans were "burning down their house in order to cook an egg."[127]

Hitler scarcely had burned down his house; rather, he had shored up his position at home and succeeded at a major diplomatic coup. To begin, while the Disarmament Conference would linger into the spring of 1934, after the events of October 14, 1933, as Hull would later write, "disarmament was dead."[128] Hitler knew this. Three days afterward he could smugly tell his ministers that the "political situation has developed as was to be expected." Nobody had done anything, Germany need do nothing. "The critical moment," the chancellor said, "has probably passed. The excitement will presumably subside itself within a short time."[129] A short while later, when Hermann Rauschning remarked of his worry about sanctions or even war against Germany, Hitler cried: "These people want war. Let them have it—but only when it suits me . . . They don't dream of making war . . . A pretty crew they are! They'll never act! They'll just protest. And they will always be too late."[130]

Hitler had many reasons for withdrawing from Geneva. Afterward he told Rauschning that it was a "liberating deed" which would be "universally comprehensible." Difficulties might be momentarily increased, but the deed was "the only sort of action, be it wise or not" that the people understood. The sterile debates of the past were over, and now people would have confidence in their chancellor, and believe that their government had restored their liberty of action with respect to other nations.[131] The results of historical analysis indicate that Hitler's assessment was valid. He wished to show the world that he was a real "Führer," while at the same time strike a decisive blow at the Geneva system which he believed worked systematically against the Reich.[132] Moreover, because in the totalitarian world foreign and domestic policy are especially bound together, this occasion allowed Hitler both to achieve a diplomatic victory that obscured earlier Nazi

127. Mussolini advice to Hitler is reported in Hassell to Hitler, Oct. 14, 1933, *DGFP*, C, I, 929; Mussolini quoted in Sir R. Graham to Sir V. Wellesley, Oct. 15, 1933, *DBFP*, 2d ser., V, 684–685.

128. *Memoirs*, I, 231.

129. Minutes of the Conference of Ministers on October 17, 1933, *DGFP*, C, II, 12.

130. Quoted in Rauschning, *Voice of Destruction*, 104.

131. *Ibid.*, 106.

132 Meinck, *Hitler und die deutsche Aufrüstung*, 47–49.

diplomatic embarrassments, such as at London, and at the same time to shield and reinforce the consolidation of domestic power.[133] Hence, by the time of the November 12 plebiscite and elections, which resulted in overwhelming affirmation of Hitler's policy, Hindenburg was willing to make a nationwide broadcast the night before praising the courageous behavior that restored German national honor and to treat with real deference, even in private, the man he once despised.[134]

Finally, while Hitler's uncanny political timing pointed up the faint-heartedness of Anglo-French solidarity and avoided having the New Order agree to any military limit on Germany (that stigma was for the founders of the Weimar government), Germany's more traditional diplomats aided his purpose. Clearly Neurath played a major role, even to the point of encouraging Hitler to go faster than he might have, as witness Hitler's hesitation on September 30. Hindenburg was persuaded without much effort, and Blomberg and Papen, momentary hesitation notwithstanding, approved the policy. So did State Secretary von Bülow, nephew of the former chancellor under Kaiser Wilhelm II, and a man whom even the bitterest critics of the new German regime found honorable.[135] Yet when some American newspapers wondered if the German aide-mémoire of October 6 violated guarantees made to America in the 1921 Berlin Treaty, Bülow drew up a long defense which argued in the main that Germany had the right to rearm because other nations had not disarmed. After Germany left the League of Nations, he wrote that undoubtedly many European countries and "so-called Neutrals" would pretend astonishment, and he encouraged German diplomats in America to seek out prominent people to contrast the political purity of the Kellogg Pact with the Treaty of Versailles which encumbered the League of Nations.[136] The case is clear too with regard to Ernst von Weizsäcker, at the time minister to

133. Karl Dietrich Bracher, "Das 'Dritte Reich' zwischen Abschirmung und Expansion," in Bracher, Wolfgang Sauer, and Gerhard Schulz, *Die national-sozialistische Machtergreifung: Studien zur Errichtung des totalitären Herrschaftssystems in Deutschland, 1933/34* (Cologne and Opladen, 1960), 220, 243. On various Nazi diplomatic setbacks in 1933, see Seabury, *Wilhelmstrasse*, 26–27, 33–37, Schmidt, *Statist auf diplomatischer Bühne*, 262–263, and Erich Kordt, *Nicht aus den Akten* . . . (Stuttgart, 1950), 55.
134. Dorpalen, *Hindenburg*, 474–475.
135. See, for example, M. Dodd, *Through Embassy Eyes,* 249–250.
136. Bülow to Delegation at Geneva, Oct. 14, and Bülow to Embassy in Washington, Oct. 24, 1933, GFM, K1868/K471951-K471956, 5747/HO35088.

Switzerland and from 1938 to 1943 state secretary, who even in his memoirs blamed "one-sided compulsion" and "reactionary" policy at Geneva for German rearmament.[137] Thus Nadolny alone opposed the decision of October 14, 1933.

Then, and later of course, German diplomats would insist that the issue was "equality," that having suffered discrimination for fifteen years, Germans could wait no longer. And it may be true, as has been suggested, that Hitler would have made his decision even had his advisers opposed it.[138] But his advisers did support his position, and in so doing they not only increased the basis for suspicion and fear of German policy, but also ironically reduced their own influence and advanced Hitler's judgment and methods against negotiation and compromise.[139]

The United States shared responsibility for the magnitude of Germany's diplomatic coup, although in fairness one must conclude that the fact that a disarmament agreement seemed as near as it did is a tribute to American hard work. Nevertheless, the Johnson amendment to the McReynolds resolution ensured against cooperation, even in the most negative way, with collective security. Roosevelt's capitulation to the Senate Foreign Relations Committee, opening the door to greater consequences, made questionable his resolve, and that of his administration, to participate in world affairs. When the United States announced on October 16 that it cared only about disarmament, not the "political aspects of peace"—which statement Herbert Feis then and later thought "momentous"—Europeans had to conclude that America knew and cared little about Old World realities, and Neville Chamberlain wrote that "the Americans are chiefly anxious to convince their people that they are not going to be drawn into doing anything helpful to the rest of the world."[140] Finally, Davis did not play his role as well as he might have. Admittedly he got along well with Nadolny, even if, as Moffat noted, he sometimes mistakenly believed a problem solved when he struck accord with the man with whom he was negotiating. But

137. Weizsäcker, *Memoirs*, 100.

138. Gordon A. Craig, "The German Foreign Office from Neurath to Ribbentrop," in Craig and Gilbert, eds., *The Diplomats*, 415.

139. Bracher, "Das 'Dritte Reich,'" in Bracher and others, *Die nationalsozialistische Machtergreifung*, 245.

140. Feis, *1933*, 305; Chamberlain quoted in Feiling, *Chamberlain*, 226.

his evaluation of Hitler as "the best one of the lot" showed little perception, and sometimes he did not appreciate the compelling French political and psychological demands for security.[141] There was little reason for Davis to write in tones as evidently satisfied as his were, shortly after Germany withdrew from the conference, that he had recently talked Simon out of taking a strong position toward the Germans, perhaps threatening to impose a treaty upon them.[142]

The Disarmament Conference had failed; the tortuous progress made since 1932 was broken at one blow. The diplomats were tired, angry. Still, on the day Hitler spoke to his ministers the American ambassador in Berlin, after a talk with him and his foreign minister, could write to the State Department that the "total effect of the interview was more favorable from the point of view of the maintenance of world peace than I had expected."[143] Perhaps there was an avenue to understanding that the ambassador might explore.

141. Diary entry for Dec. 8 and Dec. 9, 1934, Hooker, ed., *Moffat Papers,* 121.
142. Davis to Moffat, Oct. 18, 1933, Davis papers, Box 41.
143. Dodd to Hull, Oct. 18, 1933, *FR 1933,* II, 397.

# 3. DETERIORATING RELATIONS

Choosing an American ambassador to Germany in 1933 was difficult, and for three months after Roosevelt took office there was no replacement for Sackett in Berlin. Other posts were filled. Robert W. Bingham, the publisher of the Louisville *Courier-Journal* and a friend of of Hull, Secretary of Commerce Daniel C. Roper, and the aging Colonel Edward M. House, agreed to serve in London. Jesse Straus, president of R. H. Macy's in New York, accepted the Paris post. Josephus Daniels, Roosevelt's chief in the Navy Department during the Wilson era, was going to Mexico City. The career diplomat Joseph C. Grew was staying on in Tokyo. The historian Claude Bowers chose Madrid. The wealthy Breckinridge Long, assistant secretary of state from 1917 to 1920, and Roosevelt's floor manager in 1932, went to Rome.[1] The criteria usually applied to choosing an ambassador, however—friendship with the President, faithfulness to the party or contributions to its coffers, demonstration of exceptional ability as a foreign service officer—did not readily apply to the Berlin post. The *New York Times* was partly right on April 9 when it reported that Roosevelt was delaying his choice because he wanted to get a closer look at the activities of the new German government. He regarded the Berlin embassy as of "special importance" at the time.[2]

---

1. Graham H. Stuart, *The Department of State: A History of Its Organization, Procedure, and Personnel* (New York, 1949), 315–316; Robert Bendiner, *The Riddle of the State Department* (New York, 1942), 176–177.
2. Roosevelt to Cox, Mar. 9, 1933, in Elliott Roosevelt, ed., *F.D.R.: His Per-*

Conditions in Germany made heading a mission there unappealing, and a suitable and interested candidate was hard to find.

Roosevelt's early choice, James M. Cox, declined.[3] So did former secretary of war Newton D. Baker and Owen D. Young; several others were passed over. Leaders of the Democratic party in New York got into a hassle and failed to agree on a candidate.[4] Finally, during the first week in June, Secretary Roper nominated a willing, though somewhat reluctant, candidate: a professor of history at the University of Chicago, William E. Dodd.[5]

Roper and Dodd were old friends, having campaigned together for Wilson in 1916. Roper knew the professor as a fervent partisan of Jeffersonian-Wilsonian ideas of democracy and government, and he believed such ideas would help him in Berlin. Hull, too, was well acquainted with Dodd and "exceedingly fond" of him, but skeptical about his effectiveness. Dodd's loquacity, he recalled, reminded him too much of William Jennings Bryan, who had been given "to run off on tangents."[6] Roosevelt's acquaintance with Dodd was slight, but he knew something of him through his publications and the letters, filled with various advice, which Dodd wrote him in 1932. On June 8 Roosevelt telephoned Dodd, who agreed after a few hours' consideration to take the post. The Senate confirmed the nomination four days later.[7]

---

*sonal Letters, 1928–1945,* 2 vols. (New York, 1950), I, 337; hereafter cited as *FDRL.*

3. *Ibid.,* 338.

4. Edward J. Flynn, *You're the Boss* (New York, 1947), 146–148; see also Robert Dallek, "Roosevelt's Ambassador: The Public Career of William E. Dodd" (Ph.D. dissertation, Columbia University, 1964), 179–181.

5. Roper to Dodd, June 8, 1933, William E. Dodd papers, Box 41, Manuscript Division, Library of Congress. According to House, he too had suggested Dodd's name to the President some weeks earlier, but nothing came of it. House to Dodd, June 10, 1933, *ibid.*

6. Daniel C. Roper, *Fifty Years of Public Life* (Durham, N.C., 1941), 334–335; Hull, *Memoirs,* I, 182.

7. Entry for June 8, 1933, Dodd, *Diary,* 3–4. Flynn, *You're the Boss,* 148, suggested that Dodd's appointment stemmed from confusion, Roosevelt having intended to appoint Walter F. Dodd, a Chicago lawyer who had formerly taught at the University of Illinois and Yale University; Flynn retracted this story shortly after his book was published, *New York Times,* Nov. 2, 1947. There is no evidence for Flynn's story in the memoirs of Hull or Roper. Further, it is clearly refuted in an unpublished memoir left by the then consul general in Berlin, George S. Messersmith, "Some Observations on the Appointment of Dr.

Dodd was born on a small farm in Clayton, North Carolina, in 1869. He attended Virginia Polytechnic Institute and went abroad in the last years of the nineteenth century—as did so many would-be scholars from America—to earn his doctorate at the University of Leipzig. Returning in 1900 he began a long and rewarding career as writer and teacher. He wrote prolifically about the land he loved most, the Old South, and the men who made it: Jefferson, Macon, Calhoun, Lee, and Davis. Dodd was not a profound scholar. Romantic notions clouded his analyses. But by bringing to his books and classrooms compassion and judiciousness, by refusing to grind northern or southern axes, he did much to clear the way for the greater scholars and scholarship that followed in the decades after he had ended his work.

The political, economic, and social perspectives of Dodd and Hull were strikingly similar, although relations between the two men were never close and sometimes strained. Similarities in rural background prevailed over dissimilar formal education. Both men were what one might describe as classical liberal southern Democrats. Their twentieth-century hero was Woodrow Wilson, whose income tax, low tariff, trustbusting, and League of Nations Hull championed in Congress while Dodd did so in the classroom and a book, *Woodrow Wilson and His Work* (New York, 1920). Both men agreed that the way to a successful foreign policy lay in liberal trade agreements and that the best of all possible tariffs was the lowest. Highly moral in public pronouncement, Dodd and Hull made a virtue out of modest financial habits and circumstances and were suspicious of wealthier members of eastern "ivy league" business and academic circles who so often had the President's ear. Dodd and Hull differed—accounting probably for their failure to work together—in that Hull was an experienced, cautious, and shrewd politician, whereas Dodd refused to, or perhaps could not, restrain his intellectual and emotional instincts in the face of difficult and subtle aspects of politics and diplomacy. Above all, as a contemporary experienced diplomat described him, Dodd was "very sure of his opinion, and does not hesitate to call a spade a spade."[8]

---

William Dodd as Ambassador to Berlin," Messersmith papers, Box 7, Manuscript Division, University of Delaware Library, Newark, Del.
    8. Moffat to Gordon, June 21, 1933, Moffat papers.

Roosevelt's telephone call was not the first hint Dodd had that a diplomatic assignment might be forthcoming. He had corresponded with Roper and House for several months about a government position, although he was reluctant to put aside his scholarship and at first preferred working informally as a presidential adviser, a minister without portfolio.[9] He recognized that there was no precedent for this, and with no other appointment available overcame his fear that the Hitler government would be too disagreeable for his temperament and worked up enthusiasm for the new task. He always had looked back nostalgically upon his graduate school days and always—up to the outbreak of the Second World War—believed the German people "by nature more democratic than any other great race in Europe." Here, at a critical moment in history, as his daughter would explain, was opportunity for the distinguished teacher to fulfill a vision glimpsed as a young man: to return "to the Germany he loved . . . to represent his own country."[10]

In mid-June Dodd went to the White House to learn from Roosevelt what he wished him to do in Berlin, to review State Department files, and to familiarize himself with the policy his government intended to pursue with respect to the new regime in Germany.

Taking the measure of the Hitler government in the spring of 1933 was difficult because the chancellor's accession to power on January 30 had been constitutional, but Germany obviously was in the throes of an enormous revolution, whose final limits and direction were unknown. Reports American diplomats sent home were a conglomeration of certainty and guesswork, hope and despair, incisiveness and blindness. American policy moved accordingly, sometimes showing initiative and strategy—as in the case of Roosevelt's May 16 disarmament appeal—but far more often moving listlessly and without design.

Diplomatic opinion differed on the new Germany. For the American consul general at Stuttgart, Leon Dominian, Germany's new masters represented something old, "the cynical militarism of their prede-

9. Dodd to House, Feb. 25 and Mar. 4, Dodd to Roper, Mar. 4 and Mar. 15, 1933, Dodd papers, Box 41.
10. Entry for Sept. 20, 1938, Dodd, *Diary,* 447; M. Dodd, *Through Embassy Eyes,* 12.

cessors of pre-Weimar days," and, he felt, the United States should deal with them accordingly. For Douglas Miller, commercial attaché in Berlin, the average Nazi was essentially a "young, ignorant, and romantic" misfit, willing to declare the modern capitalistic world in which he had never known success a failure, voting for a "return to medieval status where the individual does not have to do his own thinking." The Nazi revolution, Miller believed, was the work of a handful of "fanatics and adventurers who had learned how to appeal to the moron majority in a period of depression and discouragement."[11] Miller and many other Americans did not yet believe the Nazis a large threat. The NSDAP represented "almost unanimous" German opinion on such critical questions as disarmament and revision of the Treaty of Versailles. Still, the National Socialist revolution was both an assertion of Germany's rights against other nations and an effort at adjusting class and occupational problems in Germany.[12] By the summer of 1933 Miller regarded Hitler and his immediate lieutenants as the moderate forces trying desperately to ward off a second revolution. Withdrawal from the Disarmament Conference hardly disturbed Miller, who remained unconvinced as to any threat of the new German government in international affairs. Having given *Mein Kampf* a careful reading, he concluded that Hitler's advocacy of deception in foreign affairs, his "inflammatory statements regarding foreign policy and Germany's mission to expand in the East," were all so much propaganda. There was no reason for concern: "The Nazis' war talk, superman talk and posing is simply designed to impress their followers and should be discounted."[13]

Davis, the American disarmament negotiator, had reached much the same conclusions. No one could understand what was happening in Germany without being there. Germany, he wrote from Berlin in the early spring of 1933, was in the midst of a "real revolution." One

11. Dominian to Hull, Apr. 4, 1933, *FR 1933,* II, 216; Miller, Report to the Bureau of Foreign and Domestic Commerce, May 10, 1933, Douglas Miller, *Via Diplomatic Pouch* (New York, 1944), 40.

12. Miller, Report to the Bureau of Foreign and Domestic Commerce, May 19, 1933, *Via Diplomatic Pouch,* 47.

13. Miller, Report to the Bureau of Foreign and Domestic Commerce, Nov. 29, 1933, *ibid.,* 80–81.

had to expect "certain excesses," though the American press probably made too much of them. He could not determine the course of the revolution and its effects on foreign policy. These would depend on Hitler's ability to withstand radicals in his party and also to shackle the semimilitary forces he had organized for purposes of the revolution. The Hitler government was committed to an early revision of the Treaty of Versailles, although the exact method was unclear.[14]

Long-term objectives of the Hitler government did not appear of immediate concern. American diplomats knew that in 1933 Germany was no threat. Politically isolated, mired in the world-wide economic collapse which saw more than 6,000,000 Germans unemployed, its army of 100,000 greatly outnumbered and outgunned by the French, the Germans could not move in any direction without running against the French alliance system.[15] Nonetheless, Germany affected American interests, and it was necessary for the government to respond to developments there.

One development, persecution of the Jews, had by no means assumed a pattern in 1933. From the end of January until the March 5 Reichstag elections, the government and NSDAP proceeded cautiously with anti-Semitic policies, attacking Jews who were opponents of the National Socialist party by virtue of their being Social Democrats or Communists. After March 5, commanding a majority in the Reichstag for the first time through support by the Nationalists, the Nazis made their attacks more frequent, arbitrary, and bloody. The government apologized, blaming undisciplined NSDAP members acting as party men, not government officials. As attacks abated everyone waited to see what would be the outcome of the government's official one-day boycott of all Jewish businesses scheduled for April 1.[16]

Ambassador Sackett reported in early March that four American Jews in Berlin had been beaten up and one of them forced to rescind an eviction notice against a Nazi tenant who owed a year's rent. Hull lodged no protest, and when Hitler on the morning of March 11 is-

14. Davis to Hull, Apr. 16, 1933, *FR 1933,* II, 216–220.
15. Alan Bullock, *Hitler: A Study in Tyranny,* rev. ed. (New York, 1962), 320.
16. Harry Schneidermann, ed., *The American Jewish Year Book, 5694* (Philadelphia, 1933), 26–27.

sued a public appeal to his followers to maintain law and order, Sackett optimistically declared anti-Jewish demonstrations at an end.[17] Violence intensified. Shortly a delegation representing American Jewish organizations called upon Hull to urge him to protest to the German government. He declined, saying at a press conference next day that the United States was still "endeavoring industriously" to gain information on conditions in Germany.[18]

While Hull and the State Department hesitated, the American Jewish Committee, American Jewish Congress, and B'nai B'rith scheduled a protest rally for March 27 in New York's Madison Square Garden. Hull became upset and, convinced that outside intercession would do no good in Germany, asked Chargé Gordon in Berlin what might calm emotions on both sides of the Atlantic before the "monster mass meeting" took place. Believing that Hitler represented the moderate element that needed strengthening, Gordon suggested that the American government affirm its "confidence in Hitler's determination to restore peaceful and normal conditions." At the same time, Ambassador von Prittwitz implied to his superiors that they ought to disregard the whole affair.[19]

Hull meanwhile sought to moderate or postpone the Madison Square Garden rally. He sent a public telegram to Cyrus Adler, president of the American Jewish Committee, and Alfred M. Cohen, president of B'nai B'rith, declaring that according to his information the physical mistreatment of Jews was now "virtually terminated." He said that restoration of equilibrium, after a period of far-reaching political readjustment, took time, and that the embassy there believed the Jewish situation in Germany was improving.[20]

The Madison Square Garden rally took place as scheduled. Before a packed house such notables as John P. O'Brien, mayor of New York, Senator Robert F. Wagner, William Green, president of the American Federation of Labor, and Bishops William T. Manning (Ro-

17. Sackett to Hull, Mar. 8 and Mar. 11, 1933, *FR 1933*, II, 321–322.
18. Memorandum Hull Press Conference, Mar. 22, 1933, *ibid.*, 327–328.
19. Hull to Gordon, Mar. 24, and Gordon to Hull, Mar. 23, 1933, *ibid.*, 330–332. Prittwitz to Foreign Ministry, Mar. 21 and Mar. 23, 1933, GFM, 5747/HO34081, 5747/HO34084-HO34085.
20. Cyrus Adler and Aaron M. Margalith, *American Intercession in Behalf of the Jews in the Diplomatic Correspondence of the United States, 1840–1938* (New York, 1943), 365.

man Catholic Church) and Francis J. McConnell (Methodist Episcopal Church) called for an end to the barbarous behavior in Germany. Hull did not know what to do. He in no way sympathized with assaults on the German Jews, yet believed it impossible for the American government to intervene. To do nothing was to allow matters to worsen, for the scheduled German boycott of April 1 brought a threat by Jewish spokesmen in America of a full-scale boycott of German-made goods. Hull, for whom the basis of harmonious international relations was good economic relations, viewed all this as senseless destruction. At the eleventh hour Under Secretary Phillips telephoned Gordon in Berlin, instructing him to tell Foreign Minister von Neurath that if Germany called off its boycott the American government would issue a statement that reports of atrocities in Germany had been exaggerated.[21] On March 31 Gordon saw Neurath who told him it was too late to prevent the boycott. Gordon, willing to give the government in Berlin every opportunity to show its best face, concluded a few days later that by any standard Germany as reflected by its present regime was "unregenerate and insatiable."[22]

The Germans increased pressure on the Jews in the weeks following, driving them out of universities, civil service, and legal and other professions. Public protest in the United States increased, with state governors and legislatures and business and professional groups sending petitions either to Berlin or Washington. Resolutions and two more visits by Adler and Cohen failed to move the State Department. The most Hull would say publicly was that he would continue to watch the situation.[23] In August Phillips informed leaders of Jewish organizations that from then on American consular offices in Europe were to give "utmost consideration" to Jews applying for visas to the United States.[24]

Jewish leaders organized boycotts of German products in 1933. By the end of the year they had built two major organizations, the Non-

21. Memorandum Phillips-Gordon Conversation, Mar. 31, 1933, *FR 1933*, II, 342.
22. Memorandum Phillips-Gordon Conversation, Mar. 31, and Gordon to Hull, Apr. 2, 1933, *ibid.*, 344, 349–350.
23. State Department Press Release, Apr. 28, 1933, *New York Times*, Apr. 29, 1933.
24. Adler and Margalith, *American Intercession*, 366.

Sectarian Anti-Nazi League to Champion Human Rights, and the Boycott Committee of the American Jewish Congress, which in August
1936 became the Joint Boycott Council of the American Jewish Congress and the Jewish Labor Committee. Samuel Untermyer, a Virginia-
born New York lawyer of German-Jewish ancestry, headed the Anti-
Nazi League; Dr. Joseph Tenenbaum, a urologist and Austrian emigré
who came to the United States in 1920, headed the Joint Boycott
Council, with Baruch Charney Vladeck, a Russian emigré and general
manager of the *Jewish Daily Forward,* as cochairman.[25]

The boycott organizations made headway in New York because of
availability of personnel and funds there and managed to establish
bases in other big cities. But as Tenenbaum complained in 1935, the
movement elsewhere was totally disorganized.[26] Complicating matters
was disagreement between organizations and leaders. When Tenenbaum asked Vladeck, who was chairman of the Jewish Labor Committee, to have that organization support tariff legislation to restrict
import of German goods, Vladeck explained that it was against his
organization's policy to support any obstacles to increased international
trade.[27] Tenenbaum preferred to keep his organization purely Jewish
and regarded Untermyer as "publicity mad." Untermyer insisted on
emphasizing the nonsectarian aspects of his organization and making
use of dramatic public statement and action. He did not hesitate to
criticize Hull and the State Department even for receiving Luther—he
called him "the propagandist masquerading as an Ambassador"—and
for failing to support the boycott as "a spontaneous uprising of all civilization against the revival of medieval savagery."[28] Probably both
the organizations and their leaders shared in their failure to unify and
thereby strengthen the boycott movement.[29]

25. Sheldon Spear, "The United States and the Persecution of the Jews in
Germany, 1933–1939" (Master's thesis, Syracuse University, 1965), 4–6.
26. Tenenbaum to Untermyer, July 2, 1935, Papers of the Joint Boycott
Council of the American Jewish Congress and the Jewish Labor Committee,
Non-Sectarian Anti-Nazi League Box, Manuscript Division, New York Public
Library, New York, N.Y.
27. Tenenbaum to Vladeck, Mar. 9, and Vladeck to Tenenbaum, Mar. 10,
1936, Baruch Charney Vladeck papers, Box A, American Jewish Congress
Folder, New York University Libraries, Tamiment Library, New York, N.Y.
28. Tenenbaum to Vladeck, June 2, 1937, Joint Boycott Council papers, Non-
Sectarian Anti-Nazi League Box; Untermyer quoted in *New York Times,* Sept. 1
and Oct. 19, 1934.
29. Spear, "United States and Persecution of Jews in Germany," 17.

The boycott movement came nowhere near accomplishing its objectives. Clearly exaggerated was Tenenbaum's declaration of hope in his organization's journal that the boycott would curb the Nazi dictatorship and thus do "what the mighty British Navy and the strongest army of France failed or dared not to do."[30] The boycott probably made its greatest impact in 1933–34, when Germany's exports to the United States declined proportionately over twice as much as its exports to the rest of the world.[31] Thereafter Germany seemed able to find new markets, especially in Latin America. While American import of German goods declined slightly in relative proportion to Germany's world-wide sales, the United States increased its dollar value import of German products from nearly $69 million in 1934 to over $91 million in 1937. Sharp decline, first to $63 million and then to $52 million, came only with the crises of 1938 and the war in 1939.[32] The American government maintained a distant attitude, neither supporting nor denouncing the boycott, which went against Hull's emphasis on more and freer trade. German representatives kept officials in Berlin fully posted on protest and boycott movements, frequently sending back long lists of cooperating companies and organizations. The boycott movement, however, was not taken too seriously. Cynically, but correctly as events would show, Reinhold Freytag, a consular official in 1933 and later Foreign Ministry adviser on American affairs, concluded that Americans would buy where it was cheapest and that the boycott movement "in the course of time will come to nothing."[33] Nevertheless, the Germans continued to complain to Hull, who replied that he would use pressure to halt the boycott only after Germany halted its assault on the Jewish people.[34]

The Nazi assault on the Jews was, of course, only one aspect of its attack on all political, economic, and religious groups that in any way

30. *Boycott: Nazi Goods and Services* (Jan. 1937), 6.
31. Allen Thomas Bonnell, *German Control Over International Economic Relations, 1930–1940* (Urbana, Ill., 1940), table 17, p. 130.
32. U.S. Tariff Commission, *Foreign Trade and Export Controls in Germany* (Washington, D.C., 1942), 150–151.
33. On boycott reports see, for example, Leitner to Foreign Ministry, Apr. 13, and Prittwitz to Foreign Ministry, Apr. 25, 1933, GFM, 5747/HO34564-HO34570, 5747/HO34537-HO34539; Freytag to Foreign Ministry, Apr. 20, 1933, GFM, 5747/HO34618-HO34622.
34. Hull Memoranda, Aug. 11, Sept. 14, and Sept. 21, 1933, *FR 1933*, II, 357–359.

opposed the New Order. Labor unions and political parties—Communist, Social Democrat, and Nationalist—had to be, and were, destroyed. The German states had to surrender their independence, Protestants had to subordinate themselves to a Reich Bishop, and the Catholic clergy, under the July 20 Concordat with the Vatican, had to remove themselves from politics. The Nazi *Gleichschaltung,* or coordination steamroller, crushed all opponents.

Events in Germany became the subject for discussion when Dodd's name went to the Senate for confirmation. Senator Joseph E. Robinson, Democratic majority leader from Arkansas, exemplified the congressional consensus. He termed recent German behavior "sickening and terrifying," and deplored German responses to "impulses of cruelty and inhumanity" which would only worsen relations between nations. But like the State Department, Robinson insisted that the United States could not intervene or attempt to determine Germany's domestic policies. Perturbed, Ambassador Luther went to considerable lengths to determine that neither the White House nor the State Department had fostered the speech; Phillips, in fact, assured Luther he had not "the slightest idea" about it beforehand, and Luther happily reported that newspapers gave it minimal space.[35]

National sovereignty of course precluded American intervention in Germany. Yet political developments there affected American interests and treaty rights, and so long as objection to German behavior was not loud and strong these interests and rights would suffer until they were nothing more than scraps of paper. American businessmen began to learn this in April 1933 as they sampled German discrimination when central, state, and municipal governments gave in to the NSDAP demand that they buy from German firms. For any foreign firm to qualify as German, it had to sign an affidavit that it was not owned or directed primarily by foreigners or Jews, and not founded on Marxist principles. George Messersmith, the extremely capable and dedicated consul general in Berlin, reported that firms such as the Remington Typewriter Company, New Burroughs Adding Machine Company, National Cash Register Company, and Watson Electrical Instrument Cor-

35. Text of speech in the American Jewish Committee, *Twenty-Seventh Annual Report* (New York, 1934), 59–60. Luther to Foreign Ministry, June 11 and June 15, 1933, GFM, 5747/HO34706-HO34707 (and copy of speech, 5747/HO34708-HO34712), 5747/HO34737.

poration could not meet these demands. These companies, owned by parent companies in the United States, had chiefly American stockholders, some of whom undoubtedly were Jewish. About all the companies could affirm, Messersmith wryly commented, was that they were not founded on Marxist principles. He also insisted that the new German requirements violated Articles I and XIII of the German-American Treaty of Friendship, Amity, and Commerce, signed in 1923, which guaranteed to American or American-owned German firms doing business in Germany the same rights as firms owned solely by Germans. In Messersmith's mind, as he said a few weeks later, the time for patience had passed; the time had arrived for the State Department to make representations of the "strongest character."[36]

Again the State Department hesitated. Phillips informed Messersmith a month later that unless he felt the situation urgent he need not hurry his reports. Meanwhile Messersmith and Gordon were able to explain to high German officials American objections to the new rules, and by mid-June the discriminatory tactics stopped. In a rare moment of optimism concerning happenings in Germany, Messersmith ventured that NSDAP leaders had seen the need "of carrying out all treaty and international obligations and of maintaining certain accepted international practices."[37] The hope was vain, for if the Nazi government was not chipping at one legal foundation it was doing so at another.

While difficulties for foreign manufacturers were temporarily—and it was only temporarily—reduced, they increased in another area, in this case foreign dollar bond investments in Germany. No one in 1933 could deny that the international monetary and trade situation was chaotic. The pound and dollar were unstable; the mark, because Germany tried to maintain its stability by clinging to the gold standard, was overvalued by 40 per cent. This situation made export difficult for German manufacturers, for on the world market they received too few marks to offset costs of production at home.[38] Tariff and other unilateral economic policies created further distress. Multiplication of regulations began to change the basis of international trade. Where formerly there

36. Messersmith to Hull, Apr. 8 and May 2, 1933, *FR 1933*, II, 422–423, 426.
37. Phillips to Messersmith, June 2, and Messersmith to Phillips, June 15, 1933, *FR 1933*, II, 432–438.
38. Edward Norman Peterson, *Hjalmar Schacht: For and Against Hitler, A Political-Economic Study of Germany, 1923–1945* (Boston, 1954), 202.

was general freedom tempered by tariff restrictions, now trade was nearly prohibited except by special permission.[39] Compounding Germany's economic woes was its tremendous foreign indebtedness. Borrowing abroad, often at exorbitant interest, had made possible the economic boom of the late twenties. But the decline in international trading meant that Germany could not export enough to raise the surplus capital to continue interest and amortization on debts, which in February 1933 stood at nearly 24 billion Reichsmarks.[40]

The Hoover moratorium of 1931–32 had been a temporary expedient. Now Schacht, who had replaced the more orthodox Luther at the Reichsbank, decided to reduce the 6 and 7 per cent interest rates on Germany's foreign debts. While in Washington in May, Schacht had told Roosevelt and Hull that he was planning to reduce payment of Germany's long-term debts entered into before July 15, 1931. American reaction, Schacht overoptimistically reported at first, was "completely calm and did not bring objections of any kind."[41] Next day, however, Hull summoned Schacht and handed him a note from Roosevelt deploring Germany's intended action, causing a ruffled Schacht to postpone Germany's announcement of its latest financial maneuver.[42]

At the end of May Schacht called representatives of foreign countries to Berlin and sought a moratorium. Failing this, the German government went ahead with its earlier plans, and on June 9 announced unilaterally that effective July 1 foreign creditors—excluding those who held Dawes or Young Plan loans and agreements made after July 15, 1931—would receive in transferable foreign currency only 50 per cent of interest due. Germany would pay the remaining 50 per cent, in the name of the particular creditor, into a *Konversionskasse für Auslandsschulden*. The creditor would then receive scrip notes for the sum due, which he could use only for purchase of German goods or convert into transferable currency by selling the scrip to the Gold Discount Bank at a 50 per cent discount. All told, the regulations meant foreign creditors—Americans held approximately $1.2 billion worth of these debts

39. League of Nations, *World Economic Survey, 1932–1933* (Geneva, 1939), 199.

40. Peterson, *Schacht*, 206.

41. Schacht to Foreign Ministry, May 8, 1933, *DGFP*, C, I, 394.

42. Cf. Hull, *Memoirs*, I, 237–238, and *My First Seventy-Six Years: The Autobiography of Hjalmar Schacht*, trans. Diana Pyke (Boston, 1955), 309–310; see also Circular of the Foreign Ministry, May 5, 1933, *DGFP*, C, I, 381–385.

—would receive 75 per cent of interest due, not a bad settlement considering the high interest rates at which the loans had been made. Nonetheless, Schacht and Germany had not negotiated the settlement, which they could have done, but had declared it.[43]

Even more disquieting for Hull was Schacht's threat to begin making interest payable to creditors dependent upon the balance of trade between creditors' countries and Germany. Because the United States had by far the largest favorable balance of trade with Germany—exports over imports—American creditors would receive the lowest interest rates. For Hull this not only was a matter of dollars and cents but challenged the most-favored-nation foundation of his traditional liberal economics.

Germany's threatened discrimination upset American bankers. John Foster Dulles, in Berlin as attorney for American creditors, asked Schacht personally and by letter not to engage in such practice. "This system," Dulles wrote, "has no moral basis; it establishes the criterion of force and is, in effect, an economic war system." The wisest course was for the Reichsbank to continue as best it could to transfer equally to all creditors of solvent debtors.[44]

The State Department, which had tried to stay out of the controversy, acted. Phillips instructed Gordon to leave an *aide-mémoire* at the German Foreign Ministry protesting Schacht's intended action. The State Department economic adviser, Herbert Feis, talked with Schacht in London, warning against economic discrimination. Schacht promised Feis he would not engage in such policy. In addition, State Secretary von Bülow assured Gordon there was no truth in rumors about Schacht's policies; Schacht, Bülow said, had meant to point out to the world that Germany could pay international debts only if the nations of the world gave it more opportunity to sell goods overseas.[45]

The economic, religious, and political situation that William E. Dodd inherited was confusing. When he went to the White House on June 16

---

43. Peterson, *Schacht*, 210. In talks with officials of National City Bank and Chase National Bank on July 3, 1933, Dodd learned that American banking interests were willing to give up their 7 per cent rates if they could be assured of 4 per cent. Dodd, *Diary*, 8–9.

44. Dulles to Schacht, June 3, 1933, *DGFP*, C, I, 538–539.

45. Phillips to Gordon, and Feis Memorandum, June 13, and Gordon to Phillips, June 15, 1933, *FR 1933*, II, 441–444.

no one knew which way the revolution in Germany was going. No one could say how domestic upheaval would affect German foreign policy, and how changes, if any, would affect the United States.

Roosevelt was not helpful. He maintained to Dodd that the Jewish problem was "not a governmental affair" and the United States could "do nothing," although its representatives might use personal and unofficial influence to moderate conditions. Trade concessions to increase American import of German goods, and thus assist Germany to raise capital to meet debt payments, were a possibility, but the drift was toward economic nationalism and the United States might have to make special arrangements with Canada and Latin America. On only one topic did Roosevelt display the least optimism. American bankers, he said, had made exorbitant profits on the 6 and 7 per cent bonds they sold for German cities and corporations during the 1920's. A moratorium, which might retard recovery in the United States, was as unacceptable as Schacht's arrogant threat to cease interest and principal payments on debts of over one billion dollars due American creditors in August. Perhaps a compromise could be reached.[46]

Dodd spent the next several days attending to details, making rounds at farewell parties—he disliked such affairs and often was unhappy, if not cranky, at them—listening to advice here and there, and visiting the small farm he owned in the Blue Ridge Mountains of Virginia. Then back to Chicago for more parties and farewells and a touching admonition by his old friend Carl Sandburg "to find out what this man Hitler is made of, what makes his brain go round, what his bones and blood are made of," but above all, in studying and dissecting the people of Europe, to "be brave and truthful, keep your poetry and integrity." At last Dodd's family left Chicago in a flurry of flowers and friends and under nervous strain which they thought unbearable but which, as his daughter Martha would sadly recall, was "only the beginning and a poor approximation of what we were to know of gnawing nerves, raw and exposed sensitiveness, and grief."[47]

Dodd and family—his wife Martha, son William, Jr., and daughter Martha—sailed on July 5, 1933. As newspapermen gathered around, Dodd talked optimistically of his coming adventure and remarked that

46. Entry for June 16, 1933, Dodd, *Diary*, 4–6.
47. M. Dodd, *Through Embassy Eyes*, 16–17.

Germany had to recognize the importance of cooperation with the
United States, as Americans needed to realize the value of economic
and social cooperation with the "land of Luther, Stein, and Bismarck."
There would be difficulties, but "an honest, frank mission to Berlin"
could not fail of results.[48]

As soon as he arrived in Berlin, he found himself beset by problems,
such as what to do with Edgar Ansel Mowrer. By and large American
newspapermen were consistently, and increasingly, critical of Germany's
regime. Sensitive to foreign opinion, the government accused reporters
of distorting news and creating bad relations. In the summer of 1933
the estrangement between the German government and the American
press focused on Mowrer, a reporter for the Chicago *Daily News* who
was also president of the Foreign Press Association. His *Germany Puts
the Clock Back* (New York, 1933), published one month before Hitler
gained formal power, characterized the Nazi movement as unscrupu-
lous demagoguery. Mowrer's reports over the next six months were un-
compromising. The Germans insisted that he resign as president of the
Foreign Press Association; his fellow journalists, by near unanimous
vote, refused a tendered resignation.[49] The Berlin government pressed
the State Department to secure his recall, but diplomats in Washington
steered clear.[50] Then, on August 20, the publisher of the *Daily News,*
Frank Knox, having assigned Mowrer to Tokyo, ordered him to leave
Berlin "immediately."[51] The reporter set his departure for the end of
the first week in September, hoping perhaps to stay long enough to
cover the Nazi party rally at Nuremberg on the first few days of that
month.

Then Dodd intervened. He had mixed feelings about Mowrer, thinking his reporting too vehement, even if the anti-Nazi part of it was
understandable. Above all, as Dodd told the State Department, the use
the Chicago *Daily News* made of sensational stories from Berlin would
curtail other journalists' opportunities there.[52] When Mowrer, whose

48. *New York Times,* July 6, 1933.
49. Lillian T. Mowrer, *Journalist's Wife* (New York, 1937), 297.
50. Hull and Moffat Memoranda, Aug. 11 and Aug. 19, 1933, *FR 1933,* II,
403–404.
51. Mowrer, *Journalist's Wife,* 307.
52. Entry for Aug. 16, 1933, Dodd, *Diary,* 24; Dodd to Hull, Aug. 22, 1933,
*FR 1933,* II, 305.

life had now been threatened, sought support from Dodd, Dodd told him crisply that he had to leave in advance of the Nuremberg rally in order not to create a diplomatic incident. Mowrer resentfully gave in.[53] Messersmith alone of the diplomatic corps bid him a meaningful farewell at the railroad station.[54]

Having managed one diplomatic problem without instruction from Washington, Dodd faced another when Hitler, as head of the National Socialist party, invited all chiefs of diplomatic mission in Berlin to be his guests at the Nazi meeting in Nuremberg on September 2 and 3. The invitation was unprecedented; the NSDAP was not the legal government of Germany and Dodd could find no diplomat in Berlin who could recall such an invitation ever being offered, let alone accepted. He "urgently" requested instruction from Washington, and after thinking about the matter for a day suggested that because the British ambassador, Sir Eric Phipps, was not in Berlin, perhaps the State Department could consult the British in Washington or through the London embassy.[55] Diplomats in Washington did not want responsibility for the decision. Under Secretary Phillips told Dodd the State Department would not take initiative or act directly on the matter; if he wished, he could consult the British or French embassy.

New at his post and understandably uncertain as to how to effect unified Anglo-American action—but absolutely certain that no representative of the great democracies should attend—Dodd repeated his request for instruction. He now had the opinion of the French ambassador, André François-Poncet, who was "strongly against acceptance," but he feared that the diplomatic corps might be "dragooned" into going, setting a "vicious precedent."[56]

Dodd's repeated request apparently angered State Department officials. As soon as Moffat, chief of the Division of Western European Affairs, received it, he went out to Phillips' house, where, along with Assistant Secretary Jefferson Caffery, they considered the matter. The three diplomats were certain that the government should neither involve itself nor approach the British and the French. They feared that

53. M. Dodd, *Through Embassy Eyes*, 39.
54. Mowrer, *Journalist's Wife*, 308.
55. Dodd to Hull, Aug. 19 and Aug. 20, 1933, *FR 1933*, II, 255–257.
56. Phillips to Dodd, Aug. 19, and Dodd to Hull, Aug. 20, 1933, *ibid.*, 257–258.

England or France might blame a joint decision, which became un-popular later, on the United States. None of the men thought it would be wrong for Dodd to accept the invitation. Caffery felt that Dodd had to establish relations with the Nazis. Phillips and Moffat believed the British and French had "more at stake than we," and that if they could go to Nuremberg, so could an American representative. If the British and French declined, a common Anglo-French-American stand "would deny criticism." Later that evening Phillips cabled as much to Dodd and promised he would be supported in whatever position he took.[57] Still uninformed as to British and French intent, Dodd declined the invitation, telling the Germans he could not absent himself from his work in Berlin; his real reasons were "disapproval of a government in-vitation to a Party convention" and belief that Nazi behavior at Nu-remberg would prove embarrassing.[58] The British and French declined their invitations, too, thus asserting, at least on the surface, Anglo-French-American solidarity. But the State Department, by failure to take initiative or act officially, had left the way open for a confusing situation four years later that would prove highly embarrassing to Dodd and the government and demonstrate the inability of major powers to coordinate action on matters even of protocol.

Trade was another problem for Dodd in 1933. To encourage do-mestic manufacturers, the German government on June 1 began to allow them to write off at once as tax-deductible expenditure the cost of all replacement machinery purchased from German corporations. Gordon insisted that the new policy was a discriminatory bounty for German as against American manufacturers, violating German-Ameri-can trade arrangements made in 1923. Upon arrival in Berlin, Dodd pursued the matter to no avail with the Foreign Ministry. The Germans insisted that write-offs of American machinery could still be in the usual manner—over a period of years—and that American firms in Germany that purchased German machinery could use the new regu-lations.[59] Protests by Hull proved useless, and as late as December

57. Diary entry for Aug. 20, 1933, Hooker, ed., *Moffat Papers,* 97–98; Phil-lips to Dodd, Aug. 20, 1933, *FR 1933,* II, 258.

58. Dodd to Hull, Aug. 23, 1933, *FR 1933,* II, 259; entry for Aug. 26, 1933, Dodd, *Diary,* 28.

59. Gordon to Hull, June 17, German Foreign Office to American Embassy, Aug. 30, and Dodd to Hull, Sept. 7, 1933, *FR 1933,* II, 460–461, 464–467.

1933 Messersmith counseled the government not to retaliate. In his opinion, which Dodd seconded, there was still going on in Germany an "obscure struggle for predominance . . . between the moderates and the extremists" and it would be best for America to do nothing that might strengthen the extremists.[60]

Tax discrimination was one aspect of Germany's new economics. In mid-September Dodd reported that for the coming year Germany had established for the United States and Yugoslavia equal import quotas of eight thousand tons of prunes. Hull was outraged. Yugoslavia's quota was twice its usual exports to Germany; the American quota was only one third. "The principles involved in this case," Secretary Hull angrily wrote, "extend far beyond the mere question of prune exports to Germany." He warned that trade relations with Germany probably would be jeopardized if it embarked upon a policy of customs quotas, and instructed Dodd to explain this to the Germans in a "forceful way."[61]

Germany, State Secretary von Bülow said, had to adopt a "hand-to-mouth economic policy," and he categorically told Dodd that Germany could not consider modifying its prune quota. The discouraged ambassador now informed the State Department that Germany would give in only "through fear of retaliatory measures rather than by argument no matter how seasoned and forceful." Hull, feeling the Germans had closed the door on "friendly discussions," instructed Dodd to protest, but also to state that American prunes covered by the quota would be cleared as usual through Hamburg and Bremen.[62]

If the Germans had lost their appetite for American prunes, they wished to increase the import of airplanes. In August the government in Berlin approached the British and asked to purchase twenty-five airplanes "for police purposes." Worried about the effect such a sale might have on disarmament, the British were counting on France, Italy, Czechoslovakia, and Belgium to uphold their May 1926 treaty which denied Germany police planes, and informally inquired whether the United States would or could tacitly agree not to sell police planes to

60. Hull to Dodd, Sept. 21, and Dodd to Phillips, Dec. 5, 1933, *ibid.,* 468–469.
61. Dodd to Hull, Sept. 18, and Hull to Dodd, Sept. 28, 1933, *ibid.,* 478, 480.
62. Dodd to Hull, Sept. 30, and Hull to Dodd, Oct. 9, 1933, *ibid.,* 481–483.

Germany. Some days later Phillips told the British that although no law forbade American manufacturers to sell arms or ammunition to Germany, the State Department would continue to dissuade American manufacturers, highly dependent on government purchases, from selling such goods to Germany. Moffat repeated this explanation to the Italians.[63]

The British now decided that the American policy on export of planes was too inclusive. Foreign Secretary Simon said he did not want to give Germany reason to feel discriminated against. "His Majesty's Government," the Foreign Office declared to the Americans five days after Germany had withdrawn from the Geneva Disarmament Conference, "did not envisage so drastic a measure as the total prohibition of the sale of aircraft to Germany." As the signatories of the 1926 treaty had now agreed they would sell planes to Germany if there were "categorical written assurance" that they would not be used for any illegal purpose.[64]

The Americans, who were not party to the Treaty of Versailles, proved themselves more fastidious than its signatories. Hull informed the British ambassador, Sir Ronald Lindsay, that the State Department never disapproved sale of civil airplanes but that German use of police or military planes would violate both the Versailles Treaty, which prohibited import or maintenance of military planes, and America's 1921 peace arrangement with Germany: the United States therefore was not in a position to respond favorably to the British proposal.[65]

As winter closed in on 1933, American diplomats, whatever their hopes for the future, had failed to moderate the policies of the Third Reich. Assaults on Jews continued, and even in cases involving American citizens Hull thought the government should avoid making a statement.[66] German finances were especially bothersome. Despite Schacht's promises, Germany negotiated separate agreements granting Swiss and Dutch bondholders 100 per cent interest due on German debts, and

63. Phillips Memoranda, Aug. 4, and Aug. 10, and Moffat Memorandum, Sept. 8, 1933, *ibid.*, 486–488.
64. British Embassy to the Department of State, Oct. 19, 1933, *ibid.*, 489–490.
65. Hull to Lindsay, Oct. 27, 1933, *ibid.*, 490–491.
66. Hull to Dodd, Oct. 12, 1933, *ibid.*, 392–393.

only after repeated protest did the Germans allow the Americans even to see the text of the agreements.[67] In December the Reichsbank announced it would continue for six months its new policy of discriminatory interest payments on long-term debts and threatened to reduce payments on bonds from 75 to 65 per cent while paying the Swiss and Dutch. Protests by Dodd and the State Department achieved no results. Finally, in January 1934 Roosevelt intervened, drafting the last paragraph of a State Department note which declared that while the American government would not even mention the possibility of retaliatory measures, it was necessary "to point out informally that if the German Government pursues a policy of discrimination . . . there will without doubt arise in the United States a serious demand for practical action to which the American Government could not lend a deaf ear."[68] The Germans at the end of the month agreed to redeem scrip payments at slightly higher value than before, actually increasing interest payments to Americans from 75 to 76.9 per cent, and to work toward an end to discriminatory payments by June 1934.[69]

Ambassador Dodd was increasingly dissatisfied. His early favorable reactions to men like Neurath, Bülow, and Schacht had brought no diplomatic rewards, and nostalgic hope to change the course of German history was proving empty. Addressing the American Chamber of Commerce in Berlin on October 12, at which meeting Schacht, Joseph Goebbels, minister for propaganda, and Alfred Rosenberg, philosopher of the Nazi party and head of its foreign office, were present, the ambassador inveighed against economic nationalism and berated "half-educated statesmen of today [who] swing violently away from the ideal purpose of Gracchus and think they find salvation for their troubled fellows in the arbitrary modes of the man who fell an easy victim to the cheap devices of the lewd Cleopatra. They forget that the Gracchus democracy failed upon the narrowest of margins and Caesar's succeeded only for a short moment as measured by the tests of history." Neurath rewarded Dodd next day by refusing to see him until evening.

67. Dodd to Hull, Nov. 16, 1933, *ibid.*, 458.
68. State Department to German Embassy, Jan. 19, 1934, *FR 1934*, II, 339–340.
69. Dodd to Hull, Jan. 31, 1934, *ibid.*, 346; Ritter to Embassy in Great Britain, Jan. 31, 1934, *DGFP*, C, II, 438–440; see also Peterson, *Schacht*, 212.

Dodd wrote in his diary: "It is evident some dislike of me is arising here now in official circles," but he optimistically attributed it to "simply Nazi opposition." A forty-five-minute interview with Hitler on October 17 touched nearly all subjects of the last nine months but brought no promise of change in German policy. The meeting showed Hitler's "belligerence and self-confidence."[70]

The German people undoubtedly bolstered that belligerence and self-confidence when 95 per cent of those voting on November 12 approved their country's withdrawal from the Disarmament Conference and the League of Nations and 92 per cent voted for the Nazi list of candidates for the Reichstag. For Dodd, even considering conditions under which people voted in Germany, these facts stood out: the German people had endorsed Hitler's foreign policy and the Nazis were in power to stay if they could "divert public attention from economic problems by pursuing a successful foreign policy."[71]

Roosevelt was not unmindful of these developments. A few days before the New Year he remarked before the Woodrow Wilson Foundation that 10 per cent of the world's population menaced peace for the other 90 per cent by seeking territorial expansion and refusing to reduce armament, or halt rearmament, even in the face of nonaggression and arms reduction agreements. Although the President stated that America was cooperating with the League of Nations more than ever before, he insisted that "we are not members and we do not contemplate membership."[72] Moffat smugly noted that the address, which the State Department had drafted, was "an exceedingly adroit piece of work." Phillips thought it a "powerful speech, splendidly rendered."[73]

During the first year of the Nazi regime relations between the United States and Germany had seriously deteriorated. The State Department, hesitant and uncertain, had proved ineffective in persuading Germany to adopt a reasonable attitude toward American interests and citizens and had not attempted to help moderate Nazi assaults on Jews. Amer-

70. *New York Times*, Oct. 13, 1933; entries for Oct. 13, Oct. 15, and Oct. 17, 1933, Dodd, *Diary*, 46–50.

71. Dodd to Hull, Nov. 15, 1933, *FR 1933*, II, 264–267.

72. *PPFDR*, II, 544–549.

73. Diary entries for Dec. 28, 1933, Hooker, ed., *Moffat Papers*, 108–109, and Phillips Diary, I, 117, Phillips papers.

ican efforts at disarmament had failed, and Anglo-American policy on disarmament, international finance, and sale of airplanes to Germany continued to diverge. Time was on the side of peace as 1934, retrospectively labeled the "crucial" year by the French ambassador, began.[74]

74. André François-Poncet, *The Fateful Years: Memoirs of a French Ambassador in Berlin, 1931–1938*, trans. Jacques Le Clercq (New York, 1949), 109.

# 4. ACCOUNTS SETTLED AND UNSETTLED

In his annual address to Congress on January 3, 1934, Roosevelt touched on foreign affairs, noting that fear of immediate or future aggression, the concomitant expense of vast sums on armament, and continued building of trade barriers stood in the way of lasting peace.[1] This international outlook clearly reflected itself in relations between the United States and Germany. Problems that strained relations in 1933—debt payments, persecution of the Jews, exasperating trade negotiations, fruitless efforts to revive disarmament —all continued into the new year. But where initially time, patience, and energy had seemed on the side of resolving difficulties, such was no longer the case. Throughout 1934 relations between the two countries worsened.

The debt settlement of January 31, 1934, was at best temporary and, contrary to public pronouncements, wholly satisfactory to neither Germany nor the United States. Two weeks before the agreement, Phillips had warned that acceptance of discriminatory terms might establish a precedent for other debtor countries. The State Department complained to the German government that discrimination by creditors on a basis of a direct bilateral trade balance would only create a new area of controversy. The Germans, Ambassador Dodd reported, told him that they had granted American creditors a slight increase not be-

1. *PPFDR,* III, 8–14.

cause they had revised estimates of their ability to pay but solely "for the sake of constructive harmony."[2]

During the first months of 1934 Schacht and other Reichsbank officials met representatives of Germany's creditors and tried to reach agreement on long- and short-term debts and Dawes and Young loans. By the second week of April, Schacht was admonishing that a complete moratorium seemed "inevitable," while the State Department continued to contend that only a settlement that treated American creditors the same as others would be acceptable.[3] Then, amidst increasingly difficult negotiations, Germany on June 14 announced that it was suspending payment on all its foreign debts.[4]

Creditors protested. Hull instructed Dodd to inform the government "energetically" that the United States did not like the recent "summary independent action." Dodd, of course, was extremely wary of bankers and financiers, perhaps to a fault. "I would not sit down to lunch with a Morgan—except possibly to learn something of his motives," he had confided in his diary only a month before these difficulties arose. Privately he told Hull that although there was no mistaking the character of the group governing Germany, a review of American tariff and other economic policies of the past decade forced him to say that he could "not for a moment overlook our own share in producing the existing chaotic world."[5]

The ambassador, however, presented his country's case as clearly as he could to State Secretary von Bülow, who insisted that Germany did not consider its action discriminatory or unilateral, that long and exhaustive negotiations made a moratorium inevitable. When Dodd charged that Germany was spending large sums on foreign planes and engines, Bülow denied knowledge of such things although a memorandum from the Reich Air Ministry of September 21, 1934, noting purchase of 10 civil aircraft and 260 engines from British and American

2. Phillips to Roosevelt, Jan. 18, Department of State to German Embassy, Jan. 19, and Dodd to Hull, Jan. 31, 1934, FR 1934, II, 336–337, 339–340, 346.

3. New York Times, Apr. 10, 1934; Department of State Press Release, May 5, 1934, FR 1934, II, 354.

4. New York Times, June 15, 1934. See also Circular of the Director of the Economic Department, June 8, 1934, DGFP, C, I, 884–885.

5. Hull to Dodd, June 16, 1934, FR 1934, II, 364; entry for May 8, 1934, Dodd, Diary, 100; Dodd to Hull, June 19, 1934, Hull papers, Box 36.

manufacturers, would confirm the suspicion. Obviously annoyed, Dodd could justifiably note in his diary after his interview that what "the Germans call financial prostration seems not to be as actual or imminent as they say."[6]

Other creditor nations, those that bought more from Germany than they sold, could deal with the situation more effectively. The English established a Debts Clearing Office to seize payments for German goods and use that money to discharge the German debt. Within a week the Germans recognized they could not afford to lose their favorable balance of trade with England and agreed to pay in full the sums due on Dawes and Young loans. Germany also offered a 40 per cent cash settlement, or ten-year bonds bearing 3 per cent interest, for all other private, nongovernment debts and guaranteed England most-favored-nation treatment in the matter of debts. The British abolished the Debts Clearing Office.[7]

The United States had a favorable balance of trade with Germany and could not seize payments for goods Americans imported from Germany. American diplomats could only protest Germany's arrangements with England and other creditors and accept Germany's eventual unilateral debt settlement terms. Having granted full service to all its other Dawes and Young loan creditors (Belgium, France, Great Britain, Italy, the Netherlands, Sweden, and Switzerland), Germany in October 1934 granted American creditors 75 per cent of the service due on Dawes loans, and one year later gave a final settlement: reduction of interest on Dawes loans from 7 to 5 per cent, on Young loans from 5½ to 4 per cent, and on other nongovernment debts, which averaged about 7 per cent, to 3 per cent, as opposed to the 4 per cent given other creditors. These arrangements remained in effect until the Second World War.[8]

The debt issue had bad repercussions. American opinion was angry,

6. Bülow Memorandum, June 18, 1934, *DGFP*, C, III, 36–39 and 39n11; entry for June 18, 1934, Dodd, *Diary*, 112.
7. Arnold J. Toynbee, ed., *Survey of International Affairs, 1934* (London, 1935), 40–41.
8. Schoenfeld Memorandum, Oct. 26, 1934, *FR 1934*, II, 386–396; Luther to Hull, Sept. 16, and Hull to Luther, Oct. 1, 1935, *FR 1935*, II, 437–438; see also Joachim Remak, "Germany and the United States, 1933–1939" (Ph.D. dissertation, Stanford University, 1956), 139.

first at Germany's failure to pay, then at the discriminatory treatment accorded American creditors, especially because the discrimination violated the German treaty obligations. The Germans were angry that whereas default on debt payments or drastic reduction of service by such countries as Austria, Bulgaria, Greece, Hungary, and Yugoslavia had been accepted as resulting from economic imperatives, Germany's action was met with reproach. Undoubtedly, as sensible American diplomats recognized, some adjustment in Germany's huge indebtedness had to be made, but as one historian of Germany's and Schacht's economics has observed, the vast sums Germany poured into rearmament, at first secretly and then openly, accounted chiefly for its inability to meet its financial obligations, which fact Hitler too acknowledged.[9]

Further, the matter established a bad precedent for settlement of international problems. The British through their Debts Clearing Office had forced Germany to pay, but thereby had established the principle that Germany would meet its obligations to only those nations that could force payment.[10] Even the British ambassador in Germany, Sir Eric Phipps, admitted to Dodd that the English had been selfish and had not served international relations as well as they might have.[11]

Such bilateral negotiations underscored the lack of unity in European politics, even when nations shared problems and interests, and Germany exploited the situation by unilaterally forcing on the United States a discriminatory settlement that disregarded a treaty obligation. The lesson would soon apply to matters military and political.

Continued German outrages against the Jews in 1934 provoked public resolutions and remonstrances, which diplomats in Washington did their best to prevent or moderate, while dissociating the government from them. Shortly after Congress convened in January, Representative Samuel Dickstein of New York City formally called for investigation into the character and extent of Nazi propaganda in the United States; the House approved the resolution on March 20.[12] The

9. Peterson, *Schacht*, 214–215; entry for April 22, 1942, *Hitler's Secret Conversations*, 350–351.

10. Peterson, *Schacht*, 215.

11. Entry for July 13, 1934, Dodd, *Diary*, 126.

12. *Congressional Record*, 73d Cong., 2d sess., LXVIII, Part 5, pp. 4934–4949.

State Department refused Dickstein's request for support. Moffat regarded the preliminary hearings, which included testimony from assorted Germans under concealed names, waiters and stewards on ships, as an *opéra bouffe*. Only Phillips, he noted with surprise, seemed "distinctly impressed." Hull did all he could to prevent passage of Dickstein's resolution.[13] Nevertheless, Congress at the end of March made an initial appropriation to the House Special Committee on Un-American Activities, which began public hearings in July that ran through the year.[14] The State Department declined an invitation from the committee's chairman, John W. McCormack of Massachusetts, to send an observer, not only because the full findings would be published but also, as Moffat noted, because there was no need to give a "false impression."[15]

German reaction to the investigation varied. When Luther first reported it was in the offing, Bülow scoffed at the investigation and at American "intimacy with Moscow!" After consultation with other officials, the Foreign Ministry decided to abide by the recommendation of its adviser on American affairs, Hans Dieckhoff, to couch its protest in language moderate enough not to arouse more suspicion (*qui s'excuse, s'accuse,* he wrote), which instruction Luther carried out.[16]

A second resolution, which Senator Millard E. Tydings of Maryland made on January 8, 1934, called for the Senate and the President to express "surprise and pain" at German treatment of the Jews and to request restoration of their civil and political rights.[17] The State Department caused this resolution to be buried in committee, Hull later explaining that the Tydings proposal would have taken constitutional initiative away from the President. Actually, as Assistant Secretary

13. Diary entry for Jan. 18, 1934, Hooker, ed., *Moffat Papers,* 109; Hull Memorandum, Mar. 23, 1934, *FR 1934,* II, 516–520.
14. U.S. Congress, *Investigation of Nazi Propaganda Activities and Investigation of Certain Other Propaganda Activities,* Hearings before the House Special Committee on Un-American Activities, 73d Cong., 2d Sess., on H. Res. 198 (Washington, D.C., 1934–35).
15. McCormack to Hull, May 30, and attached Moffat Memorandum, June 1, 1934, DS, 811.00 Nazi/126.
16. Luther to Foreign Ministry, Bülow and Dieckhoff Memoranda, Mar. 22, and Luther to Foreign Ministry, Mar. 24, 1934, *DGFP,* C, II, 653–655, 655n9, 672–673.
17. *Congressional Record,* 73d Cong., 2d sess., LXVIII, Part 1, p. 176.

R. Walton Moore advised at the time, Congress had passed such a resolution in 1867 for the people of Crete under Turkish dominion; but the present proposal, he said, although not binding on the President, might lead to embarrassing recriminations about the Negro problem in America if he acted on it, and cause recriminations at home if he did not.[18] Finally, Jewish organizations succeeded in having the resolution changed to express Senate sentiment only, and Judge Samuel Rosenman of New York, a friend of the President, urged him to support the measure. Roosevelt did instruct one of his secretaries to look into the matter, but the resolution remained in Senator Pittman's Foreign Relations Committee.[19]

The State Department again found itself in an embarrassing position when the American Federation of Labor and the American Jewish Congress sponsored a mock trial—"The Case of Civilization Against Hitlerism"—which attracted twenty thousand people to Madison Square Garden on March 7, 1934. The group of well-known personalities present was large and diverse: Al Smith; Raymond Moley; Judge Samuel Seabury; Mayor Fiorello La Guardia; the chancellor of New York University, Harry W. Chase; a member of the National Executive Committee of the American Legion, Edward McNeary; and Woodrow Wilson's last secretary of state, Bainbridge Colby, who presided over the meeting.[20]

As soon as German officials saw advertisements for the trial, they demanded that the State Department quash the proceedings. The Protocol Division, after searching law digests, concluded that precedent dictated a "hands-off" policy.[21] Hull admited to Luther he was "disappointed" that no law permitted federal intervention. Reporting to Berlin, Luther explained not only that the incident "depressed and worried" Hull but also that he frowned on the American Jewish Congress' invitation to the German embassy to provide counsel for the

18. Hull, *Memoirs,* I, 214; Moore Memorandum, Jan. 19, 1934, *FR 1934,* II, 293–294.

19. Rosenman to Roosevelt (and attached Roosevelt Memorandum to McIntyre), Mar. 18, 1934, Franklin D. Roosevelt papers, Official File 198A, Germany, Franklin D. Roosevelt Library, Hyde Park, N.Y.

20. *New York Times,* Mar. 8, 1934.

21. Southgate Memorandum, Feb. 25, 1934, DS, 862.002, Hitler, Adolf/12. Richard Southgate was assistant chief of the Division of International Conferences and Protocol.

defendant. The Germans also approached the White House through Roosevelt's press secretary, Stephen Early, but Early concluded that Roosevelt's intercession with those scheduled speakers he knew personally might cause even more adverse publicity. In Berlin, Foreign Minister von Neurath summoned Ambassador Dodd, purposely kept him waiting, then expressed vain hope that the rally could be prevented.[22]

When the affair was over, Phillips declined to comment, except to note that no member of the administration had attended.[23] Luther reported American diplomats had done all they could to prevent the rally; he blamed the affair on "the liberal, pacifistic, Jewish, Socialist, and Communist circles." Hitler said nothing publicly, although as Dodd noted after an interview with him on March 7 he cursed the Jews and threatened to eliminate them in Germany if outside agitation did not stop.[24]

The State Department maintained proper reserve and caution concerning pronouncements on Germany. Shortly after the famous Blood Purge of June 30–July 1, 1934, Hugh Johnson, the fiery head of the National Recovery Administration, declared that events in Germany "made me sick—not figuratively, but physically and very actively sick." Under instruction from Berlin, Leitner protested and reported that Hull had told him it was a difficult situation because Johnson was a "wild personality."[25] Nonetheless Hull publicly explained that Johnson did not speak for the administration.[26] In July 1935 the State Department refused a request by Jewish organizations to protest German persecution.[27] A couple of months later New York Judge

22. Hull Memorandum, Mar. 2, 1934, *FR 1934*, II, 510–511; Luther to Foreign Ministry, Mar. 3, 1934, *DGFP*, C, II, 552–554; Early Memorandum for Hull, Mar. 5, 1934, DS, 862.002 Hitler, Adolf/26; Neurath Memorandum, Mar. 5, 1934, GFM, 5747/HO35381, entry for Mar. 5, 1934, Dodd, *Diary*, 86–87.

23. *New York Times*, Mar. 9, 1934.

24. Luther to Foreign Ministry, Mar. 8, 1934, *DGFP*, C, II, 574–575; entry for Mar. 7, 1934, Dodd, *Diary*, 89. See also Dodd Memorandum (undated but Mar. 7, 1934), *FR 1934*, II, 218–221.

25. *New York Times*, July 13, 1934; Neurath to Embassy in Washington, July 13, and Leitner to Foreign Ministry, July 14, 1934, GFM, 5747/HO35633, 5747/HO37635-HO37636.

26. Hull to Roosevelt, July 13, 1934, *FR 1934*, II, 239–240.

27. Adler and Margalith, *American Intercession*, 367.

Louis Brodsky referred to the German swastika as "the black flag of piracy," and twice in March 1937 La Guardia disparaged Hitler, once as a "brown-shirted fanatic."[28] The Germans were adamant in demanding apologies, which Hull afforded them while lecturing on freedom of speech and the federal government's lack of jurisdiction.[29] Roosevelt clung to a similar policy. The furthest he went was to declare in October 1935, after passage of the odious Nuremberg Laws, which stripped all civil and political rights and privileges from Jews and made them German subjects instead of citizens, that the American people could not remain spiritually indifferent to the sufferings of others. Then, in May 1936, he allowed the secretary of the interior, Harold Ickes, to express for him, over nationwide radio at a United Palestine Appeal dinner, his distress over reversion in some parts of the world to days and deeds enlightened people had hoped would never return.[30]

The Germans of course were always interested in legitimate propaganda to their advantage.[31] For example, following conclusion of their nonaggression declaration with Poland on January 26, 1934, they quickly secured permission to publish a favorable statement by Nicholas Murray Butler, then head of the Carnegie Peace Foundation as well as president of Columbia University.[32] In the summer of 1936 German diplomats were quick to invite former Ambassador Schurman to an interview with Hitler and afterward release an official transcript in which Hitler had emphasized his peaceful effort to restore German equality while working toward international political stability

28. *New York Times,* Sept. 7, 1935, and Mar. 4 and Mar. 16, 1937.

29. On Brodsky incident, see Leitner to Foreign Ministry, Sept. 14, 1935, GFM, 5747/HO36016-HO36017; on La Guardia, see Dunn Memorandum, Mar. 4, 1937, *FR 1937,* II, 368–369; *New York Times,* Mar. 4 and Mar. 18, 1937, and Neurath to Luther and Luther to Neurath, Mar. 17, 1937, GFM, 2422/D511372-D511373.

30. *New York Times,* Oct. 3, 1935, and May 25, 1936.

31. For detail on German propaganda activities, including some unsavory efforts, see Alton Frye, *Nazi Germany and the American Hemisphere, 1933–1941* (New Haven, 1967), 32–60, 80–100; also, O. John Rogge, *The Official German Report: Nazi Penetration 1924–1942, Pan-Arabism 1939–Today* (New York, 1961), 13–172.

32. Luther to Foreign Ministry, Feb. 3, and Dieckhoff to Luther and Luther to Foreign Ministry, Feb. 5, 1934, GFM, 5747/HO35307-HO35309.

and freer world trade.[33] And in March 1938 Hitler received former President Hoover one day, while Air Marshall Göring dined him, overelaborately, the next.[34]

German officials also recognized the limits of propaganda in the United States. For example, in 1934 they forbade Nazi party members who were in the United States to propagandize there or belong to the Association of the Friends of the New Germany, which became the German-American Bund in 1936.[35] This instruction was sometimes violated, but it was enforced sufficiently to cause the Bund leader, Fritz Kuhn, to go to Berlin in March 1938 to plead in vain for Hitler to lift the ban, which now was extended to all German nationals. The Bund, whose membership did not exceed six thousand people and may have been as few as half that number, staged demonstrations during the decade which, if they misled a handful, probably succeeded only in intensifying American dislike of Nazi policies.[36]

German diplomats were also highly wary of meddling in American politics. In August 1935, for instance, former Republican Senator from Indiana Arthur R. Robinson, who had been defeated for re-election in 1934 by Sherman Minton, approached the Foreign Ministry with a plan to defeat Roosevelt in 1936. Robinson claimed that Roosevelt intended to make Senator Robert La Follette, Jr., of Wisconsin—"an outspoken radical"—his vice-president and eventually President. Robinson insisted that Germany had to organize thirty million German-Americans for the Republican party in a campaign that would contrast Germany's prior plight "under Marxism" and its pre-

---

33. German Embassy in Bern to Foreign Ministry, July 18, and Official Memorandum of Hitler Statement to Schurman, Aug. 3, 1936, GFM, 2422/D511332-D511333, 2422/D511338-D511340. The official statement did not include some favorable comments about Germany which Schurman made at the interview. See Meissner Memorandum, Aug. 3, 1936, 2422/D511335-D511336.

34. *New York Times*, Mar. 9 and Mar. 10, 1938.

35. Dieckhoff Memorandum, Feb. 16, 1934, *DGFP*, C, II, 492.

36. Joachim Remak, "'Friends of the New Germany': The Bund and German-American Relations," *Journal of Modern History*, XXIX (Mar. 1957), 38-41. Kuhn, who always exaggerated his relations with and support from Berlin, was convicted in December 1939 of embezzling Bund funds. Rogge, *Official German Report*, 128.

sent condition under Hitler as "a strong bulwark against radicalism."[37] The Germans would have none of it. State Secretary von Bülow, who knew his American history, ruled out the proposal not merely because Robinson had "no first-class political significance," but because, he insisted, the American people were extremely wary about foreign intervention in their political affairs, to wit, the clamor in 1888 when British ambassador Sir Lionel Sackville-West spoke for Grover Cleveland over Benjamin Harrison. Robinson was given only polite interviews.[38] Similarly, in 1938 Hans Dieckhoff, who had replaced Luther as ambassador to the United States, in a long report insisted that any campaign to organize German-Americans would not unite them but only intensify differences, and he branded all such efforts "conspiratorial child's play."[39] Beginning in 1939, and especially after the war had begun and throughout 1940, German agents engaged in propaganda ventures that included efforts to swing votes away from Roosevelt to Republican candidate Wendell Willkie. The significance of such efforts is questionable, and once the election of 1940 was over propaganda was in retreat. And as noted earlier, Hitler's diplomacy was aimed chiefly at avoiding direct conflict with the United States, at least until victory in Europe had been achieved.[40]

If Roosevelt and the State Department were justified in avoiding public pronouncements that could not alter conditions, the same cannot be said for their failure to seek a real solution to the German refugee problem. The League of Nations in October 1933 established the High Commission for Refugees (Jewish and other) coming from Germany and selected for its high commissioner James G. McDonald, former board chairman of the Foreign Policy Association and a Columbia University professor of political science. Representing the

37. Memorandum Fuehr-Robinson Conversation, Aug. 29, 1935, GFM, 5747/HO35988-HO35991. Carl A. Fuehr was senior counselor in Department III, which included the United States, of the Foreign Ministry.
38. Bülow to Lammers and Fuehr Memorandum, Aug. 31, 1935, GFM, 5747/HO35993-HO35997.
39. Dieckhoff to Foreign Ministry, Jan. 7, 1938, U.S. Department of State, *Documents on German Foreign Policy, 1918–1945*, series D, *From Neurath to Ribbentrop: September 1937–September 1938*, 13 vols. (Washington, D.C., 1949–64), I, 664–678.
40. On the 1939–40 propaganda schemes, see Frye, *Nazi Germany and the American Hemisphere*, 131–151, and Rogge, *Official German Report*, 238–258.

United States on the commission's Governing Board was a professor of law at Columbia, Joseph P. Chamberlain. Americans privately could contribute money or work for the commission. But when McDonald asked the government for a contribution—even a token amount—which he thought would have a "large and perhaps determining influence" in securing funds from other reluctant great powers, the State Department, replying for the President, said there could be no money forthcoming until other countries made contributions. Chamberlain hinted rather strongly that the failure to get contributions thereafter resulted from lack of American initiative.[41] Nor were the Germans helpful. In preliminary talks in August 1933 Dieckhoff indicated to McDonald that his government had no intention of assisting or cooperating meaningfully with the League organization, and in May 1934 Bülow reiterated the point.[42] According to Hanfstaengl, when in the summer of 1934 he sought to act as an intermediary for some American bankers interested in financing Jewish emigration, Hitler brushed him off with, "Do not waste my time, Hanfstaengl. I need the Jews as hostages."[43]

Fund-raising was only one part of the problem. McDonald made a crucial point when he told Dodd that in the United States there was "much interest in limited circles but no enthusiasm for taking persecuted Jews into the country."[44] The economics of the depression seemed to govern official mentality. In March 1933 Wilbur J. Carr, assistant secretary of state in charge of administration, told a House Committee on Immigration and Naturalization that he saw no reason to rescind President Hoover's executive order of September 1930, which instructed consular officials to interpret strictly the prohibition on admitting to the United States persons who were likely to become public charges.[45] Two years later Daniel W. McCormack, commissioner of immigration, said that relaxation of immigration laws would

---

41. McDonald to Carr, Jan. 2, Phillips to Chamberlain, Jan. 21, and Chamberlain to Phillips, Feb. 28, 1935, *FR 1935*, II, 412–414, 418. Wilbur J. Carr was assistant secretary of state.

42. Dieckhoff Memorandum, Aug. 30, 1933, and Bülow Memorandum, May 2, 1934, GFM, 5747/HO34980-HO34981, 5747/HO35544-HO35545.

43. Hanfstaengl, *Unheard Witness*, 221–222.

44. Entry for Feb. 7, 1934, Dodd, *Diary*, 79.

45. *New York Times*, Mar. 30, 1933.

only create more unemployment problems and perhaps heighten anti-Semitism.[46] In November 1935 Roosevelt denied a request from the governor of New York, Herbert H. Lehman, that he withdraw the 1930 executive order.[47]

The American government made its most serious effort to assist Jewish refugees after the *Anschluss* in 1938, when Hull invited thirty-two countries (only Italy declined) to establish with the United States a special refugee committee. In retrospect Hull would say that his government undertook this action "lest these victims of persecution be exterminated," but at the time he insisted that private organizations finance the operation and that no country accept more immigrants than its existing legislation allowed. In July 1938, meeting at Evian, France, representatives of the various countries formed an Intergovernmental Committee on Political Refugees.[48]

The director of the Intergovernmental Committee was George Rublee, a Washington attorney and friend of Roosevelt. Rublee worked closely with Ambassador Hugh R. Wilson (who replaced Dodd in Berlin in 1938), and preliminary conversations with Walter Funk, minister of economics, indicated some willingness on the part of the Germans to make a financial arrangement that would allow an orderly exodus from Germany.[49] The Foreign Ministry, however, was no help. At the end of July 1938 Ernst von Weizsäcker, who was now state secretary, told Ambassador Wilson that he "should not entertain any hopes" that Germany would cooperate with the Intergovernmental Committee and on October 18 rejected Rublee's request to come to Germany to negotiate. Weizsäcker insisted that because no country had yet promised to admit Jews in large numbers, and Germany would not allow them to take any foreign exchange along, Rublee's visit would be used only "to prove that it was German obstructionism that was to blame for the misery of the Jews."[50] Shortly afterward Rublee

46. *Ibid.*, Mar. 4, 1935.

47. Lehman to Roosevelt, Nov. 1, and Roosevelt to Lehman, Nov. 13, 1935, Roosevelt papers, Official File 133, Immigration 1933–1941.

48. Hull, *Memoirs,* I, 578.

49. Hugh R. Wilson, Jr., ed., *A Career Diplomat, The Third Chapter: The Third Reich* (New York, 1960), 43–44.

50. Wilson to Hull, Oct. 18, 1938, *FR 1938,* I, 799, and Weizsäcker Memoranda, July 27 and Oct. 18, 1938, *DGFP,* D, V, 895, 900–901. Weizsäcker also displayed curious interest in "the percentage of Rublee's Aryan descent." Weizsäcker Memorandum, Nov. 7, 1938, *ibid.,* 903.

proposed increased purchases of German goods to secure an orderly exodus of Jews from Germany with their property, but Hull opposed any scheme that he thought might adversely affect American trade. He insisted that Germany ought to allow the emigrants to leave with at least minimum funds for resettling and then forward the remaining funds over a period of time while private organizations supplied interim support.[51]

Agreement seemingly became possible in late 1938 after a teenaged Jewish boy, Herschel Grynszpan, distraught over Nazi treatment of his parents, shot the third secretary at the embassy in Paris, Ernst vom Rath, who died on November 9. That night the propaganda minister, Josef Goebbels, and the S.A. promulgated a pogrom which became the infamous "Week of the Broken Glass." Twenty thousand Jews were arrested while organized rioters sacked over a thousand businesses and burned hundreds of homes and synagogues. Hitler and other government officials were caught unawares by the initial rioting, and some officials, like Funk, were distressed by the wanton destruction and worried about adverse publicity abroad which would hamper political and trade relations. Nevertheless, the government on November 12 fined the Jewish people of Germany 1 billion marks ($400 million) and apparently determined to force them out of Germany.[52]

German barbarity caused considerable revulsion. Dieckhoff reported that in the United States "the outcry comes not only from Jews but in equal strength from all camps and classes, including the German-American camp," and even "the respectable patriotic circles, which are thoroughly anti-Communist and, for the greater part, anti-Semitic in their outlook, also begin to turn away from us." The same was true in England, he said, and the next day affirmed that the consulate in New York had informed him events in Germany had "without exception catastrophic effect on the American people."[53] Roosevelt, upon strong recommendation from George Messersmith, who was then as-

51. Rublee to Hull, Oct. 27, and Hull to Rublee, Nov. 9, 1938, *FR 1938*, I, 809, 816–818.

52. Raul Hilberg, *The Destruction of the European Jews*, rev. ed. (Chicago, 1967), 23–24; Woermann Memorandum, Nov. 12, 1938, *DGFP*, D, V, 904–905. Ernst Woermann was director of the Political Department of the Foreign Ministry.

53. Dieckhoff to Foreign Ministry, Nov. 14 and Nov. 15, 1938, *DGFP*, D, IV, 639–640, GFM, B21/B004971.

sistant secretary of state, ordered Ambassador Wilson home for "consultation" and publicly declared that he had thought such German barbarity impossible in modern civilization.[54]

Shortly after these events Schacht approached Hitler about allowing German Jews to emigrate. Schacht himself was a traditional anti-Semite. He believed all the clichés about a "Jewish problem," regarded Jews as a foreign minority who wielded excessive influence in industry, commerce, and the professions and arts, and approved the legislation that barred them from these fields.[55] Nevertheless, Schacht disliked violence, and he was deeply concerned about German foreign exchange and trade problems. Hence, he suggested to Hitler that a convenient solution might be found if the government would allow 150,000 wage-earners to leave Germany in the next three years, and 250,000 dependents to follow eventually; 200,000 older persons probably would remain. In return, Schacht wanted to set aside one fourth of the Jewish wealth in Germany—1.25 billion out of 6 billion marks, he estimated —in a trust fund to be used as collateral for an equivalent loan to Germany which would finance export of German goods and transport Jews out of the country, with the rest of the money remaining in Germany. "To my great astonishment," Schacht recalled, Hitler agreed to allow him to discuss the matter with representatives of the Intergovernmental Committee in London, from where Rublee on December 15 notified Washington of the tentative proposal.[56]

The State Department instinctively disliked Schacht's plan. Under Secretary Sumner Welles at first decried Germany's asking the world to ransom hostages and barter "misery for increased exports." But after thinking it over he advised against outright rejection and told Rublee that perhaps private funds could be got to finance resettlement while the Jews used their money to purchase machinery from Germany that would be needed after emigration.[57] Rublee then went to Berlin and by January 16, 1939, he and Schacht had worked out a rough

54. Messersmith to Hull, Nov. 13, and Hull to Wilson, Nov. 14, 1938, *FR 1938*, II, 396–399; Roosevelt's statement, Nov. 15, 1938, in *PPFDR*, VII, 596–597.
55. Schacht, *Autobiography*, 357–358; Hilberg, *Destruction of the Jews*, 22.
56. Schacht, *Autobiography*, 383–384; Rublee to Hull, Dec. 15, 1938, *FR 1938*, I, 873–874.
57. Welles to Rublee, Dec. 19 and Dec. 21, 1938, *FR 1938*, I, 876–880.

arrangement that would have used one fourth of the wealth of German Jews to buy German equipment and cover emigration expenses, with the rest of the money set aside to cover costs of maintaining Jews remaining in Germany, who were to be retrained and not forced to live in ghettoes. The controversial aspects of Schacht's plan, a loan and direct assistance for German exports, were omitted.[58]

Conceivably Germany's Jews might have been spared future destruction had this plan been implemented, but even this possibility faced hostile forces and adverse circumstance. First, no sooner had the Evian Conference begun in July 1938 than the German foreign minister, Joachim von Ribbentrop, informed all interested parties that "he had to reject on principle any collaboration with interested countries in the question of German Jews. This was an internal German problem that was not subject to discussion." Germany would not consider transfer of Jewish capital nor cooperate with the Evian Conference.[59] Schacht initiated discussions after the November pogrom, but the Foreign Ministry kept jealous watch. Two days after Schacht had reached tentative accord with Rublee, on January 18, 1939, Ribbentrop ruled that "initialing of any agreements with Mr. Rublee is out of the question."[60] And two days after that Hitler removed Schacht from his post at the Reichsbank, ending his connection with the negotiations.[61]

Negotiations nonetheless continued between the Intergovernmental Committee and German officials, and by mid-February they again reached tentative, but more limited, accord. The Germans were adamant in their insistence on not allowing Jews to leave with their property, they would not allow emigration to begin until pledges to receive the refugees were forthcoming from other countries, and they reserved the right to end the program at any time.[62]

Few countries were willing to admit large numbers of Jewish im-

---

58. Schacht Memorandum, Jan. 16, 1939, *DGFP*, D, V, 921–925.

59. Circular of the State Secretary, July 8, 1938, *ibid.*, 894–895.

60. Weizsäcker Memorandum, Jan. 18, 1938, *ibid.*, 925. The instruction was given to the minister to Czechoslovakia, Ernst Eisenlohr, whom Ribbentrop had designated intermediary between the Foreign Ministry and Schacht. See Weizsäcker Memorandum, Jan. 13, 1938, *ibid.*, 920.

61. Schacht, *Autobiography*, 384.

62. Minutes of . . . Committee of the Central Reich Office for Jewish Emigration . . . Feb. 11, 1939, *DGFP*, D, V, 933–936; *New York Times*, Feb. 14, 1939; Spear, "United States and Persecution of Jews in Germany," 88–89.

migrants, especially without their money. As Rublee sadly had noted in November 1938, ever since the Intergovernmental Committee had begun its work, nation after nation had closed its door to Jewish emigrants.[63] Hopeful of reversing this trend, the State Department had made clear in November 1938 that America, without increasing its quota, could take over 100,000 Jews within a period of five years, and Hull exerted what pressure he could on Latin American countries, but all to no avail.[64] Numerous schemes for colonization in such places as Alaska, Angola, Ethiopia, and the Philippines were considered but fell through.[65]

The tumult of events in the summer of 1939 and outbreak of war in September ended whatever hope remained for a rational arrangement. German leaders in 1941 determined upon their own "final solution."

A limited opportunity to save many lives had slipped away. To be sure, famous Germans and Austrians—Albert Einstein, Walter Gropius, Paul Hindemith, Thomas Mann, Kurt Weil—found refuge in America. But during 1933–1938, when the annual quota for immigrants from Germany was 26,000, including Austria's quota after incorporation into Germany in 1938, a total of approximately 160,000 for the six years, only some 46,000 German immigrants, of whom 30,000 were Jewish, actually entered the United States. Approximately another 60,000 German immigrants entered the United States in the next years through June 1941, some three fourths being Jewish.[66] American diplomats had clung to a policy that was timid, rigidly legal, and without innovation, and it scarcely improved during the Second

63. Rublee to Hull, Nov. 14, 1938, *FR 1938*, I, 880–881.

64. See Hull's Circular Letter to Certain Diplomatic Missions in Latin America, Nov. 22, 1938, *FR 1938*, I, 836–837. The nations were: Argentina, Bolivia, Brazil, Chile, Colombia, Cuba, Dominican Republic, Ecuador, Guatemala, Haiti, Honduras, Mexico, Panama, Peru, Uruguay, Venezuela.

65. Spear, "United States and Persecution of Jews in Germany," 95–98.

66. Exact figures on immigrants entering the United States, including breakdown on age, occupation, race religion, etc., for each of the years from 1933 to 1941 are available in the U.S. Department of Labor, *Annual Report of the Commissioner General of Immigration* (Washington, D.C., 1933–41). Composite figures are in Spear, "United States and Persecution of Jews in Germany," 72–73. See also Donald Peterson Kent, *The Refugee Intellectual: The Americanization of the Immigrants of 1933–1941* (New York, 1953), 12, 23.

World War.[67] Even in February 1939, Robert Pell, career diplomat, aide to Rublee, and then vice-director of the Intergovernmental Committee, wrote that he "never expected anything to come out of the conversations with the Germans," that the talks were being held largely to show them that no one would strike a trade bargain with them, and that the only solution to the refugee problem "is decent treatment of these people where they now are and we can't have that until there is a more reasonable Government in Berlin."[68] Other nations' policies were no better. As the German ambassador to England, Herbert von Dirksen, reported, the South Americans "made fine speeches to empty galleries" but remained suspicious that Europe was merely trying to "unload their undesirable elements on them," while the Poles presented a "bulky memorandum" indicating they had three-and-a-half million Jews "whom they also wanted to get rid of."[69] German policy, of course, remains a blot on civilization.

The problem in American-German relations in 1934 that the State Department and the German Foreign Ministry probably considered most important was trade. The 1923 Treaty of Friendship, Commerce and Consular Rights, which became effective in 1925, expired a decade later.[70] If either country intended to denounce it, or not to renew it, one year's notice was required. The barrier to renegotiation of the treaty was Article VII, which guaranteed each country most-favored-nation treatment. The Germans wanted a new treaty to allow greater opportunity for export to the United States but to omit most-favored-nation status. Thus they could negotiate bilateral tariff and import quotas that excluded American goods. For Hull and many others of similar outlook in the State Department, the most-favored-nation idea was the heart of the new reciprocal trade program, and they refused to compromise an economic program they regarded as a near-panacea for the world's ills. Also, they remembered the arbitrary manner in

---

67. See Dwight MacDonald, "Old Judge Hull and the Refugees," *Memoirs of a Revolutionist: Essays in Political Criticism* (New York, 1957), 154–158.
68. Pell to Messersmith, Feb. 16, 1939, Messersmith papers, Box 2.
69. Dirksen to Foreign Ministry, Feb. 18, 1939, *DGFP*, D, V, 937–938.
70. For text, see *FR 1923*, II, 29–46.

which Germany had imposed discriminatory quotas on American imports in 1933.

Neurath told Luther in February 1934 that their government was alarmed at continued deterioration of its foreign exchange and that it must do "everything" in its power to improve it, especially through increased sales to the United States, with which Germany had its largest unfavorable balance of trade. Luther saw Hull in March and Assistant Secretary Francis Sayre in April. Both men told him that although they would like to see more trade between the United States and Germany the time was not propitious for discussions and that advance commitments might endanger passage of the Reciprocal Trade Agreements Act, which was to give the President authority to alter tariffs by as much as 50 per cent.[71]

The real reasons for the State Department's reluctance to talk trade with the Germans were more involved. Commercial relations between the United States and Germany, as the State Department economic adviser, Herbert Feis, described them on March 28, were "closely approaching trade warfare." Reports that continued to flow into Washington, especially those written by George Messersmith, were even more discouraging. Messersmith had been in the Foreign Service since 1914, and he was consul general in Berlin from 1930 until April 1934, when he became minister to Austria. He was a brilliant career officer, and Under Secretary Phillips was right when he described him as "probably better informed than anyone else about Nazi programs and activities." Roosevelt, not easily given to praising career officers, considered him "one of the best men we have in the whole Service," and and freely admitted that "I count greatly on his judgment."[72] To various members of the State Department, Messersmith habitually wrote long letters—up to eighteen or twenty pages single-spaced—and as was the case specifically with those concerning Germany at this time, these letters circulated through the department's higher echelons. In

71. Neurath to Embassy in the United States, Feb. 27, and Luther to Foreign Ministry, Mar. 3, 1934, *DGFP*, C, II, 537–539; Sayre Memorandum, Apr. 12, 1934, *FR 1934*, II, 420–421.

72. Feis to Hull, Mar. 28, 1934, DS, 611.6231/320; Phillips Memorandum, Mar. 16, 1934, DS, 123M561/411; Roosevelt to Julian W. Mack, Dec. 4, 1935, Roosevelt papers, President's Personal File 2211.

the spring of 1934 he waged a long and important campaign to block trade negotiations with Germany.

Messersmith believed and hoped that economic instability would bring down the Hitler regime. But even if the collapse did not come, he argued on March 24, the United States should not sign with a nation "not willing to protect existing interests, getting ready to repudiate its debts, and asking for new agreements and new credits with which to get raw materials, a good deal of which are destined for a rearmament program." Perhaps, he concluded, the best thing the United States could do for "the general world interest" was to allow Germany's economic difficulties to "come to a crisis." Five days later he commented suspiciously on Germany's recent purchase from American manufacturers of long-range mail planes "easily convertible to bombers" and noted that unstable conditions were forcing the Germans, not truly interested in economic programs, to "want a bargain fast for political reasons." Nazi officials, he said, "think we are getting ready to play Santa Claus."[73] His views remained unchanged in April. He had had enough of Schacht, whom he regarded as "arrogant, prideful, cynical." Worsening conditions, he reported, had put merchants in Hamburg and Bremen "in a panic," and the Hitler regime seemed on the brink of collapse. Messersmith advised against even a favorable treaty and thought that "the Germans have nothing to offer and we have nothing to gain but much to lose." Besides, "I don't believe any agreement we make with the present government means anything." In May he added flatly that "a government with really peaceable intentions does not produce armaments, train its people in military exercises, and create such an extraordinary spirit in the schools, even among the very young."[74]

Messersmith's recommendation received a strong second from the commercial attaché in Berlin, Douglas Miller. His earlier optimism about the German regime diminished, Miller submitted a brief in April arguing that Germany needed American cotton, copper, and petroleum, but aside from large quantities of potash there was nothing

73. Messersmith to Phillips, Mar. 24 and Mar. 29, 1934, DS, 862.00/3418, 862.00/3419.
74. Messersmith to Phillips, Apr. 13 and May 3, 1934, DS, 862.00/3420, 862.00/3423.

other than small manufactured articles—"none of which are of staple character and many of which are subject to changes in popular taste"— that the Germans could hope to market in America in large enough quantities to increase their foreign exchange. He added several other reasons commercial negotiations could serve no purpose: German import quotas on American products—such as lard, the second most important export to Germany—changed too quickly to guarantee a steady market; Germany's currency problem resulted largely from maintaining the mark at an artificially high gold rate, which meant that foreigners could not take currency out of Germany; finally, the Nazis were not satisfied with the map of Europe and "the more completely their experiments succeed the more certain large scale war is today." In June, Miller reported disapprovingly of the Reich government's currency system, which through different types of marks gave advantages to German manufacturers over foreign manufacturers by restricting the use of certain marks to purchase of German goods and prevented foreigners with businesses in Germany from taking capital out of the country. The National Socialist experiment, Miller wrote, was "leading Germany further away from normal commercial relations with the western world," and there was possibility that out of it all might come an internal revolution or war.[75]

The campaign proved effective. Phillips had told Messersmith in May that his observations on economics and finance were of "extreme importance" and on June 5 forwarded to Roosevelt a memorandum from the State Department Economic Office that urged against negotiations and cited numerous passages from Messersmith's letters. Further, the memorandum argued exactly as had Messersmith that there was no good reason to assist the German government's effort to shore up either its political prestige or economic credit.[76] Interestingly, that same day Congress passed Hull's cherished Reciprocal Trade Agreements Act. But when Luther next day offered repeated

75. Miller, Reports to the Bureau of Foreign and Domestic Commerce, Apr. 17 and June 19, 1934, Miller, *Via Diplomatic Pouch*, 133–162, 171–188.

76. Phillips to Messersmith, May 10, 1934, DS, 862.00/3421; Phillips to Roosevelt, June 5, 1934, Roosevelt papers, President's Secretary's File, Diplomatic Correspondence: Germany; hereafter cited as PSF.

congratulations while renewing his country's request for trade negotiations, Hull turned him down.[77]

Events of the summer of 1934 confirmed the State Department in its decision. Unstable conditions in Germany climaxed in the Blood Purge of June 30–July 1. The murders of Ernst Roehm, General Kurt von Schleicher, and Gregor Strasser, the arrest of Franz von Papen, and summary execution of scores of S.A. officials stunned the world and seemed to corroborate rumors of Europe's whispering gallery that the Hitler regime was on its way out. The Soviet foreign minister, Maxim Litvinov, told Ambassador William Bullitt that Hitler could not hold out much longer. President Eduard Beneš of Chechoslovakia opined to the American chargé, J. Webb Benton, that the Reichswehr and conservative industrial elements would force the Nazis into the background. In France the Quai d'Orsay ventured to the American chargé, Theodore Marriner, that Hitler would probably become a figurehead for the ruling Reichswehr. From England came word from Ambassador Bingham, who himself referred to "so many madmen in Europe and in the Far East," that by and large British officials now felt that the old Junkers and industrialists were in control. In Italy the foreign minister, Fulvio Suvich, assured Ambassador Long that the majority of the German people opposed Hitler, who could not remain in power much longer.[78]

Messersmith at his new post in Vienna concurred in the judgment that the purge would undo the Nazi regime. Everything evil he believed about Hitler stood verified: "There is no brutality he will not sanction to gain his ends," he wrote on July 5. Perhaps now that the world had seen for itself the barbarity of National Socialism, "maybe the people will believe the press reports." At any rate, he added, "I do not see how our policy or that of the rest of the world towards Germany can change. What has happened can only strengthen us in our attitude of refraining from giving any moral or material support whatever." Less than a week later he admitted to Moffat that the German people pos-

77. Hull Memorandum, June 6, 1934, FR 1934, II, 426–428.
78. Bullitt to Hull, July 3, 1934, DS, 862.00/3288; Benton to Hull, July 4, 1934, 862.00/3290; Marriner to Hull, July 3, 1934, 862.00/3291; Bingham to Hull, July 23, 1934, Hull papers, Box 36; Long to Hull, July 17, 1934, 862.00/3309.

sessed "a callousness and cruelty" which he had not thought they did, but there was still "a lot of decency" in Germany that, combined with the shocking events of June 30, would overturn the National Socialist dictatorship. He reiterated his view on July 17. Germany now was "definitely isolated," the present government unable to halt the flow of events that would ultimately undo it. When the time was ripe the Reichswehr would install a reasonable government.[79]

The prognostications—and hopes—of the diplomats proved wrong. The Third Reich did not collapse. Far from it. Hitler and his followers even were able to withstand the embarrassment of the brutal July 25 murder by Austrian Nazis of the Austrian chancellor, Engelbert Dollfuss, and the pressure of mobilization of Italian troops on the Brenner Pass. Then, following passage on August 1 of a law combining the offices of chancellor and president, and the death of President von Hindenburg next day, on August 19 Hitler won overwhelmingly in a plebiscite authorizing his assumption of both posts.

Schacht tightened economic controls through his "New Plan," which went into effect on September 1. From then on Germany was to buy only what it could pay for—transactions on imports were not allowed until foreign exchange was in the Reichsbank—and imports would have to equal German exports to each country. The New Plan meant that Germany had turned its back on its two greatest suppliers of raw materials, the United States and Western Europe, to deal primarily with Latin American and Balkan nations.[80]

The State Department had to make a final decision on trade policy with Germany in the autumn of 1934. A special State Department committee, under the chairmanship of Professor Alvin Hansen of the University of Minnesota, presented its findings and recommendations. There were four alternatives: America could negotiate a new treaty with Germany, inaugurate trade warfare, denounce the existing commercial treaty, or maintain the *status quo*. The committee declared

79. Messersmith to Phillips, July 5, 1934, DS, 862.00/3424; Messersmith to Phillips, July 11 and July 17, 1934, Messersmith papers, Box 6.
80. Peterson, *Schacht*, 218–222. As one example of the effect of the new policy on trade, Peterson points out that whereas in 1933 three fourths of Germany's cotton imports came from the United States, in 1935 only one fourth did, the difference being made up in purchases from Argentina, Brazil, Peru, Egypt, and India. *Ibid.*, 224–226.

that after study of economic possibilities in a new treaty, the probability of meeting German demands was "altogether remote." Trade warfare, the committee said, would mean total loss of America's export trade to Germany, endanger nearly a billion dollars American citizens had invested in Germany, and antagonize a large group of German-Americans. Denouncing the existing treaty was meaningless if not accompanied by trade war. The committee recommended maintaining the *status quo*, reasoning that if the New Plan were successful, trade with Germany would be "of little value" to the United States. If Schacht's program failed, America might then gain more favorable terms. Hull concurred.[81] The next move was up to Germany.

Luther told Phillips in October that Germany was giving the required year's notice of intent to denounce the commercial treaty.[82] Thus the situation remained until the spring of 1935. Then officials of both nations reasoned that lack of any treaty would create a terribly complicated situation over consular rights, guarantees for private investments, and a host of other problems connected with daily relations. Hence, on June 3, 1935, the United States and Germany negotiated a new Treaty of Friendship, Commerce and Consular Rights, omitting both new trade concessions for the Germans and those provisions of Article VII that guaranteed both sides most-favored-nation status.[83] In the next years the Germans frequently mentioned trade negotiations with a view to increasing exports to the United States, holding out promises to purchase one or another type of goods—cotton especially—at higher-than-world-market prices. The State Department refused such proposals, and from 1935 on German goods were excluded from the special tariff concessions afforded the goods of the sixteen nations that by 1938 had entered into reciprocal trade agreements with the United States, all enjoying most-favored-nation privileges.

The most serious challenge to the State Department's trade program and principles came from Roosevelt's own special adviser on foreign trade, George N. Peek, who was also president of the Export-Import

81. Memorandum by a Special State Department Committee on Proposed American Policy with Respect to Germany, Oct. 12, and attached Hull Memorandum, Oct. 17, 1934, *FR 1934*, II, 448–453.
82. Phillips Memorandum, Oct. 13, 1934, *ibid.*, 454.
83. For text, see *FR 1935*, II, 451.

Bank, created in 1934 to foster and underwrite foreign trade. Peek felt it was futile for the United States to lead the way toward freer and increased trade through general tariff reduction and most-favored-nation arrangements. He believed the protective tariff system fundamentally sound, and preferred bilateral commercial agreements, with nations negotiating them on a *quid pro quo* basis and concerning themselves only with selling or bartering as much as they could.[84] In 1934 Peek's views coincided with Schacht's.

Schacht had approached Dodd in February and said that Germany would agree to purchase $500 million worth of American cotton over the next few years at a fixed price higher than the world price if the United States agreed to lower interest rates on German bonded indebtedness and perhaps increase import of German manufactures.[85] The State Department apparently made no response to this proposal. Then, in November 1934, Peek's office announced it had negotiated a trade agreement with Germany. The United States would sell Germany 800,000 bales of cotton through the Export-Import Bank. Germany would pay 25 per cent of the price in American dollars, and the remaining 75 per cent, plus a 22½ per cent premium, in German currency which could be used only for purchase of certain German goods. The Export-Import Bank could then sell these marks, at a discount, to Americans interested in importing German goods.[86]

Roosevelt was receptive to the scheme. It is true, as one analyst recently has written, that traditional principles governed New Deal foreign policy, which "rejoined the mainstream" in 1934 after passage of the Reciprocal Trade Agreements Act.[87] But Roosevelt apparently was not yet convinced that Hull's trade program was the only one appropriate for the United States. His attitude, at least as Phillips has recalled it, toward Hull's views and the Trade Agreements Act was "well, all right, let the old gentleman go ahead and have his fill."[88] Hence, on November 19, 1934, the President sent his secretary of state an informal note explaining that although they generally agreed

84. Gilbert C. Fite, *George N. Peek and the Fight for Farm Parity* (Norman, Okla., 1954), 271–272.

85. Dodd to Hull, Feb. 20, 1934, DS, 611.6231/384.

86. Hull, *Memoirs*, I, 371.

87. Lloyd G. Gardner, *Economic Aspects of New Deal Foreign Policy* (Madison, Wis., 1964), vii.

88. "The Reminiscences of William Phillips," 170, The Oral History Collection of Columbia University, Columbia University Library.

in theory "every once in a while we have to modify a principle to meet a hard and disagreeable fact! Witness the avalanche of cotton goods into the Philippines during the past six months." Roosevelt instructed Hull to work out a compromise with Peek who, he said, "represents the very hard-headed practical angle of trade." A meeting between Hull and Peek, however, produced no agreement.[89]

Then, while Hull went to speak in Nashville, Peek went to the White House and got Roosevelt on December 12 to approve the barter scheme. Phillips learned of this the same day and at once called Roosevelt's secretary, Marvin McIntyre, and told him that Hull would be "heartbroken" if the deal went through.[90] As Phillips would explain, events had developed "with a suddenness which was unexpected," and thereupon "as urgently as I possibly could [I] begged FDR should do nothing," at least until after Hull returned. McIntyre conferred with Roosevelt, who acceded to the request.[91]

Shortly afterward Hull presented Roosevelt with a long series of arguments in opposition to the Peek plan. Most important was that the deal violated principles the State Department had been preaching so fervently to Congress and other nations. A special bilateral arrangement with Germany, he said, violated the most-favored-nation principle. Acceptance of special conditions—cotton at a higher price than the world price for discounted marks exchangeable in Germany only for German goods—was granting advantages to German exports not granted to other countries. Already, Hull declared, Chile had threatened to retaliate by dumping nitrates, and Brazil had warned that its trade negotiations with the United States would have to be postponed in event of an American-German barter agreement. Roosevelt thereupon agreed to withdraw support of the plan, cutting off whatever hopes Peek might have had about barter with other countries as well.[92]

Hull and the State Department had won a decided victory over Peek, who made some unsuccessful last efforts in March and April 1935 to revive his plan.[93] Finally, in November 1935, Peek resigned from the administration to continue his battles in various books and

89. Quoted in Hull, *Memoirs*, I, 372.

90. Entry for Dec. 13, 1934, Phillips Diary, IV, 547, Phillips papers.

91. Phillips to Hull, Dec. 13, 1934, Hull papers, Box 36.

92. Hull, *Memoirs*, I, 373–374.

93. Peek to Roosevelt, Mar. 5, and Roosevelt to Peek, Mar. 7 and Apr. 8, 1935, Roosevelt papers, Official File 198A, Germany.

articles. His departure, as the New Deal historian Arthur M. Schlesinger, Jr., has written, marked the triumph of Hull's brand of internationalism.[94]

Despite their triumph, one must conclude that Hull and the State Department were not altogether adroit in their bargaining with Germany. First, as later disputes with the Treasury Department would show, they backed off their policy sufficiently so that those who wished to barter with Germany could do so through clever devices. Second, analysis of trade statistics for the years 1929 through 1938 shows that the great decline in American-German trade took place between 1929 and 1933. As noted earlier, the absolute dollar value of exports between the two countries increased in the period 1933–1938, although in relative export-import percentage Germany in 1933 took 8.4 per cent of the total of American exports and only 3.7 per cent in 1938, whereas in 1933 the United States took 5.4 per cent of Germany's exports and only 3.3 per cent in 1938. In the areas of such critical products as chemicals and pharmaceuticals, oil and base metals, American exports to Germany increased. American petroleum interests in 1934 sold over $12 million worth of oil to Germany; increases in each of the next years jumped sales to over $34 million in 1938— America thereby becoming a major supplier, along with the Soviet Union, Rumania, and Mexico for the German navy, which in turn had to supply the army just before the spring 1940 offensive.[95]

The State Department's strictures went unheeded as American firms pursued private profit even to the detriment of public and national long-range interest, frequently using methods that were not only frowned upon by the government but illegal. General Motors, having purchased the Adam Opel automobile works in Germany in 1929, placed at its disposal in 1931 facilities of the world-wide General Motors Export Corporation and opened new markets for its subsidiary in Latin America. This, of course, put the General Motors subsidiary in competition with both other American firms and domestic divisions of the parent company. By March 1937 officials of Adam Opel were encouraging their representatives in various countries to suggest barter

94. *Coming of the New Deal*, 258–259.

95. U.S. Tariff Commission, *Foreign Trade and Export Controls*, 150–151; Grand Admiral Erich Raeder, *My Life*, trans. Henry W. Drexel (Annapolis, 1960), 209–210.

arrangements to increase sales, and by 1939 Graeme K. Howard, vice-president in charge of exports for General Motors, was openly attacking both Hull's trade program for its opposition to Germany's efforts at bilateral trade policies and the State Department for not making agreements under the Reciprocal Trade Agreements Act with "have-not" nations.[96] Numerous other American manufacturers, including E. I. du Pont de Nemours and Union Carbide and Carbon, entered into restrictive agreements with German corporations, under which they promised not to produce critical chemical and metal products. Standard Oil of New Jersey, having agreed in 1929 not to enter chemical manufacture, in return for which I. G. Farben promised not to develop a high-grade gasoline from inexpensive materials, actually kept this arrangement secret until the Justice Department uncovered it in 1941. Standard also refused to develop 100-octane aviation fuel for the United States army, because the army would not allow it to give complete technical reports to I. G. Farben, as the 1929 arrangement provided.[97]

More meaningful even in retrospect then is Messersmith's lament, in 1936, that American firms were allowing their capital to be "used for the maintenance of the German industrial program and in some important directions for German rearmament, which is obviously not intended for defensive but for aggressive measures." American businessmen, he commented sadly, "are not blind to all of this . . . Perhaps they may yet find themselves in a position where they will consider it better policy to let the investments go to nothing rather than permit this capital and their organizations being used as a part of this tremendous armament program so definitely directed against the peace of the world."[98] Messersmith hoped in vain. American businessmen publicly opposed war as much as anyone else.[99] But it would seem that the one price they would not pay for peace was private profit.

96. Edward Tenenbaum, *National Socialism vs. International Capitalism* (New Haven, 1942), 105–106.

97. Gabriel Kolko, "American Business and Germany, 1930–1941," *Western Political Quarterly*, XV (Dec. 1962), 720–723. See also Michael Sayers and Albert E. Kahn, *Sabotage!: The Secret War Against America* (New York, 1942), 55–59.

98. Messersmith to Hull, July 2, 1936, Hull papers, Box 39.

99. Roland N. Stromberg, "American Business and the Approach of War, 1935–1941," *Journal of Economic History*, XIII (Winter 1953), 58–78.

American diplomacy in 1934 neither moderated German behavior nor improved relations with Germany. Ambassador Dodd was especially distressed. The Blood Purge shocked him.[100] Doubts crept into his mind about the succes of his mission. His task, he felt, was to work for peace and better relations, but, he confided in his diary a week after the purge, "I do not see how anything can be done so long as Hitler, Goering and Goebbels are the directing heads of the country . . . Ought I to resign?" On July 13 he recorded his reaction to Hitler: "I have a sense of horror when I look at the man." Next day he wrote Hull that there was "nothing more repulsive than to watch the country of Goethe and Beethoven revert to the barbarism of Stuart England and Bourbon France."[101]

Virtually alone among American or European diplomts, Dodd refused to subscribe to the notion that the Hitler government would soon collapse. On July 21, two days after Hitler's plebiscite victory, he wrote that Hitler would "continue to dominate the German people" through "mass propaganda, backed by the energetic activity of the 'Brown Shirts,' and with the tacit acquiescence of the Reichswehr." There seemed to be no quarter in Germany, he said, that could bring about a fundamental change. In September he wrote Hull that events since the Blood Purge had not weakened the hold of Hitler, whose prestige and power "seem to be tremendous," and whose regime was secure and only strengthened by "the absence of a united opposition animated with a definite program."[102] In November the ambassador persisted in this vein by indicating that reports of discontent in Germany had to be evaluated with "great caution," and probably had no "definite political significance." The peace that prevailed, Dodd conceded in his diary, would last only "until Germany can be entirely ready to command Europe."[103]

Little that American diplomats proposed in 1934 might have prevented Dodd's worst fears from becoming reality. Roosevelt, however,

100. His daughter said it was a shock he "never got over." M. Dodd, *Through Embassy Eyes,* 155.

101. Entries for July 8 and July 13, 1934, Dodd, *Diary,* 123, 126; Dodd to Hull, July 14, 1934, DS, 862.00/3707.

102. Dodd to Hull, Aug. 21 and Sept. 17, 1934, *FR 1934,* II, 247, DS, 862.00/3410.

103. Dodd to Hull, Nov. 17, 1934, *FR 1934,* II, 252; entry for Nov. 9, 1934, Dodd, *Diary,* 187.

did consider certain possibilities intermittently and fleetingly. He was not yet as distressed as was his ambassador in Berlin, but at an April 28 luncheon with Hull and Norman Davis he proposed that the United States, Great Britain, and France take up the matter of German rearmament in violation of the Treaty of Versailles and inform the Gemans that they wanted to send an investigating commission. If the Germans refused, as Roosevelt expected, the cooperating nations were to announce that although they would never invade, as a matter of protection they were cutting off all trade with Germany. Davis thought it a good plan, though he and Hull wondered whether it would be unfair to take a stand against German rearmament without considering the whole problem of disarmament. Roosevelt also thought he would not be able to enforce a non-export-import program, but he would implore the American people not to trade with Germany. At any rate, he authorized Davis to discuss administrative aspects of the idea with the British.[104]

Nothing more was said of the scheme until mid-May, when Emile Francqui, head of a special Belgian mission to announce the accession of Leopold III, told Phillips that Roosevelt had suggested to him that if Germany refused to go along with gradual disarmament, there should be a boycott of German goods.[105]

The matter drifted again until late October. Then Roosevelt proposed to Phillips that the United States, Great Britain, France, and possibly others ought to consider an arrangement whereby, if any nation crossed another's frontier, every signatory power would refuse to trade with the aggressor. Phillips referred Roosevelt's scheme to Moffat, who immediately wrote a memorandum pointing up weaknesses in it. Among other things, Moffat said, the envisaged pact, instead of keeping the United States out of a European war, would lead to involvement, for trade sanctions were "pretty close to a *casus belli,* and would in any event be inconsistent with the duties of neutrality." A pact that defined an act of aggression as crossing a frontier, Moffat said, would also allow every nation to pursue treaty violations within its own borders, as, for example, Germany rearming. In addition, determining whether a nation had committed aggression would be diffi-

104. Davis-Hull-Roosevelt Memorandum, Apr. 28, 1934, Davis papers, Box 9.
105. Phillips Memorandum, May 25, 1934, *FR 1934,* I, 70.

cult because there were many disputed frontiers. And in certain "backward parts of the world," Moffat added, such as China, nations had to send their soldiers across frontiers to protect their citizens. Finally, "if the proposed pact were not universalized, I reach the reluctant conclusion that it would in effect constitute an alliance in fact if not in form between the signatory powers." After reading Moffat's memorandum, Roosevelt agreed, as Phillips reported, to "let this matter rest."[106] Davis made one final effort to resurrect the plan in March 1935 when he approached the British ambassador, Sir Ronald Lindsay, just after Germany publicly announced rearmament. Davis admitted that the plan might be "Utopian and probably unacceptable," but at least a guarantee that Germany would not be invaded would undercut its chief claim to need arms. Lindsay, as Davis noted, "didn't think much of the idea."[107]

Whether anything might have come of Roosevelt's scheme is doubtful. Moffat's objections were important, although these might have been overcome had the parties to the proposed agreement determined to do so. But that determination, which implied need for real cooperation, probably was lacking. In August 1934, Colonel House complained to Phillips that the two most powerful men in the British government, Stanley Baldwin, lord president of the Council, and Neville Chamberlain, chancellor of the Exchequer, were "distinctly unfriendly" toward the United States. At least part of the British explanation for this attitude was forthcoming at nearly the same time in October that Roosevelt's boycott scheme was under consideration. When approached about Anglo-American cooperation, Lindsay said, as Phillips recorded, that "the British Government was not in the least interested in playing ball with us . . . partly because they had made up their minds that the United States Government was a hopeless proposition to play ball with."[108]

106. Phillips to Moffat, Oct. 22, Moffat to Phillips, Oct. 23, and undated Phillips Memorandum to Moffat, 1934, *ibid.*, 170–172 and 170n85.
107. Davis Memorandum, Mar. 19, 1935, Davis papers, Box 9.
108. Entries for Aug. 14 and Oct. 15, 1934, Phillips Diary, III, 336–338, 447, Phillips papers.

# 5. THE COMING OF AGGRESSION

The fifteen months from January 1935 through March 1936 were critical for the United States and Germany, and for the future peace of the world. Developments at this time, one could reasonably argue, contributed as much if not more than those of any comparable period to making inevitable that war which Winston Churchill later insisted was "unnecessary."[1] For men like Ambassador Dodd, convinced that one needed to look no further than *Mein Kampf* to discover the aims of German foreign policy, the course was clear: "Roosevelt must act this year or surrender in matters of relations to distraught Europe."[2]

Hitler too had to act. The British and the French in the first months of 1935 were pressing him to extend the Locarno guarantees to Central and Eastern Europe and to sign an agreement covering unprovoked aggression by air. In return Germany probably would have been allowed to continue rearmament openly. For Hitler the test of his diplomacy was to avoid agreeing to the British proposals and still announce with righteousness and justification German rearmament, which, having grown to enormous proportions, could no longer be carried on secretly.[3]

In January 1935 two diplomatically unrelated events symbolized forthcoming developments. The first was the Saar plebiscite on January

---

1. Winston S. Churchill, *The Second World War: The Gathering Storm,* 6 vols. (Boston, 1948–53), I, iv.
2. Entry for Jan. 17, 1935, Dodd, *Diary,* 210.
3. Bullock, *Hitler,* 331–332; Meinck *Hitler und die deutsche Aufrüstung,* 94.

13; the second, the Senate vote on January 29 on the administration proposal that the United States join the Permanent Court of International Justice at The Hague (the World Court). The decision of the people of the Saar to reunite with Germany surprised no one, although the fact that more than 90 per cent of the half-million people voting elected union with Germany, only 1 per cent elected France, and the remainder chose the *status quo* caused concern.

As Ambassador Long in Italy wrote to Roosevelt, diplomats in Europe worried that the Saar plebiscite would affect the Germans like "a big drink of Schnaps" and that Hitler would "be emboldened now to pursue his Pan Germanic ideas into the fields of former German territories and Austria."[4] In fact, Long only recently had written that in a conversation with him the day before Mussolini had given the "definite and uneradicable impression that he expects war with Germany within a comparatively short time." Long added that he too thought war "must come. We have all known it must come. It is only that the day is actually approaching. We must be realists." And he seriously suggested that Roosevelt supply diplomatic and consular offices with gas masks. A few weeks later he reiterated his view that he saw "no escape from a real cataclysm."[5]

While diplomats fretted in anticipation of Germany's next move, the Roosevelt administration attempted to bring about American adherence to the World Court, which functioned independently of the League of Nations and generally was restricted to matters of minor international importance because it had jurisdiction only when authorized by all parties to a dispute. Proposing membership in 1935 was hardly a new or bold idea; each of the previous three Republican administrations had done so, and so did the platforms of both parties, with various reservations, in 1924 and in 1932.[6] Isolationists in the Senate had always managed to tie up deliberation on the matter. In the autumn of 1934 Secretary Hull and his aides revived the proposal and secured Roosevelt's support. The Senate Foreign Relations Committee on January 9 reported favorably on a measure to join, and one

4. Long to Roosevelt, Feb. 8, 1935, Long papers, Box 114.
5. Long to Roosevelt, Feb. 3 and Feb. 21, 1935, *ibid.*
6. Kirk Porter and Donald Bruce Johnson, eds., *National Party Platforms, 1840–1960* (Urbana, Ill., 1961), 251, 260, 332, 345–346.

week later in a special message Roosevelt noted the criticalness of the days and implored the Senate to allow the United States "to throw its weight into the scale in favor of peace."[7]

Throughout the heated debate that followed, State Department officials remained confident their measure would receive support.[8] But a furious last-ditch radio and telegram campaign, led by the chauvinistic publisher William Randolph Hearst, the demagogic Detroit radio priest Father Charles E. Coughlin, and the folksy entertainer-philosopher Will Rogers, sufficiently fired Senators William E. Borah, Hiram Johnson, and Huey P. Long, to coerce their colleagues into defeating the administration effort. When the roll call came on January 29, the administration could muster only a 52–36 majority, seven votes short of the two thirds required.[9]

The defeat was bitter for those who longed for a more thoughtful and resolute foreign policy. Dodd, in Washington at the time, offered to resign as a protest, but Hull and Assistant Secretary R. Walton Moore, Dodd's close friend, though sharing his anguish, convinced him the gesture would do no good.[10] Hull apparently considered declaring publicly that the fight would continue, but his advisers talked him out of it, feeling that most people backed the Senate.[11] Roosevelt was "fighting mad," Norman Davis reported to the State Department.[12] The President said nothing publicly, but privately wrote majority leader Joseph T. Robinson, who had led the floor fight for the administration, that if the senators who voted against the measure ever got to heaven they would be "doing a great deal of apologizing for a very long time." And to former secretary of state Stimson, Roosevelt explained that the opposition was able to get away with its appeal only because "these are not normal times; people are jumpy and very ready to run after strange gods. This is so in every other country as well as our own." At a cabinet meeting, noted the secretary of interior,

---

7. Hull, *Memoirs*, I, 387–389; *PPFDR*, IV, 40–41.
8. Entry for Jan. 23, 1935, Phillips Diary, IV, 631, Phillips papers.
9. Leuchtenburg, *FDR and the New Deal*, 216.
10. Entries for Feb. 1 and Feb. 2, 1935, Dodd, *Diary*, 211–213.
11. Entries for Jan. 29 and Jan. 30, 1935, Phillips Diary, Phillips papers, cited in Pratt, *Hull*, I, 273.
12. Moffat to Mayer, Feb. 2, 1935, Moffat papers.

Harold Ickes, the President showed that his defeat had "cut pretty deeply. At times there seemed to be a bitter tinge to his laughter and good humor."[13]

The World Court setback was more than a personal defeat for advocates of responsible American policy on matters international. It demonstrated that a vocal and vociferous minority could block any effort, no matter how symbolic or innocuous, at constructive commitments in world affairs. It underscored another point. As Moffat remarked, if the Roosevelt administration, fresh from scoring the greatest congressional victory of any party in the nation's history in November 1934, was unable to put through the World Court measure, what likelihood was there now of its being able to sponsor even more serious legislation or action to support treaties or halt aggression? A group of senators visiting Paris told Chargé Marriner that the administration's defeat "put a complete stop" on increased cooperation with the League of Nations.[14]

The Saar vote itself did not cause Hitler to do more than he already intended, and he could claim only limited credit because the Weimar regime had ensured the plebiscite.[15] But whereas Hitler had to be cautious before the voting in order not to jeopardize the outcome, his hands were now freer. Thus on January 16, for instance, he ordered increased speed in naval rearmament, indicative of his intention no longer to bargain to increase armaments but rather to increase armaments to be able to bargain better.[16] The British, meanwhile, continued their overtures to seek extension of the Locarno guarantees, and on February 22 Neurath agreed to receive Foreign Secretary Simon in Berlin, whose visit was scheduled for March 7.[17]

The Germans, however, seized the first opportunity to stall. The

13. Roosevelt to Robinson, Jan. 30, and Roosevelt to Stimson, Feb. 6, 1935, *FDRL*, I, 450–451; entry for Feb. 2, 1935, *The Secret Diary of Harold L. Ickes: The First Thousand Days, 1933–1936,* 3 vols. (New York, 1953–55), I, 287.

14. Moffat to Mayer, Jan. 29, 1935, Moffat papers; entry for Jan. 29, 1935, Marriner Diary, Marriner papers.

15. Bracher, "Das 'Dritte Reich,' " in Bracher and others, *Die nationalsozial-istische Machtergreifung,* 257.

16. Meinck, *Hitler und die deutsche Aufrüstung,* 92, and Robertson, *Hitler's Pre-War Policy,* 46.

17. Neurath Memorandum, Feb. 22, 1935, *DGFP,* C, III, 958–959, 980n3.

British rather tactlessly issued a white paper on March 4 announcing that in view of Germany's defiant rearmament they felt compelled to increase their own armaments.[18] Hitler at once contracted a cold, and Neurath informed the British on the eve of Simon's departure that the visit would have to be postponed.[19] Then, on March 9, the Germans made official what everyone knew all along: Germany had a military air force, Reich Air Minister Hermann Göring said to Ward Price, editor of the *Daily Mail*.[20] As Dodd would insist, this announcement was not specifically a retaliatory measure against the British white paper, but had been decided upon in advance of it to be used as a "trial balloon" to test attitudes before making a more serious move.[21]

The second and more serious move followed shortly. The United States and the rest of the world remained silent about Germany's announced air force, and Simon even told Parliament that he and Lord Privy Seal Eden still hoped to go to Berlin, a fact that apparently surprised the German Foreign Ministry but delighted Hitler.[22] The French shortly afterward, insisting that they had to compensate for the decline in eligible military draftees resulting from the diminished birth rate of the war years, lowered the age for conscription and made clear their intention of lengthening service first from twelve to eighteen months, and then to two years. Hitler, meanwhile, having left Berlin to "recuperate" from his feigned illness, decided the time had come for his second stroke.[23] He summoned his Wehrmacht adjutant, Friedrich Hossbach, and told him on March 14 that he intended to announce universal military service as soon as the French concluded their discussion on conscription. Hossbach apparently indicated he thought the

18. Text in John W. Wheeler-Bennett and Stephen Heald, eds., *Documents on International Affairs, 1935*, 2 vols. (London, 1936–37), I, 38–47. (Heald edited vol. II alone.)

19. Neurath to the Embassies in France, Italy, and Great Britain, Mar. 6, 1935, *DGFP*, C, III, 979–980, 979n2.

20. Arnold J. Toynbee, ed., *Survey of International Affairs, 1935*, 2 vols. (London, 1936), I, 140.

21. Dodd to Hull, Mar. 20, 1935, DS, 862.00/805. Historical analysts concur with Dodd. See Bullock, *Hitler*, 332, Meinck, *Hitler und die deutsche Aufrüstung*, 96, and William L. Shirer *The Rise and Fall of the Third Reich: A History of Nazi Germany* (New York, 1960), 283.

22. Kordt, *Wahn und Wirklichkeit*, 70–71.

23. Kordt, *Nicht aus den Akten*, 93.

appropriate ministers ought to be notified, and Hitler authorized him to arrange a cabinet session. At the meeting next day only War Minister von Blomberg expressed concern over foreign reaction, but Ribbentrop cut him short with, "That's a lot of nonsense."[24]

The following day, March 16, Hitler announced to the German people and the ambassadors from England, France, Italy, and Poland that the Reich government had reintroduced conscription and would build Germany's peacetime forces to thirty-six divisions, or approximately half a million men.[25] Although the Germans unilaterally had abrogated their separate peace treaty of 1921 with the United States, as well as the military clauses of the Treaty of Versailles, they had not even given the Americans the benefit of private diplomatic notification.

The American response to proceedings of the last weeks was feeble. On the day that Göring was announcing Germany's construction of an air force, Roosevelt was writing sadly to Breckinridge Long in Italy that the United States was still suffering from a "bad case of Huey Long and Father Coughlin influenza—the whole country aching in every bone." He believed that current events made things as "hair-trigger" dangerous as any days of their lives had been, including those of June and July 1914.[26] But neither Roosevelt nor his advisers had any program. That same day Roosevelt read to his cabinet one of Ambassador Long's letters predicting war in Europe within a year and expressing hope that the United States would not involve itself. Every member of the cabinet, as Ickes recorded, thought it would be a "dreadful thing if we should again be dragged into a war."[27]

What the United States was willing to do about preventing such a war was another matter. Thus, when newspapermen following Germany's announced rearmament on March 16 asked Hull if the government at least was going to protest, Hull declined comment on the entire situation.[28] When the counselor of the Belgian embassy, Prince Eugene de Ligne, expressed hope that the United States of-

24. Friedrich Hossbach, *Zwischen Wehrmacht und Hitler, 1934–1938* (Wolfenbüttel and Hanover, 1949), 94–96.
25. Hitler's proclamation, and text of the law, are in Wheeler-Bennett and Heald, eds., *Documents 1935*, I, 58–64; Neurath to the Embassies in Italy, Great Britain, France and Poland, *DGFP*, C, III, 1005–1006.
26. Roosevelt to Long, Mar. 9, 1935, Long papers, Box 114.
27. Entry for Mar. 11, 1935, Ickes, *Diary*, I, 312.
28. *New York Times*, Mar. 19, 1935.

ficially would deplore the German act, Moffat said that it was too early to say what the United States would do, that reports from overseas were still coming in.[29] Those reports told Washington little that might not have been guessed. The British protested formally, but at the same time requested that Hitler receive the Simon mission, now scheduled for late March, to discuss a general peace and armaments settlement.[30] The "principal desire" of British policy, wrote Chargé Ray Atherton from London, was "to get Germany back into the League again and a part of the collective security system from which she would find it extremely difficult to withdraw."[31] The French too protested the German act and called for an extraordinary session of the League Council although, Marriner noted, the "press and people seemed to take the whole thing much more calmly than anyone could have anticipated."[32] If anything, Ambassador Straus reported, the French were in a state of "despair and smouldering resentment" against the British for their decision to proceed with negotiations without even consulting them or the Italians.[33] From Poland, Ambassador John Cudahy reported that the foreign minister, Josef Beck, was angry, but Poland would not protest because "protests without action are no good." In Austria, Chargé A. W. Kliefoth wrote, even the most violent anti-Hitler newspapers "agreed cordially and wholeheartedly" with Germany's rearmament; there was objection only to the "method of gaining it." From Czechoslovakia came word from Minister J. Butler Wright that President Beneš—speaking "with frankness which might appear to be even brutal in part"—regarded the League of Nations as hereafter restricted to "study, counsel, and advice." Never would the League be able to recommend unanimously the use of force. This admission was, Wright remarked, unusual from someone consistently dedicated to the League.[34]

29. Moffat Memorandum, Mar. 18, 1935, *FR 1935*, II, 303.

30. British Note to the German Government, Mar. 18, 1935, Wheeler-Bennett and Heald, eds., *Documents 1935*, I, 64–66.

31. Atherton to Hull, Mar. 18, 1935, *FR 1935*, II, 304.

32. Text of French notes to League of Nations and Germany in Wheeler-Bennett and Heald, eds., *Documents 1935*, I, 66–68; entry for Mar. 18, 1935, Marriner Diary, Marriner papers.

33. Straus to Hull, Mar. 20, 1935, *FR 1935*, II, 305.

34. Cudahy to Hull and Kliefoth to Hull, Mar. 22, and Wright to Hull, Mar. 25, 1935, DS, 862.20/829, 862.20/831, 862.20/920.

Hull and his advisers did prepare for Roosevelt a tentative protest note restricted to criticism of Germany's violation of its 1921 peace settlement with the United States.[35] When Davis drafted a slightly harsher note next day, Phillips told him to make it more general—put it on a "high plane"—and less specific. A few days later when the French ambassador, André Lefebvre de Laboulaye, called Phillips to ask that the American government make its position clear before the British opened negotiations with the Germans, Phillips consulted Roosevelt, who said that at present he preferred not to involve the United States in European affairs through a protest note.[36]

Ambassador Long maintained that the United States was not bound to joint action because it had not signed the Treaty of Versailles, and therefore American diplomats should tell Europe that they were "considering the matter." Ambassadors Bingham and Straus jointly told Hull that although the United States should let it be known European events were watched with concern, "we should continue not to interfere with the evolution of European decisions." In fact, if the European nations called a meeting, the United States "should not attend or send an observer . . . even if so suggested."[37] Even Davis decided finally that America should do nothing about Germany's rearmament. He favored a fairly strong protest at the outset, but considering that the Allies and Germany had discussed revision of the Treaty of Versailles "both sides were responsible for creating the situation which led Germany to denounce the Treaty, and since protest could do no good and might do some harm and be construed as our taking sides in the other issues involved, we all agreed that we should not send a protest." Personally, Davis contended that Germany had "much justification" for announcing rearmament but "no justification for doing it at the time and in the way she did." It was, after all, "stupid for France to think she could keep Germany forever in a position of inequality."[38]

Ambassador Luther perhaps best summed up the American attitude when he reported to Berlin that the "swing of opinion" during March was toward "conviction . . . that the German step was justified." Were

35. Entry for Mar. 18, 1935, Phillips Diary, IV, 723, Phillips papers.
36. Entries for Mar. 19 and Mar. 22, 1935, *ibid.*, 727, 731.
37. Long to Hull, Mar. 21, 1935, *FR 1935,* II, 309–310; Bingham to Hull, Mar. 29, 1935, DS, 862.20/798.
38. Davis to Welles, Mar. 27, 1935, Davis papers, Box 63.

Americans piqued because Germany had not informed them of the decision to rearm? Not really, he wrote. In fact, "I have the impression that the fact that they were not informed is rather welcome here."[39] Two days later, on March 22, Hull told a press conference that the United States followed European events carefully, that the moral influence of the American people and their government always encouraged people to live up to treaties, and that the United States hoped current efforts in Europe "will succeed in their purpose of bringing about a general appeasement."[40] Three days later Roosevelt left for a fishing trip off the Florida coast, always within reach by telephone, of course, but the move was hardly indicative of any immediate development in American diplomacy.[41] Not even the joint resolution of Great Britain, France, and Italy at Stresa on April 14, condemning Germany's behavior, and the League of Nations resolution of censure on April 17—politically meaningless as these gestures were—could move the American government to protest Germany's unilateral abrogation of treaty obligations.[42] When a member of the Rumanian embassy called at the State Department on April 19 and asked if the United States now intended to protest, Moffat replied that the wide circulation of Hull's March 22 press statement made comment unnecessary.[43]

No one invited the United States to Stresa; nor did American diplomats wish to go. The question remains what the Americans would have been willing to contribute to collective action had the conferees at Stresa, and then at Geneva, done more than speak angry words. Shortly after returning from his fishing trip Roosevelt indicated that the contribution at best would have been very small. Seemingly hopeful that some day all nations would blockade Germany, he wrote Colonel House that he had heard rumors that the Stresa powers were

39. Luther to Foreign Ministry, Mar. 20, 1935, *DGFP*, C, III, 1028.
40. Memorandum of Hull Press Conference, Mar. 22, 1935, DS, 862.20/808. Interestingly, in citing this memorandum in his *Memoirs*, I, 243, Hull omitted the passage with the word "appeasement," obviously not wishing to associate himself with the word that later had a sinister connotation.
41. Entry for Mar. 25, 1935, Ickes, *Diary*, I, 327.
42. Joint resolution of Stresa Conference in Toynbee, ed., *Survey 1935*, I, 159–161; League of Nations resolution in Wheeler-Bennett and Heald, eds., *Documents 1935*, I, 98–99.
43. Moffat Memorandum, Apr. 28, 1935, *FR 1935*, II, 328.

considering some joint action and that he hoped it would take the form of "a complete blockade of Germany." If it proved effective, "recognition of the blockade by us would obviously follow." A blockade, he went on, was neither a boycott nor an economic sanction, and the chief executive was therefore able to recognize it without having to ask for congressional approval. Roosevelt's "plan," of course, left initiative completely to the European countries, and were a blockade effective, he would have had to recognize it, unless he intended American shippers to offend every country in Europe. A clearer estimate of Roosevelt's—and America's—current position came from what he said to his ambassador in Germany: "As I told you, I feel very helpless to render any particular service to immediate or permanent peace at this time."[44]

The Stresa conference never produced a blockade, and Americans had little reason to take the proceedings seriously. Two days before the conference opened, Bingham reported from London that although the British had no illusions about Germany's ultimate needs and ambitions, neither the public nor the government was prepared to sanction an anti-German defensive alliance; in fact, the Foreign Office was determined to prevent France and Italy from realizing their encirclement policy which would only ruin chances of "Christianizing" Germany.[45] In a dispatch next day, which Hull thought important enough to pass along to Roosevelt, Bingham said he had just seen Simon, who regarded Hitler as the "one great figure" whose sincere purpose was to "rehabilitate Germany morally" and help the people there to regain their "self-esteem, and overcome their inferiority complex." It was obvious, Bingham concluded, that Simon did not expect the Stresa conference to produce "tangible" results.[46]

Bingham was right. As he reported shortly, "high Foreign Office opinion" believed that the conferences of the past week merely had given the French and Italians a chance "to blow off steam."[47] Nor did the British want the conferences to achieve more. As Hugh Wilson reported from Geneva on April 17, Simon had just told him that he

44. Roosevelt to House, Apr. 10, and Roosevelt to Dodd, Apr. 26, 1935, *FDRL,* I, 472–473, 475.
45. Bingham to Hull, Apr. 9, 1935, DS, 862.20/870.
46. Bingham to Hull, Apr. 10, 1935, DS, 862.20/853.
47. Bingham to Hull, Apr. 17, 1935, DS, 862.20/895.

"deplored" the fact that the French had brought the matter of German rearmament before the League Council, and that he would "not tolerate any attempt to isolate and surround Germany."[48] The only American diplomat who seemed to think Stresa had "put a military ring around Germany" was Breckinridge Long. But, he added, Germany will not give up its ambitions; rather, the ring "will yield in spots in the east and south" and eventually the European powers will "accept something of German leadership rather than French leadership." This, he added, might not be so bad, because only two countries were capable of dominating Europe: Germany or the Soviet Union. "I shudder to think of a Russian domination," he said, and while at first German domination would be "hard and cruel . . . it would be an intensification of a culture which is more akin to ours." Further, Germany would "act as a bulwark against the westward progress of Russia."[49]

The papier mâché Stresa front fell apart in less than two months. The British were chiefly responsible; Hitler helped with his "peace" speech of May 21. The United States provided subtle reassurance that there was reason to believe Hitler's offers in that speech sincere and some basis for beginning negotiations that might lead to long-range settlement.

When Simon and Eden visited Berlin on March 25–26, Simon indicated interest in agreement on a naval construction program over a number of years, that is, one which would place absolute limits, as did the Treaty of Versailles, on the size and number of ships and gun calibre. Hitler expressed surprise at what he considered a new approach and said he preferred the system of ratios among navies which previous conferences had laid down. Germany, he said, would be willing to limit itself to a navy 35 per cent the size of the British navy. Simon replied that preliminary conversations in London were clearly necessary.[50]

48. Wilson to Hull, Apr. 17, 1935, DS, 862.20/901.
49. Long to Roosevelt, Apr. 19, 1935, Long papers, Box 114.
50. Unsigned Memorandum (Record . . . of the Conversation Between the Führer and Simon), Mar. 25–26, 1935, *DGFP*, C, III, 1064–1067. See also Schmidt, *Statist auf diplomatischer Bühne*, 310. On British naval building policy see D. C. Watt, "The Anglo-German Naval Agreement of 1935: An Interim Judgment," *Journal of Modern History*, XXVIII (June 1956), 164–166.

Following conversations in late April, the British invited the Germans to send a delegation to London. The Germans accepted, stipulating that no date for the talks be set until the Reich government had made a statement on foreign policy in reply to the League's April 17 censure vote.[51] The German reply was Hitler's May 21 speech in the Kroll Opera House.[52] The chancellor, as one reporter noted, was in "great form" and in an "easy, confident" mood; he offered the world as much, if not more, than anyone dared hope.[53] Hitler spoke eloquently about the absolute stupidity of war, insisting that the "dynastic egoism, political passion, and patriotic blindness" that caused rivers of blood to be shed had brought about significant political changes that only scarcely had "touched the skin of nations" and had not altered their fundamental character. "If these states had applied merely a fraction of their sacrifices to wiser purposes," he said, "the success would certainly have been greater and more permanent." Concretely, Hitler offered a program for peace which included Germany's respecting all remaining Versailles provisions (he declared Germany did not intend to annex Austria or remilitarize the Rhineland), signing non-aggression pacts with all its neighbors (expect Lithuania, which still retained Memel), strengthening the Locarno treaties by an agreement on air attack, and negotiating various arrangements to limit or abolish arms. Germany also would restrict its navy to 35 per cent of the size of the British. "Earnest and emphatic as Hitler appeared," Ambassador Dodd wrote in his diary after sitting through the performance, "he certainly does not fool me."[54] The chancellor had, however, created an atmosphere conducive to Anglo-German agreement.

Before these negotiations got under way, the Soviet foreign commissar, Litvinov, approached Ambassador Bullitt, commented that American diplomats did not seem distresed by the prospect of an Anglo-German naval agreement, and asked whether the United States intended to protest the reconstruction of the German navy, which violated the Versailles Treaty and the American treaty of 1921. Bullitt, reporting this conversation to Hull, said that he had told Litvinov

51. Bülow Note, Apr. 26, 1935, *DGFP*, C, IV, 86.
52. Text in Baynes, ed., *Hitler's Speeches*, II, 1218–1247.
53. Entry for May 21, 1935, William L. Shirer, *Berlin Diary: The Journal of a Foreign Correspondent, 1934–1941* (New York, 1941), 37–39.
54. Entry for May 21, 1935, Dodd, *Diary*, 246.

he had no information. Hull felt compelled to define things more explicitly. Aside from the matter of violation of treaty rights shared by the United States, he cabled Bullitt, America's interest in German naval rearmament was "primarily an indirect one." Relations in the Pacific were the first concern. The "immediate influence" of the Continental navies was in the Eastern Atlantic and European waters, where "our interest is relatively small." Thus, "regional discussion of German naval rearmament as now envisaged is the most appropriate method of dealing with the issue at present." None of this information could be given to Litvinov, Hull concluded, but might be used informally.[55] One month later the State Department would go a step further in approval of an Anglo-German accord.

For Hitler, accord with Great Britain—even as a temporary expedient—was part of the policy he had sketched in *Mein Kampf,* and in February 1933 he told Admiral Erich Raeder, chief of the German Naval Command, that he hoped to secure a formal 3:1 naval ratio between England and Germany. Raeder recognized the military and political advantages—repudiation of the Treaty of Versailles—of such an agreement and requested only that Hitler increase the German claim to a 35 per cent ratio. After the March–May 1935 diplomatic exchanges, Hitler decided to send Ribbentrop as ambassador extraordinary to London to negotiate. Raeder, fearful that Ribbentrop might make some concession at the navy's expense, insisted that no discussion among technical experts concerning construction or future building plans be allowed until the British accepted the 35 per cent ratio. Hitler agreed, and further instructed Ribbentrop that if the British balked he was to break off negotiations and return to Berlin.[56]

At the initial meeting in London on June 4 Simon declared that fixing ratios generally had been difficult, and he proposed turning discussion over to the technical experts. Ribbentrop thereupon caught him off guard with a prepared statement that talks could proceed only if "this ratio of Great Britain 100 to Germany 35 is accepted as an inviolable and firmly established relationship." After Simon countered that perhaps such a demand belonged at the end rather than the

55. Bullitt to Hull, May 4, and Hull to Bullitt, May 7, 1935, *FR 1935* I, 272, 162–163.
56. Raeder, *My Life,* 165–167, 176.

beginning of negotiations, Ribbentrop testily replied that the ratio was "not simply a demand to be put forward by the German side but *a final decision by the German Chancellor.*" Simon excused himself from the meeting.[57]

Within twenty-four hours the British made a hasty decision, based on admiralty rather than political advice.[58] Simon informed the Germans that his government accepted the "final decision" and was prepared to sign an agreement, although it would be necessary to inform other governments of England's intention and give them "an opportunity to offer any observations they may desire to make."[59]

The British promptly explained recent developments in a "secret" *aide-mémoire* they circulated among delegations in London the next day. After viewing it, Bingham cabled Hull that preliminary Anglo-German talks represented a "constructive contribution" and that it would perhaps be a good idea, if the State Department looked favorably upon the proposed agreement, to convey this information to the British Foreign Office, "where I have reason to believe that it would be welcome."[60] Hull at once had the Division of Western European Affairs prepare a memorandum. State Department experts were not blind to the unfavorable aspects of approving the proposed naval agreement. It would not seem fitting, they said, for the United States to approve unilateral scrapping of a treaty obligation which it had "informally regretted" in the case of German land and air armaments. Nor was it desirable to favor an agreement that created a sixth naval power and that might begin an increase in armaments by other nations, for example, France. But, the advisers reasoned, disapproval of the German project might be unwise "since *per se* it does not affect our own naval policy directly." The German position seemed "in several respects more reasonable than might have been feared," and demand for a navy 35 per cent the size of the British navy would leave Ger-

57. Kordt, *Nicht aus den Akten*, 104. (Kordt was secretary of the Legation and present at the meeting.) Unsigned Memorandum, June 4, 1935, *DGFP*, C, IV, 253–262.

58. Watt, "Anglo-German Naval Agreement," *Journal of Modern History*, 168–170.

59. Kordt, *Nicht aus den Akten*, 105; Unsigned Memorandum, June 6, 1935, *DGFP*, C, IV, 277–281.

60. Bingham to Hull, June 7, 1935, *FR 1935*, I, 163–164.

many's navy smaller than that of France. Application of tonnage limitations was to be made not on a general basis but category by category, which accorded with procedure advocated by the United States. The German offer and acceptance by Great Britain was "in one sense undoubtedly a constructive factor in European and world pacification." Further, the British attitude foreshadowed a "definite push towards resumption of general naval negotiations and the United States should not in any way hamper the effort." All in all, the State Department advisers concluded, despite the "astonishing" fact that England was allowing Germany submarines (England had just threatened to build more destroyers if France did not reduce its number of submarines), and considering that France was now "isolated," it seemed best to instruct the London embassy to "indicate a detached and non-committal but friendly attitude."[61]

Three days later Hull told Bingham to inform the British that the American government appreciated the detailed information and that it noted with "particular satisfaction" Germany's acceptance of a permanent, category by category naval tonnage ratio. As for determination of the absolute size of the two navies, that problem was "primarily one for British decision."[62]

When Jules Henry, counselor of the French embassy, called at the State Department on June 15 and asked if press reports stating that the United States approved the German demand for a navy 35 per cent the size of the British were correct, Moffat told him they were inaccurate. The United States, Moffat said, looked upon the naval problem as twofold. First there were the fleets of the United States, Japan, and England in the Pacific; second, the fleets in Europe. America's chief interest was in the size of the former, but naturally it hoped that agreement concerning the size of the latter would lead to further naval reduction. Four days later the Italians called and learned the same thing.[63]

Hitler obtained more than a navy from the Anglo-German Naval Agreement of June 18, 1935. For the past two years he had achieved diplomatic success largely at the cost of isolating Germany. Now he

61. Field Memorandum, June 8, 1935, DS, 862.34/146.
62. Hull to Bingham, June 11, 1935, *FR 1935*, I, 164–165.
63. Moffat Memoranda, June 15 and June 19, 1935, DS, 862.34/149, 862.34/150.

broke through the isolation and secured England's recognition of German rearmament, which marked the "first epoch occurrence of the policy of appeasement" and paved the way for further revisionist, and ultimately expansionist, policy. In addition, Ribbentrop, who would encourage Hitler all the more, had his prestige enhanced.[64] Hitler could also set German shipyards to work at maximum activity for perhaps ten years, providing jobs as well as ships. The Germans fully recognized their political and military gains at the time.[65]

As in the case of the debt settlement of the previous June, the British had made an agreement which they thought to their advantage but which had only allowed Germany to exploit and emphasize European political disunity. The Stresa front was smashed. The French were furious, insult being added to injury as the signing of the agreement took place on the anniversary of Waterloo.[66] Diplomats in Paris were now less likely to oppose Mussolini's latest adventures as long as Italy, under the Locarno arrangements, was a guarantor against German maneuvers in the Rhineland and Austria. The Italians, offended too because the British bypassed them, were now militarily and politically freer to operate against Ethiopia and more likely to look cynically upon British strictures. The Soviets were no less angry; Litvinov told Bullitt that the British were "blacklegs."[67]

Although England was chiefly responsible for this critical blunder of June 1935, American diplomats were not without fault. To some extent they probably believed their options were limited. The speed with which Anglo-German negotiations moved surprised them, as indeed it did the British. The Americans knew from reports on the rearmament crisis and Stresa meeting how reluctant the British were

64. Bracher, "Das 'Dritte Reich,'" in Bracher and others, *Die nationalsozialistische Machtergreifung*, 258–259.

65. Unsigned Memorandum, Aug. 28, 1935, *DGFP*, C, IV, 587–588. See also Churchill, *Gathering Storm*, 138, and Watt, "Anglo-German Naval Agreement," *Journal of Modern History*, 171–174.

66. Andre Géraud (Pertinax), "France and the Anglo-German Naval Agreement," *Foreign Affairs*, XIV (Oct. 1935), 51–61; entry for June 19, 1935, Marriner Diary, Marriner papers; Straus to Hull (copy), July 2, 1935, Davis papers, Box 36.

67. Watt, "Anglo-German Naval Agreement," *Journal of Modern History*, 158–159; Robertson, *Hitler's Pre-War Policy*, 63; Kirk to Hull, July 20, 1935, DS, 862.34/164 (Alexander Kirk was chargé ad interim in Rome); Bullitt to Hull, June 27, 1935, *FR 1935*, I, 168.

to take a strong stand. Further, immediately after the British decided to accept the German naval demand Stanley Baldwin, as had been anticipated, replaced Ramsay MacDonald as prime minister. Bingham had earlier reported after a meeting with Baldwin that he "had no intention of shutting the door on Hitler."[68] Also, American diplomats probably did not feel that German naval policy, which prior to the spring of 1938 really only anticipated a war with France, the Soviet Union, and Czechoslovakia, truly threatened American security.[69]

Nevertheless, American diplomats obviously could have protested when the British asked for observations on the impending agreement, whether or not they thought it would change England's immediate course. Far from doubting the wisdom of the British maneuver, with all its political implications, the State Department said that though its primary concern was the Pacific, not the Atlantic, the agreement seemed a step in the right direction. The United States thus recognized the correctness of the British attitude and the legitimacy of German rearmament. Replies given to the French and Italian inquiries further drove home the point.

Hitler's biographer, Alan Bullock, has pointed out that "appeasement is not to be understood unless it is realized that it represented the acceptance by the British government, at least in part, of Hitler's views of what British policy should be."[70] The same might be said for any other government, and, interestingly, on the same day that England and Germany inked their agreement Ambassador Luther, with apparent good reason, reported from Washington that "a more sober assessment of political events in Europe and a more objective attitude to our foreign policy have for some time been observable amongst the public here. This applies to both political circles, in particular to Congress and to Government quarters, and to the press." Several recent developments, he said, accounted for the mellowing attitude. First was the Stresa conference, which when it came to nothing made the public "realize that Europe could not be pacified by the methods pursued under the leadership of France"; second was Hitler's speech of May 21, which "had a lasting effect on the new attitude"; third was

68. Bingham to Hull, April 29, 1935, Hull papers, Box 38.
69. Raeder, *My Life*, 167–168, 193; Raeder testimony, *Nazi Conspiracy and Aggression*, VIII, 684; Compton, *Swastika and Eagle*, 142–146.
70. *Hitler*, 338.

the influence of the British policy of reconciliation and voluntary disarmament, which "has been accepted with a sympathy as great as was the surprise with which the German-British naval conversations came about." It would be wrong to assume that "American opinion has everywhere finally come down on our side." There were many fierce opponents of German policy. But most important, "with the exception of those who are entirely hostile, people today regard our course as a just one, whilst not always approving our methods. And ultimately, the restoration of Germany's military power is viewed with respect, regarded as a fact about which the other nations could, in effect, do nothing."[71] Perhaps Luther overstated the case; nonetheless, by mid-1935 American diplomats had given Germany cause to believe that Americans objected to the methods of German foreign policy but not its claims.

The focus of international diplomacy shifted in the autumn of 1935 from Germany to Italy. Climaxing months of incidents, crises, and negotiations, without a declaration of war Italian troops invaded Ethiopia on October 3. Since the first clash of troops at Wal-Wal in December 1934, the French and British had been trying to appease Mussolini. The French foreign minister, Pierre Laval, in talks in Rome in January 1935 had offered shares in the French-owned Djibouti-Addis Ababa railroad (France would maintain its interest in the railway zone) and additional land for Somaliland and Eritrea; conceivably this also meant Mussolini had a free hand against Ethiopia.[72] In June 1935 Eden went to Rome but failed to reach agreement although he offered the province of Ogaden, economic concessions, and yet undetermined advantages. To induce the Ethiopians to agree, the British were prepared to give them the small bay of Zeila in British Somaliland and some additional territory. But Mussolini clearly wanted more, and he turned down the proposal.[73] Eden made several other

71. Luther to Foreign Ministry, June 18, 1935, *DGFP*, C, IV, 316–319.

72. William C. Askew, "The Secret Agreement Between France and Italy on Ethiopia, January 1935," *Journal of Modern History*, XXV (Mar. 1953), 47–48; D. C. Watt, "The Secret Laval-Mussolini Agreement on Ethiopia," *Middle East Journal*, XV (Winter 1961), 69–74.

73. Mario Toscano, "Eden's Mission to Rome on the Eve of the Italo-Ethiopian Conflict," in Sarkissian, ed., *Studies in Diplomatic History*, 134–142. See

efforts, but by mid-August he was telling Marriner that he was very much discouraged and did not think negotiations would succeed.[74]

Emperor Haile Selassie meanwhile was looking about for support, but found none. The Germans in December 1934 had decided upon a policy of strict neutrality in an Italian-Ethiopian clash, and in the spring of 1935 determined not to ship war matériel to Ethiopia. When a confidant of Haile Selassie in July suggested a loan from Germany to buy thirty thousand rifles and other supplies from German firms with branches in Sweden and Switzerland, the Foreign Ministry ignored the proposal.[75] From Rome Ambassador von Hassell sent long dispatches saying that Mussolini had told him Italy must be allowed to go its own way and would not tolerate tripartite negotiations. On the eve of the conflict Hassell said Mussolini, "who has never quite understood the Anglo-Saxons and who frequently overestimates his own strength," was determined on the war despite uncertainty about foreign response.[76]

Haile Selassie could not find support in the United States either. From mid-1934 on, State Department officials were well informed on Italian military preparations and British and French negotiations, but they did not want to become involved.[77] Ambassador Long as early as February 1935 warned Roosevelt about Italian manufacture of "guns and ammunition—even large cannon" and insisted that despite considerable popular opposition in Italy to the forthcoming war "the troops go." Roosevelt replied that he regretted the difficulty of these "hair-trigger times."[78]

By the summer of 1935 Haile Selassie was desperate. He managed through some shrewd statements to get Hull to declare that the United

---

also Brice Harris, Jr., *The United States and the Italo-Ethiopian Crisis* (Stanford, 1964), 10, 12–13, 17–19.

74. Entry for Aug. 18, 1935, Marriner Diary, Marriner papers.

75. Dieckhoff to Legation in Ethiopia, Dec. 27, 1934, *DGFP*, C, III, 760; Frohwein Memorandum, May 10, and Bülow to Neurath, July 18, 1935, *DGFP*, C, IV, 146, 454–455.

76. Hassell to Foreign Ministry, July 15 and Oct. 3 (two cables), 1935, *DGFP*, C, IV, 443–446, 684–691.

77. Harris, *United States and Italo-Ethiopian Crisis*, 31–32.

78. Long to Roosevelt, Feb. 3 and Feb. 21, and Roosevelt to Long, Mar. 9, 1935, Long papers, Box 114.

States still regarded the Kellogg Pact as binding.[79] But that scarcely would halt Mussolini. Haile Selassie then tried to involve the United States and England by granting a huge mineral concession to a British adventurer for lease to Socony Vacuum and Standard Oil of New Jersey. But the alarmed State Department quashed the project.[80] Roosevelt did send a note to Mussolini on August 18 asking him to seek a peaceful settlement, but Mussolini replied he had invested too many men and too much money to hold back now; or, as Roosevelt apparently indicated to a visitor in March 1936, Mussolini had told him to go to hell.[81]

When Italy's undeclared war began on October 3, Roosevelt was on a vacation cruise off the coast of lower California. By cable he discussed the matter with Hull. Under the terms of the Neutrality Act of August 31, 1935, rushed through Congress partly in anticipation of this conflict, the President was empowered to declare an embargo, which applied to all belligerents in a dispute, on export of arms, munitions, and implements of war.[82] Diplomatic opinion divided over whether the United States should act before or after the League of Nations. Hugh Wilson, in Geneva, thought the United States should wait because American action might undermine collective security efforts; Hull wanted to act first to prevent anyone from charging that the government followed or cooperated too closely with the League of Nations.[83] Furious over the undeclared aggression, Roosevelt saw no reason to delay. He irately declared to his close friend and relief administrator, Harry Hopkins, that the Italians "are dropping bombs on Ethiopia—and that is war. Why wait for Mussolini to say so."[84]

Late on the evening of October 5, at Roosevelt's authorization, the State Department invoked the embargo, warned against travel on belligerent ships, and issued a statement by Roosevelt that citizens who

79. Harris, *United States and Italo-Ethiopian Crisis,* 32–35.

80. *Ibid.,* 35–38; Hull, *Memoirs,* I, 423–424.

81. Hull, *Memoirs,* I, 422; Roosevelt paraphrased in Dorothy Detzer, *Appointment on the Hill* (New York, 1948), 186.

82. For a full account of the controversy around this legislation, see Divine, *Illusion of Neutrality,* 85–116.

83. Hull, *Memoirs,* I, 429.

84. Quoted in Robert E. Sherwood, *Roosevelt and Hopkins: An Intimate History* (New York, 1948), 79.

trafficked with either belligerent did so at their own risk.[85] Clearly, these measures were intended to hurt Italy because Americans did a great deal of business with the Italians and little with the Ethiopians, who had no fleet that would suffer loss of passenger tolls and no submarines to sink the German ships on which Americans had been warned against traveling. Spurred by the British, the League Council declared on October 7 that Italy's action violated Article XII of the League Covenant. Four days later the League's Co-ordination Committee prohibited shipment of arms and munitions to Italy, and in the next several weeks agreed to embargo, effective November 18, a long list of materials, not including oil.[86] Here was the critical error: Mussolini admitted to Hitler in autumn 1938 that oil sanctions would have forced him to quit his adventure in a week, and that would have been disastrous for him.[87] Nor did the League or, really, the British and French, close the Suez Canal or impose a naval blockade; Laval and the British foreign secretary, Sir Samuel Hoare, had agreed in advance to restrict collective action to economic and financial pressure and thus did not invoke the measures that probably would have brought Mussolini to heel.[88]

Despite the fact that their government clearly opposed trade with the belligerents, American businessmen took advantage of the limited embargo to increase sale of essential raw materials to Italy. Oil exports were double the peacetime level in October and were triple in November.[89] This trend continued despite Hull's statement on November 15 that shipment of oil, copper, trucks, tractors, scrap iron, and scrap steel was "contrary to the policy of this Government" and "contrary to the general spirit of the recent Neutrality Act."[90] Few paid attention to this embargo which Hull called "moral."[91] Led by oil and shipping

85. Hull, *Memoirs*, I, 431; statement by Roosevelt, Oct. 5, 1935, *Peace and War*, 283.

86. Report of the Council Committee, Oct. 7, 1935, and Resolutions adopted by the Co-ordination Committee, Oct. 11–Nov. 2, 1935, Heald, ed., *Documents 1935*, II, 202–212.

87. Schmidt, *Statist auf diplomatischer Bühne*, 342.

88. Harris, *United States and Italo-Ethiopian Crisis*, 64–66, 72.

89. Herbert Feis, *Seen From E.A.: Three International Episodes* (New York, 1947), 307–308.

90. Statement by Hull, Nov. 15, 1935, *Peace and War*, 292–293.

91. *Memoirs*, I, 428.

interests, American business assailed it and insisted that so long as the United States maintained relations with Italy, they could sell, within the law, whatever and however much the Italians could buy.[92]

Washington did not intend to go further than a moral embargo. At the outset of the crisis Hull made clear that on the matter of sanctions the United States would chart its course independent of the League of Nations.[93] In December the British asked whether the United States would embargo oil shipments to Italy if they and the League of Nations did so. Hull replied to Ambassador Lindsay: "We have gone as far as we can."[94] Later on some Englishmen would insist that the American position made an oil sanction "impracticable."[95] But even Neville Chamberlain conceded in his diary at the time that "U.S.A. has already gone a good deal further than usual," and he thought the British ought to take the lead and not "leave the Americans in the air."[96]

The Germans meanwhile pursued a policy that had to work to their advantage. On October 5 Neurath proposed absolute neutrality—no shipment of war matériel to either side—but he also resolved that Germany should not take part in any League sanctions against Italy. Hitler agreed, but decided to forego a formal declaration of neutrality.[97] Hitler's cautious policy stemmed from the relatively little progress Germany had made in rearmament and the military estimate that Italy would take three years to win.[98] Neurath advised Mussolini it would probably be in his interest "not to push matters to extremes but to liquidate the Abyssinian undertaking as soon as possible by means of a suitable compromise." The Germans however, saw their advantage in the conflict, and although they were "*non-participant*," as Ambassador

---

92. Stromberg, "American Business and the Approach of War," *Journal of Economic History,* 64–65.

93. Hull to United States Delegation at Geneva, Oct. 9, 1935, *Peace and War,* 283–284.

94. Quoted in James MacGregor Burns, *Roosevelt: The Lion and the Fox* (New York, 1956), 247.

95. Viscount Simon, *Retrospect* (London, 1952), 212.

96. Quoted in Feiling, *Chamberlain,* 272.

97. Kotze Memorandum, Oct. 5, and Köpke Memorandum, Oct. 12, 1935, *DGFP,* C, IV, 703–704, 727, 727n2. Hans von Kotze was an official of the Foreign Minister's Secretariat.

98. Robertson, *Hitler's Pre-War Policy,* 63–64.

von Hassell put it, "this does not mean we are not interested." The war, he hoped, though "premature" in terms of a clash between "dynamic and static conceptions of the present political and economic world situation," might destroy the League and the Stresa front and weaken Anglo-French friendship. A crushing defeat for Italy would be unfavorable for Germany; triumph might increase Italy's "Great Power megalomania," but that was a "slight" danger; a compromise solution, the most likely arrangement, might make Italy dependent on France. But above all, current developments and Germany's assisting Italy by refusing cooperation with sanctions might lead Italy to give Germany a guarantee of "non-interference in the internal affairs of Austria under *all* circumstances."[99]

The British lead was revealed in December 1935, and the Italian-Ethiopian war shortly reached its discreditable end. On December 9, news of the plan worked out by Hoare and Laval, who was now premier as well as foreign minister, was prematurely divulged. The Hoare-Laval plan, proposing to carve Ethiopia largely to Italy's benefit, shamed England and France; Hoare had to resign a week later, and the Laval government was sufficiently undermined so as to collapse a month later.[100] Public opinion everywhere was outraged. The chief of the Near Eastern Division in the State Department, Wallace Murray, concluded that the schemes seemed "almost to place a premium on aggression"; Roosevelt thought the proceedings outrageous.[101]

Germany delighted in the discord and embarrassment. At the end of the year Dieckhoff told Under Secretary Phillips, in London for naval negotiations, that Germany's position on the League and sanctions "was very like that of his government." More to the point, however, was Hassell's report that Mussolini had told him he regarded German neutrality as "benevolent," that it would be to Italian and German benefit if Austria became "a German satellite," and that he

99. Neurath Memorandum, Oct. 12, and Hassell to Foreign Ministry, Oct. 17, 1935, *DGFP*, C, IV, 728, 743–746.

100. Text of the plan in Heald, ed., *Documents 1935*, II, 460–462. For an account of this bungle, see Arthur H. Furnia, *The Diplomacy of Appeasement: Anglo-French Relations and the Prelude to World War II, 1931–1938* (Washington, D.C., 1960), 168–182.

101. Quoted in Hull, *Memoirs*, I, 440; entry for Dec. 11, 1935, Ickes, *Diary*, I, 484.

regarded Stresa "as dead and buried once and for all." With respect to the present war, Hassell told Mussolini that "the world preferred to bow to accomplished facts and that clear military successes for Italy were doubtless the most important thing at present."[102]

The military victories came soon. The United States lost even its slim chance to hurt the Italian cause directly, or spur the League to action, when Congress at the end of February 1936 extended the Neutrality Act and refused to allow the President the discretion he had asked for to apply the embargo only against the aggressor. Mussolini was delighted with this act, which he called a service to world peace. Shortly thereafter a final effort to solve the conflict dissolved amidst the furor of the Rhineland crisis and the rout of Ethiopian troops, fighting bravely but vainly against the mechanized Italians who came with airplanes and poison gas.[103]

Emperor Haile Selassie had to flee his country in May 1936 and the Italian government announced that Ethiopia had been annexed, with King Victor Emanuel III the new emperor of Ethiopia. The fact that the United States never recognized the annexation did not change the *de facto* situation. Haile Selassie's poignant pleas before the League of Nations in June 1936 fell on deaf ears, and on July 4 the League voted to end sanctions against Italy. The United States had already done so on June 16.[104]

The pillars upon which the peace in Europe rested suffered severe cracks and strains in 1935. Germany had for the first time directly assaulted the Treaty of Versailles and Italy assaulted Ethiopia. Both aggressors achieved their goals. The French had failed to mobilize resistance against Germany—the Franco-Soviet Defensive Pact of May 2, 1935, which set off a nine-month dispute over ratification, was their best effort—and they had been partner to the Hoare-Laval scheme. The British had behaved inconsistently, seemingly without scruple or reason. They wrecked what unity there might have been by entering a naval agreement with Germany and, after a strong initial show against Italian aggression, reprehensibly backed off. The League of Nations, as Beneš had noted at the time of German rearmament, was hereafter

102. Dieckhoff Memorandum, Dec. 31, 1935, GFM, 5747/HO36114-HO-36116; Hassell to Foreign Ministry, Jan. 7, 1936, *DGFP*, C, IV, 974–977.
103. Harris, *United States and Italo-Ethiopian Crisis*, 131–137.
104. *New York Times*, July 5 and June 17, 1936.

restricted to "study, counsel, and advice," if ever it had been capable of more. In a rebuke aimed at British and French policy, Erich Kordt later said that the outcome of the Ethiopian war decided the question of war or peace in Europe.[105] This assumption is an exaggeration, of course, and relieves German diplomats too much of the responsibility for the way in which they were willing to exploit the Italian-Ethiopian war for their purposes, as events would show. Nonetheless, aggression had triumphed, and the alignment for a second world war was that much closer.

The year's events had disastrous effects upon American foreign policy. Timid and reserved as were Roosevelt, Hull, and the State Department about taking part in European politics, the divisive, discordant policies of Europe's major powers made an American contribution highly difficult. Worse, the administration apparently guessed that Italy would never really challenge England, or that at least British pressure would cause Mussolini to back down.[106] Consequently, Ethiopia's betrayal left American internationalists uncertain and despondent. Isolationists could jeer that European diplomats again had gulled Uncle Sam and the public was confused.[107]

Events within the United States conspired to cripple efforts at collective security. Two highly popular books in 1934 had been *Iron, Blood, and Profits: An Exposure of the World-Wide Munitions Racket* (New York), by George Seldes, and *Merchants of Death, A Study of the International Armaments Industry* (New York), by Helmuth C. Engelbrecht and Frank C. Hanighen. *Merchants of Death* in fact was a Book-of-the-Month Club selection, a best seller. Since mid-1934 a Senate committee under Gerald P. Nye of North Dakota had been investigating the munitions industry, and whatever the final verdict on the Nye committee investigations, the attendant publicity confused the public about the relations between bankers, munition makers, and America's entry into the First World War.[108] In 1935 Walter Millis in

105. Kordt, *Nicht aus den Akten,* 114.

106. Henderson Braddick, "A New Look at American Policy During the Italo-Ethiopian Crisis, 1935–1936," *Journal of Modern History,* XXXIV (Mar. 1962), 67.

107. Burns, *Roosevelt,* 260.

108. For a full appraisal which contrasts with previous standard interpretations, see John E. Wiltz, *In Search of Peace: The Senate Munitions Inquiry, 1934–36* (Baton Rouge, 1963).

*Road to War: America, 1914–1917* (Boston), a Book-of-the-Month Club selection that sold over 200,000 copies, demonstrated that propaganda and American political and economic ties to England and France had as much to do with bringing America into the war as did Germany's submarine warfare.

The Roosevelt administration in 1935 retreated in the face of this growing suspicion about international entanglements. Instead of battling down to the wire for legislation that would have allowed the President an embargo against the aggressor nation only, Roosevelt and his advisers settled in August for the temporary measure that prescribed an embargo against all nations involved in war. Whatever arguments might have been used then and later to justify this law because it denied arms and munitions to Italy did not change the fact that if the United States had restricted the embargo to Italy a way might have been found to ship arms to the Ethiopians on credit. Italy needed oil, not weapons, from the United States and oil was never embargoed.

These events disheartened the American ambassador in Germany. Hitler's insistent claim that he was seeking only peace did not deceive him; all evidence he had gathered, Dodd scrawled in a note to Under Secretary Phillips in May, did nothing but confirm the view that Hitler aimed "to annex part of the Corridor, part of Czechoslovakia, and all of Austria." What good, Dodd asked rhetorically, to ridicule tanks, bombs, and submarines when "inside Germany arms manufacture of every kind goes on night and day"?[109] The Anglo-German Naval Agreement, too, disappointed Dodd. "This is the first time, I believe, in modern history," he wrote Roosevelt in June, "that England has sided with a threatening imperialist power, rather than guide a combination of weaker powers against the threatening one." The Senate's action on the neutrality legislation and the subsequent Italian invasion further upset Dodd. If Italy were "forced out of Ethiopia," he wrote Roosevelt in October, it would be a setback for Germany's "autocratic military procedure." If Italy were successful, "it is the common feeling the two dictatorships would unite on a policy of aggression."[110]

109. Dodd to Phillips, May 29, 1935, Dodd papers, Box 44.
110. Dodd to Roosevelt, June 29 and Oct. 31, 1935, DS, 862.00/3518½, 862.00/3558½.

Roosevelt was disappointed. "A year ago I was fairly optimistic," he told Dodd in August; "today I am the opposite." But the President was always the politician and ever the optimist. Some things did look black, he wrote in December, but "if you'd been here I don't think you'd have felt the Senate bill last August was an unmitigated evil." The country was being "fairly well-educated," he said, and "I hope that next January I can get an even stronger law, leaving, however, some authority to the President."[111]

Dodd was a scholar, not a politician, and decidedly not an optimist. He had tired of Germany and of offering unheeded advice. In September he told his good friend, Assistant Secretary Moore, that he wanted to go home to complete the three-volume history of the Old South that would culminate his life's researches and that now seemed —"at least for me"—more important than continuing in Berlin.[112] Moore brought the matter to Roosevelt, who was of another mind. He appreciated Dodd's reports and efforts; in fact, he was just about to write Long in Italy that he thought him and Dodd "far more accurate in your pessimism for the past two years than any of my other friends in Europe."[113] Thus, Roosevelt told Moore that Dodd might come home for a short rest—"if things are peaceful"—but "in any event, we most certainly do not want him to consider resigning. I need him in Berlin."[114]

Roosevelt did not say why he wanted Dodd to remain in Berlin. But the President's wish was good enough for the ambassador. Dodd remained, rightly fearful that events in 1936 would bring the world closer to war. Perhaps, though, he could do something at Roosevelt's bidding that would help avert the catastrophe the future so surely held.

111. Roosevelt to Dodd, Aug. 14 and Dec. 2, 1935, *FDRL,* I, 501, 530–531.
112. Dodd to Moore, Sept. 3, 1935, R. Walton Moore papers, Box 5, Franklin D. Roosevelt Library, Hyde Park.
113. Roosevelt to Long, Sept. 19, 1935, Long papers, Box 114.
114. Roosevelt Memorandum for Moore, Sept. 11, 1935, Moore papers, Box 5.

# 6. NEIGHBORS GOOD AND BAD

Dodd took heart during the first weeks of 1936, reassured that Roosevelt wanted him to remain at the troublesome and unrewarding Berlin post. The ambassador began to feel that his warnings and pleadings were doing some good. Roosevelt's annual address to Congress, in particular, cheered him. Unlike previous yearly messages, in which there were only fleeting references to foreign relations, Roosevelt in January 1936 clearly insisted that nations needing to expand, find new trade outlets, or rectify injustices springing from previous wars, ought to seek legitimate objectives through patient and peaceful negotiation. He did not fail to add, however, that if nations reverted to "the law of the sword" America had one recourse: "a well ordered neutrality."[1]

Dodd was so delighted with even this qualified statement that he at once sent a congratulatory telegram to the President for his "masterly and unanswerable" speech.[2] He believed Roosevelt's words "a marvelous but very shrewd indictment of all dictatorships," which no German official could read "without serious concern."[3] Probably remembering that Roosevelt had told him in December that he hoped to get a new neutrality law permitting him discriminatory authority, Dodd rushed to tell the French ambassador, André François-Poncet, that despite what journalists in Berlin thought, Roosevelt would compromise American neutrality in a way highly unfavorable to an ag-

1. *PPFDR*, V, 8–18.
2. Dodd to Roosevelt, Jan. 4, 1936, Roosevelt papers, PSF, Germany: William E. Dodd.
3. Entry for Jan. 4, 1936, Dodd, *Diary*, 293.

gressor. François-Poncet at once reported this prospect to his superiors.[4]

The French Foreign Office was not so optimistic. Laval told Ambassador de Laboulaye in Washington he regretted that the neutrality legislation currently before Congress did not discriminate between aggressor and victim, and that it was unclear whether the United States would embargo trade only with those belligerents directly involved in a conflict (as the French hoped), or extend an embargo to nations entering a conflict after it was under way, including even those joining in collective action against an aggressor under the auspices of the League of Nations. Still, the fact that the American government would not protect its nationals who traded with belligerents meant surrendering freedom of the seas and throwing aside England's chief objection to leading a collective effort against an aggressor on the grounds that a blockade would lead to conflict with the United States.[5]

Laboulaye replied that it was too early to conclude absolutely what the United States would do in case of world conflict, that though the American people were devoted to peace—"peace at any price even"—this commitment was no stronger than it had been in 1917 and one could not foresee what circumstances might cause a sudden change in attitude.[6] Meanwhile, Roosevelt thanked Dodd for his congratulatory telegram and told him that his recent reports from Berlin had confirmed his uneasiness about European affairs: "hence the serious and, at the same time, clear note of my Message to the Congress. I am glad you liked it." As for its effect on autocratic nations, "I do not anticipate much of a response," but perhaps the message would help keep the peace another year. A few days later Roosevelt wrote Norman Davis, attending the London Naval Conference, that he was "a little afraid" the speech would arouse bitterness in Germany, Japan, and Italy, but he had made it "not only for the record, but in order to solidify the forces of non-aggression."[7]

The address did create a stir in Germany—at least in the newspapers.

---

4. François-Poncet to Laval, Jan. 5, 1936, Ministère des Affaires Etrangères, *Documents Diplomatiques Français, 1932–1939,* 2d series (1936–1939), 3 vols. (Paris, 1963———), I, 14; hereafter cited as *DDF.*

5. Laval to Laboulaye, Jan. 6, 1936, *ibid.,* 19–20.

6. Laboulaye to Laval, Jan. 6, 1936, *ibid.,* 20–21.

7. Roosevelt to Dodd, Jan. 6, and Roosevelt to Davis, Jan. 14, 1936, FDRL, I, 543–545.

Virtually every German daily, Joseph Goebbels' *Der Angriff* in particular, rebuked Roosevelt.[8] But one public pronouncement by the President of the United States could scarcely change German foreign policy, and, François-Poncet said, official circles attributed it largely to domestic political considerations.[9] Within two months events took a sinister turn.

At the start of 1936 diplomats were concerned not only about the Italian-Ethiopian war, but also about the possibility that Germany intended to reoccupy the demilitarized Rhineland. In his May 21, 1935, peace speech Hitler had proclaimed that the as yet unratified Franco-Soviet Pact of May 2, 1935, which provided for mutual assistance in case of "an unprovoked attack on the part of a European state," had "brought an element of legal insecurity into the Locarno Pact."[10] In an interview with François-Poncet in November 1935, Hitler assailed the Franco-Soviet agreement, causing François-Poncet to report to Paris that he thought Hitler would use it as an excuse to reoccupy the Rhineland. In another interview, on January 1, 1936, Hitler denied that was his intention, but François-Poncet remained skeptical.[11] When the French Chamber of Deputies ratified the pact on February 27, François-Poncet concluded that although the Germans maintained the pact was incompatible with Locarno, they probably would not carry out a sudden military occupation of the Rhineland but would seek to achieve their end by diplomatic pressure.[12]

Dodd was even more suspicious. On February 6 Dieckhoff told the embassy counselor, Ferdinand L. Mayer, that although Germany disliked the Rhineland arrangements, it would keep to the Locarno provisions "provided others did so." Dodd put little faith in the assurance. When the Chamber of Deputies ratified the pact, he warned that though Hitler might not act immediately, "the record is to be kept clear" so that at a future date Germany could use the Franco-

8. Entries for Jan. 4, 1936, Shirer, *Berlin Diary*, 44, and Dodd, Diary, 293–294; see also Remak, "Germany and the United States," 68.

9. François-Poncet to Laval, Jan. 5, 1936, *DDF*, I, 16.

10. On the Franco-Soviet Pact see William Evans Scott, *Alliance Against Hitler: The Origins of the Franco-Soviet Pact* (Durham, N.C., 1962), 246–250.

11. François-Poncet, *Fateful Years*, 188–189; François-Poncet to Flandin, Jan. 1, 1936, *DDF*, I, 1–2. Pierre-Etienne Flandin was foreign minister.

12. François-Poncet to Flandin, Feb. 27, 1936, *DDF*, I, 340–344.

Soviet alliance as "an excuse" for sending troops into the Rhineland and breaching the Locarno arrangements.[13] On February 29 Dodd saw Neurath, who told him that Germany might rejoin the League of Nations if the other powers returned Germany's colonies and allowed its troops into the Rhineland. Neurath's emphasis on Hitler's conciliatory mood surprised Dodd, who warned, according to François-Poncet, that unilateral renunciation of the Locarno Pact would lead to suicidal conflict for Germany. There would be no indulgence by the United States: the White House would not hesitate to invoke strict sanctions against Germany (no export of oil, steel, or cotton) and it soon would be in desperate straits. Neurath said he would not fail to tell Hitler.[14]

Dodd's warning did no good; Neurath in fact knew more than he had let on and probably had been hinting without real hope that somehow a way might be found to alter developments well under way. From the spring of 1935 the military had expressed grave concern over Germany's vulnerability to concerted Franco-Soviet-Czech action, and on May 2, 1935, War Minister von Blomberg issued a directive instructing the military branches to draw up plans for a speedy reoccupation of the Rhineland.[15] Hitler waited, and on February 12, 1936, decided by himself that the favorable opportunity had come. Blomberg and General Werner von Fritsch, commander in chief of the army, agreed, but did not want to risk war. On February 14 Hitler told Ambassador von Hassell that despite Germany's military unpreparedness and the original intention of reoccupying the Rhineland in the spring of 1937, considering the current international situation the appropriate psychological moment was at hand. Hassell was to try to convince Mussolini that it would be to Italy's advantage to denounce Locarno first, but regardless, Germany would proceed on its own. In the meantime, preparations were ordered with the instruction that the troops would retreat if France offered military resistance.[16]

13. Dodd to Hull, Feb. 6 and Feb. 28, 1936, DS, 862.00/1102, 762.65/176.
14. Entry for Feb. 29, 1936, Dodd, *Diary,* 314–316; François-Poncet to Flandin, Mar. 6, 1936, *DDF,* 403–404.
15. Meinck, *Hitler und die deutsche Aufrüstung,* 149; Shirer, *Rise and Fall,* 290.
16. Hossbach, *Zwischen Wehrmacht und Hitler,* 97–98; Hassell Memorandum, Feb. 14, 1936, *DGFP,* C, IV, 1142–1144.

Less than a week later Hassell returned to Berlin to discuss matters. The Italian ambassador, Bernardo Attolico, did not know what his country would do about Locarno. Neurath, who had word from the German embassy in London that the British were preparing a Working Agreement for England, France, and Germany, thought Italy would not renounce Locarno, and in a later conversation with Hitler and Ribbentrop, Neurath and Hassell expressed preference for waiting for future opportunities. Hitler insisted that "passivity was, in the long run, no policy," and thought the Franco-Soviet Pact should be used as a "pretext." He would wait only until the Chamber of Deputies ratified it, not the Senate.[17]

Hassell saw Mussolini on February 22 and reported that he regarded Stresa as "finally dead," agreed with Hitler's assessment of events, and said Italy "would not take part in action by Britain and France against Germany occasioned by an alleged breach by Germany of the Locarno Treaty."[18] Reports from London, meanwhile, that the British were trying to delay passage of the Franco-Soviet Pact were disregarded; Hitler was not really interested in tying himself to the conclusion of debates in Paris. He granted an interview to the French writer Bertrand de Jouvenel on February 21 and spoke of his desire for peace, but such talk was propaganda. He was already at work on the speech he would deliver after German troops marched into the Rhineland.[19] When various American newspapermen saw Hitler on February 26, he seemed unusually edgy and preoccupied.[20]

Although Hitler had decided to go ahead with his move, on March 2 he reproached François-Poncet because the French press had not published the interview with Jouvenel until the day after the vote by the French Chamber of Deputies. François-Poncet reported that there was still a chance Hitler would do nothing until after the Senate

---

17. Hassell Memorandum, Feb. 20, 1936, *DGFP,* C, IV, 1163–1166. On the British Working Agreement see Bismarck to Dieckhoff, Feb. 13, 1936, *ibid.,* 1135–1139. Prince Otto von Bismarck was counselor at the German embassy in London.

18. Hassell to Foreign Ministry, Feb. 22, 1936, *ibid.,* 1172–1177.

19. Robertson, *Hitler's Pre-War Policy,* 75–77; Meinck, *Hitler und die deutsche Aufrüstung,* 150–151. For interview see Baynes, ed., *Hitler's Speeches,* II, 1266–1271.

20. Entry for Feb. 27, 1936, Dodd, *Diary,* 313; entry for Feb. 28, 1936, Shirer, *Berlin Diary,* 48.

acted.[21] But on the same day Blomberg issued the order to deploy the troops; next day Hassell reported that the Italians had given him a corrected memorandum of his interview with Mussolini which reaffirmed Italy's intention to have nothing to do with an Anglo-French response to Germany's reaction to the Franco-Soviet Pact.[22] Hitler grew tense on March 5 when it appeared that the British and French might put forward some proposals, and he inquired of Hossbach whether troop movements could be halted and how late.[23] Nevertheless, on March 5 Neurath sent instructions and explanations to the German embassies about the imminent maneuver.[24] Wild rumors circulated in Berlin, and on March 6 the American journalist, William L. Shirer, inquired at the Foreign Ministry whether Germany was about to occupy the Rhineland. According to Shirer's record, the head of the Press Department, Gottfried Aschmann, "kept giving the most categorical denials" and insisted that to do so "would mean war."[25] Early the next morning, March 7, German soldiers, amidst cheering and flower-throwing crowds, marched into the Rhineland.

The timing of the maneuver caught everyone off guard, even the wary French.[26] Dodd learned something was afoot only when he reached his office at 9:30 in the morning and heard that the Foreign Ministry had summoned the embassy counselor, Mayer, who returned an hour and a half later with reports of the move and a summary of the speech and proposals Hitler was about to deliver to the Reichstag. Dodd proceeded to the Kroll Opera House to hear Hitler's hour-and-a-half oration.[27]

Hitler now offered to replace the repudiated Locarno Pact by treaties with France and Belgium demilitarizing the frontiers on a basis of equality and to sign a twenty-five-year nonaggression pact with those countries, to be guaranteed by England, Italy, and possibly the Netherlands. He offered to negotiate nonaggression pacts with all of Ger-

21. François-Poncet to Flandin, Mar. 2, 1936, *DDF*, I, 375–377.
22. Hassell to Foreign Ministry, Mar. 3, 1936, *DGFP*, C, IV, 1214–1220.
23. Hossbach, *Zwischen Wehrmacht und Hitler*, 98.
24. Neurath to Missions in Great Britain, France, Italy and Belgium, *DGFP*, C, V, 11–19.
25. Entry for Mar. 6, 1936, Shirer, *Berlin Diary*, 48–49.
26. Straus to Hull, Mar. 7, 1936, *FR 1936*, I, 207.
27. Entry for Mar. 7, 1936, Dodd, *Diary*, 317–320. The English, French, Soviet, and Polish ambassadors absented themselves.

many's neighbors, even Lithuania if Memel were given autonomy, and to bring Germany into the League of Nations provided the Treaty of Versailles and the League Covenant were separated and a promise made to discuss Germany's colonial claims. Surrounded as these proposals were with Hitler's usual masterful attacks on the horrors and stupidities of war and appeals to replace "useless strife" with the "rule of reason," even Dodd had to concede grudgingly that it was all "cleverly planned."[28]

The French military, according to the accurate recollection of Pierre-Etienne Flandin, who had replaced Laval as foreign minister in January 1936, were prepared only for defensive action and had no intention of driving German troops from the Rhineland.[29] Further, Flandin, who has insisted that the military's attitude and lack of preparation came as a "great surprise" to him, as late as March 3 had indicated to British Foreign Secretary Eden that in event of a breach of the Locarno Pact France would not act on its own.[30] The British did not want the French to undertake military action, and in a series of frantic telephone conversations on March 7 and 8 prevailed on them to wait until Eden could get to Paris and everyone had a chance to consider the situation.[31] In this interim Flandin appealed to the United States. He knew that American military intervention in Europe at this time was out of the question, but during these critical hours he sought moral support. Receiving Ambassador Straus on the afternoon of March 8, he told him he would be extremely grateful if either Roosevelt or Hull would publicly condemn on moral grounds any unilateral treaty repudiation. Straus told Flandin that he did not know what the response to such a request would be (admitting he had a good idea in view of public opinion) but that he would convey the message to the State Department that evening. At about the same time the ambassador in Mexico, Josephus Daniels, cabled Roosevelt, via the State Department, that he hoped FDR would use good offices to help settle matters.[32]

28. *Ibid.*, 319; text of address in Baynes, ed., *Hitler's Speeches*, II, 1271–1293.
29. Pierre-Etienne Flandin, *Politique Française, 1919–1940* (Paris, 1947), 195–196. For military discussion of the problem, see *DDF,* I, 444–448.
30. Flandin to Corbin, Mar. 5, and Aide-Mémoire, Flandin to Eden, Mar. 3, 1936, *DDF,* I, 396–398. Charles Corbin was French ambassador to Great Britain.
31. Furnia, *Diplomacy of Appeasement,* 191.
32. Straus to Hull, Mar. 8, and Daniels to Hull, Mar. 9, 1936, *FR 1936,* I, 217, 219.

For a variety of reasons American officials were unwilling to become involved. Although the French certainly had the military capacity to drive German troops from the Rhineland, Straus's reports on the situation in France were extremely bleak. At the end of January he found the French air force, in contrast to Germany's, "insignificant, poorly equipped and unprepared." Taxes were high in France, "business here is rotten," and the Chamber of Deputies "poor looking and bad acting." The French were "looking for a miracle to happen, but they have no miracle man," he said, and the current "dirty picture . . . portends no very brilliant future for France." Roosevelt replied a couple of weeks later, "I feel as you do about France and the French future"; the "whole European panorama is fundamentally blacker than at any time in your life time or mine."[33]

Nor were matters much better in the United States. Hardly more than a week before the Rhineland crisis, on February 29, Roosevelt had signed the congressional resolution that extended the 1935 Neutrality Act to May 1937. Worse, the new measure not only kept the arms embargo and denied credit to any belligerent, but, confirming French fears, made it mandatory for the President to extend the arms embargo to countries entering a war already under way, thus denying support even to members of the League of Nations who were joining a collective effort to halt an aggressor.[34] The administration was unhappy with the law, but felt it could do little about it. The whole neutrality question was so complicated, Hull explained amidst the controversy, that even well-informed persons kept changing their minds. Consequently "we are . . . acquiescing in the extension of the so called Neutrality Act."[35]

The government decided to acquiesce in the Rhineland crisis as well. By the time the appeals from Flandin and Daniels reached Washington, the State Department had drawn a memorandum, which Hull passed along to Roosevelt for approval, outlining the American position. Germany's action, the memorandum stated, contravened the Locarno and Versailles treaties. The United States had taken no part in the 1925 Locarno arrangements and thus could not concern itself. And because those sections of the Versailles Treaty pertaining to the Rhineland were

33. Straus to Roosevelt, Jan. 20, and Roosevelt to Straus, Feb. 13, 1936, Roosevelt papers, PSF, France: Jesse Straus.
34. *New York Times*, Mar. 1, 1936; Divine, *Illusion of Neutrality*, 156–158.
35. Hull to Davis, Feb. 13, 1936, Hull papers, Box 38.

not included among rights and privileges guaranteed the United States by its 1921 peace treaty, Germany technically had not violated any American treaty.[36] Roosevelt's response to the memorandum is unrecorded, but there is every reason to believe he accepted it as American policy. Next day, March 10, Hull told Straus it would be impossible for the United States to say anything. Straus passed the message on to Flandin, who was visibly disappointed.[37] Hull wrote the reply to Daniels, Phillips sent it to the White House, where Roosevelt scrawled his "O.K. F.D.R.," and on March 12 Hull cabled Daniels that Roosevelt thanked him for his suggestion and "the spirit in which it was offered" and said that events in Europe were being watched closely.[38]

European events unfolded quickly. Eden had gone to Paris on March 9 and persuaded Flandin to come to London, where the League Council would meet. Flandin arrived two days later and discovered his pleading would do no good. The English told him in no uncertain terms that military or economic sanctions were out of the question. The Germans, said Lord Lothian, who had been private secretary to Prime Minister Lloyd George and recently under secretary for India, had only marched "into their own back-garden," and war could not be risked.[39] The League of Nations, unable to act without English support, did what it had done in the 1935 rearmament crisis: solemnly condemned and censured Germany.

American diplomats had sensed what would be the outcome of the Rhineland crisis. The chargé in London, Ray Atherton, had told Hull on March 9 that conversations in the Foreign Office made clear that England "would make every endeavor to prevent the imposition of military and/or economic sanctions against Germany." Prentiss Gilbert, consul in Geneva, said any thought that the League might vote sanctions was utterly "fantastic." The "Italian precedent carries no weight," he insisted, and neither England nor the Balkan nations would

36. Hull Memorandum to Roosevelt, Mar. 9, 1936, DS, 740.0011 Mutual Guarantee (Locarno)/395, and Hull to Roosevelt, Mar. 9, 1936, Roosevelt papers, PSF, Diplomatic Correspondence: Germany.
37. Hull to Straus, Mar. 10, and Straus to Hull, Mar. 11, 1936, *FR 1936*, I, 228, 234–235.
38. Phillips to Roosevelt, Mar. 11, 1936, DS, 740.0011 Mutual Guarantee (Locarno)/436; Hull to Daniels, Mar. 12, 1936, *FR 1936*, I, 237.
39. Lothian quoted in Churchill, *Gathering Storm*, 196–197.

support the effort. Further, the ministers of almost all these nations had told him that sanctions would be "totally impracticable," as the economies of their countries and Germany were closely intertwined.[40] In Berlin, Truman Smith, the military attaché who was rather favorably disposed to the Hitler regime, was mistakenly convinced that "Germany will accept the battle the moment one French soldier crosses the French frontier."[41] He believed Germany intended only to break France's hold on the Continent. The German General Staff, he wrote, "no more thinks of attacking . . . Alsace and Lorraine than it dreams of attacking Peoria, Illinois." The German maneuver challenged France's political domination, not its security. "By one single daring move on the diplomatic chess board," Smith continued, more tragically than he was aware, Hitler "has cut the military basis from under the whole series of French post war alliances." At last, he said, the World War was coming to a close. "Versailles is dead. There may possibly be a German catastrophe and a new Versailles, but it will not be the Versailles which has hung like a dark cloud over Europe since 1920."[42]

Nor would there be a war, at least not at this time, Ambassador Long recorded in Rome. He was under "no delusions" that Germany would withdraw its troops from territory over which it was sovereign. But no one was going to fight. "Italy is not going to join England and France while under sanctions. Czechoslovakia is afraid. Russia is too far away. And France is not going in alone! So they will talk it to death —with England supporting Germany all she can."[43] A few days later he comforted himself that the German move into the Rhineland was not offensively against France but defensively against Russia—"the one

40. Atherton to Hull, Mar. 9, 1936, DS, 740.0011 Mutual Guarantee (Locarno)/381; Gilbert to Hull, Mar. 11, 1936, *FR 1936*, I, 230–231.

41. Report by Military Attaché Truman Smith, Mar. 14, 1936, DS, 740.0011 Mutual Guarantee (Locarno)/586. George Messersmith thought Smith a man of "considerable capacity," but with "no political judgment" and far too willing to gloss over things. On more than one occasion they exchanged sharp opinions. "Some Observations on . . . Dodd," 8, Messersmith papers, Box 7. According to Hanfstaengl, *Unheard Witness,* 32–33, 222, he had helped Smith get the post because he had known him since 1923 and knew he was impressed with Hitler.

42. Report by Military Attaché Truman Smith, Mar. 20, 1936, *FR 1936,* I, 260.

43. Entry for Mar. 21, 1936, Long Diary, 328, Long papers, Box 4.

real hostile objective of Germany in Europe"—and he wrote a long memorandum for the State Department.[44] Even Dodd had mixed feelings. The failure of England, France, and the League of Nations to act disappointed him. He disapproved, he said on March 11, of the shift of conference talks from Paris to London because he felt the Germans would consider it a "most favorable" development intended to curb French action. He knew that the episode once again sadly demonstrated "the old story of European balancing of interest and powers, not the sacredness of treaties or League decisions." But, he concluded the next day, it would be better for France to "consider the constructive aspects of Hitler's proposals" than to create a situation wherein Hitler, convinced that military or economic sanctions against Germany were forthcoming, "might then decide instantly on action."[45] Perhaps, he told François-Poncet, France ought to open negotiations by revoking whatever military precautions it had decided upon and allowing Germany "equality of treatment" through a "symbolic occupation."[46]

American diplomats determined to steer clear of the affair. When Atherton asked if he could accept visitors' tickets to the League Council meeting convening in London, as Hugh Wilson, minister to Switzerland, frequently did when the Council met in Geneva, Phillips told him that "considering all the circumstances" it would be "preferable" if he did not. Next day Phillips told the Turkish ambassador, Münir Ertegün, that the position of the American government was the same as always, based on the "historical attitude of the American people": strictly "hands off." Americans were concerned about European politics, he added, but could not become involved.[47] Laboulaye thus correctly informed his government that although the move into the Rhineland shocked Hull's devotion to the sanctity of treaties, and members of the administration, State Department, and Congress disliked the German action and felt some shame at American neutrality, they were glad that at least for the time being Congress had placed the United States outside European complications.[48]

44. Entry for Mar. 24, 1936, Long Diary, 331, *ibid.*
45. Dodd to Hull, Mar. 11 and Mar. 12, 1936, *FR 1936*, I, 235, 238.
46. François-Poncet to Flandin, Mar. 12, 1936, *DDF*, I, 518–519.
47. Atherton to Hull and Phillips to Atherton, Mar. 13, and Phillips Memorandum, Mar. 14, 1936, *FR 1936*, I, 244–245.
48. Laboulaye to Flandin, Mar. 19, 1936, *DDF*, I, 609–610.

Similarly, Ambassador Luther reported on March 9 that the State Department "felt that the German step was to have been expected, that it is indeed understandable, since, after all, it is German territory which is involved, and that it promises a pacification of the European atmosphere." Less than a week later he noted that Americans were taking some delight in the fact that Germany, by forcing the Rhineland issue, had "for the sake of something that would have fallen into our laps anyway . . . lost not only our friends but also Britain's and Italy's guarantee of our security."[49] But, the United States had no intention of involving itself, and if the point needed emphasis, Roosevelt, who had gone fishing during the rearmament crisis of March 1935, again went fishing on March 22, 1936.[50]

No blood was shed in the Rhineland. Long afterwards Hitler boasted of "my unshakeable obstinacy and my amazing aplomb" in resisting pressure during the crisis.[51] He had, of course, given orders to retreat if the French advanced, and the period of March 7–8 was was one of acute tension and strain: Kordt said Hitler was near "nervous collapse" and his interpreter, Paul Schmidt, said Hitler afterwards referred to those forty-eight hours as the most tension-filled of his life.[52] Nevertheless, even in the face of reports about French military activity and wavering by Blomberg, Hitler determined not to withdraw.[53] Whether this was the critical moment that England and France might have converted into a disastrous defeat for Hitler remains at best another of history's might-have-beens. Developments bore out Hitler's judgment and thereby enhanced his prestige and control. On March 22, having dissolved the Reichstag two weeks earlier and called for new elections and a referendum on his policy, Hitler proclaimed that Versailles could only be the gravestone of the New Order, never its foundation. One week later the German people approved his policy by an over-

49. Luther to Foreign Ministry, Mar. 9 and Mar. 15, 1936, *DGFP*, C, V, 164–165.

50. Roosevelt would have left sooner had it not been for a change for the worse in the health of the ailing secretary of the navy, Claude Swanson. Entry for Mar. 25, 1936, Ickes, *Diary*, I, 548.

51. Entry for Jan. 27, 1942, *Hitler's Secret Conversations*, 211.

52. Kordt, *Nicht aus den Akten*, 134; Schmidt, *Statist auf diplomatischer Bühne*, 93.

53. Hossbach, *Zwischen Wehrmacht und Hitler*, 98.

whelming 98.8 per cent majority.[54] Six weeks later Ambassador Bullitt, passing through Berlin to the United States, stopped off to talk to Neurath, who assured him that Germany planned no more diplomatic maneuvers until "the Rhineland has been digested." As soon as fortifications in the Rhineland were constructed, Neurath went on, "and the countries of Central Europe realize that France cannot enter Germany at will, all those countries will begin to feel very differently about their foreign policies and a new constellation will develop."[55] Three days later in Paris, Bullitt saw the secretary general of the French Foreign Office, Alexis Léger, who tried to maintain a front. He told Bullitt that to permit the Germans to complete their Rhineland fortification would be to allow them to build a Chinese wall across Europe which would place all of Central and Eastern Europe at their mercy. If the British would not call a halt to Germany's action, Léger said, "the French Army would march alone." Bullitt pressed the matter until the Frenchman admitted that unless the Germans committed some enormous blunder that aroused all France, nothing would be done. In the end, as Bullitt told Hull, "I derived the impression from . . . Mr. Léger that the French Foreign Office has in fact no constructive ideas whatsoever."[56] And thus passed what Hull later called an "obvious . . . seven league step toward war," but a development "in which we were not involved."[57]

Throughout the Rhineland crisis the President and State Department had maintained, almost to a fault, a position of correctness. So long as Germany's act did not legally affect American rights or interests, American diplomats generally agreed there was no alternative to aloofness. The State Department was not interested in trying to force Germany to change tactics. Even in matters affecting the United States, where the law seemed to prescribe action, the State Department preferred to interpret the law, if not to disregard it, so as not to involve itself. Such policy, while not sympathetic toward Nazi aims, obliged Germany in certain demands. The dispute over invoking countervailing duties on German imports, which reached its peak in the months immediately

54. Baynes, ed., *Hitler's Speeches*, II, 1313–1315; Bullock, *Hitler*, 346.
55. Bullitt Memorandum, May 18, 1936, *FR 1936*, I, 300.
56. Bullitt to Hull, May 21, 1936, Hull papers, Box 36.
57. *Memoirs*, I, 453.

after Germany's march into the Rhineland, demonstrated this State Department attitude that one of the principals in the dispute, Secretary of the Treasury Henry Morgenthau, Jr., later derided as "constitutional timidity."[58]

According to Section 303 of the 1930 Smoot-Hawley Tariff the Treasury Department was under mandate, if it discovered that foreign governments provided bounties or subsidies for export of goods to the United States that were dutiable upon entrance, to impose additional, or countervailing, duties upon those goods equal in amount to the subsidy. Certain German currency practices, notably the use of Aski, or registered, marks, indicated subsidy of exports to the United States. Under the Aski system, applied similarly to many countries, German importers paid American exporters for goods in Aski marks. These marks could neither be exchanged for dollars nor taken out of the country; they could be used only in Germany for purchase of specific German products. Normally American exporters might have hesitated to sell under such restrictive circumstances, but the German government, which regulated German import-export transactions, established Aski mark prices for American goods that were considerably higher than world market prices. American exporters therefore could afford to sell their Aski marks at a discount to importers who purchased German goods. The importers thus got more marks for their dollars than if they had exchanged them at the official rate, and obtained more German goods for their money. In this roundabout way—similar procedures being applied to other types of currency and bonds—the German government subsidized its export manufactures that competed with American goods.[59] Chiefly involved were cameras, surgical and optical instruments, bicycles, and various cotton, rayon, calf, kid leather, and paper items which constituted about 15 per cent of the total German export to the United States.[60]

In late November 1935 the State Department informed the German

58. "The Morgenthau Diaries," *Colliers,* 73.

59. Schoenfeld Memorandum, Dec. 4, 1935, *FR 1935,* II, 473–474; see also John Morton Blum, *From the Morgenthau Diaries: Years of Crisis, 1928–1938* (Boston, 1959), 149–150.

60. Johnson to Sayre, Jan. 16, 1936, DS, 611.623/110. William R. Johnson was acting chief counsel for the Customs Bureau; Francis B. Sayre was assistant secretary of state.

embassy that if Germany subsidized exports to the United States the Treasury Department would have to impose the countervailing duties. The Germans replied one week later that currency manipulations did not constitute a subsidy within the meaning of the Smoot-Hawley Tariff because the German government made no payments to exporters, and that if the restrictive mark system resulted in additional costs then German consumers paid them.[61] The Customs Bureau thought otherwise and notified Herbert Feis, State Department economic adviser, that Germany was subsidizing exports and that in the near future the secretary of the treasury would impose countervailing duties.[62] State Department advisers opposed higher duties. They believed Germany used the Aski system with American exporters and importers because German goods were otherwise too expensive in dollars to sell in the United States, and that higher duties would eliminate these German goods from the American market. The Germans might curtail purchases of American raw materials. All in all, they concluded, the Germans were only devaluing their currency and employing devices that did not give an "extraordinary advantage" over American manufacturers. Further, countervailing duties had never before been imposed on a country because it had depreciated its currency. Higher duties at this time, they felt, might kill what hope there was that Germany might end its discriminatory practices against American business.[63] Nonetheless Herman Oliphant, general counsel for the Treasury Department, informed Hull on February 3 that it was "common knowledge that practically all, if not all" German exports to the United States were being subsidized and that his department would impose countervailing duties.[64] A special delegation of German officials failed to persuade the Treasury Department to alter its intention.[65]

The Treasury Department regarded imposition of countervailing duties as a matter of "extreme urgency."[66] Nevertheless, throughout the critical month of March it awaited Germany's response to its re-

61. Schoenfeld Memoranda, Nov. 27 and Dec. 4, 1935, DS, 600.628/13½, *FR 1935*, II, 473–474.
62. Johnson to Feis, Jan. 3, 1936, DS, 611.623/113.
63. Unsigned Memorandum, "Comments on the Treasury Proposal to Impose Countervailing Duties on German Products," Jan. 27, 1936, DS, 611.623/115.
64. Oliphant to Hull, Feb. 3, 1936, DS, 611.623/118.
65. Schoenfeld Memorandum, Feb. 3, 1936, *FR 1936*, II, 213–214.
66. Taylor to Hull, Mar. 16, 1936, DS, 611.623/119. Wayne C. Taylor was assistant secretary of the treasury.

quest, submitted through Dodd in January, for full explanation of the reason for use of the registered marks. The Germans explained late in March that their special measures resulted from international economic conditions beyond their control.[67] The special German trade delegation in Washington proposed several measures to improve trade with the United States, including, perhaps, restoration of the most-favored-nation standard. Although aspects of the plan were unclear, German willingness to depart from discriminatory bilateral arrangements appealed to the State Department.[68] In April the Executive Committee on Commercial Policy, consisting of the secretaries of state, treasury, commerce, agriculture, and the chairmen of the Tariff Commission, National Recovery Administration, and Agricultural Adjustment Administration, which Roosevelt had established in November 1933 to coordinate America's international commercial policies, submitted a unanimous report—the Treasury's representative abstained—supporting State Department contentions. Currency manipulation, the committee said, was just another form of currency depreciation, practiced by many countries including the United States. Allowances had to be made for abnormal economic conditions. If duties were invoked against Germany, they would have to be invoked against other countries—Argentina, Brazil, Chile, Uruguay, Hungary. Germany was having dollar-exchange difficulties and if German purchases of American goods were not to decline further, the Germans had to use Aski marks to bolster sales. Imposing duties would eliminate all possibility of a new trade agreement with Germany. Above all, the committee insisted, high duties ran counter to the trade agreements program, the object of which was to reduce tariffs and surpluses and reopen foreign markets.[69] Along with this report, Hull sent a letter to Morgenthau declaring strong support for the committee's recommendations and warning that it would be "regrettable" if duties were imposed and conversations with Germany about them ended.[70]

Morgenthau, strongly and outspokenly anti-Nazi, now took his

67. Dodd to Neurath, Jan. 28, and Dodd to Hull, Mar. 23, 1936, *FR 1936,* II, 211–212, 215–216.

68. Grady Memorandum, Mar. 30, 1936, *ibid.,* 221–223. Henry F. Grady was chief of the Division of Trade Agreements.

69. Blum, *Morgenthau Diaries,* 150.

70. Hull to Morgenthau, Apr. 2, 1936, DS, 611.00w1 Executive Committee (on Commercial Policy)/497.

case to Roosevelt, with whom he had a close friendship and sympathetic views. Roosevelt told him that "if it is a borderline case, I feel so keenly about Germany that I would enforce the countervailing duties." But first, he advised, get an opinion from the Justice Department.[71] Morgenthau did so, and on April 30 the assistant solicitor general, Golden W. Bell, reported that German practices clearly constituted bounties or grants within the meaning of the Smoot-Hawley Tariff. The State Department's concern over economic policy, he said, had made it difficult to dissociate policy from law. But he concluded that it might be best to resubmit the question to the President, and perhaps even consider asking Congress to change the law.[72]

The State Department made a final appeal to Bell, reiterating its own and executive committee arguments, adding that if countervailing duties were imposed on Germany it would only be fair to impose them on Latin American countries that had depreciated their currency. That would cause retaliation and prove "very unfortunate" in view of the forthcoming conference in Buenos Aires.[73] Later Hull would insist that Morgenthau "rushed blindly ahead with a project that stood to throw a crowbar into the machinery of our foreign relations."[74] Such was not the case, for Morgenthau did take the State Department's latest objections to Roosevelt, who deliberated and told him to go ahead. "I am convinced," Roosevelt said, "that we have to act. It may be possible to make the action apply to Germany only."[75]

At a meeting with Morgenthau and Attorney General Homer Cummings, Hull persisted in the State Department position, but admitted finally that the law demanded that the Treasury Department impose the duties. Morgenthau, concerned that his department's action might be misconstrued as based on his personal contempt for Germany, reported back to Roosevelt, who said that as long as the law was clear "there is nothing for you to do but carry it out."[76] Cummings officially

71. Quoted in Blum, *Morgenthau Diaries,* 151.
72. *Ibid.,* 151–152.
73. Sayre to Bell, May 4, 1936, DS, 611.623/126A.
74. *Memoirs,* I, 473.
75. Roosevelt to Morgenthau, May 22, 1936, Roosevelt papers, Official File 614-A. A copy was sent to the State Department, DS, 611.623/183.
76. Quoted in Blum, *Morgenthau Diaries,* 153. Remak, "Germany and the United States," 124, contends that Hull's arguments were "better" than Morgenthau's, and wrongly states that Roosevelt "would not intervene in the dispute."

ruled that the Treasury Department's proposed action fell within the meaning and requirements of the Smoot-Hawley Tariff, and at a press conference Morgenthau announced that Treasury Decision 48360 would be made public on June 11, 1936, and that thirty days from then countervailing duties, ranging from approximately 20 to 55 per cent—depending on the amount of subsidy—would be imposed on the appropriate German goods.[77]

The Treasury decision brought protests from Germany and from American cotton and tobacco merchants and importers of German wares, who complained either directly to the secretary of state or to their congressmen.[78] Not even a German commission headed by Rudolf Brinkmann, a Reichsbank and Economics Ministry official, could cause the Treasury Department to halt application of the new duties.[79] Morgenthau's policy quickly brought dividends. Within a month from the time the countervailing duties went into effect, the German government notified the State Department it would no longer allow payments from Aski accounts for German goods delivered to the United States, and the Treasury Department removed the countervailing duties.[80]

The Treasury Department's "triumph" was short-lived. After the Second World War, Morgenthau wrote that the Treasury plan represented "the first check to Germany's career of economic conquest."[81] The truth was that although the countervailing duties had forced Germany, for the first time, to give in to American demands, a few months after the duties were removed the State Department and

---

Remark drew on Hull's *Memoirs,* which omit mention of Roosevelt's decisive role, for his information.

77. Cummings to Morgenthau, June 2, 1936, DS, 611.623/157; *New York Times,* June 5, 1936.

78. Livesey Memorandum, June 15, 1936, *FR 1936,* II, 231. For examples of protest, see New Orleans Spot Cotton Merchants Association to Hull, June 11, 1936, DS, 611.623/138; Southern Cotton Shippers Association to Hull, June 11, 1936, 611.623/119; Congressman J. D. Fernandez (La.) to Roosevelt, June 11, 1936, 611.623/147; Senator Joseph W. Bailey (N.C.) to Hull, June 24, 1936, 611.623/166.

79. Schoenfeld and Livesey Memoranda, July 6, 1936, *FR 1936,* II, 241–244.

80. Luther to Phillips, Aug. 12, and Roche to Hull, Aug. 14, 1936, *ibid.,* 249, DS, 611.623/227. Josephine P. Roche was assistant secretary of the treasury.

81. "The Morgenthau Diaries," *Colliers,* 77.

American businessmen pressed the Treasury to alter its interpretation of the law so that by clever bookkeeping and financial devices the old Aski practices could be taken up in new guise. In October 1936 government economic experts from both countries and the Treasury Department agreed there should be no countervailing duties on German goods that Americans purchased with Aski marks provided that the person or firm using these marks owned them originally and continuously, that is, had received these marks for goods he had sold to Germany, and had not, therefore, bought the marks at a discount from some other American exporter.[82]

The bookkeeping procedure worked in the following manner. An American importer, "A," ordered from a German exporter, "B," chemicals costing 9,000 registered marks. Then "A" purchased $2,700 worth of cotton from an American firm, "C," $2,700 equaling only three fourths the real dollar value of 9,000 registered marks. Then firm "A" sold the cotton to a German firm, "D," interested in buying American cotton, and "D" in turn deposited a credit of 9,000 registered marks with the German chemical firm, "B," or its bank, in the name of the American importer of German chemicals, firm "A." Whereupon "B" shipped the chemicals to the American importer, "A."[83] To facilitate matters, American cotton firms never shipped the cotton to American importers of German goods but only invoices for such goods, and importers in turn shipped the invoices to German purchasers of the cotton.[84]

The "cotton barter" scheme, as this system was known, worked equally well for copper and petroleum. Fluctuations in these dealings resulted chiefly from the amount of discount the German government allowed American businesmen on their money and merchandise and how quickly the Germans delivered promised goods. Bartering continued uninterrupted until March 1939. Then Germany's seizure of what remained of Czechoslovakia caused the attorney general, Frank Murphy, at the behest of Roosevelt and his advisers (especially Morgenthau and Under Secretary Sumner Welles), to rule on March

---

82. German Embassy to the Department of State, Oct. 22, 1936, *FR 1936*, II, 251. See also Luther to Schacht, Oct. 2, 1936, *DGFP*, C, V, 1027.

83. The example used follows closely that described by the American consul in Bremen, J. Webb Benton, to Hull, Apr. 24, 1937, DS, 611.623/935.

84. Tenenbaum, *National Socialism*, 110.

18 that the barter system violated the Smoot-Hawley Tariff, and Murphy again imposed countervailing duties.[85]

The saddest aspect of this affair was not that Germany had benefit of American cotton, copper, petroleum, and other goods for three extra years, for countervailing duties alone would not have altered the course of German history. Rather, it was that American diplomats took so long to make up their minds to take such a small step.

The second half of 1936 brought further strife to Europe, dramatic gains for Germany and fascism, and retreat by American diplomats. On July 17 a group of Spanish generals, consummating an old plot to destroy the Republic of Spain, revolted against the Popular Front government. The generals had assumed they would win quickly but soon found that without foreign assistance they would lose to determined Republican resistance.[86] Mussolini had been interested in the destruction of the Spanish Republic at least since 1934 and had supplied arms for that purpose.[87] Germany too was interested in Spain and various Nazi organizations had been at work there and in North Africa, but there is no record of any government plan to foment or aid the revolt.[88] On July 23 the German embassy counselor in Madrid, Karl Schwendemann, did point out the advantages that would accrue from a victory by the forces under General Francisco Franco. But the Foreign Ministry, aware of requests about to be made, opposed helping Franco move his forces from Morocco, or any other aid, and Hitler was even reluctant to allow the navy to use the fleet to assist German citizens in Spain.[89]

Franco soon decided to accept the offer of several German citizens,

85. *New York Times,* Mar. 19, 1936; see also Tenenbaum, *National Socialism,* 110–112.

86. Dante A. Puzzo, *Spain and the Great Powers, 1936–1941* (New York and London, 1962), 41, 58, 96.

87. William C. Askew, "Italian Intervention in Spain: The Agreements of March 31, 1934 with the Spanish Monarchist Parties," *Journal of Modern History,* XXIV (Mar. 1952), 181–183.

88. Manfred Merkes, *Die deutsche Politik gegenüber dem spanischen Bürgerkrieg, 1936–1939* (Bonn, 1961), 14–17.

89. Schwendemann to Foreign Ministry, July 23, Dieckhoff to War Ministry, Foreign Department, July 24, and Dieckhoff Memorandum, July 25, 1936, *DGFP,* D, III, 5–7, 10–11; Raeder, *My Life,* 221.

in particular a businessman resident in Morocco who sold supplies to the army, Johannes Bernhardt, and a Nazi *Auslandsorganisation* official, Adolf Langenheim, to appeal directly to Hitler, who was in Bayreuth. They reached Hitler on July 25, and after consultation with Göring and Blomberg, Hitler authorized the dispatch of the transport planes necessary to move Franco's troops to the mainland. A Franco victory would ring France with yet a third hostile power, upset the Anglo-French balance of power in the Mediterranean, perhaps increase the strain between England and France on the one hand and Italy on the other, and give Germany further access to Spanish raw material and bases. Whether Hitler thought of all these things at the time cannot be determined, but at any rate he made his decision for initial support and did not consult his Foreign Ministry officials, who were playing a passive role in light of the fact that they certainly knew Franco would be appealing for aid.[90] Additional German and Italian supplies followed shortly, and by early August Franco had landed fifteen thousand troops in Seville under a protective air convoy.[91]

Europe and the United States preserved their neutrality; only the Soviet Union and Mexico (which had little matériel to offer) would support the Republicans. First reports to the State Department from France indicated that the Popular Front government of Léon Blum inclined to honor the Spanish government's legitimate request to buy planes and munitions.[92] But the French were worried about British reaction, and Blum, urged by the French ambassador in London, Charles Corbin, and the secretary general at the Quai d'Orsay, Alexis Léger, agreed to go to London for discussions.[93] The British were determined not to antagonize Germany or Italy—Bingham reported that Eden warned Blum about the "grave international consequences" that would arise from active support of the Madrid government—and after his return Blum announced on July 25 that France would not send arms.[94] Admittedly Blum, in power only two months at the time,

90. Merkes, *Die deutsche Politik gegenüber dem spanischen Bürgerkrieg*, 18–22, 26–27; Furnia, *Diplomacy of Appeasement*, 207–209.

91. Puzzo, *Spain and the Great Powers*, 64–65; Gabriel Jackson, *The Spanish Republic and the Civil War, 1931–1939* (Princeton, 1965), 248–249.

92. Hull, *Memoirs*, I, 476.

93. Elizabeth R. Cameron, "Alexis Saint-Léger Léger," in Craig and Gilbert, eds., *The Dipomats*, 391.

94. Straus to Hull, July 27, 1936, *FR 1936*, II, 447–449. See also Hugh

was under pressure from the British, French conservatives who favored Franco, and liberals like Léger who feared France might be isolated, but the fact remains, as one scholar has noted, that the French decision not to help the Spanish Republicans was perhaps "the most important single act in the history of the diplomacy of the Spanish Civil War."[95]

Within six weeks the British and French set up the International Nonintervention Committee which met in London in early September and shortly secured pledges of twenty-seven nations—Germany and Italy included—not to intervene in any way in the Spanish civil war.[96] Virtually everyone in Europe, Eden and Churchill included, insisted nonintervention was the alternative to general war. Churchill persisted in April 1937 that although he knew there were "swindles and cheats" in the Nonintervention Committee, it was encouraging to have German, French, Soviet, Italian, and British naval officers "officially acting together, however crankily, in something which represents, albeit feebly, the concert of Europe . . . The man who mocks at the existence of the Nonintervention Committee I put on the same level as the man who mocks at the hope of Geneva and the League of Nations."[97]

The American government did not mock the "concert of Europe" or the Nonintervention Committee, although it never signed the non-intervention pledge because it would have nothing to do with European politics. Hull informed American diplomatic and consular officials in Spain, and made the statement public, that although the Neutrality Act of 1936 applied only to war between or among nations, not civil war, he was calling on the American people to follow the example of their government, which was to "scrupulously refrain from any inter-ference whatsoever in the unfortunate Spanish situation."[98] On August 14 Roosevelt placed emphasis on the moral embargo. In a famous speech at Chautauqua, New York, he reiterated how the United States had shunned political commitments that might have led to war,

---

Thomas, *The Spanish Civil War* (New York and Evanston, 1961), 219–220, and Wm. Laird Kleine-Ahlbrandt, *The Policy of Simmering: A Study of British Policy during the Spanish Civil War, 1936–1939* (The Hague, 1962), 6–9.

95. Puzzo, *Spain and the Great Powers,* 241.
96. Furnia, *Diplomacy of Appeasement,* 210–213.
97. Quoted in Hull, *Memoirs,* I, 482.
98. Hull Circular Letter of Aug. 7, 1936, *FR 1936,* II, 471.

had avoided connection with the League of Nations' political activities, and insisted that Americans were not isolationists except in seeking isolation from war. There were people who might drag their country into war, "thousands of Americans who, seeking immediate riches— 'fools' gold'—would attempt to break down or evade our neutrality." Following a moving description of his own wartime experiences—"I have seen blood running from the wounded. I have seen men coughing out their gassed lungs. I have seen the dead in the mud. I have seen cities destroyed."—Roosevelt reminded the American people that no neutrality legislation could foresee every contingency and called for support of the government's moral embargo.[99] Shortly afterward the State Department turned down as too risky a proposal by Uruguay that the American Republics together offer to mediate the war in Spain, and in October Hull informed the Spanish ambassador in Washington, Fernando de los Ríos, that despite America's traditional attitude of favoring legal governments the United States would not aid the legal Spanish Republican regime.[100]

The administration maintained its nonintervention policy. True, the forthcoming November presidential election partly accounted for the restraint and timidity, but following Roosevelt's smashing victory—he captured every state but Maine and Vermont—and considering that both Germany and Italy recognized the Franco regime on November 18 and continually and flagrantly violated their nonintervention pledges, the United States did have opportunity to maneuver. Rather than relax its neutrality, however, it chose to intensify it. At first the State Department, unable to prohibit legally the export of arms to Spain, publicized each license granted for arms export in order to embarrass the shippers. When in December one exporter secured a license to ship nearly $3 million worth of airplanes and engines to the Republican government, the State Department said it had granted the license "reluctantly" and at a press conference Roosevelt said shipping arms was legal but "unpatriotic."[101] Further, the State Department through the embassy in Berlin apologized to the German government for being unable to prevent the shipment and assured it that repairs and

99. *PPFDR*, V, 285–292.
100. Hull, *Memoirs*, I, 480, 484–485.
101. *New York Times*, Dec. 28 and Dec. 29, 1936.

other complications would delay shipment for two to six months.[102]

The Roosevelt government then decided to clamp a legal embargo on top of the moral one. The President conferred with party congressional leaders and State Department officials, and on January 6, 1937, Senator Pittman and Representative McReynolds introduced in the Senate and House respectively a resolution prohibiting export of arms, munitions, and implements of war to either side in the Spanish struggle.[103] The Senate passed the measure unanimously that afternoon, although Senator Nye, insisting he did not favor one side over the other, objected to it "in the name of neutrality, for, strictly speaking, neutrality it is not."[104] In the House numerous congressmen of highly divergent points of view, distressed at the lack of time for debate, insisted that it was senseless to apply such a measure to Spain alone and unneutral to deny a legal government access to arms. Once again administration pressure prevailed, applied by McReynolds, who said he had the personal approval of Roosevelt and Hull. Farmer-Laborite John Bernard of Minnesota cast the single dissenting vote, explaining afterward that "Fascism is engaging in the open rape of Spain" and that the neutrality measure was a "sham" intended to "choke off democratic Spain from its legitimate international rights at a time while it is being assailed by the Fascist hordes of Europe."[105] Roosevelt signed the measure into law on January 8. The Germans were pleased, regretting only, as the semiofficial *Diplomatische Korrespondenz* put it on January 7, that the present definition of neutrality had not been adopted twenty years sooner. General Franco remarked that Roosevelt had behaved like a "true gentleman" and that the rapid passage of the new neutrality law was "a gesture we Nationalists shall never forget."[106]

102. Erdmannsdorf Memorandum, Dec. 31, 1936, *DGFP*, D, III, 198. Otto von Erdmannsdorf was head of the Extra-European Section of the Political Department in the Foreign Ministry.

103. Text of resolution in *Peace and War*, 353–354.

104. *Congressional Record,* 75th Cong., 1st sess., LXXXI, Part 1, p. 79; see also F. Jay Taylor, *The United States and the Spanish Civil War* (New York, 1956), 78.

105. *Congressional Record,* 75th Cong., 1st sess., LXXXI, Part 9, pp. 65–66.

106. *New York American,* Feb. 1, 1937, cited in Taylor, *United States and the Spanish Civil War,* 81. Two points are worth noting. First, in his *Memoirs,* I, 490–492, Hull says that the legislative and executive branches joined "in sin-

The administration never deviated from its chosen course. In March 1937 Senator Nye proposed that the government extend the embargo to Germany and Italy, but the Foreign Relations Committee tabled the resolution after Hull and the State Department persisted that the United States could not proclaim there existed a state of war between those countries and Spain when the Spanish government had not done so.[107] A few weeks later Roosevelt, thinking he would have to apply the Neutrality Act to Germany and Italy, asked Hull to poll American ambassadors in Europe on the extent of German and Italian participation in the Spanish war. He dropped the idea, however, as the State Department insisted that no state of war existed between Spain and Germany and Italy and that the latter two had recognized the Franco forces as the legal government. Also, there would have been complications in applying the law because there were citizens of numerous other countries in the fighting. Reflecting the attitude of European leaders, British Foreign Secretary Eden told Ambassador Bingham that an arms embargo against Germany and Italy would be "to say the least, premature."[108]

The drive for repealing the Spanish embargo reached new intensity in the spring of 1938, encompassing such diverse prominent Americans as former Secretary of State Stimson and the leading Socialist, Norman Thomas, as well as liberal journals, clergymen, college faculties, and peace movement people.[109] On May 2 Nye introduced another resolution proposing to lift the embargo on the Spanish Republican government and allow it to purchase war goods on a cash-and-carry basis, with American shippers excluded from the carrying trade in order to

---

gular harmony" in advocating the embargo. Despite Hull's statement, and the fact that Bernard cast the only negative vote, there was considerable opposition which the administration steamrollered, recognizing that prolonged debate might delay, if not prevent, passage of the law. Second, Welles, in his *Time for Decision* (New York, 1944), 60–61, says that Roosevelt signed the bill with "regret" and that had the President not been occupied in December with the Buenos Aires Conference he might have gone to the public to fight the embargo. Clearly, Roosevelt and his advisers prepared the bill themselves and engineered its passage.

107. Hull, *Memoirs*, I, 510–511.
108. *Ibid.*, 511–513; Bingham to Hull, July 6, 1937, *FR 1937*, I, 353–355,
109. Divine, *Illusion of Neutrality*, 224,

avoid incidents. According to a front-page story by Arthur Krock in the *New York Times* of May 5, the administration now supported repealing the embargo and had sufficient congressional support to do it. At once there was a furor, and precise developments are not easy to discern. Apparently Roosevelt, after conferring with Hull and congressional leaders, decided not to offend the Catholic hierarchy, and the British and French, who still supported nonintervention, or to further disintegrate the New Deal coalition which was suffering from the fight of the past year over Roosevelt's Supreme Court packing plan.[110] Hull seemingly never had his heart in the effort and wrote Pittman, chairman of the Senate Foreign Relations Committee, that in light of international conditions, to change course might cause "complications."[111] Pittman called a special meeting of his committee, distributed copies of the letter to each senator, and after less than thirty minutes' consideration they tabled Nye's resolution.[112] The embargo remained in effect until April 1, 1939, when, following the fall of Madrid and Valencia, the United States recognized the Franco regime as the legal government of Spain and, two days later, established diplomatic relations.[113]

When Ambassador Claude Bowers, a consistent critic of his government's policy, returned from Spain in March 1939, both Roosevelt and Pittman quickly and frankly admitted to him that they had "made a mistake."[114] At the height of the Second World War, Welles wrote that American policy with respect to the Spanish civil war was "of all our blind isolationist policies, the most disastrous."[115] Of the major figures in the government only Hull did not think, either at the time or in retrospect, that a mistake had been made. He insisted then and later not only that he did not see how the United States might have

110. *Ibid.*, 226–227. See also Allen Guttmann, *The Wound in the Heart: America and the Spanish Civil War* (New York, 1962), esp. 116, 120–121, and J. David Valaik, "Catholics, Neutrality, and the Spanish Embargo, 1937–1939," *Journal of American History*, LIV (June 1967), 73–85.

111. Hull, *Memoirs*, I, 516.

112. Israel, *Pittman*, 157.

113. Pratt, *Hull*, I, 230; see also *FR 1939*, II, 771–772.

114. Claude Bowers, *My Mission to Spain: Watching the Rehearsal for World War II* (New York, 1954), 418–419.

115. *Time for Decision*, 57.

pursued any other policy, but that the elected one improved American relations with England and France, and thereby did not "encourage" Germany or Italy.[116]

Hull was wrong. The bloody conflict in Spain, like the Italian-Ethiopian struggle, worked to German and Italian advantage even if events did not proceed according to plan. Italy's expenditure of $400 million and fifty thousand troops was larger than Germany's $200 million and sixteen thousand soldiers and civilians, but Germany's contribution, especially including essential personnel to man heavy bombers and artillery, was probably the critical one in determining Franco's victory.[117] But the fascist powers could not make the war move according to their proposed schedule: Germany believed that commitment of the "Condor Legion"—which would take part in bombing the little Basque town of Guernica—and recognition of the Franco regime in November 1936 would bring speedy victory; time and again, however, Germany and Italy had to commit more men, money, and matériel than anticipated or desired.[118] Further, the Germans and Italians found Franco obstinate in pursuing strategy and tactics they disapproved, just as Hitler would find at Hendaye in October 1940 that Franco could not be moved to do what he did not want to do.[119]

Ironically, too, the Spanish civil war marked a serious decline for the German Foreign Ministry,[120] whose officials probably contributed to their own demise. Weizsäcker, who had returned from Switzerland to head the Political Department and take the Spanish question as his specialty, has contended that Hitler made the decision to supply arms without consulting the Foreign Ministry; yet even at

116. *Memoirs,* I, 517.

117. Thomas, *The Spanish Civil War,* Appendix III, 634–635; Puzzo, *Spain and the Great Powers,* 65.

118. Merkes, *Die deutsche Politik gegenüber dem spanischen Bürgerkrieg,* 169.

119. On complaints about Franco see, for example, Hassell to Foreign Ministry, Dec. 20, 1937, *DGFP,* D, III, 533; entries for May 3, 1937, and Aug. 29 and Sept. 3, 1938, Malcolm Muggeridge, ed., *Ciano's Diplomatic Papers,* trans. Stuart Hood (London, 1948), 115, 148, 150. On German efforts to involve Spain in the Second World War, see Puzzo, *Spain and the Great Powers,* 202–238.

120. Watt, "The German Diplomats and the Nazi Leaders," *Journal of Central European Affairs,* 156.

the time, Weizsäcker noted in his own records, Germany's and Italy's goals were to prevent "a Soviet Spain."[121] As noted before, the Foreign Ministry played a passive role, doing nothing to get Hitler to change his course. In the Foreign Ministry's constant references to Communist influence in Spain they of course overlooked the facts that prior to the revolt of the generals there is no evidence of Communist or Soviet effort at insurrection and that Soviet intervention did not begin until late August or early September 1936, when its essential purpose was to shield the Soviet Union from expected German aggression.[122] Neurath's circumlocutions to the French in early August 1936 that the German government was not aiding Franco were hollow; hollower still were Dieckhoff's insistences to Dodd that Germany was "strictly neutral," and that if Italy and Portugal were not it was because Republican Spain intended to annex Portugal.[123]

The purpose of British—and French—policy was to contain the war and maintain Spain's integrity.[124] The war was "contained" but not without allowing fascist forces to invade, and such integrity as the Nationalists maintained bore little resemblance to that of the Republic. Would Hitler have backed down—and Italy, too, because it could not have persisted alone—had the British, French, and Americans merely given the Republicans the aid to which they were legally entitled? The answer is probably yes for before November 1936 and only perhaps for any time after that. Support for the Republicans in the summer of 1936 probably would have caused Franco's defeat, thus making irrelevant the question of what Hitler might have done after November. And if the British had hoped in 1936 to appease Mussolini to gain his support for their future endeavors, they failed miserably. When the British in April 1938 reached tentative accord with Italy over recognition of the Italian claim to Ethiopia in return for troop withdrawal from Spain, the Italian foreign minister, Count Galeazzo Ciano, privately noted that "we shall not modify our policy towards

121. Weizsäcker, *Memoirs,* 106, 113–114.
122. Puzzo, *Spain and the Great Powers,* 38–39; David T. Cattell, *Soviet Diplomacy and the Spanish Civil War* (Berkeley and Los Angeles, 1957), 32, 37.
123. Neurath Memorandum, Aug. 4, 1936, *DGFP,* D, III, 29–30; entry for Sept. 16, 1936, Dodd, *Diary,* 351–352.
124. Kleine-Ahlbrandt, *The Policy of Simmering,* 140–141.

Franco in the smallest degree and the agreement with London will come into force when God pleases, if indeed it ever will."[125] Thus British and French policy failed, as did that of the American administration, which subsequently admitted its failure. The position of the German Foreign Ministry declined. Only Hitler's gamble, and Franco's revolt, succeeded. The Spanish civil war constituted, besides a devastating defeat for the people of Spain, a shocking demonstration of the political and moral bankruptcy of democratic foreign policy and an assist to aggression.

Autumn 1936 was a period of more ominous developments. Hitler was determined to win Mussolini's confidence, and Germany's "Gentlemen's Agreement" of July 11, 1936—affirming Austrian independence and promising a relaxation of tension between the two countries—and the common German-Italian effort in Spain seemed to make the circumstances favorable.[126] Hitler's minister of justice, Hans Frank, went to Rome in September to discuss with Mussolini possible areas of cooperation. At Hitler's invitation Ciano journeyed to Berlin where on October 23 he and Neurath signed secret protocols calling for cooperative foreign policies with respect to Spain, Ethiopia, and the Danubian countries, proposals for a new Locarno settlement, and recognition of Japan's puppet state of Manchukuo. One week later, on November 1, Mussolini spoke for the first time of the new Axis "around which the European states animated by the will to collaboration and peace can also collaborate."[127] As has been pointed out, the secret protocols reflected Italy's distrust of Germany more than cooperative policy between the two countries and were breached more than observed; the Axis, although intended as an instrument of propaganda for political purposes, was not an alliance involving real

125. Entries for June 22 and June 30, 1938, Malcolm Muggeridge, ed., *Ciano's Diary, 1937–1938,* trans. Andreas Mayor (London, 1952), 130, 133–134.

126. Text of German-Austrian "Gentlemen's Agreement," in *DGFP,* D, V, 756–760.

127. Bullock, *Hitler,* 350–352; Memorandum Frank–Mussolini Conversation, Sept. 23, 1936, Ciano, *Diplomatic Papers,* 143–148; German-Italian Protocols in *DGFP,* C, V, 1136–1138; Mussolini speech in Wheeler-Bennett, ed., *Documents 1936,* 346.

coordination of policy and security for the signatories.[128] For the United States, probably, the significant aspect of the German-Italian rapprochement was the decision concerning Manchukuo. Neurath had told Ciano that Hitler "wishes to take the step of recognizing Manchuokuo" but intended "to delay this gesture so as not to compromise certain German economic interests in China."[129] The implications of this decision for German policy, developments in the Far East, and the United States would be great.

Since 1932 Germany had gone along with the Hoover-Stimson doctrine of nonrecognition, which the League of Nations adopted, built a lucrative arms trade with China, and sent various generals to advise the forces of Chiang Kai-shek. According to Kordt, Hitler admired the Japanese army and sympathized with Japan's departure from the League in February–March 1933, but the only concession he made to the Foreign Policy Office of the Nazi party in 1933 was to appoint a "German Delegate for Manchuokuo."[130] Numerous diplomatic, economic, and cultural exchanges between Germany and Japan during 1933–1935 caused considerable comment and suspicion by observers, but there were no agreements between the countries.[131]

Meanwhile Ribbentrop, who shortly after the Blood Purge of 1934 had set up his *Büro* or *Dienststelle Ribbentrop* to compete with the Foreign Ministry, and whose eye was always on Neurath's job, apparently glimpsed a way to enhance his prestige and further alienate Hitler from his diplomats. In the spring of 1935 Ribbentrop used an intermediary to suggest to the Japanese military attaché in Berlin, Major General Hiroshi Oshima, that it was his personal idea to conclude a defensive pact against the Soviet Union. The Japanese grew interested after the summer of 1935, when the Seventh Comintern

128. D. C. Watt, "The Rome-Berlin Axis, 1936–1940: Myth and Reality," *Review of Politics*, XXII (Oct. 1960), 520–521, 531, 542–543.

129. Memorandum Neurath-Ciano Conversation, Oct. 21, 1936, Ciano, *Diplomatic Papers*, 55.

130. Kordt, *Nicht aus den Akten*, 122; Gerhard L. Weinberg, "German Recognition of Manchuokuo," *World Affairs Quarterly*, XXVIII (July 1957), 149–151, 153.

131. Frank William Iklé, *German-Japanese Relations, 1936–1940* (New York, 1956), 15–16, 24–28; Ernst L. Presseisen, *Germany and Japan: A Study in Totalitarian Diplomacy, 1933–1941* (The Hague, 1958), 55–86.

Congress called for a Popular Front against fascist aggression and Japanese troops skirmished with Soviet troops in Inner Mongolia and North Manchuria, and in the fall they sent a representative of the General Staff, Lieutenant Tadaichi Wakamatsu, to Berlin for further talks. At about this time, in November 1935, an employee of Ribbentrop's *Büro* who had worked in East Asia and was knowledgeable in geopolitical matters, Hermann von Raumer, sketched what would be the basis of the Anti-Comintern Pact a year later. In November 1935 Ribbentrop took the proposal to Hitler, who approved it and authorized additional talks.[132]

Negotiations moved slowly in 1936 as Japan became embroiled in the February army revolt and Germany in the Rhineland crisis. At the end of April Germany concluded a trade agreement with Manchukuo, which implied *de facto* recognition, and following the outbreak of the Spanish civil war Hitler determined upon agreement with Japan.[133] In Japan the army had shown the most enthusiasm for agreement; the government's response had been tepid, partly out of desire not to offend Great Britain or the United States. But the army gained more leverage following conclusion of a defense pact in April between the Soviet Union and Outer Mongolia and the start of the Spanish civil war. The government also saw the proposed pact as a means to coerce China. By the end of September 1936 it agreed to conclude a pact, wishing only to delay formal announcement until the signing of a fisheries agreement with the Soviet Union.[134] On November 25, 1936, Ribbentrop and the Japanese ambassador, Viscount Kintomo Mushakoji, signed the Anti-Comintern Pact in Berlin. Publicly it provided for collaboration against the spread of communism within German and Japanese borders; secretly, each country pledged that if the Soviet Union without provocation attacked, or threatened to attack, one of them, the other would not do anything that would ease the

132. Theo Sommer, *Deutschland und Japan zwischen den Mächten, 1935–1940: Vom Antikominternpakt zum Dreimächtepakt. Eine Studie zur diplomatischen Vorgeschichte des Zweiten Weltkriegs* (Tübingen, 1962), 23–28.

133. Weinberg, "German Recognition of Manchuokuo," *World Affairs Quarterly,* 154–155; Sommer, *Deutschland und Japan,* 31–34, also indicates Hitler told Ribbentrop his "greatest wish" was to have England join the pact.

134. Iklé, *German-Japanese Relations,* 34–38; Presseisen, *Germany and Japan,* 103–105; Sommer, *Deutschland und Japan,* 36–37.

position of the Soviet Union, nor would Germany or Japan, without mutual consent, conclude a political treaty at any time with the Soviet Union that contravened the spirit of this agreement.[135]

The full meaning of these arrangements was not discernible in 1936, and numerous diplomats believed that the German-Japanese accord contained secret military arrangements between the General Staffs, perhaps for a venture against the Soviet Union.[136] No such arrangement existed, but Dodd rightly pointed out that the Anti-Comintern Pact went a long way toward connecting such geographically distant areas as Spain and Czechoslovakia (anticommunism could be used as an excuse for aggression) and confirmed his "fearful understanding" that the initiative and proceedings for the pact had been the work of Ribbentrop, "Hitler's real confidant for foreign affairs whose influence we consider unfortunate and inclined toward ever greater adventure."[137]

One scholar has labeled the Anti-Comintern Pact "an international kiss on the cheek," and this description is partly true. Certainly the arrangements implied no specific obligations and allowed both sides latitude in pursuing policies to their separate interests.[138] Nevertheless, the agreement not only indicated the direction in which German policy had been moving[139] but would hasten that movement by facilitating Japanese pressure on China which led up to the July 7, 1937, incident and the following war. With its vital interests in the Far East threatened, England would be more cautious about opposing Hitler.[140] German Foreign Ministry officials did not like the agreement.[141] But they could muster no serious opposition to it and only found their prestige

135. Text in Arnold J. Toynbee, ed., *Documents on International Affairs, 1939–1946*, 2 vols. (London, 1951), I, 4–5.

136. Grew to Hull, Dec. 4, 1936, *FR 1936*, I, 404. Joseph Grew was ambassador to Japan.

137. Dodd to Hull, Nov. 28, 1936, ibid., 402–403.

138. Sommer, *Deutschland und Japan*, 49. See also Gerhard L. Weinberg, "Die geheimen Abkommen zum Antikominternpakt," *Vierteljahrshefte für Zeitgeschichte*, II (Apr. 1954), 196, and Robertson, *Hitler's Pre-War Policy*, 99.

139. Weinberg, "German Recognition of Manchuokuo," *World Affairs Quarterly*, 156.

140. Iklé, *German-Japanese Relations*, 38–39, 50; Presseisen, *Germany and Japan*, 121–123; Robertson, *Hitler's Pre-War Policy*, 102.

141. DeWitt C. Poole, "New Light on Nazi Foreign Policy," *Foreign Affairs*, XXV (Oct. 1946), 137.

diminished and ultimately Germany's policy in the Far East reversed.[142] For the United States, of course, these developments would prove momentous. In 1937–38 American diplomats would make various efforts to curb the conflict in the Far East and ease the problems in Europe, but they would find that in both worlds their proposals ran behind the pace of aggression. The initiative had been surrendered to Germany and Japan, and as time would make clear, the consequences for everyone would be tragic as well as ironic.

American diplomats in 1936 were not aware of the threat of German foreign policy. There were exceptions, Dodd being one, Messersmith another. Nine days after Hitler concluded his 1936 agreement with Austria, Messersmith, then American minister there, wrote Hull that if "one knows Mr. Hitler one must realize that his burning ambition is to impose his will on Europe by force of arms." It would be a mistake, he said, to think that the Austro-German accord meant that conservative elements favoring peace had gained the upper hand. "Germany's so-called conservative elements," he wrote with a prescience rare among men of his era, "are conservative in the sense that they believe Germany is not ready and must not take any precipitate action. They are by no means conservative in the sense that they do not share the political expansionist aims of Hitler and the more radical members of the Party."[143]

Dodd agreed. In September 1936 he believed that whereas two years before the German people would have responded negatively to a declaration of war, and that the loyalty of the Reichswehr would have been doubtful, now the reverse was true. Hitler's political and economic policies at home and abroad—everything from luxury liner vacations for workers who had never been aboard anything more pretentious than small lake craft, to the brilliant rearmament and Rhineland coups—had brought a new dawn for people who had been

142. According to Weizsäcker, *Memoirs*, 116, he told Ambassador Mushakoji in July 1937 that Japan's policy in China fostered rather than prevented communism there, and further, "it was no business of ours to fight Communism in other countries." That was a different attitude than the one Weizsäcker himself assumed in the Spanish civil war, where he justified German policy as preventing "a Soviet Spain," *ibid.*, 113.

143. Messersmith to Hull, July 20, 1936, Hull papers, Box 39.

groping, unsure of their future. "This was existence as Hitler had promised it," and this was the New Reich that would grow ever stronger and invincible under guidance of a Fuehrer who would scrap the Treaty of Versailles and restore his adopted country to the sovereignty it claimed. Dodd concluded that whether Hitler made his aggression outright or in the "guise of repelling an invader," he could count on the overwhelming majority of Germans for support "in any measure he might undertake."[144]

Such warnings, combined with newly critical developments, did bestir the American government to some response to Germany's challenges. The first undertaking was the Buenos Aires Conference.

Since the late 1920's the United States had been moving toward a policy of nonintervention, that is, not landing troops, in Latin America. At the Seventh International Conference of American States in Montevideo in December 1933, the United States agreed with the participating nations not to intervene in one another's foreign or domestic affairs, appending only an ambiguous reservation allowing America to pursue such policy as had prevailed since Roosevelt's inauguration. The Senate approved the agreement in June 1934 and Roosevelt proclaimed it in January 1935.[145] From the time of the Montevideo Conference, the Latin American countries wanted the United States to go one step further and renounce its reserved claim to use of force in instances that threatened American lives or property.[146] From 1935 on the State Department, alarmed over the political, economic, and ideological inroads Germany was making in Latin America through barter arrangements, radio and news service propaganda, and even exchange training programs for military personnel, sought a conference to strengthen friendship with and among the Latin American countries. Hence on January 30, 1936, Roosevelt proposed to the presidents of the Latin American countries that they meet in Argentina at a special conference to determine how peace among the countries might best be safeguarded, and in August the

144. Dodd to Hull, Sept. 18, 1936, *FR 1936*, II, 149–156.
145. Edward O. Guerrant, *Roosevelt's Good Neighbor Policy* (Albuquerque, N.M., 1950), 6–8; text of the convention in *Peace and War*, 199–204.
146. Bryce Wood, *The Making of the Good Neighbor Policy* (New York, 1961), 118–119.

president of Argentina, Augustín P. Justo, issued the formal invitation to confer in Buenos Aires beginning on December 1.[147]

Roosevelt did not expect the conference to alter German policy. A week before he sailed on his dramatic seven-thousand-mile battleship voyage to address the delegates, he told Dodd that the visit would have "little practical or immediate effect in Europe but at least the forces of example will help if the knowledge of it can be spread down to the masses of the people in Germany and Italy."[148] Greeted by a cheering crowd of over half a million people on November 30, Roosevelt next day told the opening session of the conference that other nations were constructing vast supplies of arms to create "false employment." These nations, he warned, would one day have to choose between using the weapons against each other or allowing unsound economies to collapse "like a house of cards." The Americas, he said, whether or not involved in future wars, would suffer. Perhaps the nations of the New World could help the Old World avert disaster by demonstrating to any nation "driven by war madness or land hunger" that aggression would find a hemisphere prepared to consult for mutual safety and good.[149]

Following Roosevelt's address Hull proposed that the attending nations agree to compulsory consultation among their foreign ministers in event of a threat to the hemisphere. The proposed agreement also called for a permanent Inter-American Consultative Committee and outlined a neutrality policy—including an arms embargo—in event of war.[150] The United States had balked at a compulsory consultative pact at the Geneva Disarmament Conference in 1933; now Latin American countries opposed the American plan. The leading critic was the foreign minister of Argentina, Carlos Saavedra Lamas, who in 1936 had presided over the League of Nations, and earlier had won the Nobel Prize for a special Anti-War Treaty signed in Rio de Janeiro in 1933. Saavedra Lamas was for the League first and Pan Americanism second. He would not endorse a consultative pact that he thought detracted from the League, and he would not agree to an embargo that ran counter to the League policy of permitting arms shipments to nations under

147. Hull, *Memoirs,* I, 494–496.
148. Roosevelt to Dodd, Nov. 9, 1936, Roosevelt papers, PSF, Germany: William E. Dodd.
149. *PPFDR,* V, 604–610.
150. Hull, *Memoirs,* I, 498.

attack. Hull and Saavedra Lamas held several conferences, and in the end they exchanged sharp words and parted on bad terms.[151]

The compromise the delegates reached was closer to Saavedra Lamas' position than Hull's, but marked important gains for American foreign policy. The Convention for the Maintenance, Preservation, and Reestablishment of Peace provided for consultation if the American Republics were menaced, or if war broke out between American nations, or if international war menaced their peace. In the latter case the consulting nations could "if they so desire" determine necessary cooperative measures to preserve peace in the Americas.[152] (The Argentinians had insisted on the phrase "if they so desire," causing Hull to feel they had emasculated the resolution.)[153] The convention affirmed a neutrality policy, but allowed the nations to act in accord with their League obligations and domestic laws. Hull's plan for a permanent Inter-American Consultative Committee was dropped. In return the United States in another and famous resolution agreed with other nations not to intervene "directly or indirectly, and for whatever reason, in the internal or external affairs of any of the other Parties."[154]

Despite Hull's pique with the Argentinians, and his failure to achieve all his goals, the Buenos Aires conference was a success for American policy and looked to further achievement at the Eighth International Conference of American States in Lima in December 1938.[155] Here the United States again ran into Argentine opposition and had to accept a morally binding declaration rather than a treaty. But the Latin American nations adhered to a Declaration of Lima in which, carrying out the Buenos Aires decisions, they agreed that their foreign ministers would consult, on initiative of any one of them, in event of a threat

151. Sumner Welles, *Seven Decisions That Shaped History* (New York, 1950), 104–105. Welles, at the time assistant secretary of state, and a member of the delegation, interpreted for Hull and notes that at the last meeting he had to temper Hull's remarks to Saavedra Lamas "to prevent an open brawl."

152. *Report of the Delegation of the United States of America to the Inter-American Conference for the Maintenance of Peace, Buenos Aires, Argentina, December 1–23, 1936* (Washington, D.C., 1937), 116–124.

153. *Memoirs*, I, 500.

154. *Report of the Delegation*, 124–131; see also Pratt, *Hull*, I, 169–172.

155. In 1944 Welles, *Time for Decision*, 206, said the Buenos Aires conference was "intrinsically the most important inter-American gathering that has ever taken place."

from abroad.[156] This decision marked the first time these countries had agreed to work together in the face of foreign encroachments, and the arrangement greatly facilitated cooperative defense measures prior to and during the Second World War.[157]

The Germans, meanwhile, had made little headway, Nazi propaganda activities notwithstanding. In 1937 they recognized that their effort to get the Latin American nations, especially Argentina, Brazil, and Chile, to sign the Anti-Comintern Pact was futile.[158] And in August 1938 the ambassador to Argentina, Edmund von Thermann, told the Foreign Ministry that he and his colleagues in Brazil, Chile, and Uruguay were convinced that Germany could not combat the United States politically in South America and would have to confine itself to economic and cultural efforts.[159] The most any German diplomat could say was that the Lima Declaration, directed against Germany, was "a poor substitute for a military alliance."[160]

Shortly after the war began, in September 1939, the Declaration of Panama announced the neutrality of the American nations, excluding Canada, and by the Declaration of Havana of July 1940, the American nations declared they would not allow transfer of any colony in the Western Hemisphere from one non-American country to another. Germany could not gain control of Dutch and French possessions in the New World.[161] The Havana Conference marked the end of effective German influence on the American continent.[162]

The United States before December 1941 arranged executive agreements with eleven Latin American countries, providing for military defense missions. After America entered the war every Latin American nation (including Argentina at the late date of March 24, 1945) declared war on the Axis powers. To its credit the Roosevelt administration, in what was undoubtedly its most ambitious and successful

156. *Peace and War*, 436–440.

157. Guerrant, *Roosevelt's Good Neighbor Policy*, 139–141; for details of wartime measures, see Pratt, *Hull*, II, 677–717.

158. Frye, *Nazi Germany and the American Hemisphere*, 101–102.

159. Thermann to Foreign Ministry, Aug. 2, 1938, *DGFP*, D, V, 863–868.

160. Noebel to Foreign Ministry, Dec. 28, 1938, *ibid.*, 885–886. Edward Noebel was minister to Peru.

161. Guerrant, *Roosevelt's Good Neighbor Policy*, 143, 150–154; Havana Declaration in *Peace and War*, 562–563.

162. Friedländer, *Hitler et les Etats-Unis*, 109.

response to German foreign policy, had begun in 1936 to convert the Monroe Doctrine into a defensive alliance. This development could not change the course of German, or world, history.

The second of Roosevelt's undertakings to proscribe German advances was neither policy nor procedure but one of his typical ventures in personal diplomacy.

In the midst of the Rhineland crisis the President asked Dodd to notify him immediately of any opportunity during the present unpredictable events where "a gesture, an offer or a formal statement by me would, in your judgment, make for peace," which would be just and would "endure without threat for more than a week or two."[163] That proper moment did not arrive; Dodd sent no word. Roosevelt did not give up on his idea. Following Dodd's vacation in the United States in the late spring and early summer of 1936, the President wrote him asking "in the utmost confidence" what he thought would happen if he, Roosevelt, were "personally and secretly" to ask Hitler to outline the limit of German foreign policy over the next ten years, and if Hitler would "have any sympathy with a general limitation of armaments proposal."[164] Dodd, ever eager to see the United States undertake a constructive policy, was convinced the "animosity here is such that one may not easily get a quiet answer to such an inquiry as you suggest," but he visited Schacht on August 18, reporting back that mere mention of Roosevelt's plan brought about repetition of German demands "for expansion and colonies."[165]

Dodd continued his assignment. He visited Dieckhoff, Ribbentrop's brother-in-law and then director of Department III in the Foreign Ministry, which encompassed the British Empire, United States, Far East, Central and South America, and colonial matters. Dodd considered Dieckhoff "the most sympathetic representative of the Government in the Foreign Office," but, as he reported, frank discussion led both men to conclude that Hitler would not attend any conference outside of

163. Roosevelt to Dodd, Mar. 16, 1936, *FDRL*, I, 571.

164. Roosevelt to Dodd, Aug. 5, 1936, *FDRL*, I, 606. Roosevelt sent carbon copies to Hull, Phillips, and Moore, Roosevelt papers, PSF, Germany: William E. Dodd.

165. Dodd to Roosevelt, Aug. 19, 1936, Roosevelt papers, PSF, Germany: William E. Dodd.

Germany. Further, Dodd added, Hitler would accept nothing less than subordination of the Balkans to Germany.[166] Dodd next saw Neurath, who said that Germany would have nothing to do with a Locarno or world peace conference "unless the main points are agreed to beforehand." This, Dodd wrote, meant granting colonies to Germany and Italy and condemning the Franco-Soviet rapprochement.[167]

Two months later Dodd made his last conciliatory efforts. He called on Dieckhoff early in December and asked what would be Germany's response if the Buenos Aires Conference called for a world peace conference. Dieckhoff thought the idea had possibilities, especially if Roosevelt asked for the conference. Dodd was skeptical and told Roosevelt that in truth no one, not even the Foreign Ministry, could predict Hitler's response. The ambassador believed that "Hitler is simply waiting for his best opportunity to seize what he wants."[168] Two days before the year's end Dodd again visited Schacht. Response to inquiries about possibilities of a world peace conference, perhaps in the spring or summer of 1937, Dodd wrote Hull, was the same: Germany would not consider any conference until guaranteed colonies.[169]

Dodd abandoned hope that Roosevelt might summon a conference that would include Germany and lead to lasting settlement. He explained his reasoning in a thirty-five-page report to the State Department, a report Assistant Secretary Moore thought important enough to send to Roosevelt at the White House and to then report back to Dodd that the State Department wished to commend him and his staff for their analysis.[170]

166. Dodd to Roosevelt, Sept. 21, 1936, Roosevelt papers, PSF, Germany: William E. Dodd. See also entry for Sept. 16, 1936, Dodd, *Diary*, 351–353, and Dieckhoff Memorandum, Sept. 17, 1936, *DGFP*, C, V, 979.

167. Dodd to Roosevelt, Oct. 19, 1936, DS, 862.00/3616½. See also Neurath Memorandum, Oct. 16, 1936, *DGFP*, C, V, 1103.

168. Dodd to Roosevelt, Dec. 7, 1936, Roosevelt papers, PSF, Germany: William E. Dodd. (Dodd sent this letter enclosed in another to Moore dated Dec. 8.) See also entry for Dec. 5, 1936, Dodd, *Diary*, 351–354, and Dieckhoff Memorandum, Dec. 5, 1936, *DGFP*, D, III, 153–154.

169. Dodd to Hull, Dec. 31, 1936, Hull papers, Box 40. See also entry for Dec. 29, 1936, Dodd, *Diary*, 376–377.

170. Dodd to Hull, Nov. 28, Moore to Roosevelt, Dec. 30, 1936, and Moore to Dodd, Jan. 6, 1937, DS, 762.00/140. Doubtless members of the embassy worked on the report, but the approach to the subject—"A Survey of German National Socialist Foreign Policy"—and the manner and style of presentation were strictly Dodd's.

Foreign statesmen, Dodd began in this report dated November 28, 1936, had been viewing each new bold German move with surprise and dismay "as though it were something which, having no particular precedent, simply could not be true." The only thing surprising about Hitler's maneuvers, he said, was the exact time and manner in which they were carried out. Everything Hitler had done followed *Mein Kampf* "and will do so increasingly." There was no reason to doubt that Nazi foreign policy would continue to follow the fundamentals of *Mein Kampf* and "there is even less reason for guessing at what the National Socialist government has in mind for the future." After analytical comparison of *Mein Kampf*, the 1920 National Socialist party platform, and the present one, Dodd explained how Europe's statesmen played into Hitler's hands. The Anglo-German Naval Agreement, he said, went along with Hitler's strategy of rapprochement with England and at the same time "gave Germany domination of the Baltic and *de facto* recognition" of the breaching of the Treaty of Versailles. French prestige, diminished because England had acted alone, suffered greater impairment by the Rhineland occupation which "shut off France from her eastern allies" and ended French hegemony in Central Europe. Hitler's practical successes "convinced the dubious elements of the army, headed by General von Fritsch . . . of the national efficacy of the party." In this manner Dodd continued to analyze Hitler's success in winning Mussolini's friendship and committing their two countries in Spain, and in creating an anticommunist front that served as an anti-Semitic weapon and as a tool to isolate the Soviet Union from Western Europe. As for the future, Dodd said, "there does not appear to be any vital force or combination of forces which will materially impede Germany in the pursuit of her ambitions." Possibly Hitler would run into trouble at home or in Spain, or Mussolini would prove an unreliable friend, but this seemed improbable. Hitler was an "instinctively adroit opportunist, and a devout student of the methods of Frederick Wilhelm I, during whose reign Germany's power, without resort to war, flourished as it never has since." The same principles were at work in the mid-1930's, Dodd warned, and "Germany will realise her aims without war, if possible, if not——."

This analysis, simple, direct, suffered only in that what its author saw as obvious other men could not or would not see. Whatever the case, American diplomats, even those who recognized the truth of Dodd's assertions, had no answer for problems that German foreign policy imposed on the world. Whether Germany's leaders wished to listen or take seriously an American effort is questionable. Just after Roosevelt's Chautauqua speech in August Luther cynically reported that it was the work of "this experienced mass psychologist" whose nation had subdued a continent through wars and broken treaties, but that if the speech signified anything it was "a definite departure from the . . . spirit that brought America into the World War." When the Foreign Ministry queried the ambassador about Dodd's soundings, he reported that the State Department had not inspired them but rather they stemmed from Roosevelt's informal requests to his ambassadors to seek means of peace through better distribution of the world's economic resources; Roosevelt would undertake no peace initiative, he said, and Americans regarded Europe's political problems as "hopeless."[171] Later in October and again in November, Rudolf Leitner, the chargé from the Washington embassy who was now senior counselor on American affairs in the Foreign Ministry, reported that relations between the United States and Germany were worse than ever and there were no signs of improvement.[172] And at the end of the year Hassell told William Phillips, now ambassador to Italy, that if Roosevelt wanted to do anything for the world peace he ought to send two men he trusted to Germany and Italy; they would see things diffierently after being there.[173]

For the moment the President and his advisers had given up on any American intervention in Europe's affairs. But in a short while they would weigh and consider several schemes, only to find they offered too little too late. For the ambassador in Berlin, too, time was running out.

171. Luther to Foreign Ministry, Aug. 18 and Oct. 24, 1936, *DGFP,* C, V, 915–917, 1141–1142.
172. Leitner Memoranda, Oct. 27 and Nov. 20, 1936, GFM, 2422/D511347-D511348, 2422/D511350.
173. Hassell to Foreign Ministry, Dec. 23, 1936, GFM, 2422/D511355-D511356.

# 7. INVITATIONS DECLINED

Rumors were current late in 1936 and throughout 1937 that American diplomats, their aloofness and near estrangement during the past four years notwithstanding, planned to intervene in the diplomatic affairs of the Old World. Norman Davis, now far more against German policy than he had been in 1933, thought that an effort by Roosevelt to halt the arms race, or to secure an international embargo against an aggressor, would be futile. "It is not possible to reason with Dictators like Hitler or Mussolini," he wrote Hull in November 1936, "who have a frankenstein that forces them to keep on the move."[1] A month later, from Warsaw, Ambassador John Cudahy worriedly wrote Roosevelt that a Wilsonian pronouncement would be forgotten in two weeks, and it would be a grave mistake to intervene without a program to improve economic conditions in Germany, where "a proud, capable, ambitious and warlike people . . . are denied a full and happy life while . . . the Russians, crude and uncouth, three hundred years behind present day civilization, are in possession of the wealth of an empire. The day of reckoning is coming on this issue." Roosevelt replied that he agreed with Cudahy's conclusions, but reassured him that he did not contemplate "any move of any kind in Europe—certainly under the conditions of the moment."[2] When a few European diplomats in January 1937 approached William Bullitt, now ambassador to France, to inquire if

1. Davis to Hull, Nov. 17, 1936, Hull papers, Box 40.
2. Cudahy to Roosevelt, Dec. 26, 1936, and Roosevelt to Cudahy, Jan. 15, 1937, *FR 1937*, I, 24–27.

rumors about American intervention were true, he replied only "that God and the United States help those who help themselves."[3]

To be sure, there would be no startling developments on the horizon of American diplomacy in 1937. But more than once the President, top State Department officials, and others in high circles of the administration considered schemes to circumscribe the demands and undertakings of German foreign policy. These schemes ranged from secret bilateral negotiations with the British, to unilateral declarations, to contemplating an international conference to meet at the White House. Each effort failed, revealing imprecise thinking, poor planning, and a cleavage among diplomats in Washington and between American diplomats and their European counterparts. Combined with the embarrassing circumstances that surrounded Dodd's recall from Berlin at the end of the year, the events of 1937 demonstrated how unprepared the American democracy was to meet the problems Germany posed for it and the rest of the world.

Hitler proclaimed to the Reichstag on January 30, 1937, that the new year would see no German undertaking as dramatic as the announcement of rearmament or the Rhineland occupation, that "the time of the so-called surprises has ended."[4] He kept his word for a year. Political consolidation at home, determining the long- and short-range limits, objectives, and alternatives in German foreign policy, and, above all, courting Benito Mussolini, were the primary items on the agenda for 1937. In fact, between January and June, Hitler sent Göring, Neurath, and Blomberg on visits to the Italian dictator. The visits were not unqualified successes; Mussolini was not yet ready to surrender his role as guarantor of Austrian independence or to cast his lot wholly with Hitler. But the talks did produce international uncertainty about Italy's future position with regard to Austrian independence, and in September Mussolini would undertake a fateful trip to Germany.[5]

While the Germans pressed their attentions on the Italians, American

3. Bullitt to Moore, Jan. 8, 1937, Moore papers, Box 3.

4. Text of speech in Baynes, ed., *Hitler's Speeches*, II, 1334–1347. Luther reported that the Americans were pleased with the conciliatory tone of the speech but the State Department still maintained a "cool reserve." Luther to Foreign Ministry, Feb. 3, 1937, GFM, 2422/D511358.

5. Bullock, *Hitler*, 312–314; Watt, "Rome-Berlin Axis," *Review of Politics*, 532; Ulrich Eichstadt, *Von Dollfuss zu Hitler: Geschichte des Anschlusses Österreichs, 1933–1938* (Wiesbaden, 1955), 220–229.

diplomats considered what role their own nation might now take in world affairs. Shortly after Hitler's Reichstag address, Hugh Wilson, minister to Switzerland, wrote Hull that he thought he detected in Hitler's thinking "a slow evolution in favor of better understanding with his neighbors," and for this reason he hoped that the British and the French would look favorably on Hitler's moderation, continue to seek a peaceful settlement, and show whatever sympathy they could for the German point of view.[6] The State Department apparently was of like mind, prepared to adopt a sympathetic attitude toward the German point of view as the basis for an American contribution to Europe's search for peace.

In a long secret memorandum drawn up for Davis in mid-February 1937, the Division of Western European Affairs weighed the possibilities of an American "Contribution to a Peace Settlement," taking for granted that the United States had an "indirect interest" only in the political settlement of Europe as opposed to a "direct interest" in the resolution of the turmoil in the Far East. Approaching their subject historically, the experts declared that Germany after the World War had been "shorn of colonial resources" and "hampered by treaty shackles" which National Socialism "set out to throw off." Amidst crisis, National Socialism "naturally" began to look abroad. In a word, Germany had to fight against a political *status quo* and a much more serious economic *status quo*. Germany was at the center of the problem of war and peace; a solution in favor of peace lay in the answer to this question: "Can a compromise be found, or a price paid, which will satisfy the economic necessities of the German people, without war, and without making Germany paramount on the continent? If so, there will be no war: if no, war is possible, if not probable." The "immediate objective" of American intervention, the memorandum confirmed, was to precipitate events that would lead to a general political and economic settlement "which would obviate the necessity for Germany to strike out to obtain resources of raw materials in markets deemed by German leaders necessary to maintain the standard of living of the German people." Davis was to begin the "preliminary spade work" in "strictest confidence," using negotiations for naval limitation as a "screen."[7]

6. Wilson to Hull, Feb. 4, 1937, *FR 1937*, I, 39.
7. Department of State, Division of Western European Affairs, Memorandum for the Honorable N. H. Davis, Feb. 16, 1937, Davis papers, Box 24.

While the State Department deliberated, Secretary of the Treasury Morgenthau urged Roosevelt to take initiative. Morgenthau was convinced that Hull's strictures were insufficient to meet the new and ugly challenge of European fascism. And although he dared not tell the President, he thought that neither Hull nor Davis would ever find a solution to the armaments race because "they just don't have guts enough."[8] At a meeting with Roosevelt on February 9, Morgenthau suggested he be allowed to make a confidential overture to Britain's chancellor of the Exchequer, Neville Chamberlain. Roosevelt agreed.[9] Encouragingly, according to Ambassador Bingham in London, leading members of Parliament, and the army and navy, were doing everything possible to express good will toward the United States; in fact, he said, government officials in daily contact with the Embassy had publicly and privately demonstrated "almost bewildering friendliness that cannot pass unnoticed."[10]

Morgenthau conferred with Kenneth Bewley, the British commercial attaché who was slated to return to London shortly. First he explained he spoke confidentially, and at Roosevelt's behest, and asked Bewley to ask Chamberlain if he had any suggestions to help halt the armaments race and its ensuing financial crises. He also offered to have a destroyer escort Bewley home. At a second meeting Morgenthau indicated that Roosevelt thought some bold Anglo-American initiative might preserve peace in Europe, and that they would like Chamberlain's views on the matter.[11]

When Chamberlain received the oral message he referred it to the foreign secretary, Eden, who consulted Ambassador Lindsay in Washington. In December 1936 Lindsay had indicated that Roosevelt might be thinking of a conference to "pillory Hitler," and he advised his superiors in London to do nothing to discourage the effort.[12] Now, early in March 1937, he thought that the "extraordinarily youthful and sensitive" America would be flattered to cooperate with Great Britain, and

8. Entry for Feb. 6, 1937, Morgenthau Diary, as cited in Blum, *Morgenthau Diaries,* 457.

9. Entry for Feb. 9, 1937, Morgenthau Diary, as cited *ibid.,* 457–458.

10. Bingham to Roosevelt, Jan. 5, 1937, Roosevelt papers, PSF, Great Britain: Robert Bingham.

11. Eden, *Facing the Dictators,* 597.

12. *Ibid.,* 596.

conversely, hurt if cooperation were withheld. On the whole Lindsay thought his country should abstain from taking initiative with the United States on a major political issue. Eden conferred as well with Bingham, who said he did not believe the time for American initiative had come. Eden concurred, stating that premature effort might cause Germany to believe England's increased armaments program a bluff.[13]

Eden drafted the formal reply, bearing Chamberlain's signature, which reached the United States at the end of March. The British ruled out a disarmament conference and declared the main source of war fears to be German determination to be so strong that no one could oppose whatever demands it might make for European or colonial territory. By way of recommending American action, the British opined that an embargo was an indirect "but potent encouragement to aggression" and said that the "greatest single contribution" the United States could make to the peace effort would be to amend the neutrality legislation, which was, interestingly, exactly what Bingham had advised in his recent letter to Roosevelt. Further, Chamberlain proposed that America lend a hand in the Far East. The German-Japanese agreement, he said, indicated that if England were seriously involved in Europe, it could not count even on Japanese neutrality. Anything the United States could do to "stabilize the situation in the Far East *pro tanto*" would be of great help. So would the conclusion of an Anglo-American commercial agreement.[14]

Morgenthau referred this response to the State Department and within two days Economic Adviser Feis had drafted a reply to two of Chamberlain's three proposals. He said it was "not easy to estimate" why the British said the neutrality legislation encouraged aggression. Regardless, new legislation before Congress would allow the President to place goods other than war matériel on a cash-and-carry basis, and although even this procedure might make the British position in time of war "somewhat less advantageous than it would have been were there no such legislation," it was an improvement over a total embargo. As for a trade agreement, Feis caustically noted that the British "could share more vigorously" in the effort to lower trade barriers generally

13. *Ibid.,* 598–599.
14. *Ibid.,* 597; Chamberlain to Morgenthau, undated, *FR 1937,* I, 98–102; see also Blum, *Morgenthau Diaries,* 463–466.

by modifying their "restrictive schemes of production in rubber and tin, which produce extortion and crisis," and by liberalizing their preferential tariff policies within the empire.[15]

More than six weeks elapsed before Hull and Welles, now under secretary, prepared a reply to Chamberlain which agreed in the main with Feis. In a slightly miffed tone they declared that if the United States appeared to emphasize, more than England, the economic aspect of things, it was not because Americans minimized political or military matters but because "broadened trade relations ease political tensions." On the crucial matters of neutrality legislation and the Far East the diplomats were defensive or evasive. They contended that the new neutrality law of May 1 gave the President "considerable discretion": when he found a state of war between nations, only arms, ammunition, and implements of war would be embargoed; in case the security of the United States demanded it, he could place all other goods on a cash-and-carry basis, that is, insist that title to the goods transfer to the belligerents before the goods left port, and he could also prohibit shipment of certain goods in American vessels. In event of aggression in the Far East, the United States would do as much as possible "within the limits of our general policy" to protect American interests, "but we are not, as we assume the British Government would not be, in position to state in advance what methods of protection this country would employ." Further, Hull and Welles said, forces were apparently at work within and between China and Japan "operating in the direction of peace." At the moment they could not say anything definite about a trade agreement, but it seemed "wholly within the range of practical possibilities." Welles forwarded this draft message to Roosevelt, who approved it. No one, he informed Welles after reading the eleven pages of the text, could possibly object to them: "They are completely pious—I can think of no other characteristic."[16] At Hull's request, Ambassador Lindsay called at the State Department on the morning of June 1, where he received America's "completely pious" answer.[17]

If Roosevelt and the State Department were thinking seriously about

15. Feis Memorandum, Apr. 1, 1937, DS, 740.00/184.
16. Welles to Roosevelt, May 27, and Roosevelt Memorandum for Welles, May 28, 1937, DS, 740.00/184.
17. Hull Memorandum, June 1, 1937, DS, 740.00/184; text of the informal State Department note appears in *FR 1937*, I, 102–106.

a joint venture with the British, the reply to Chamberlain was curious, especially in view of Davis' activities in London at this time. In May he told Eden that Roosevelt would be glad to see either him or Chamberlain, who would become prime minister at the end of the month, visit the United States, perhaps in the fall after Congress had adjourned.[18] Washington diplomats had reason to believe that important members of the British government favored such a venture. That same month Eden told Bingham he would heartily welcome an invitation to the United States, and Bingham in reporting this to Roosevelt added that Eden, "highly intelligent, candid and sincere," was unlike some of his countrymen in that he expected his own country "to do its full share instead of expecting, as some of them do, to receive and not to give." Two weeks later Bingham reported that currently the British were campaigning to "persuade the United States . . . that the frontier of democracy lies somewhere in the North Sea." Personally, the ambassador added, he did not think the United States could contribute more than economic agreements and discretionary neutrality laws to European peace efforts "without raising false hopes on this side of the Atlantic."[19]

Chamberlain and Eden discussed the matter with Bingham, who agreed that neither of them should go to the United States unless the journey seemed likely to produce results.[20] Chamberlain then replied to Davis that a visit would be feasible only if so carefully planned that there was little or no chance it would disappoint high expectations. Davis forwarded the letter to Roosevelt, who on July 28 wrote Chamberlain that he accorded fully with his receptive but cautious attitude. On the assumption that steps could be taken, Roosevelt invited Chamberlain to come to America early in autumn and said that in the interim he would welcome "any suggestions as to additional preparatory steps that might be taken as between ourselves in the near future to expedite progress towards [the] desired goal."[21]

Roosevelt's letter did not reach Chamberlain, vacationing in Scot-

---

18. Eden, *Facing the Dictators,* 601. Eden adds that Davis' "good intentions outran his discretion," for Roosevelt had intended an invitation be extended to Chamberlain only.
19. Bingham to Roosevelt, May 22 and June 5, 1937, Roosevelt papers, PSF, Great Britain: Robert Bingham.
20. Eden, *Facing the Dictators,* 601.
21. Roosevelt to Chamberlain, July 28, 1937, *FR 1937,* I, 113. Chamberlain's letter of July 8 is not in the State Department files but is summarized in Roosevelt's letter.

land, until late August, and he decided not to answer until he returned to London. When he wrote on September 28, he told Roosevelt that whatever earlier enthusiasm he might have had was now diminished. He said that although the democracies and totalitarian states were far from resuming cordial relations, "at the same time various circumstances have combined to ease the tension and to encourage the friends of peace." Still, Japan and China were at war and the situation in the Far East had deteriorated so that there was "little prospect of being able to improve it by action on the part of the Western powers." Circumstances made a meeting impossible between the two heads of state; it would be necessary to wait a little longer.[22]

The Americans would raise the matter sooner than Chamberlain was aware, but meantime events would demonstrate how valuable an autumn meeting might have been. Eden, who favored a conference but acted cautiously enough to discourage one, writes in his memoirs that the British had no alternative but to reject a conference, although he regrets he did not visit the United States in 1937, "for if the meeting had met with some success, its steadying effect upon the dictators could have been important."[23] How much success and importance can only be conjecture, but the meeting might have prevented the failure of the forthcoming Brussels Conference, and united Anglo-American policy in the Far East might have persuaded or allowed the English to take a stiffer position toward Germany in Europe. Such developments might have encouraged Mussolini, who at just this time was making vague overtures toward the United States, to resist Hitler's pressures, at least for a while longer.

Throughout Roosevelt's first term in office he and Mussolini had paid scant attention to each other. Roosevelt did not like Mussolini, but did not regard him, as he did Hitler, as a threat to civilization. Italy might overrun Ethiopia, but that was the extent of its military might. Whatever comparisons either of the two leaders or members of their governments might have made about efforts of the New Deal and Italian fascism to

22. Chamberlain to Roosevelt, Sept. 28, 1937, *ibid.*, 131–132. Hull, *Memoirs*, I, 549, says that on July 8 Chamberlain declined a future meeting with Roosevelt; Chamberlain did not do so, of course, until September, and Hull makes no mention of the intervening "pious" American note to Great Britain.
23. *Facing the Dictators*, 601.

cope with problems of an industrial society amidst economic collapse were meaningless. Between 1933 and 1936 the two heads of state made official exchanges only in 1933 when Breckinridge Long presented his credentials as ambassador to Italy, and in the summer of 1935 when Mussolini rejected Roosevelt's appeal to seek a peaceful solution to the crisis over Ethiopia. When Roosevelt won a landslide victory in November 1936, Mussolini took the occasion to write him personally. The dictator said he regretted that events had not allowed both men to pursue their first letters "with the continuity which was our intention." He congratulated Roosevelt upon re-election and hoped that "our relations, now reestablished, may not undergo any further interruption."[24]

Roosevelt put off responding and there might not have been a second Italian approach were it not for other events. First, on April 19, 1937, the British Laborite George Lansbury announced, after an interview with Hitler, that Germany would be "very willing" to attend a conference and take part in a united effort to establish world-wide economic cooperation and mutual understanding "if President Roosevelt or the head of another great country will take the lead in calling such a conference." The statement created a sensation, although Lansbury's enthusiasm for his own diplomatic effort went far beyond Hitler's interest in the proposal and the German press explained it was only a reaffirmation of an old principle, no departure.[25] In the *New York Times* one day later was a story that the Belgian prime minister, Paul van Zeeland, then touring Europe on a Mission to Investigate Obstacles to International Trade, and due to visit the United States June 18–June 20, had conferred with European leaders about the United States calling a world conference.

State Department officials opposed any such scheme. Feis said that for the United States to take responsibility in European affairs by convoking or even urging an international conference would be dangerous. Working out a program would be "quite impossible," as the failure in London in 1933 indicated. From the political point of view James C. Dunn, who had replaced Moffat as chief of the Division of Western European Affairs, agreed that the United States could not take initia-

---

24. Mussolini to Roosevelt, Nov. 19, 1936, *FR 1937,* I, 662–664.
25. Arnold J. Toynbee, ed., *Survey of International Affairs, 1937,* 2 vols. (London, 1938), I, 32; Schmidt, *Statist auf diplomatischer Bühne,* 343–344.

tive, that economic agreement was "inconceivable" without political settlement, and that an economic conference could too easily become the forum for justification of rearmament programs some nations long had been carrying out and others were beginning.[26]

Amidst these rumors of conferences economic and political, Mussolini apparently had been trying to determine what new role, if any, the United States might play in European affairs. Early in April his foreign minister, Ciano, told Ambassador Phillips that Italy would support an American-sponsored conference to limit armaments.[27] Phillips relayed this information to Roosevelt a few weeks later, adding that Mussolini had said recently, "I must have peace."[28] About a month later Mussolini inquired of the publisher of the Chicago *Daily News*, Colonel Knox, who was interviewing him in Rome, what progress Roosevelt had made of late toward world peace.[29] Then on May 24 Mussolini granted an interview to William Philip Simms, foreign editor of the Scripps-Howard papers, and told him that "if Roosevelt would take the initiative of calling a conference for the limitation of armaments in the immediate future this gesture would certainly have a great success." Italy would back it to the "utmost." He emphasized that he spoke not of disarmament nor of reduction, but of future limitation.[30] Phillips at once cabled Hull—"deeply impressed"—that he hoped the proposal would be received sympathetically in the United States. He cautioned that a rebuff might jeopardize the policy of peace and cooperation to which Mussolini appeared to have committed himself in the statement to Simms.[31]

Nonetheless, the State Department publicly acknowledged Mussolini's comments only indirectly. At a press conference on May 26, Welles said he had read reports of the Simms interview with great in-

26. Feis Memorandum to Hull, Apr. 20, and Dunn Memorandum, Apr. 27, 1937, *FR 1937*, I, 652–655. England had just begun serious rearmament.
27. Memorandum Ciano-Phillips Conversation, Apr. 2, 1937, Phillips papers.
28. Phillips to Roosevelt, Apr. 2, 1937, Italian Diary, III, Phillips papers.
29. Phillips, who reported the conversation, deemed it so confidential that he avoided regular diplomatic channels and wrote a personal letter to Hull, May 20, 1937, Hull papers, Box 41.
30. Stephen Heald, ed., *Documents on International Affairs, 1937* (London, 1939), 286–287; a slightly different version appears in Phillips to Hull, May 25, 1937, *FR 1937*, I, 655–657.
31. Phillips to Hull, May 25, 1937, *FR 1937*, I, 657.

terest but that as Mussolini's message was not official, no comment was possible.[32] Privately Welles told the Italian ambassador in Washington, Augusto Rosso, who confirmed the authenticity of the interview, that he considered Mussolini's remarks highly important and encouraging and immediately authorized Phillips in Rome to inform the Italian government of the State Department's attitude. Phillips did so on May 29, asking Ciano what he and Mussolini had in mind with respect to an American initiative, so that Washington could take the next step. Ciano said he would have to speak with Mussolini, who was out of town for a few days.[33]

Whatever plans Mussolini might have been entertaining he apparently discarded, for on May 31 a lead editorial, regarded as speaking for him, in the *Giornale d'Italia* declared he had not invited Roosevelt to call a conference; rather, Simms had asked Italy's view if Roosevelt called a conference, and Mussolini replied only that such a move could be successful, and that Italy would support it.[34] Phillips, who at first found this new explanation "very puzzling," a few days later went to see Ciano, who told him that because London, Paris, and Moscow had not responded to the overture in the Mussolini-Simms interview, there was nothing else to do.[35] Phillips' conversations with officials at the British embassy in Rome confirmed that their government felt that their own armaments program, and a public hostile toward Italy, did not allow any response.[36]

There remained Mussolini's November 1936 letter to Roosevelt, who did not answer until July 29, 1937. Roosevelt explained he had delayed writing in hope the international situation would "clarify" itself, but unfortunately things had gone from bad to worse. He assured Mussolini they shared a fear that the present international trend was "ominous to peace," and he had frequently thought he would like to speak with him "frankly and in person." Nonetheless, Roosevelt concluded (and just one day after he had extended an invitation to Chamberlain to come to the United States), "international difficulties

32. *New York Times,* May 27, 1937; Welles to Phillips, May 27, 1937, *FR 1937,* I, 658.
33. Entries for May 28 and May 29, 1937, Italian Diary, IV, Phillips papers.
34. Phillips to Hull, May 31, 1937, *FR 1937,* I, 660.
35. Entries for May 31 and June 3, 1937, Italian Diary, IV, Phillips papers.
36. Phillips to Hull, June 4, 1937, *FR 1937,* I, 661.

as well as the distances of the Atlantic Ocean and the Mediterranean Sea" prevented a meeting.[37]

A little more than a month later, on September 4, the Italian government announced that Mussolini would journey to Germany. Three weeks later Hitler received the Italian dictator amidst enormous fanfare. There was little time for political talk, but Mussolini clearly was almost spellbound by the display of the industrial and military might of the Third Reich, and both he and Ciano were more firmly convinced of the advantages of pursuing a pro-German policy.[38] Five weeks later Ribbentrop went to Rome, where on November 6 Mussolini signed the Anti-Comintern Pact. The Duce also let it be known that although it was best not to aggravate matters and cause an international crisis, he was tiring of defending Austrian independence, that he had warned the Austrians he would do nothing in event of a crisis in their country and could not impose independence on it.[39]

These events marked the beginning of the surrender of Italian independence in foreign policy, the first step by Mussolini toward his inglorious demise, and a turning point in German foreign policy. Now Hitler, having maneuvered Italy out of the way in Eastern Europe, could sit down on November 5 with Neurath, Blomberg, and the commanders in chief of his armed forces and, although not positive of Italian response in every situation, discuss the cases in which their country might have to go to war for *Lebensraum*. The Fuehrer insisted that Germany could not fight later than 1943–1945, when its military power as opposed to that of other nations would have reached its peak. Civil war in France would provide an occasion for war, as would a war involving England and France against Italy growing out of tensions in the Mediterranean. In these cases, Germany would have to seize the opportune moment for strikes at Austria and Czechoslovakia.[40]

37. Roosevelt to Mussolini, July 29, 1937, *ibid.,* 662–664.

38. Schmidt, *Statist auf diplomatischer Bühne,* 365–370; entry for Sept. 29, 1937, Ciano, *Diary,* 16.

39. Bullock, *Hitler,* 315–316; Eichstadt, *Von Dollfuss zu Hitler,* 230–231.

40. The famous Hossbach Memorandum, Nov. 10, 1937, is in *DGFP,* D, I, 29–39. Hitler's explanation of alternatives is discussed in Bullock, Hitler, 367–371, and Robertson, *Hitler's Pre-War Policy,* 106–113. A. J. P. Taylor, *The Origins of the Second World War* (London, 1961), 131–135, disputes traditional interpretations and argues that Hitler's real purpose at this meeting was to isolate

One cannot say that international developments would have been much different had Mussolini visited the United States instead of Germany in the autumn of 1937. Roosevelt had no particular reason to invite him to America, and had he done so, and had the invitation been accepted, he undoubtedly would have run afoul of both isolationists and liberal interventionists. Roosevelt undoubtedly felt he had no meaningful proposals. Mussolini would have liked the United States to recognize Italy's conquest of Ethiopia, and Ambassador Phillips favored this, even though the prospect was "unpleasant."[41] But the American government had no current intention or desire to alter its position. There was little to discuss. Thus, when a reporter in mid-July queried Roosevelt about Mussolini's interest in a conference, Roosevelt replied that Europeans were increasingly looking to him to pull a rabbit out of a hat but "I haven't got a hat and I haven't got a rabbit in it."[42]

There is little reason to believe that Mussolini wanted a conference either, or that he could have been induced to alter his present course.[43] In particular, he showed no real interest in diplomatic reports from Washington and in September 1937 was denouncing the United States as a country of "niggers and Jews."[44] When Ribbentrop was in Rome to secure his signature to the Anti-Comintern Pact, which outwardly aligned Italy with Germany and Japan in a front that favored Japan over China, Mussolini remarked that the agreement would increase the ill-humor of the Americans, but again they "will do nothing."[45] Hence although Roosevelt and Hull might have given Mussolini some hint that the Atlantic and Mediterranean were easily traversed, and possibly strengthened his resistance to Hitler's advances, a real meeting of the

---

Schacht, who opposed increased expenditure on armaments, from other conservatives. No mention was made of the United States in any capacity, except in a fleeting reference to the vulnerability of the British empire; for example, the possibility of an American attack on Canada.

41. Phillips to Roosevelt, July 30, 1937, Roosevelt papers, PSF, Italy: William Phillips.

42. Quoted in Dorothy Borg, *The United States and the Far Eastern Crisis of 1933–1938: From the Manchurian Incident Through the Initial Stage of the Undeclared Sino-Japanese War* (Cambridge, Mass., 1964), 374.

43. Felix Gilbert, "Ciano and His Ambassadors," in Craig and Gilbert, eds., *The Diplomats,* 530–533.

44. Entries for Aug. 24 and Sept. 6, 1937, Ciano, *Diary,* 3, 9.

45. Entry for Nov. 6, 1937, Ciano, *Diplomatic Papers,* 142–143.

minds or concrete achievement at a conference were improbable. Events in the fall of 1937 would serve only to show how impotent the democracies had become in the face of aggression.

The efforts at tête à tête diplomacy during the spring and summer had gotten nowhere. At the same time members of the administration began to recognize that the further America removed itself from the world scene the more American interests were jeopardized. This observation seemed especially true for the Far East. Chinese and Japanese troops clashed near the Marco Polo Bridge outside Peiping on July 7, 1937, and despite a lull in the fighting the "incident" soon escalated into relentless undeclared war. Extreme caution marked the American response. Within a week Hull and the State Department replied to inquiries from the Chinese, Japanese, and English that although the United States supported efforts at preserving peace it did not believe it could undertake any useful action in the Far East and would not consider any form of mediation.[46] On July 16 Hull issued a statement urging peaceful solution of problems, which elicited silence from the Japanese, approval from the British, and delayed acknowledgment from the Germans.[47] According to Welles, around this time Roosevelt consulted him about the United States and Great Britain using their navies to force an embargo on Japan, but as so frequently happened with such Rooseveltian schemes, nothing proceeded beyond this initial stage.[48] Then in September, Hull and Davis approached the President to ask if he would make a speech about international cooperation on his forthcoming transcontinental trip. Roosevelt agreed, and the State Department complied wih his request for a draft.[49]

In Chicago on October 5, 1937, Roosevelt made his famous declaration, in a passage he had written, that "when an epidemic of physical disease starts to spread, the community approves and joins in a quarantine of the patients in order to protect the health of the commu-

46. Borg, *United States and Far Eastern Crisis,* 255–258.
47. Hull Statement in Bucknell Memorandum, July 16, and replies in Grew to Hull, July 19, Lindsay to Welles, Aug. 6, and Mayer to Hull, Aug. 9, 1937, *FR 1937,* I, 699–700, 703, 756, 768. See also entries for July 14 and July 20, 1937, Dodd, *Diary,* 423–424.
48. Sumner Welles, *Seven Decisions That Shaped History* (New York, 1950), 71.
49. Hull, *Memoirs,* I, 544–545.

nity against the spread of the disease." He also hinted at the message he had earlier tried to convey to Chamberlain by emphasizing the need for peace-loving nations to make a concerted effort to uphold laws and principles, to oppose treaty violations and inhumane action that created international anarchy and instability "from which there is no escape through mere isolation or neutrality."[50] National response to the address was mixed. Hearst newspapers and others of similar outlook assailed it, but enthusiasm came from many other papers, including several papers in midwestern strongholds of isolation, and numerous public and congressional leaders.[51] Roosevelt's advisers, including Hull, were pleased with the strong tone—at least at first.[52] Many foreign officials responded favorably. French Foreign Minister Yvon Delbos termed the address "magnificent," "an act of the highest importance," and Premier Camille Chautemps, declaring that he did not wish to embarrass Roosevelt by exaggerating the meaning of the address, said it was moral assistance and that he would give a great deal to sit down quietly with him and ask exactly what he had in mind when he spoke of a "concerted effort."[53] British Prime Minister Chamberlain publicly responded favorably, although privately he wrote that "it is always best and safest to count on nothing from the Americans but words."[54] The German ambassador, Dieckhoff, went to the State Department and asked for an "exact interpretation." Welles told him it spoke for itself, but that he might wish to give emphasis to the last paragraph, in which the President had said that America hated war and was searching for peace. Dieckhoff informed his superiors that the quarantine passage

50. *PPFDR*, V, 406–411. Dorothy Borg, "Notes on Roosevelt's 'Quarantine' Speech," *Political Science Quarterly*, LXXII (Sept. 1957), 413–417, explains that in piecing together the speech Roosevelt put his "quarantine" passage in place of one Davis had written that referred to America's willingness to fight for certain principles. Thus Roosevelt had toned down the speech.

51. Travis Beal Jacobs, "Roosevelt's Quarantine Speech," *The Historian*, XXIV (Aug. 1962), 489–499; Borg, "Roosevelt's 'Quarantine' Speech," *Political Science Quarterly*, 426–427.

52. Hull, *Memoirs*, I, 545, categorized response to the speech as "quick and violent," and said it set back the effort to educate the public "for at least six months." However, Hull and Moffat together watched the speech come over the ticker tape and Hull, at first, was "delighted" with Roosevelt's words. Diary entry for Oct. 5, 1937, Hooker, ed., *Moffat Papers*, 153.

53. Wilson to Hull, Oct. 6 and Oct. 7, 1937, *FR 1937*, I, 132–133, 135.

54. Quoted in Feiling, *Life of Chamberlain*, 325.

was Roosevelt's idea and that it was "aimed principally at Japan." Further, Roosevelt had made derogatory comments about dictators only to defend himself against similar reproaches at home. "Aggressor nations," the ambassador declared, "referred only to Japan, and perhaps to Italy." The United States had no intention of intervening in the Far East or in Europe, except—and this would be a recurrent theme in his reports over the next year and thereafter—in case of a world conflict involving Great Britain, in which case "the weight of the United States will be thrown into the scales on the side of the British at the very beginning of the conflict or shortly thereafter."[55] According to Kordt, Hitler took no note of the speech because of his low estimate of American power.[56] As will be seen, Hitler was also concerned with the possibility of German mediation of the Far East crisis.

It is difficult to say what Roosevelt had in mind when he made his address other than that he was searching for peace but had no program in mind. As he told reporters off-the-record the next day, sanctions were "out of the window."[57] The quick favorable response had caught him both without a plan and without endorsement and assistance of his advisers, and he retreated.[58] But though he had no plan for Asia or Europe he was willing to listen to ideas. And Welles had a plan; at least so Welles thought.

The under secretary had a special relationship with Roosevelt. Both came from New York's aristocracy; Welles had the same godmother as did Eleanor Roosevelt, and in 1905 at age thirteen had been a page at her wedding to the future President. Welles too went to Groton and Harvard, and then turned career diplomat, becoming the youngest division chief in State Department history when at age twenty-eight he became head of the Division of Latin American Affairs. He left diplomatic service in the mid-1920's but Roosevelt brought him back as assistant secretary in 1933. In April of that year Roosevelt sent him as ambassador to revolution-torn Cuba, only to have to recall him for

55. Welles Memorandum, Oct. 11, 1937, *FR 1937*, I, 138–139; Dieckhoff to Foreign Ministry, Oct. 15, 1937, *DGFP*, D, I, 639–641. See also Dieckhoff to Foreign Ministry, Oct. 7 and Oct. 9, 1937, *DGFP*, D, I, 633–634.
56. Kordt, *Wahn und Wirklichkeit*, 141.
57. Press Conference, Oct. 6, 1937, *PPFDR*, V, 414–425; Borg, "Roosevelt's 'Quarantine' Speech," *Political Science Quarterly*, 423–424.
58. Jacobs, "Roosevelt's Quarantine Speech," *Historian*, 500–501.

getting too involved in Cuban politics. Welles returned to his post as assistant secretary.[59] Following Phillips' departure as ambassador to Italy, Welles moved up to under secretary, after having won out over Hull's choice, Assistant Secretary R. Walton Moore.[60] Frequently Welles bypassed Hull in consulting Roosevelt, who apparently did not object to the procedure. Strikingly different in background and bearing, Welles and Hull often disagreed; Welles regarded himself as more of a realist and thought the United States ought to recognize Italy's conquest of Ethiopia, while Hull remained steadfastly opposed.[61] Their ten years of uneasy association would end in 1943 when Hull forced Roosevelt to request Welles's resignation by threatening his own, which Roosevelt could not afford at the time for political reasons.[62] In 1937, however, Welles had Roosevelt's ear.

The day after the quarantine message, Welles drew up a memorandum in which he suggested that Roosevelt ask the other governments of the world if they would participate in a conference, which America would call, to set principles in international relations, laws and customs of land and naval warfare, and rights and obligations of neutrals, and to guarantee freedom of access for all peoples to raw materials. This latter category was clearly of major importance to Welles—as his later memoranda would show—and he believed German and Italian, though probably not Japanese, cooperation could be secured at such a conference.[63] On October 8 he discussed his plan with Roosevelt, who liked the idea but wanted to move even more cautiously. Roosevelt preferred to approach other nations through regular diplomatic channels, and if they expressed interest the United States would work with a smaller group of powers in elaborating the principles of international conduct. These principles would be communicated to the other powers, and if a majority seemed in accord, then he would call a world conference.[64]

59. Bendiner, *Riddle of the State Department,* 150–159.
60. Pratt, *Hull,* II, 283–285.
61. Phillips too favored recognition and was distressed that he and Welles could not budge Hull, who in March 1938 told Phillips that world peace could be secured only through "international law and order." Entry for Mar. 24, 1938, Italian Diary, IV, Phillips papers.
62. Pratt, *Hull,* II, 615–616.
63. Welles Memorandum, Oct. 6, 1937, *FR 1937,* I, 665–666.
64. Welles Memorandum, Oct. 9, 1937, *ibid.,* 667.

Three days later Messersmith, who had returned from Austria to serve as assistant secretary, added his analysis. He told Hull he thought that Japan and Italy and the conflicts they had brought were important, but "the most important factor is still Germany." He insisted the conclusion was inescapable that "the United States are the ultimate object of the powers grouped in this new system of force and lawlessness," and that when the aggressors finally focused attention on the United States "that country will be practically alone for the rest will have been cleared out of the way." Then, in intelligible understatement he said the Department of State was the President's adviser and instrument through which American foreign policy was conducted, and it was the department's responsibility to face present dangers by designing long-range policy that looked at facts. He insisted that no matter how much Americans wished to be aloof or wished to find shelter behind neutrality legislation, they had to recognize that the question was whether to follow "a temporizing policy or one which really offers hope of maintaining peace." He concluded that the State Department bore heavy responsibility for "informing and guiding public opinion in its own interest."[65]

Hull took Messersmith's memorandum to Roosevelt, and it may well have persuaded him to allow Welles to expand their effort at a peace proposal in belief that German problems might now be solved through negotiation.[66] Hence Welles, after discussion, submitted to Roosevelt plans for a world peace conference, with an accompanying note recording even the ever-cautious Hull's approval of the plan as "entirely sound." Welles asked Roosevelt to summon to the White House on Armistice Day, November 11, the ambassadors of nations represented in the United States and propose that nations of the world meet in conference to achieve agreement on "essential and fundamental principles which should be observed in international relations," methods through which "all peoples may obtain the right to access upon equal and effective terms to raw materials and other elements necessary for their life," "methods by which international agreements may be pacifically revised," and finally, in event of war, neutral rights and obligations. There can be no doubt that emphasis on equal access to raw

65. Messersmith to Hull, Oct. 11, 1937, *ibid.,* 140–145.
66. Langer and Gleason, *Challenge to Isolation,* 22.

materials and pacific revision of treaties was an effort in the tradition of Woodrow Wilson. Welles was making an effort to appease Germany, for as he said in the note accompanying his outline, the statements were intended to, and "almost inevitably [would,] create a favorable reaction on the part of Germany." In fact, he was so concerned about making the lure attractive that in his final draft he said he felt it would be necessary for the President to declare that before lasting peace could be secured it would be necessary to "remove those inequities which exist by reason of the nature of certain settlements reached at the termination of the Great War." America, the President would have to add, could not play a part in determination of political readjustments, but these might be made more easily if the principles of international action were agreed to beforehand.[67] Roosevelt liked the scheme and told Welles he would revise the draft and return it in a day or two.[68]

The conclave Welles envisioned, which seemingly appealed to Roosevelt's sense of the dramatic, might have become reality had not Hull abruptly shifted his position from lukewarm acceptance to determined opposition. In a series of meetings with the President, Hull, at least as he later wrote, argued the entire project was "illogical and impossible," that a "peace congress" would serve only to "lull the democracies into a feeling of tranquility" when efforts should be directed toward rearmament, that the Axis powers would only laugh at the whole affair, that American public opinion needed to be aroused to the dangers abroad, not turned toward disarmament, which was "a completely collapsed movement." He said that in his statement of principles at a press conference on July 16, 1937, he had made America's attitudes and position clear on procedure in international conduct and need for every country to be economically stable.[69] Roosevelt discussed these objections with Welles, who did his "utmost" to persuade him to go through with the proposed conference.[70] Hull prevailed; Roosevelt abandoned the project.

67. Welles to Roosevelt, Oct. 26, 1937, *FR 1937*, I, 667–670.
68. Welles, *Seven Decisions*, 22.
69. *Memoirs*, I, 547–548. Hull's additional argument that the conference would have played into Axis hands "as completely as did the later neutrality policies of Belgium and Holland" is clearly after-the-fact reasoning.
70. Welles, *Seven Decisions*, 24.

Thirteen years afterward Welles in his chapter "The Last Frail Chance . . ." remarked with bitterness that he regretted few things so much as that an opportunity which Roosevelt "was so singularly qualified to grasp should thus have so needlessly been thrown away." Welles insisted his plan was not a "peace congress," and would not have lulled the democracies into tranquility. It was a "concrete proposal" which, had the Axis turned it down, would have served better than anything "to convince the democracies that isolation and neutrality in the modern world could never insure their safety."[71] The historian can only speculate about changes such a congress might have worked on ensuing events. Hull probably was right to oppose the conference, at least on the basis Welles proposed, although it is likely his opposition stemmed from fear that America would be going too far rather than not far enough, and also from pique at what he regarded as encroachment upon his jurisdiction. The Welles proposal lacked teeth, and Hull was not the man to add them. Emphasizing the need to remove the "inequities" of postwar settlements and assuring equal access to raw materials—which seemed to imply granting colonies to Germany—would scarcely have interested Hitler; in fact, the question of whether Germany was entitled to colonies was academic now because at that fateful November 5, 1937, meeting Hitler had underscored that Germany needed not colonies but Eastern Europe. Further, it is doubtful that America could have effected a change in the course of European events so long as it maintained it would have nothing to do with political problems. Perhaps the best proof of how little the Welles conference, however well intended, might have achieved was about to be demonstrated by events at Brussels.

On October 6 the League of Nations invited members who were signatories of the Nine Power Treaty of 1922, and other interested nations, to work out an agreement to end the Sino-Japanese war. After some maneuvering the meeting was set for Brussels, beginning November 3, with invitations extended at the request of the British and with American approval.[72] The Japanese did not attend. Hitler refused an invitation, although Welles, through Ambassador Dieckhoff,

---

71. *Ibid.*
72. Borg, *United States and Far Eastern Crisis*, 399–400.

made an effort to get German representation and insisted that the purpose of the conference was not to condemn Japan but to work out a constructive agreement.[73] Hitler's intentions were different. He had decided to do nothing to curb Japanese designs and he wanted the conference to collapse. In fact, he hoped that Italian accession to the Anti-Comintern Pact on November 6, three days after the conference had opened, would hasten that collapse.[74]

The Italians attended, but acted to obstruct. According to Ciano, they were sure Japan would triumph, and Mussolini looked upon the signing of the Anti-Comintern Pact as an anti-British maneuver which would help defeat the conference, as well as make up for the isolation Italy had felt since 1935 and the Ethiopian campaign.[75] Only Italy voted against a conference resolution of November 15 urging Japan to join in negotiations to end the war, and on November 29, less than a week after the conference had adjourned, Italy recognized Japan's conquest of Manchuria.[76]

The French were deeply worried about a Japanese thrust at Indochina, and had already prohibited shipment of supplies to Chiang Kai-shek over the Indochina railroad. They insisted the decision was irreversible unless the Nine Power Treaty signatories promised "physical support" against any Japanese reprisals. No one would offer such a guarantee before or during the Brussels talks.[77] Clearly the burden for achievement at Brussels rested with the United States and Great Britain.

According to Eden, some time after the July 7 clash Ambassador Bingham asked him if the British might want to enlist the United States in an embargo on trade with Japan. Eden referred the matter to Chamberlain, who said he hoped the proposal would go no further: it smacked of sanctions and would antagonize Japan and cost England

73. Dieckhoff to Foreign Ministry, Oct. 21, 1937, *DGFP*, D, I, 770–771.

74. Sommer, *Deutschland und Japan*, 66–67.

75. Entries for Sept. 16, Nov. 1, Nov. 2, Nov. 6, and Nov. 7, 1937, Ciano, *Diary*, 13, 27, 29; Memorandum Mussolini–Ribbentrop–Ciano Conversation, Nov. 6, 1937, Ciano, *Diplomatic Papers*, 142–143.

76. Entries for Nov. 14, Nov. 16, and Nov. 28, 1937, Ciano, *Diary*, 32–33, 38. The Scandinavian countries abstained, fearful the resolution implied future sanctions that would hurt them more than the great powers. Borg, *United States and Far Eastern Crisis*, 427.

77. Borg, *United States and Far Eastern Crisis*, 420–422, 634–635n66.

millions of dollars in Far East defense measures.[78] Clearly, judging from events surrounding Roosevelt's October 5 speech, the United States did not intend to push for sanctions against Japan. On October 19 Norman Davis, who headed the delegation to Brussels, went to Hyde Park to confer with Roosevelt. The President's sympathies were with China, and he said that if Japan refused all conciliation then other powers ought to give China all the supplies it needed and perhaps "ostracize Japan, break off relations," if the "overwhelming opinion of the world would support it." Then, after reminding Davis about public opinion in the United States, Roosevelt warned that the administration did not want to be "pushed out in front as the leader in, or suggestor of, future action"; nor could it appear to be "a tail to the British kite."[79]

Roosevelt's vagueness about specific intentions or undertakings stemmed from the fact that he wanted to do something to halt Japan, but did not know what, and from his fear of lack of support at home and abroad. Hull was even more cautious. Amidst rumors of various kinds about strong action against Japan, on November 15 he reminded Davis to limit himself to "a strong re-affirmation of the principles which should underlie international relationships."[80]

The British were equally uncertain and evasive. Chamberlain (with Eden's concurrence) had already turned down Roosevelt's invitation to visit the United States, opposed sanctions, and said the Americans could be counted on only for words. Eden meanwhile had been unsuccessful in efforts to get Neurath or Ciano to come to Brussels for talks with him.[81] Then on November 1, in a speech to Parliament, Eden declared his willingness to travel "not only from Geneva to Brussels, but from Melbourne to Alaska" if that would secure full

78. Eden, *Facing the Dictators*, 603–604.
79. Memorandum from the Files of President Roosevelt's Secretary, undated, *FR 1937*, IV, 85–86. See also Borg, *United States and Far Eastern Crisis*, 406–407.
80. Hull to Davis, Nov. 15, 1937, *FR 1937*, IV, 187–188.
81. Richthofen to Foreign Ministry, Oct. 27, and Hassell to Foreign Ministry, Oct. 29, 1937, *DGFP*, D, I, 20–21. (Herbert von Richthofen was German minister to Belgium.) See also entries for Oct. 28, Oct. 29, and Nov. 11, 1937, Ciano, *Diary*, 25–26, 31. Ciano at first wanted to meet with Eden—"It's a good way of shelving the Far East question—all the spotlights of the world will be on the Eden-Ciano meeting"—but Mussolini ruled against it. By November 11 Ciano had concluded that a meeting at Brussels would smack too much of "League atmosphere."

cooperation of the United States in a conference. During his first conversation with Davis in Brussels, Eden emphasized that his country based its policy on American policy, that it would support but not go further than American action, and that though the British fleet had to remain in Europe, England would consider moving a few ships about to influence the Japanese.[82]

A while later he indicated willingness to talk about sanctions, although he emphasized that the case of Italy demonstrated the futility of the kind of economic pressure Davis seemed to be talking about. Further, when Eden returned to London for consultation, Chamberlain said, "On no account will I impose a sanction!"[83] Eden did not report this remark to Davis, but on November 13 Ambassador Lindsay in Washington saw Welles, who indicated clearly that Davis' exploration of possibilities had gone beyond his instructions, and that there was no legislation that would authorize Roosevelt "to take part in any economic sanctions or in any of the other measures mentioned."[84] Two days later there followed Hull's telegram reminding Davis he had to restrict himself to discussing the principles of international relations.

The Brussels conference adjourned *sine die* on November 24. The British clearly were not ready to undertake sanctions or other coercive measures to halt Japan, at least not unless the United States forced the issue. American diplomats—perhaps Davis excepted on this matter— never intended to take the lead on their own, nor be a "tail to the British kite," nor do anything unless everyone else first proclaimed sanctions and thereby made it impossible for the United States to resist the movement. Even Roosevelt did not believe such a miracle would come to pass.[85] By failing to agree on concerted action, however, the United States and Great Britain were jointly responsible for throwing away what was, in Feis's postwar judgment, "the last good chance to work out a settlement between China and Japan."[86]

82. Eden speech in Heald, ed., *Documents 1937*, 60–70; Davis to Hull, Nov. 2, 1937, *FR 1937*, IV, 145–147.
83. Quoted in Eden, *Facing the Dictators*, 610–612.
84. Welles Memorandum, Nov. 13, 1937, *FR 1937*, IV, 152–155.
85. Borg, *United States and Far Eastern Crisis*, 439–440.
86. Herbert Feis, *The Road to Pearl Harbor: The Coming of the War Between the United States and Japan* (Princeton, 1950), 16.

America's diplomats seemingly were hoping that someone else would find a peaceful way to halt Japan. Virtually by default, because the Japanese would have preferred Great Britain or the United States to act as intermediary, the initiative fell to Germany.[87] At the beginning of 1937 Germany was enjoying the best of two worlds, namely profitable commerce with China while maintaining military missions there, and increasing political friendship with Japan and expanded trade through Manchuria.[88] At the same time some diplomats, like the ambassador to China, Oskar Trautmann, recognized that although Germany had a China policy and a Japan policy, it had no East Asia policy.[89] Most Foreign Ministry officials and diplomats were disposed toward China rather than Japan, or at least felt that Japan's aggression would only devastate China (while exhausting Japan) and open the way to extended Soviet influence—an argument that even various Nazis who preferred closer ties with Japan conceded had merit.[90] Shortly after hostilities began, therefore, the Foreign Ministry instructed German representatives to maintain absolute neutrality and prevailed upon Hitler to make this official policy.[91] Similarly, Neurath remained opposed to Italian accession to the Anti-Comintern Pact as a foil to the British and the Brussels Conference, and in late November Ciano was complaining about Wilhelmstrasse efforts to delay Italian recognition of Manchukuo.[92]

Ribbentrop, who had done so much to bring about Germany's agreement with Japan in 1936, opposed Neurath and Foreign Ministry policy. He apparently accepted Japanese assurances of a quick victory,

87. Borg, *United States and Far Eastern Crisis*, 456.
88. Presseisen, *Germany and Japan*, 124.
89. Sommer, *Deutschland und Japan*, 56.
90. On the prospects of a Sino-Japanese war see, for example, Dirksen to Foreign Ministry, Aug. 3, 1937, *DGFP*, D, I, 748–749, and Weizsäcker, *Memoirs*, 116. See also Robertson, *Hitler's Pre-War Policy*, 100, and Presseisen, *Germany and Japan*, 129. Dirksen also argued that Japan aimed at overthrowing the government of China, and Germany therefore should put more pressure to negotiate on China. Dirksen to Foreign Ministry, Aug. 23, 1937, *DGFP*, D, I, 754–755.
91. Mackensen Circular, July 20, and Neurath Memorandum, Aug. 17, 1937, *DGFP*, D, I, 733–734, 750.
92. Sommer, *Deutschland und Japan*, 67; entries for Nov. 21 and Nov. 24, 1937, Ciano, *Diary*, 35–36.

and on September 19 assured Hitler that Japan had successfully flouted the United States and Great Britain over military activities in the "demilitarized" area of Shanghai and had passed "brilliantly the test of strength."[93] By mid-October Ribbentrop's views had prevailed at least to the extent, as noted earlier, that Hitler agreed to do nothing to discourage the Japanese and agreed to Italian accession to the Anti-Comintern Pact.[94] At the same time, however, apparently in an effort to avoid an absolute choice between Japan and China and between Ribbentrop and Neurath, Hitler allowed German officials to act as letter carriers in an effort to find peace terms suitable to the belligerents.[95]

The Japanese passed their terms to Ambassador Herbert von Dirksen, who sent them to Trautmann for presentation to Chiang Kai-shek on November 5. In sum the Japanese demanded Chinese *de facto* if not *de jure* relations with Manchukuo, an autonomous Inner Mongolia, cessation of "anti-Japanese" activities, and a common front against communism. Chiang Kai-shek refused the proposal as too extreme and said that even if he accepted public outrage would topple his government. He also alluded to the intention of the powers at Brussels to seek peace.[96] Although he did not say so, it is likely he hoped the meeting there would bring more favorable terms.[97]

The Brussels Conference produced no results, and shortly afterward Welles told the British that it would be "inconceivable" for the United States to mediate the Sino-Japanese dispute on any basis that would impair the Nine Power Treaty.[98] Early in December, however, Chiang Kai-shek told Trautmann that he was prepared to negotiate along the lines proposed in November, if the Germans would sit in on the negotiations so China would not have to deal directly with Japan. But when Dirksen relayed this information to the Japanese, Foreign Minis-

---

93. Kordt, *Nicht aus den Akten,* 163; Ribbentrop Memorandum for Hitler, Sept. 19, 1937, *DGFP,* D, I, 758.

94. See also Robertson, *Hitler's Pre-War Policy,* 102.

95. Sommer, *Deutschland und Japan,* 67–68.

96. Dirksen to Foreign Ministry, Nov. 3, and Trautmann to Foreign Ministry, Nov. 5, 1937, *DGFP,* D, I, 778–781.

97. Borg, *United States and Far Eastern Crisis,* 460–462.

98. Welles Memorandum, Dec. 8, 1937, *FR 1937,* III, 775–777.

ter Koki Hirota said that he thought the November terms were now insufficient.[99] Indeed, the military situation had outrun the diplomatic, both in China where Japanese forces were about to take Nanking, and in Japan where expansionist groups in the army, and frenzied public opinion, were demanding the breaking of relations with Chiang Kai-shek's government, or at least its admission of "war guilt," and establishment of a puppet regime.[100]

Toward the end of December the Japanese offered a four-point proposal which included the establishment of special regimes "wherever necessary," close economic cooperation, the end of anti-Japanese and anti-Manchurian policies, and an indemnity for Japan. Further, hostilities would continue until direct Sino-Japanese negotiations concluded the peace.[101] The Germans knew that there was no chance the Chinese would agree to these terms, but forwarded them anyway.[102] The Chinese meanwhile made a final appeal to Roosevelt, who rather casually told Hull, "I suppose . . . that some reply ought to be made. What do you recommend?"[103] The State Department drafted a reply on January 7, which reached Chiang Kai-shek about two weeks later, assuring him that the United States was still searching for ways to establish lasting peace and that it hoped the conflict in the Far East would be resolved.[104]

The Chinese reply to the Japanese proposal, delivered on January 14, 1938, termed it "rather too broad in scope" and asked for further explanation. Foreign Minister Hirota, who noted that China had failed to secure American aid, said that because the Chinese had waited so long, and their reply was perfunctory, negotiations were ended.[105]

99. Trautmann to Foreign Ministry, Dec. 3, and Dirksen to Foreign Ministry, Dec. 7, 1937, DGFP, D, I, 787–789, 799.

100. Borg, United States and Far Eastern Crisis, 474–475; Presseisen, Germany and Japan, 136–137.

101. Dirksen to Foreign Ministry, Dec. 23, 1937, DGFP, D, I, 802–804.

102. Trautmann to Foreign Ministry, Dec. 26 and Dec. 27, 1937, ibid., 809.

103. Chiang Kai-shek to Roosevelt, Dec. 24, 1937, FR 1937, III, 832–833. (The letter was handed to Roosevelt by the Chinese ambassador on Dec. 31.) Roosevelt quoted in Hull, Memoirs, I, 567.

104. Hull to Johnson (transmitting letter of Roosevelt to Chiang Kai-shek, Jan. 11, 1938), Jan. 14, 1938, FR 1938, III, 36–37. Nelson Johnson was ambassador to China.

105. Trautmann to Foreign Ministry, Jan. 13, and Dirksen to Foreign Ministry, Jan. 14 and Jan. 16, 1937, DGFP, D, I, 815–817, 819–820.

Two days later the Japanese government issued a formal proclamation to that effect.[106]

Developments in Germany's Far East policy followed logically if not inevitably from the direction in which German policy had been moving and from the collapse of negotiations in January 1938. Significantly, the irresponsible Ribbentrop, who aimed at buying Japanese favor through concessions, replaced Neurath as foreign minister on February 4.[107] In a speech before the Reichstag on February 20, Hitler, while proclaiming Germany's intention never to return to the League of Nations, also recognized Manchukuo. He insisted that Japan's defeat "would never benefit Europe or America, but only Bolshevist Russia." Germany regarded Japan as safeguarding the culture of mankind, he said, and "we are perfectly certain that Japan's greatest victory would not affect the civilization of the white races in the very least."[108] In the course of the next several months Germany signed a friendship treaty with Manchukuo, recalled its military advisers and ended arms shipments to China, and recalled a dejected Trautmann in June 1938. Despite these concessions, however, Germany never realized the economic advantages it had hoped for in Manchukuo.[109]

The way in which the "new" orientation in German policy in the Far East led to conflict with the United States is not the subject of this book and has been carefully studied elsewhere.[110] There are significant points to be noted, however. According to Kordt, in the spring of 1938 Hitler dismissed concern over American interest in Asian developments by insisting that the United States was incapable of military leadership and would confine itself to empty warnings.[111] Nevertheless, Dieckhoff had warned after Roosevelt's quarantine address

106. Text in U.S. Department of State, *Foreign Relations of the United States, Japan: 1931–1941*, 2 vols. (Washington, D.C., 1943), I, 437–438. See also Robert J. C. Butow, *Tojo and the Coming of the War* (Princeton, 1961), 106–132.

107. Sommer, *Deutschland und Japan*, 102.

108. Text in Monica Lewis, ed., *Documents on International Affairs, 1938*, 2 vols. (London, 1942–43), I, 7–9.

109. Presseisen, *Germany and Japan*, 145–147; Sommer, *Deutschland und Japan*, 103–116. Dirksen supported the new policy as realistic; Trautmann opposed it. See, for example, Dirksen to Foreign Ministry, Jan. 26, and Trautmann to Foreign Ministry, Mar. 8, 1938, *DGFP*, D, I, 826–831, 844–850.

110. See Bibliographical Essay, below.

111. *Wahn und Wirklichkeit*, 142.

that although the United States would remain aloof from European and Asian politics, a conflict that menaced Great Britain would eventually lead to American intervention. Regardless of Hitler's estimate and of whether he even cared if the United States entered a war in progress, Hitler could use this specter of American intervention to try to achieve his diplomatic purpose.

Although Italy did not agree to conclude a military alliance until May 22, 1939—the Pact of Steel—in June and October 1938 Ribbentrop tried to convince the skeptical Italians of his and Hitler's stated belief that a German and Italian military alliance, especially if Japan joined, would ensure American neutrality under all circumstances.[112] Similarly, in pursuing an alliance with Japan, German officials emphasized, as Weizsäcker instructed the embassy in Japan, that "only a perfectly clear alliance is calculated fully to ensure American neutrality."[113] Hitler did not achieve an agreement with Japan in 1939, and instead determined to push for the Nazi-Soviet Nonaggression Pact of August 22. When it became clear, however, that the war in Europe would be protracted, he returned to the effort with Japan. The result was the Tripartite Agreement of September 27, 1940, which recognized the German and Italian claim to lead a New Order in Europe, and Japan's claim to lead a New Order in Asia.[114] The defensive agreement, which provided for assistance in case one of the signatories was attacked by a power not then involved in the European or Sino-Japanese war, was less than the straightforward military alliance against the United States the Germans would have preferred. But the purpose of the agreement remained the intimidation of the United States. As Ribbentrop wrote at the time, "The alliance is exclusively directed against the American warmongers. Its exclusive purpose is to bring

112. Compton, *Swastika and Eagle*, 182, citing Mario Toscano, *Le Origini Diplomatiche del Patto d'Acciaio* (Florence, 1956), 24–29; entries for May 5 and May 12, 1938, Ciano, *Diary*, 112–113, 115; Memorandum Mussolini–Ribbentrop–Ciano Conversation, Oct. 28, 1938, Ciano, *Diplomatic Papers*, 243, and Schmidt Memorandum, Oct. 28, 1938, *DGFP*, D, IV, 515–520. Text of Alliance in *DGFP*, D, VI, 561–564. See also Watt, "Rome-Berlin Axis," *Review of Politics*, 536–537.

113. Weizsäcker to Embassy in Japan, June 17, 1939, *DGFP*, D, VI, 737. See also Compton, *Swastika and Eagle*, 183–185.

114. Text in Arnold J. Toynbee, ed., *Documents on International Affairs, 1939–1946*, 2 vols. (London, 1951), II, 81–82.

the element pressing for America's entry into the war to their senses."[115]

The factors that accounted for American "neutrality" during 1939–1941 had far less to do with fear of German alliances than with the reluctance of the majority of the American people to undertake what they feared would be another dubious battle to make the world safe for democracy and with matters of military preparedness. Admittedly whether and when the United States would have entered the war in Asia or Europe must remain a matter for speculation. Japan, however, determining its policy in secret and according to its interest but encouraged to greater risks throughout 1941 by the Germans, resolved the first part of the question by the attack on Pearl Harbor on December 7, 1941. Although Germany was not bound by the Tripartite Agreement because Japan had attacked the United States, Hitler resolved the second part of the question by declaring war on the United States on December 11, 1941. In his speech to the Reichstag, Hitler blamed everything on Roosevelt and "the full diabolical meanness of Jewry rallied around this man" for having committed "a series of the worst crimes against international law."[116] The Second World War had begun.

In autumn 1937 diplomats only dimly perceived these events. They suggest, however, how little the Welles plan probably would have accomplished in Europe or Asia. It probably would not have achieved any more than did the British, French, and other foreign-policy makers in 1938 and 1939.

American diplomacy in 1937 was muddled and confused. It needed a new approach, not shopworn phrases. Unfortunately, there was no one to lead. This confusion and timidity, this hope that matters would care for themselves, was sadly reflected in events surrounding Ambassador Dodd's recall from Berlin.

Dodd was suffering physically and emotionally by the spring of 1937.

115. Ribbentrop to Schulenberg, Sept. 25, 1940, in R. J. Sontag and J. S. Beddie, eds., *Nazi-Soviet Relations 1939–1941: Documents from the Archives of the German Foreign Office* (Washington, D.C., 1948), 195–196. (Count Friedrich Schulenberg was ambassador to the Soviet Union.) See also Compton, *Swastika and Eagle,* 80–81, 192–196, and Sommer, *Deutschland und Japan,* 436–444.

116. Text of speech in Gordon W. Prange, ed., *Hitler's Words* (Washington, D.C., 1944), 367–377.

On at least a half-dozen occasions since July 1934 he had considered resigning. By the spring of 1936 he found his usual nervous disposition aggravated by indigestion and headaches so severe that he could hardly sleep.[117] He also found difficulty performing necessary official duties. He was able to get on reasonably well with men like Bülow ("perhaps the most sensible and charming man in the Foreign Office"), Neurath, and Schacht.[118] But in June 1936 Bülow was dead, and in 1937 Neurath and Schacht had little power. The ambassador had nothing but contempt for Germany's new masters and he did little to hide it. The feeling was mutual. For a variety of reasons, political, economic, and social, the unhappy Dodd had moved to the periphery of diplomatic life in Berlin.

Now he became entangled with Congress and the State Department. In early March 1937 he wrote a letter to Senator Robert Bulkley of Ohio, and sent copies to Senators Carter Glass of Virginia and Joseph T. Robinson of Arkansas, in which he urged support of Roosevelt's Supreme Court packing bill, deplored the "anti-democratic urging" of men like Senator Borah, and alleged there was someone in the United States "who owns near a billion dollars" and who was ready to support a dictatorial movement in behalf of individuals like Huey Long. Foolishly he sent a copy to his good friend Moore, now counselor for the State Department, for publication in the Richmond *Times–Dispatch*, where it appeared on May 11, 1937. [119] Roosevelt let Dodd know he was "frankly delighted" with the letter, but Senator Nye attacked him as a "scandal monger," "a disgrace to his country," and declared the dictatorship idea to be the "figment of a disturbed mind."[120] In short order the Senate had before it resolutions demanding that Dodd reveal the name of his "billionaire" and that he be recalled.[121] Roosevelt and Hull interceded through Senator Pittman and the resolutions were buried in committee.[122] Despite this support from his superiors, Dodd's

117. Entries for July 8 and Sept. 14, 1934; July 24, 1935; Apr. 22 and Dec. 25, 1936, Dodd, *Diary*, 123, 163, 262, 334, 375.

118. Entry for Apr. 16, 1936, Dodd, *Diary*, 332.

119. Entry for May 12, 1937, *ibid.*, 407; Dodd to Hull, May 17, 1937, Hull papers, Box 40.

120. Roosevelt to Dodd, May 25, 1937, *FDRL*, I, 684; *New York Times*, May 12 and May 13, 1937.

121. *New York Times*, May 14 and May 20, 1937.

122. Hull to Pittman, May 17, 1937, DS, 123 Dodd, William E./167.

position was in jeopardy, and Arthur Krock of the *New York Times* was right when amidst the flare-up he wrote it was "no secret that a change in Berlin has long been desired."[123]

Plans for Dodd's retirement were going forward. Roosevelt knew that Dodd needed and wanted to leave Germany and at least as early as August 1936 had told Joseph E. Davies, the new ambassador to Moscow, to be ready to transfer to Berlin within the year.[124] Dodd in March 1937 asked relief from his post on September 1, and on April 5 Roosevelt agreed.[125]

No sooner had Dodd's resignation date been determined than he grew worried over the choice of successor. He wanted Roosevelt to appoint James T. Shotwell of Columbia University, an outspoken advocate of collective security. When Moore wrote that Davies was certain to get the Berlin post, Dodd replied that if his replacement were not going to be Shotwell or a man of similar background he would "stay a while longer."[126] Sympathetically disposed toward Dodd as were his friends, they urged him to retire as soon as possible. Moore advised against delay and Colonel House hinted strongly that Dodd accept the Harmsworth professorship at Oxford which Ambassador Bingham had said was both "ideal" and available.[127] Dodd gave in, with mixed feelings. Through Moore he requested only that, because he could not book passage to the United States until the end of July and his family would remain behind to care for personal matters, the date of his resignation be postponed one month to October 1. Roosevelt, who as Moore had indicated to Dodd on May 20 "spoke warmly, and I may add even affectionately of you," was in no hurry to remove his ambassador; he informed Hull that the delay was "entirely agreeable."[128]

---

123. May 14, 1937.

124. Joseph E. Davies, *Mission to Moscow* (New York, 1941), xii–xiii.

125. Dodd to Moore, Mar. 28, Roosevelt to Moore, Apr. 5, and Moore to Dodd, Apr. 8, 1937, Moore papers, Box 6.

126. Moore to Dodd, May 4, and Dodd to Moore, May 7, 1937, *ibid.* Davies' Diary entries of Jan. 2, Apr. 5, and Apr. 7, 1937, *Mission to Moscow*, 7, 139–140, 143, suggest that Roosevelt at least at the time, apparently intended to make him Dodd's successor.

127. Moore to Dodd, May 15, 1937, Moore papers, Box 6; House to Dodd, June 20, 1937, Dodd papers, Box 46.

128. Moore to Dodd, May 20, Moore Memorandum for Roosevelt, July 17, and Roosevelt Memorandum for Hull, July 23, 1937, Moore papers, Box 6.

Events now seemed to conspire against Dodd. When he arrived at Norfolk, Virginia, on August 4, he remarked to interviewing newsmen that "the basic aim of some powers in Europe is to frighten and even cajole democracies everywhere."[129] The German government at once protested. Hull insisted to Ambassador Dieckhoff that there was no offense because Dodd had not mentioned a specific country, although Hull commented that Dodd had "almost an obsession on the question of peace and democracy." Dodd apologized to Neurath and the Germans decided nothing could be gained by pursuing the matter and let it go.[130]

Barely had the reaction to this incident subsided when Dodd publicly crossed swords with the State Department over a minor but emotionally charged policy matter. The State Department in 1933 had avoided a decision on whether the American ambassador should accept an invitation to the annual Nazi Party Congress at Nuremberg. Dodd had decided against attending, the British and the French had agreed with Dodd, and for four years no representative of the three governments had attended the September spectacles. Things were different in 1937. In April Sir Nevile Henderson had replaced Eric Phipps at the embassy in Berlin. Henderson's appointment was to underscore the approach to Germany of the new prime minister, Chamberlain, and as the British envoy recalled, he had determined to do his "utmost to see the good side of the Nazi regime as well as the bad."[131] Even before Dodd left Berlin for the United States in July, François-Poncet told him the other ambassadors probably would attend the Nuremberg rally "to avoid trouble." Dodd said he would never do so, unless ordered by his government—in which case he would resign.[132] Before sailing he told his staff he did not want any of them to go to Nuremberg in September.[133]

---

129. *New York Times,* Aug. 5, 1937.

130. Hull Memorandum, Aug. 5, 1937, *FR 1937,* II, 317–318. (In the German version, Dieckhoff Memorandum, Aug. 5, 1937, GFM, 2422/D511383-D511385, Hull is quoted as saying Dodd was "somewhat insane" on the issues of Jeffersonian democracy and world peace.) Dodd to Neurath, Aug. 31, 1937. *DGFP,* D, I, 628.

131. *Failure of a Mission: Berlin 1937–1939* (New York, 1940), viii.

132. Entry for July 20, 1937, Dodd, *Diary,* 425.

133. M. Dodd, *Through Embassy Eyes,* 355–356, says that her father left explicit instructions on the matter; I have not found them or any reference to

Shortly after Dodd left Berlin, François-Poncet again called at the American embassy and told the counselor, Ferdinand L. Mayer, that because the Nazi party had become the State in Germany it would be "conspicuous if not antagonistic" to refuse an invitation. He said he had consulted with the British and together they had decided to attend one day out of the eight days the rally lasted. François-Poncet did not request that America do likewise, but Mayer reported he "implied this would be welcome." Mayer added he had talked with Prentiss Gilbert, the new chargé whose appointment took effect after Dodd had sailed, and they agreed that an American refusal might create a wrong impression and prove harmful in other areas of American relations with Germany.[134] Jay Pierrepont Moffat, who returned from duty in Australia to head the Division of European Affairs, commented to Welles on August 13 that whatever America did would stir criticism but that the choice should be left to the Berlin embassy because "it would be easier to support a decision made locally with full knowledge of the implications than a decision made here." Moffat enclosed for Welles's signature the draft of a note authorizing Mayer and Gilbert to do as they deemed appropriate.[135]

The State Department authorized Gilbert to attend the rally, and on August 25 he wired that Hitler, in his capacity as Reich chancellor, had sent him a formal invitation, which he had accepted. During the past two weeks, Gilbert added, he had talked with both François-Poncet, who had tried to make the French and British decision to attend seem joint policy, and Henderson, who had taken pains to point out that such was not the case, and that all Anglo-German relations had to be independent and bilateral.[136] Only a few hours before Gilbert's telegram arrived Welles grew, in his words, "a little concerned" about press reports concerning the announced British and French decisions. He asked that the decision be reviewed by Hull, who at once called a meeting of his advisers. Messersmith said he had always opposed going, but because England and France had "deserted"

---

them. Regardless, the ambassador's position on attending the rallies was known, and he probably instructed his staff orally.

134. Mayer to Hull, Aug. 11, 1937, DS, 862.00/3664.
135. Moffat to Welles, Aug. 13, 1937, DS, 862.00/3664.
136. Gilbert to Hull, Aug. 25, 1937, DS, 862.00/3668.

the United States, there seemed no alternative. Assistant Secretary Hugh Wilson agreed. So did Moore, but he wondered whether Dodd—whom he knew would be upset by the decision—had discussed the problem with the President. No one knew, but they all guessed that if Roosevelt had expressed an opinion either he or Dodd would have so indicated. Moffat agreed, and Hull concurred. "I doubt if we would have gotten far in combatting Naziism merely by falling back in company with the Soviets alone in this connection," the secretary would answer to a Roosevelt query about the affair in January 1938. The officials left the decision in Gilbert's hands.[137] The chargé already had decided.

Protests poured into the State Department as soon as the newspapers announced an American in official capacity would attend the Nuremberg rally. The reply to each was the same: the chief of state had extended the invitation and virtually every other government had accepted.[138] Nothing more might have come of the affair had there not been unexpected newspaper publicity. The New York *Herald Tribune* on September 4, 1937, published a letter Dodd had written to Hull in late August urging against American representation at Nuremberg. The *Herald Tribune* also printed a telegram Dodd had sent to Hull on September 3 from Williamstown, Massachusetts, asking if there was no way to reverse the decision which to Dodd seemed to violate America's 150-year-old diplomatic tradition. When Hull late in the afternoon on September 3 asked Moffat about the inquiries the *Herald Tribune* had been making prior to releasing early editions of the September 4 paper, Moffat at once concluded, unfairly in light of having no evidence, that Dodd had released the letter in an act of "disloyalty to the Secretary, among his [Dodd's] other shortcomings." Hull and Wilson decided to protect Gilbert.[139] They arranged

137. Moffat Memorandum, Aug. 25, 1937, DS, 862.00/3671; Diary entry for Aug. 25, 1937, Hooker, ed., *Moffat Papers,* 147–148; Hull Memorandum for Roosevelt, Jan. 25, 1938, Hull papers, Box 42.
138. See for example Congressman Emanuel Celler (N. Y.) to Hull, Aug. 27, and Hull to Celler, Aug. 28, 1938, DS, 862.00/3673.
139. Dodd to Hull, Sept. 3, 1937, DS, 862.00/3690; entry for Sept. 4, 1937, Dodd, *Diary,* 427; Diary entry for Sept. 3, 1937, Hooker, ed., *Moffat Papers,* 148. Dodd apparently did not release his letter or telegram to the press and was as surprised as anyone by their public appearance; the "leak" possibly was in the State Department.

for a question about the Nuremberg attendance at a September 4 press conference, and Hull declared that an American could be loyal to his own flag only, that it was usual to accept an invitation from a chief of state, that the decision had been reached with the British and French, and that Dodd had been overruled. The answer apparently satisfied the press, and the matter, to the delight of Hull, faded.[140]

The State Department had escaped the embarrassing situation. Dodd was not so fortunate. Two days after Hull's statement, the German chargé, Hans Thomsen, told Moffat that he did not think that Dodd "could go usefully on with his mission." Three days later Assistant Secretary Wilson informed Thomsen that Dodd would be returning to Berlin around October 1, but that he would remain only briefly, retiring early in 1938. When Thomsen asked if he could make this news official to Berlin, Wilson said yes, provided he did not mention these conversations.[141] Shortly Welles, returning from a trip to Europe, met Ambassador Dieckhoff on board and told him he found Dodd "incomprehensible," and that although now the date of Dodd's resignation seemingly had been postponed, he would take up the matter as soon as he got back to Washington.[142]

Welles was true to his word. Engrossed in his aborted Armistice Day scheme to placate Germany, obviously desiring to ease tensions, he told Dieckhoff on October 1 that Hull had authorized him to tell the German government informally but confidentially that Dodd would return to Germany but "definitely" leave after the New Year. Under those circumstances Dieckhoff replied that there would be no more protests about Dodd.[143]

Matters were not as definite or explicit as Hull, Welles, and Wilson had made them seem. In October, Dodd conferred with Roosevelt, who said nothing about the ambassador's leaving Germany in January. Dodd was anxious to leave, but preferred to wait until at least March

140. Diary entry for Sept. 4, Sept. 5, and Sept. 6, 1937, Hooker, ed., *Moffat Papers*, 148–149; *New York Times*, Sept. 5, 1937.

141. Moffat Memoranda, Sept. 7 and Sept. 10, 1937, *FR 1937*, II, 375, 381; see also Diary entry for Sept. 7, 1937, Hooker, ed., *Moffat Papers*, 149–150, and Thomsen to Foreign Ministry, Sept. 7, 1937, GFM, 2422/D511386-D511387.

142. Dieckhoff to Foreign Ministry, Sept. 27, 1937, *DGFP*, D, I, 630–631.

143. Welles Memorandum, Oct. 1, 1937, *FR 1937*, II, 382.

1938 (when the weather would make traveling easier) in order to avoid the appearance that the German protests had forced his recall. Roosevelt apparently agreed on the later resignation date, or at least did not indicate otherwise, and when Dodd sailed for Germany at the end of the month he believed he was to remain for at least another four or five months.[144] He had good reason to be shocked and hurt when a few weeks after his return to Berlin, Hull wired that "because of the complications with which you are familiar and which threaten to increase" he was to end his mission between December 15 and Christmas.[145] Dodd could never be positive who had arranged this embarrassing recall, but he had a good idea. He knew he was not popular with State Department officials generally and that he and Welles disliked each other—Welles's huge house, servants, and lavish entertainment (and close friendship with Roosevelt) distressed the ambassador who at times overemphasized the virtues of Jeffersonian simplicity.[146] Dodd rightly placed major responsibility for his dismissal on Welles. Moore, who was upset over Welles's influence and who did not hide the fact that his relations with the under secretary were "not at all intimate," confirmed Dodd's suspicions.[147]

The tragedy of Dodd's recall was not the recall but rather the manner in which it was executed and what it showed about American foreign policy. When the ambassador wrote in his diary on October 29, 1937, "In Berlin once more. What can I do?" he knew the answer was nothing.[148] In his heart of hearts he had to know that he should have been gone from Berlin no less than a year or two before. He had done all that he could: he was more right in his analysis of Nazi Germany, and its menace to civilization, than any of his professional colleagues in Berlin—François-Poncet and Henderson especially. As Messersmith, perhaps the most astute American diplomat of the era, would judge in retrospect, Dodd for all his undiplomatic methods saw through all Nazi pretense and was not deceived even for a

144. Entries for Nov. 3 and Nov. 23, 1937, Dodd, *Diary,* 430, 433–434. The Nov. 3 entry reads: "It has been decided that I am to leave Berlin for good about March 1, 1938. The President indicated that date."
145. Hull to Dodd, Nov. 23, 1937, *FR 1937,* II, 383.
146. Entry for June 30, 1937, Dodd, *Diary,* 421–422.
147. Moore to Dodd, Nov. 12 and Dec. 14, 1937, Moore papers, Box 6.
148. *Diary,* 430.

moment.[149] Nor did he seek to deceive himself. It is equally clear that Roosevelt was fond of Dodd, that he agreed with him even if political reality constrained him not to act upon that agreement, that he took curious delight in maintaining a Jeffersonian Democrat in the Third Reich. What is sad, and puzzling, is Roosevelt's failure, for Dodd's sake if no other, to relieve him of the strain of duty earlier and in more gallant fashion.

The ambassador quietly and quickly put his affairs in order and without public notice set sail for the United States on December 29, 1937. Once returned to the land of Jefferson, the wearied but indefatigable scholar-diplomat would spend his remaining days in dwindling health in a crusade to awaken his countrymen to the tragedy that would soon come upon them and the rest of the world. Dodd died on February 9, 1940, five months after outbreak of the Second World War, the final two volumes of that long-planned trilogy on the Old South unwritten.[150]

The State Department had blundered.[151] If Dodd had remained a while longer it would not have made much difference and would have spared him and his government some embarrassment. Attendance at the Nuremberg rally was technically correct but unnecessary, and diplomatically unprofitable. Since the basis for attending was that the Nazi party had become the State, and the rally was therefore a government function, it is hard to explain why, in light of the fact that this situation had existed since December 1933, the same reasoning

149. "Some Observations on . . . Dodd," Messersmith papers, Box 7.

150. For a sketch of Dodd's life and the sad details of his activities from 1938 to his death see Franklin L. Ford, "Three Observers in Berlin: Rumbold, Dodd, and François-Poncet," in Craig and Gilbert, eds., *The Diplomats*, 447–460; L. F. Gittler, "Ambassador Extraordinary," *Survey Graphic*, XXVII (July 1939), 388–389; and Arnold A. Offner, "William E. Dodd: Romantic Historian and Diplomatic Cassandra," *The Historian*, XXXIV (Aug. 1962), 451–469.

151. Although the Nuremberg incident obviously merely triggered the recall long intended, interestingly enough Nevile Henderson wrote that "Dodd went on leave in the summer and never returned to his post, having disagreed with the policy of his government in authorizing the American representative to attend the Nuremberg rally in September," *Failure of a Mission*, 39. Of course Dodd did return to Berlin from October 29 to December 29, 1937, but what is striking, aside from Henderson's unawareness of Dodd's presence, is that Henderson, like so many others, must have linked Dodd's dismissal with the Nuremberg incident.

did not apply to the years 1934, 1935, and 1936. The decision to go to Nuremberg reversed American policy and demonstrated that American diplomats, indecisive and uncertain, intended to follow the British lead. Hitler did not fail to tell Henderson at Nuremberg in September 1937 that he regarded American, French, and British attendance as an "innovation" springing from the Englishman's initiative.[152]

American diplomacy had become nearly pathetic. Every step or half-step toward a concerted effort had resulted in a step back. The British, or at least Chamberlain, remained aloof and unapproachable. Roosevelt did not want to approach Mussolini; Hitler profitably did. The quarantine address led only to confusion, and the Brussels Conference was a dismal failure. Dodd's dismissal, at least its time and manner, made no sense. Japanese sinking of the American gunboat *Panay* and attack upon the British ship *Ladybird* on December 12 commented tragically on the year's events. Eventually, Japan apologized for the *Panay* incident and paid an indemnity of over $2 million, but the most important possibility never developed. The British suggested to the Americans that the two countries register their protests jointly. Hull, through Lindsay in Washington, informed Eden that joint action, in protest or demonstration of force, was impossible.[153] Rather snidely Ciano noted that "if the Americans don't want bombs, they must get out," although he also advised the Japanese that they ought to go easier on the Americans if they wished to keep them divided from the British.[154]

Ciano had pointed to a critical factor. Relations between the United

---

152. *Ibid.,* 71; see also Offner, "William E. Dodd," *Historian,* 466–467n51. In 1938 and 1939 the State Department again agonized over attendance at the Nuremberg rally. Roosevelt, basing his decision on what State Department information counseled, directed the American embassy to send a representative for one day only. Ambassador Hugh Wilson attended in 1938; Chargé Alexander Kirk would have done so in 1939, but the war caused the rally to be canceled. See Wilson to Roosevelt, May 12, 1938, and Roosevelt to Welles, June [?], 1938, DS, 862.00/3777¼; Messersmith to Welles, June 7, 1938, 862.00/3777¾; Welles to Roosevelt, June 7, 1938, and Roosevelt to Wilson, June 10, 1938, 862.00/3777¾; Wilson to Hull, Sept. 2, 1938, 862.00/3778; Welles to Kirk, Aug. 22, 1939, 862.00/3865; Kirk to Hull and Hull to Kirk, Aug. 26, 1939, 862.00/3866; Kirk to Hull, Aug. 26, 1939, 862.00/3870.

153. Cf. Hull, *Memoirs,* I, 559–563, and Eden, *Facing the Dictators,* 615–616. See also Borg, *United States and Far Eastern Crisis,* 486–518.

154. Entries for Dec. 16 and Dec. 25, 1937, Ciano, *Diary,* 44, 49.

States and Great Britain during the past year were not good or at least the countries could not agree on a common policy. Chamberlain apparently did not want American intervention in Europe, although he might have wanted more assistance in the Far East; he had reason to be skeptical of how much the Americans would contribute to maintaining peace. The Americans, even those like Messersmith who believed Germany to be bent upon a policy of conquest, were suspicious or resentful of the British. Anglo-American cooperation, Messersmith wrote at the year's end, "is the only safe anchor left to the world." But the British had to stop playing "a game" in which they sought advantage for themselves and realize that "we are really a greater and stronger country and that therefore we cannot merely follow her but that any association must be a full partnership. It is too bad that things are so bad and that there is a lack of understanding, which I agree is not always on one side."[155] Sooner, perhaps, than Messersmith anticipated, events in 1938 would go a long way toward determining whether the Americans and British would resolve their difficulties, and whether the world would have peace or war.

155. Messersmith to Daniel Heineman, Dec. 21, 1937, Messersmith papers, Box 1.

# 8. LAST OPPORTUNITIES

Whole sections of the European peace structure collapsed in 1938. Before the year was out Austria fell, Czechoslovakia was fatally compromised, and Mussolini gained British recognition of his Ethiopian conquest. To Italian and German delight, Anthony Eden left the Foreign Office. In Spain, Franco's forces stood close to victory; British and French recognition of the dictator's regime would come in February 1939, shortly before Germany took what remained of Czechoslovakia. The American role in these events was not decisive; neither was it insignificant. There were almost two sides to American diplomacy in 1938. One manifested itself in an undertaking at the start of the year that, if successful, might have matured into the most important development of the decade; the other reflected the thinking of the man who represented the United States in Germany, an individual who agreed in the main with the mixed and confused assumptions that caused his European colleagues to commit the diplomatic blunders leading to catastrophe.

Hugh R. Wilson was a highly capable career diplomat, esteemed by his colleague, Moffat, for belonging to the "realist" as opposed to the "messianic" school of thought.[1] He had entered the foreign service in 1911 and served successively in Guatemala, Argentina,

1. Entry for Jan. 31, 1938, Moffat Diary, Moffat papers. According to Joseph Davies, Roosevelt gave the appointment to a career man in order to make the appointment "distinctly formal" and of "no special significance." Diary entry for Dec. 8, 1937, *Mission to Moscow*, 255–256.

Switzerland, Austria, Germany, and Japan. President Coolidge appointed him minister to Switzerland, a position he held for a decade until he returned to Washington in the spring of 1937 as assistant secretary of state. In January 1938 Roosevelt named him to succeed Dodd in Germany.[2] The new ambassador was well acquainted with diplomats the world over and with the finer aspects of diplomacy. He recognized that Europe's complex problems of nationality and economics did not lend themselves to easy solution by moral stricture; yet like so many individuals of his generation who considered themselves sophisticated in *Realpolitik,* he showed himself blind to the dangers in appeasement. He had good reason in 1936 to insist that war could be averted only if Germany were prosperous and reasonably contented, politically and economically in the mainstream of European life. But although willing to respect the Germans and their demands, he let dislike and distrust of the Soviets blind him to the possibility of their contributing to the balance of peace he sought. Rather unfairly, without perceiving errors everyone else had made, he charged that ever since the Soviet Union had entered the League of Nations its delegation, "pleading always the noblest grounds of democracy among states and fidelity to treaties, has thrown its influence repeatedly for decisions which endanger the peace of Europe."[3] For all his sophistication Wilson could write with marked annoyance even after the *Anschluss* that the Jewish problem "had done more than any other to keep alive the continuous and bitter attacks in our press on Germany." Shortly thereafter he noted in his diary that the Germans "have got something" in their Strength Through Joy program "which is going to be beneficial to the world at large."[4]

Wilson deceived himself in other ways. Germany's plans, he insisted at the end of March 1938, "do not necessarily involve the Western powers." The Munich settlement, he wrote in October of that terrible year, probably opened the way "to a better Europe," and he would "deplore" any American undertaking that might "spoil such a possibility"; the press, therefore, ought to halt its "hymn of hate" against Germany. More than three months after the Second World War began

2. Wilson, *Career Diplomat,* 9–14.
3. Wilson to Hull, Oct. 9, 1936, Hull papers, Box 39.
4. Wilson to Hull, Mar. 23, 1938, DS, 711.62/145; Diary entry for Apr. 12, 1938, Wilson, *Career Diplomat,* 65.

he declared that he would "enthusiastically applaud" the end of hostilities in western Europe so that Germany would be free to "take care of the Russian encroachment" and thus further "the ends of civilization."[5] Like so many of his contemporaries who argued that the best solution for all would be to stand aside and let the Germans and the Soviets have it out, Wilson never considered that German victory might mean concentration camps for millions of people in Europe and beyond the Continent, nor what, if the contemptible Bolsheviks were as much a threat to civilization as he believed, Europe's fate might be if they defeated Germany.

His political vision was obstructed. He could not see that there were issues between Germany and the Western world that went beyond the Treaty of Versailles. Clearly the disillusionment prevalent among his generation gripped him. At the outset of the long and critical summer of 1938 he expressed his feelings this way: "Twenty years ago we tried to save the world and now look at it. If we tried to save the world again, it would be just as bad at the end of the conflict. The older I grow the deeper is my conviction that we have nothing to gain by entering a European conflict, and indeed everything to lose."[6] Clearly the words came from conviction, sincerity, even sadness; nonetheless, they missed the mark. Whatever his feelings, he did not arrive in Berlin until February 1938, by which time the Roosevelt administration had failed in its latest and last significant effort to secure peace in Europe.

Two things were clearly on the mind of Roosevelt and his diplomatic subordinates at the start of the new year: appeasement and power. In his annual message of January 3, 1938, the President not only talked of highminded efforts in behalf of international order but stressed the "responsibility" of every nation striving for peace "to be strong enough to assure the observance of those fundamentals of peaceful solution of conflicts." A few weeks later, in support of an increased military budget that was the first part of a vast rearmament

5. Wilson to Hull, Mar. 24, 1938, Hull papers, Box 42; Wilson to Hull, undated, and Wilson to Kirk, Dec. [?], 1939, *Career Diplomat*, 51–53, 80–81. Wilson wrote his undated dispatch to Hull just after the Munich conference, but did not send it.

6. Wilson to Welles, June 20, 1938, *Career Diplomat*, 38–39.

program, Roosevelt sought to impress legislators that current military spending was "inadequate for national security," and that so long as nations of the world had not reached an arms agreement, America would have to build forces strong enough to "keep any potential enemy many hundred miles away from our continental limits."[7]

In the days between these two messages Representative Louis Ludlow of Indiana had been trying to force out of committee a proposed constitutional amendment that would have made mandatory—except in cases of attack upon the United States, its territories, or the Western Hemisphere—a national referendum on a declaration of war. Roosevelt wrote the speaker of the house, William B. Bankhead of Alabama, on January 6 that the proposed amendment "would cripple any President in his conduct of our foreign relations" and "would encourage other nations to believe that they could violate American rights with impunity."[8] Bankhead read the President's message in measured tones to the House on January 10; by the small margin of 209–188 Congress refused to discharge the amendment from committee.[9]

The same day that the House voted on the Ludlow amendment, Under Secretary Welles, having smoothed over difficulties with Hull, sensed that Roosevelt was in a mood to explore diplomatic possibilities and submitted to him a memorandum outlining a proposal to call a conference to settle Europe's difficulties. According to Welles's scheme, which envisioned the attending nations drawing up programs for international conduct, arms reduction, methods of war, and equal access to raw materials, Roosevelt was to initiate proceedings by summoning European representatives in the United States and handing them copies of the conference proposal. If their governments responded favorably, the secretary of state would ask the American Republics to choose two representatives from among themselves (United States officials excluded) to meet in Washington, along with one delegate each from Sweden, Switzerland, the Netherlands, Hungary, Turkey, Belgium, and Yugoslavia. These delegates, with the American government serving as "a channel of information, and no more," would write the elaborate codes, which would go to all nations

7. *PPFDR*, VII, 3–14, 68–71.
8. *Ibid.*, 36–37.
9. Divine, *Illusion of Neutrality*, 219–221; see also Wayne S. Cole, *Senator Gerald P. Nye and American Foreign Relations* (Minneapolis, 1963), 120–121.

for ratification. What would happen beyond that, Welles said, was "impossible . . . to forecast with any precision." He was certain, falsely optimistic as he was over the talks in November 1937 between Hitler and Lord Halifax, lord president of the Council, that the recommendations would "lend support and impetus" to British and French efforts "to reach the bases for a practical understanding with Germany on colonies and security." Solution of these difficulties, Welles felt, would undercut Axis support of Japan and "obligate Japan to make peace with China upon terms not inconsistent with the Nine Power Treaty." The only question before engaging upon the undertaking was whether England should be informed secretly and its opinion obtained before communicating the plan to the French, Germans, and Italians, or whether to approach everyone simultaneously. Welles favored the first procedure; Norman Davis advised the second.[10] Hull already had made securing British approval privately a condition of Welles's even suggesting the conference.[11]

Once again Welles's design appealed to Roosevelt, who chose to operate in secrecy with the British. On January 11 Welles called on Ambassador Lindsay and asked him to communicate the plan to his government, explaining that Roosevelt wanted to summon the conference on January 22 but that he would drop the whole matter if the English did not express "cordial and wholehearted support" of it within five days.[12] Lindsay, like Eden an advocate of closer Anglo-American cooperation, told Welles it was "the first hope I have had in more than a year that a new World War can be prevented." He promptly sent two telegrams to his superiors arguing that the best way to avert disaster was to gain support of both the Roosevelt administration and American public opinion, and that although there

10. Welles Memorandum for Roosevelt, Jan. 10, 1938, *FR 1938*, I, 115–117. Welles was not alone in his false view of the Hitler-Halifax conversations. Chamberlain too felt the way was now open to discuss a practical settlement with Germany. But that was dogged wishful thinking. Halifax's conversations offered little real encouragement. Halifax's account of his talks are in *Fullness of Days* (New York, 1957), 184–193. See also Feiling, *Life of Chamberlain*, 332, Bullock, *Hitler*, 366–367, and *DGFP*, D, I, 39–71.

11. Welles, *Seven Decisions*, 25.

12. *Ibid.*, 26–27; Eden, *Facing the Dictators*, 623. No text of the message has ever been found in the State Department files or Roosevelt papers; English government officials, however, have quoted from it in various of their memoirs.

was no need to be anxious over the administration's position, the scheme would have a "profound effect" on the public. He stressed that even though the Welles plan did not define terms and issues, the British government ought to give this "invaluable initiative . . . a very quick and cordial acceptance."[13]

London officials disagreed. Horace Wilson, chief industrial adviser and increasingly an intimate of the prime minister, opposed the plan from the start, and in later discussions dismissed it as "woolly rubbish."[14] Alexander Cadogan, the under secretary for foreign affairs, had reservations but felt his government should welcome the proposal; at least, he thought, no reply ought to be given until Foreign Secretary Eden, traveling as hastily as he could from the French Riviera in response to Cadogan's frantic phone call to him, reached London.[15] Chamberlain did not like the proposal at all, and his view prevailed. He called the American initiative "a bolt from the blue,"[16] "a bomb,"[17] "fantastic," and "likely to excite the derision of Germany and Italy."[18] He also determined quickly that England alone had to undertake initial efforts to appease Germany, and that if the United States joined in, it would have to be at the end rather than at the start of negotiations. This he made clear in a letter, of curious logic, which he wrote to a relative on January 16, three days after receiving the American proposal. Chamberlain said he intended doing everything in his power to further cooperation between the United States and England because both wanted "the same fundamental things in the world, peace, liberty, order, respect for international obligations." Unfortunately, certain governments, notably the German, Japanese, and Soviet, were in the grip of unreasonable dictatorships that would heed only force, and "U.S.A. and U.K. represent a force so over-whelming that the mere hint of the possibility of its use is sufficient to make the most powerful of dictators pause." (France, he said, "keeps pulling her own house down about her ears.") The dictators "are too often regarded as though they were entirely inhuman"; true

---

13. Welles, *Seven Decisions,* 27; Eden, *Facing the Dictators,* 624–625.
14. Quoted in Eden, *Facing the Dictators,* 639.
15. *Ibid.,* 622, 625.
16. Templewood, *Nine Troubled Years,* 270.
17. Feiling, *Life of Chamberlain,* 336.
18. Iain Macleod, *Neville Chamberlain* (New York, 1962), 212.

what made them dangerous was their human side, but it was also this side that allowed one to approach them. And this he intended to do shortly, he explained. Then, after "a certain amount of spade-work," and if agreement seemed near but not quite within grasp, "a friendly and sympathetic President might be able to give just the fresh impetus we required."[19]

Consequently, without waiting for Eden's return, Chamberlain cabled Roosevelt that it seemed the American proposal would hurt British efforts to reach lasting settlements with Germany and Italy. He added that his government, "if possible with the authority of the League of Nations," was considering recognizing *de jure* Italy's con-quest of Ethiopia if the Italians "were ready to give evidence of their desire to contribute to the restoration of confidence and friendly relations." He wondered if it might not be best then for Roosevelt "to consider holding his hand for a short while to see what progress we can make in beginning to tackle some of the problems." He feared that if Roosevelt's suggestions were put forward presently, "Germany and Italy may feel constrained to take advantage of them, both to delay the consideration of specific points which must be settled if appeasement is to be achieved and to put forward demands over and above what they would put forward to us if we were in direct negotiation with them."[20]

Chamberlain's response troubled Washington diplomats, particu-larly Welles, who later called it "a douche of cold water."[21] He and Hull quickly drafted another message for Roosevelt to send Chamber-lain. In this second appeal, of January 17, the President said he was willing to defer for "a short while" his intention of calling a con-ference, but he argued that Britain's proposal to give *de jure* recogni-tion to Italy's conquest of Ethiopia meant surrendering the principle of nonrecognition, which would have a bad effect upon events in the Far East and American public opinion. "The recognition of the conquest of Ethiopia," Roosevelt said, "*which at some appropriate time may have to be regarded as an accomplished fact,* would seem to me to be a matter which affects all nations which are committed

19. Chamberlain to Mrs. Morton Price, Jan. 16, 1938, quoted in Feiling, *Life of Chamberlain,* 322–324.
20. Chamberlain to Roosevelt, Jan. 14, 1938, *FR 1938,* I, 118–120.
21. *Time for Decision,* 66.

to the principles of nonrecognition *and which should consequently be dealt with as an integral part of measures for world appeasement,* in which all nations of the world have previously demonstrated their common interest and their willingness to bear individual responsibility." He hoped the English would advise him of their negotiations with Germany and Italy, though the United States could have nothing to do with the politics of such negotiations.[22]

Privately, Hull and Welles were more emphatic. On the same day the secretary of state told Lindsay in typically rustic phraseology that if Great Britain abandoned nonrecognition "the desperado nations" would regard this move as "a virtual ratification of their policy of outright treaty wrecking and the seizure of land by force of arms." This assumption might have a terrible effect in the Pacific, where Japan would possibly "destroy solemn treaties and make this a universal precedent." On the future of nonrecognition, Hull conceded that it would have to be "modified by some general arrangement entered into by all or most of the nations of the world in an orderly manner."[23]

Welles, speaking at Roosevelt's instruction, angrily warned that recognition of Mussolini's conquest would "rouse a feeling of disgust," revive the old concern about "pulling the chestnuts out of the fire," and stir charges that the United States and England were engaging in a "corrupt bargain" in Europe at the expense of American interests in the Far East. When Lindsay said that England, having begun talks with Italy, might confront an ultimatum to recognize Italy's conquest of Ethiopia as a price for continuing negotiations, Welles insisted that to give in would be to surrender to blackmail, and that in turn would only lead to unconscionable demands from Germany.[24]

While American diplomats fretted and fumed, Eden, back in London, at a private meeting with Chamberlain on January 18 sought to induce him to respond more enthusiastically to the American proposal. Eden said that English negotiations with Italy, even if successful, coupled with rejection of the American overture, might

22. Welles to Roosevelt and Roosevelt to Chamberlain, Jan. 17, 1938, *FR 1938,* I, 120–122, italics added.
23. Hull, *Memoirs,* I, 580–581.
24. Quoted in Eden, *Facing the Dictators,* 632–633; see also Langer and Gleason, *Challenge to Isolation,* 27, who do not mention Welles's conversation.

make the President "withdraw more and more into isolation"—the "greatest possible disaster to the peace of the world"—and destroy the last six months of patient British effort to encourage American cooperation. He insisted that it was imperative to choose an Anglo-American venture over "a piecemeal settlement approached by way of problematical agreement with Mussolini," and that closer cooperation with the United States would strengthen England's ability to deal with Germany. To agree to Roosevelt's initiative, Eden concluded, would also justify asking him to modify the comments he made in his message about "inequities" in the peace treaty and his insistence on America's "traditional policy of freedom from political involvement." Two hours of wrangling failed to move the prime minister; he conceded only that there was a deep difference between himself and his foreign secretary.[25]

Chamberlain stood firm. At a critical meeting of the cabinet's Foreign Affairs Committee on January 19, he noted on a slip of paper that "Eden's policy to line up the U.S.A., Great Britain and France, result war." Eden asserted that such a line-up would prevent war. After two days of bitter debate, in which Horace Wilson became enraged at the thought that the Americans might leak news of the secret negotiations and threatened a full government attack upon Eden and the Foreign Office, and Eden talked of resigning, the foreign secretary gained a compromise. Chamberlain sent two messages to Roosevelt on January 21 declaring he welcomed "warmly" the President's initiative and would do his best to make Roosevelt's scheme work "whenever he decides to launch it." *De jure* recognition of Italy's conquest, the prime minister explained in the second message, would be given only as part of a broad European settlement or appeasement. Eden too sent two messages to Lindsay. The first explained that the British were walking a tightrope: they did not want to share responsibility with Roosevelt for his proposals "lest these proposals receive . . . a bad reception"; nor did they want Roosevelt to be able to blame them for encouraging him to undertake an effort that undoubtedly would cause the dictators "intense irritation," and which they

---

25. Eden, *Facing the Dictators*, 634–635, 699–700. Eden only refers to Roosevelt's statement about American involvement; the passage in which it appears is quoted in Templewood, *Nine Troubled Years*, 270.

might reject out of hand. The second telegram emphasized the urgent need to come to terms with Italy, but explained that talks would be put off at least a week. The compromise arrangements, Eden noted personally, were the best he could achieve, and he hoped they would encourage "growing Anglo-American confidence."[26]

What followed remains uncertain. According to Churchill and Eden, on January 22 Lindsay called on Welles, who said that Chamberlain's latest response would please Roosevelt because he regarded *de jure* recognition of Mussolini's conquest of Ethiopia "as an unpleasant pill which we should both have to swallow and he wished that we should both swallow it together."[27] The historians for the Council on Foreign Relations, William L. Langer and S. Everett Gleason, have argued that Welles's statement seems "hardly plausible" and that in enthusiasm for Anglo-American unison Lindsay overstated Welles's account.[28] Likely Welles said very nearly, if not exactly, the words Lindsay attributed to him. Americans generally might have looked unfavorably upon abandoning nonrecognition, but Welles did write Roosevelt's message to Chamberlain (which Hull approved) that recognition of Mussolini's conquest of Ethiopia "at some appropriate time may have to be regarded as an accomplished fact." Apparently, the prospect of the British independently giving immediate recognition, without making it an "integral part of measures for world appeasement," distressed American diplomats. Unfortunately, they did not make their distress as clear as they should have to the British, for Roosevelt expressed "deep gratification" at Chamberlain's second message, and Lindsay reported that the proposed British course, including support of Roosevelt's conference, "entirely met the President's views."[29] The English thus could assume that the Americans had reached similar conclusions about measures to preserve peace and now had only to await their next move.

That move never came. Ten days after Chamberlain's messages to

26. Eden, *Facing the Dictators*, 636–642; see also Macleod, *Chamberlain*, 213. Templewood, *Nine Troubled Years*, 272, says nothing about the bitter British debates, only that Chamberlain now realized more fully the importance Roosevelt attached to his plan and did not wish to disappoint him.
27. *Gathering Storm*, 253; *Facing the Dictators*, 643.
28. *Challenge to Isolation*, 28.
29. Macleod, *Chamberlain*, 213.

Roosevelt, the British grew restive over American silence, and, following inquiries from Chamberlain on January 28 and Eden on February 1, Lindsay called Welles to ask about Roosevelt's plans. Welles spoke to Roosevelt and then told the British ambassador that the President expected to give some indication of his plans shortly, but at the moment had "nothing more definite to say."[30] A week passed. Events in Germany complicated matters. On February 4, following allegations about Field-Marshal von Blomberg's marriage to a prostitute and false charges of homosexuality against General von Fritsch, Hitler announced the resignations of the two men. He abolished Blomberg's post of minister of war and assumed the role of commander in chief of the armed forces, placing the malleable General Walther von Brauchitsch in Fritsch's post as commander in chief of the army. Göring was elevated to field marshal, making him the highest-ranking officer. Ribbentrop, ambassador to Great Britain, replaced Neurath at the Foreign Ministry, and Hitler recalled Papen and Hassell from their posts in Vienna and Rome. The weak-willed Walter Funk assumed Schacht's position at the Ministry of Economics.[31]

American officials worried about these changes, particularly Ribbentrop's ascendancy. Welles could get no information from Ambassador Dieckhoff.[32] Reports from overseas were discouraging. Prentiss Gilbert, the chargé in Berlin who had broken with Dodd over attendance at Nuremberg the past September and who had made an effort to get closer to Nazis in power, thought Ribbentrop's appointment suggested "a more radical tendency" in German policy, although he did think the high office might have a sobering effect. But, he concluded, there was absolutely no unity of view among the most experienced diplomats in Berlin.[33] The Italians were delighted with the changes, Phillips reported; Ciano had told him they marked the development of a "revolutionary government."[34] The British, reported

30. Welles Memorandum, Feb. 2, 1938, *FR 1938*, I, 122–123.
31. This purge is discussed at length in Bullock, *Hitler*, 416–420, Shirer, *Rise and Fall*, 314–321, and Walter Goerlitz, *History of the German General Staff, 1657–1945*, trans. Brian Battershaw (New York, 1953), 304–323.
32. Welles Memorandum, Feb. 8, 1938, DS, 862.00/3773½.
33. Gilbert to Hull, Feb. 5 and Feb. 11 (two cables), 1938, DS, 862.00/3726, 762.00/160, 862.00/3735.
34. Phillips to Hull, Feb. 11, 1938, DS, 862.00/3748. See also entry for Feb. 5, 1938, Ciano, *Diary*, 70.

the chargé in London, Herschel Johnson, were highly upset. Everyone knew that Ribbentrop's year-and-a-half stay in England had been a social and political failure, and he had left with "a bad case of wounded vanity" and little regard for the English. His promotion then came as "a very unpleasant surprise" for British leaders who were inclined to "look wistfully" toward the Secret Cabinet Council which Neurath headed (and which never met) as the source of power.[35]

Thus, when Lindsay inquired on February 9 about the proposed American conference, Welles said that the President wished the British to know he had delayed because of the "acute situation" in Germany, and that until things appeared clearer "it would be unwise to go ahead." Roosevelt would proceed with his plan "in the relatively near future," Welles assured Lindsay, and would communicate further. In the meantime the Americans awaited suggestions from the British, whose recent silence "might be construed as an indication of apathy" toward the plan. Lindsay reassured Welles that his superiors were "committed to support with every means within their power the successful realization of the President's objectives," and would carry out their commitment "with the utmost loyalty and energy."[36]

The British never had to honor their commitment. The "relatively near future" in which Roosevelt was to act became a confusing and ominous present in which both statesmen and citizens floundered from one crisis to the next until war broke in September 1939. Eden, the one member of Chamberlain's cabinet who might have created closer Anglo-American relations, resigned on February 20, 1938, at odds with Chamberlain over negotiations with Mussolini. The resignation meant not only that the British would seek a "piecemeal" settlement with Italy, but also, as Lindsay informed Welles on March 3, that the prime minister, who had determined "to push actively for an understanding with Germany," would instruct Ambassador Nevile Henderson in Berlin to seek an interview with Hitler about the "precise extent and nature of Germany's colonial ambitions and . . . Germany's attitude with regard to a permanent Central European appeasement."[37]

35. Johnson to Hull, Feb. 8, 1938, DS, 862.00/3745.
36. Welles Memorandum, Feb. 9, 1938, *FR 1938*, I, 124–125.
37. Welles Memorandum, Mar. 3, 1938, *ibid.*, 31–32.

Conversations had not proceeded far when the Austrian crisis intervened. At a stormy meeting at Berchtesgaden on February 12, 1938, Hitler made a number of demands upon Austrian Chancellor Kurt von Schuschnigg, including making the Austrian Nazi, Arthur Seyss-Inquart, minister of interior and lifting the ban on Nazi activities.[38] The American chargé in Vienna, John C. Wiley, was well informed about what had taken place, and he reported that Schuschnigg had told him he would meet Hitler's demands to avert the "worst" and that although Italy preferred an independent Austria, in a crisis Mussolini would not give material support. Wiley also reported that he had told the Austrian foreign minister, Guido Schmidt, that the American government hoped he would "firmly resist threats against the independence of Austria."[39] Hull merely instructed Wiley never to say anything that "in any sense" suggested that the United States concerned itself with European politics. Approving Hull's response, Moffat wrote in his diary that Wiley's remark to Schmidt had been a "blunder" and that it was out of the question for the United States to assume any responsibility in Europe—"legal or moral."[40]

By the end of February the Nazis in Austria had so undermined Schuschnigg's government that it seemed only a matter of time before it would collapse.[41] On March 9 Schuschnigg announced his decision to hold a plebiscite on March 13 to determine whether Austria would remain independent. Wiley thought the decision was an "encouraging" sign that the government had not yielded to "defeatism." Moffat thought Schuschnigg had "sacrificed wisdom for cleverness" and that

38. Protocol of the Conference of Feb. 12, 1938, *DGFP*, D, I, 515–517. See also Gordon Brook-Shepherd, *The Anschluss* (Philadelphia and New York, 1963), 42–63.

39. Wiley to Hull, Feb. 14 and Feb. 15, 1938, *FR 1938*, I, 391–394. On Feb. 16, 1938, Ciano wrote the Italian ambassador in London, Count Dino Grandi, that if the Nazis march into Austria and "present us with a fait accompli, then there would exist no alternative and we would have to direct our policy in a spirit of sharp, open, immutable hostility toward the Western Powers." Ciano, *Diplomatic Papers*, 161–162.

40. Hull to Wiley, Feb. 15, 1938, *FR 1938*, I, 396; Diary entry for Feb. 15, 1938, Hooker, ed., *Moffat Papers*, 189.

41. Eichstädt, *Von Dollfuss zu Hitler*, 354.

the plebiscite would be a "travesty."[42] Mussolini, questioned in advance of the decision, had advised against the plebiscite.[43] In London on March 10, Eden's successor, Lord Halifax, tried to prevail upon the visiting Ribbentrop to persuade Hitler to agree to a peaceful solution of the crisis regardless of what he thought of the plebiscite.[44]

Hitler was not interested in advice. He had told a group of Austrian Nazis on February 26 that if they followed "evolutionary processes" the Austrian problem "would be automatically solved."[45] Now he decided to conclude matters, by force if necessary. On the night of March 10–11 he signed orders for an invasion of Austria, to take place by noon on March 12 if he did not have his way. During the course of the afternoon of March 11 he and Göring forced Schuschnigg to cancel the plebiscite and then to resign. They also insisted that Seyss-Inquart become chancellor, a demand that the Austrian president, Wilhelm Miklas, resisted until shortly before midnight. Nevertheless, about 9:00 P.M. Göring dictated instructions to Seyss-Inquart to request, for purposes of preserving law and order, German troops, whose instructions for marching Hitler had already signed. About an hour and a half later a delighted Hitler received word from Prince Philip of Hesse, his special emissary dispatched to Rome earlier in the day, that Mussolini had agreed to acquiesce in the developments.[46] Not even a request from Seyss-Inquart's government at 2:00 A.M. on March 12 could deter Hitler from sending his troops, and shortly after noon he too entered Austria.[47]

Neither England nor Italy nor France was happy with these developments, but no one seriously proposed to do anything about

42. Wiley to Hull, Mar. 9, 1938, *FR 1938,* I, 416; entry for Mar. 10, 1938, Moffat Diary, I, Moffat papers.

43. Weizsäcker Minute, Mar. 11, 1938, *DGFP,* D, I, 572; Brook-Shepherd, *Anschluss,* 117–118.

44. Ribbentrop Memorandum for Hitler, Mar. 10, 1938, *DGFP,* D, I, 264–265. See also Halifax to Henderson, Mar. 10, 1938 (2 cables), *DBFP,* 3d ser., I, 4–6, and Robertson, *Hitler's Pre-War Policy,* 118–119.

45. Unsigned Memorandum, Feb. 28, 1938, *DGFP,* D, I, 548–549. The memorandum is from the files of Wilhelm Keppler, adviser on economic matters and Austria in the Reich Chancellery.

46. For a close account of the events of Mar. 11, 1938, see Eichstädt, *Von Dollfuss zu Hitler,* 371–422, and Brook-Shepherd, *Anschluss,* 137–179.

47. Bullock, *Hitler,* 431–433. See also Weizsäcker, *Memoirs,* 123.

them. Early in the afternoon of March 11 Chamberlain had given Ribbentrop a message for Hitler expressing his desire to "clear up German-British relations"; when Ribbentrop mentioned the plebiscite, Chamberlain said only that he hoped to better German-British understanding "once we had all got past this unpleasant affair and a reasonable solution had been found."[48] When word came that pressures were being exerted on Schuschnigg, Halifax told Ribbentrop that threats of force were "*intolerable*" and he suggested that an international police force hold the plebiscite at a later date. Chamberlain hastily suggested that this was not necessary, and while he disapproved of the threats, he thought that the plebiscite should be cancelled.[49] Later in the day the British informed Austria they could not advise any course of action or guarantee protection.[50] The British and French did make overtures to Mussolini about the possibility of joint action, but he would not even receive the inquiries.[51] As Ciano noted in his diary, Austria's loss of independence was no advantage for Italy, but given the differences of the last two years Stresa could not be rebuilt in an hour "with Hannibal at the gates." The British and French were reduced to protests to the German Foreign Ministry, which were rejected as "inadmissible."[52]

On the evening of March 11 Lord Halifax addressed a summary of the day's events to Roosevelt. He confessed that German "brutal disregard for any argument but force shows the difficulty of reasoning with them," and he thought further negotiations were useless, at least for some time to come. He said he did not believe anything other than the threat of force could have averted the *fait accompli,* and had the threat been ignored action that would have plunged Europe into war would have been necessary. "In these circumstances," Halifax concluded, "I am bound to confess that one of the twin efforts His Majesty's Government was anxious to make to prepare the way for

48. Ribbentrop Memorandum, Mar. 13, 1938, *DGFP,* D, I, 276–277.

49. Ribbentrop Memorandum, Mar. 11, 1938, *ibid.,* 273–275. The substance of the conversation was telephoned to Berlin at 5:05 P.M.

50. Halifax to Palairet, Mar. 11, 1938, *DBFP,* 3d ser., I, 13.

51. Earl of Perth to Halifax, Mar. 11, 1938, *ibid.,* 20.

52. Entry for Mar. 11, 1938, Ciano, *Diary,* 87; Henderson to Neurath and François-Poncet to Neurath, Mar. 11, and Weizsäcker to Various German Diplomatic Missions, Mar. 12, 1938, *DGFP,* D, I, 578–579, 586–587.

an appeasement, and on account of which we asked the President to postpone his initiative, has failed."[53]

Hitler and his troops strolled into Austria on March 12, and on March 13 the German government proclaimed Austria a province of the German Reich. That same day Roosevelt cabled the British that his plan was indefinitely postponed and opportunity for its use "would not recur."[54]

There have been strong differences of opinion over the failure of the Americans and British to undertake some joint enterprise in January 1938. Ten years later Churchill condemned Chamberlain for rejecting the American proposal—"the last frail chance to save the world from tyranny otherwise than by war"— and for his "limited outlook, inexperience in European affairs, and misguided self-sufficiency" that led him to "wave away the proffered hand stretched out across the Atlantic."[55] Welles, convinced that Hull made the major mistake by preventing the calling of a world conference on Armistice Day in 1937, placed equal blame for the failure in 1938 on him and Chamberlain.[56] Alfred Duff Cooper, the first lord of the Admiralty, who would resign after the Munich Conference, thought that the scheme was "open to criticism," but that Roosevelt's offer of intervention presented "an immense opportunity which, if it had been seized upon, might have proved one of the turning-points in European history and would probably have averted the coming war."[57] The historian A. L. Rowse, during the thirties a fervent Labor candidate opposed to appeasement who frequently dined with high government officials and friends at All Souls College, Oxford, has noted that Roosevelt "*needed* that conference; for us it was a lifebuoy thrown to a drowning man." But the "besotted Chamberlain" turned it down.[58] Eden has written that although the American proposal "admittedly might have failed," Chamberlain and his cabinet "did not

53. British Embassy to Department of State, Mar. 11, 1938, *FR 1938*, I, 130–132.
54. Templewood, *Nine Troubled Years*, 273.
55. *Gathering Storm*, 254–255.
56. *Seven Decisions*, 27–30.
57. *Old Men Forget: The Autobiography of Duff Cooper* (New York, 1954), 210.
58. *Appeasement: A Study in Political Decline, 1933–39* (New York, 1961), 67.

look beyond the Roosevelt plan itself . . . to the beneficent conse-quences which might have flowed from it, even in failure." He has agreed with Welles, whom he felt had clearer perception of world affairs than any other American, that neither before nor after did there arise a comparable opportunity to avert the Second World War.[59]

Other participants and observers have not been so certain. Two whom Chamberlain consulted at the time were Sir Samuel Hoare (Viscount Templewood), formerly foreign secretary and then secre-tary for home affairs, and Lord Halifax, who was then president of the Council. Templewood has written that they were "deeply suspici-ous" of American readiness to undertake any practical action and that "American isolationism" forced him and Chamberlain to conclude that they had to rely "chiefly upon ourselves" in the immediate crisis facing Europe. It would have been "dangerous in the extreme" to put off the action they saw as appeasing Europe in hope that eventually America would join in "salvaging the ruins." They were "impatient of American lectures on international conduct, and American reiteration of moral principles," and had determined upon negotiating "specific, and probably limited, agreements, first with Mussolini and secondly with Hitler."[60] Halifax, in full agreement with Templewood, con-cluded that Chamberlain did not rebuff the initiative from Roosevelt, who, he said, did not resent the British response; further, different handling of the initiative would not have prevented war.[61] Even Langer and Gleason consider the American plan "very modest," akin to Hull's moral strictures to which every nation probably would have assented but which would not have satisfied Nazi ambitions. Only a stand by the United States in support of Great Britain might have

59. *Facing the Dictators,* 645.

60. *Nine Troubled Years,* 263, 268.

61. *Fullness of Days,* 196–197. To support his judgment, Halifax, who be-came ambassador to the United States in January 1941, cites a wartime con-versation with Roosevelt concerning the failure to achieve Anglo-American cooperation in January 1938, a factor that weighed heavily in Eden's decision to resign. Halifax says that Roosevelt merely referred to the famous "Good man" telegram he sent Chamberlain at the height of the Munich crisis. Eden therefore "was more royalist than the King," for, Halifax concludes, Roosevelt was not angered by Chamberlain's policies in 1938. The latter aspect of Hali-fax's judgment is at least partly correct, but it is also likely that Roosevelt preferred, during wartime, to make light of old differences.

changed things, they contend, but the American government had "no thought of assuming any political or military commitment in connection with it," thus making it perfectly safe for Hitler to discount American influence.[62]

Unquestionably, the Americans handled the Roosevelt-Welles scheme of 1938 ineptly. Surely the determining factor at that juncture was Chamberlain's intention of proceeding alone in appeasing Europe, and he neither wanted nor trusted American overtures. Yet the United States had not demonstrated resolve to help Europe; and the current proposal seemingly did not put forth anything the British were not preparing to do themselves by way of appeasing Germany and Italy. Seemingly one could not expect England to surrender its role as Europe's arbiter to a nation that intended to retain, as Roosevelt had said in his first message, "its traditional policy of freedom from political involvement."

The Germans were not interested in any conference in January 1938. Ribbentrop, not yet foreign minister, was extremely hostile toward the British, and while on a visit to Berlin in early January advised Hitler that German success depended upon building an overpowering alliance system—specifically the Rome-Berlin-Tokyo Axis—before the British, who were deliberately stalling for this purpose, had a chance to build an equal force through accommodation with the United States. A few weeks later Weizsäcker reviewed various subjects touched on in talks with the British and advised that conceivably armaments limitation offered a chance "to pay in cheap coin, or perhaps even make a virtue of necessity," but apparently the British were considering only colonies in exchange for maintaining the political *status quo*. "The net result of such an accounting," he concluded, "will in all probability be zero."[63] Ribbentrop and Weizsäcker, of course, represented contending factions about Hitler, who was largely determining matters according to his own counsel. But to judge from the fact that in January and February 1938 he was formally reversing German policy in the Far East in direct opposition to American and British interests, and from his impatience in the

---

62. *Challenge to Isolation,* 31–32.
63. Ribbentrop Memorandum for Hitler, Jan. 2, and Weizsäcker Minute, Jan. 17, 1938, *DGFP,* D, I, 168–169, 182.

Austrian crisis and willingness to use force without assurances that he would not meet concerted opposition, one must conclude that he would not have been interested in a conference sponsored by a politically, and militarily, uninvolved United States.

Eden knew this and had wanted Roosevelt to modify his statement, recognizing that the United States would have to assume obligations. Perhaps the tragedy was Chamberlain's shortsightedness, his failure to exploit that precious little opportunity he now had at least to call into being that Anglo-American alliance which he had described in his letter of January 16 as "a force so overwhelming that mere hint of the possibility of its use is sufficient to make the most powerful of dictators pause." Equally tragic, the triumph of Chamberlain's view meant that Eden would have to resign. That resignation would not come until February 20, and publicly the issue would be negotiations with Italy, but from the moment Chamberlain and Eden disagreed over the American initiative, the two men could not work together. In fact, Eden has confessed, even after the conciliatory telegrams of January 21, he would have resigned "there and then" had not the whole affair been secret.[64]

Had Roosevelt determined on a peace conference he might have summoned one between the time Chamberlain pledged British support on January 21, and the time Hitler reorganized his government on February 4, or even up until the *Anschluss* on March 12. Roosevelt's decision not to call a conference suggests not only hypersensitivity to Chamberlain's first rebuff but, as with the quarantine address aftermath and the Brussels Conference, lack of substantial peace programs. The Americans obscured their position first by failing to defend their interests in the Far East and then by scolding the British for suggesting recognition of Mussolini's conquest while at the same time talking about recognition as "an integral part of measures for world appeasement." Developments in the next two months further demonstrated the confusion and rancor in Anglo-American relations.

American diplomatic views differed on Eden's resignation. Moffat was convinced that Chamberlain intended to "play ball with Hitler and Mussolini" and regretted that "belief will grow that Britain's interest in principles and in democracy was skin deep," to be played

64. *Facing the Dictators*, 642.

up to only when it affected British material interests and otherwise discarded. Ambassador Wilson said he had "much affection" for Eden, but was "out of step with him politically ever since the spring of 1936."[65] When Lindsay asked Welles's opinion of recent developments in England, he replied evasively that he trusted that Chamberlain's "realistic and energetic efforts" to achieve peaceful settlement of political problems might prove successful, opening the way "for a general world appeasement" and reestablishment of the principles of international conduct which the United States considered necessary for permanent peace.[66] Lindsay apparently reported these remarks to his government, and on March 8 he told Welles that Halifax was gratified that Roosevelt and the American government considered British efforts to achieve political appeasement "to be right." Welles irately replied that the Americans had never said that, they had said only that "the President frankly recognized that certain political appeasements in Europe with which this Government had no direct concern and in which this Government could not participate were evidently an indispensable factor in the finding of bases for world peace."[67]

In April, the British neared agreement with Italy on recognition of Italian sovereignty over Ethiopia in return for withdrawal of Italian troops from Spain, the presumption being that the civil war there was near its end. On April 14 Halifax appealed through Joseph P. Kennedy, who had replaced the deceased Robert Bingham as ambassador at the start of the year, for Roosevelt to give public indication of approval of the Anglo-Italian agreement and the principles that inspired it.[68] Hull was not in Washington, and Welles apparently prevailed upon Roosevelt to issue a statement, in which Hull, relating afterward, "reluctantly concurred."[69] Following the Anglo-Italian agreement on April 16, Roosevelt declared that the United States advocated negotiation and "economic appeasement" to resolve controversies, but would not judge the political aspects of agreements. It did view the Anglo-Italian agreement with "sympathetic interest

65. Moffat to Wilson, Feb. 21, and Wilson to Moffat, Mar. 7, 1938, Moffat papers.
66. Welles Memorandum, Feb. 25, 1938, DS, 740.00/299½.
67. Welles Memorandum, Mar. 8, 1938, *FR 1938*, I, 126–130.
68. Kennedy to Hull, Apr. 15, 1938, *ibid.*, 143–145.
69. *Memoirs*, I, 581.

because it is proof of the value of peaceful negotiations."[70] Rumors circulated that Hull, angry that the statement suggested too much, would resign. He had no intention of following Eden's example.[71] Whether the United States, which never recognized Italy's conquest of Ethiopia, intended to follow the British example, is less clear. The Roosevelt administration was divided and confused; relations between the United States and Great Britain were poor. When in March 1938 Hull wrote his good friend Davis that "we do not know what is ahead on the West," it is likely he anticipated only more ominous developments.[72]

The *Anschluss* outraged Americans, the brutal diplomacy perhaps even more than the development itself. Newspapers denounced the Nazi takeover, and even the isolationist Senator Borah lamented Austria's loss of independence, although he insisted it was "not of the slightest moment" to the United States.[73] Assistant Secretary Messersmith wrote Wiley that "words would be inadequate to tell you how I feel . . . and how much my heart goes out to our Austrian friends." Even Ambassador Wilson, given to admiring the "efficiency of the action," conceded that morally one had to judge the action "with condemnation" and "deplore the brutality of it."[74] When Ambassador Dieckhoff went to the State Department on March 14 to inform officials about formal German control of Austrian representation, first Hull and then Welles received him with icy silence. Dieckhoff made some nervous remarks about Germany's "great and wonderful day," which met further silence, and then much to the surprise of Welles, who had known him well and liked him for fifteen years, he burst into a "tirade," accusing everyone of being far too ready to question Germany's good faith.[75]

---

70. Text of Roosevelt's statement is in Welles to Kennedy, Apr. 19, 1938, *FR 1938*, I, 147–148.

71. Hull, *Memoirs*, I, 512.

72. Hull to Davis, Mar. 4, 1938, Davis papers, Box. 27.

73. Borah is quoted in Arnold J. Toynbee and R. G. D. Laffan, eds., *Survey of International Affairs, 1938*, 3 vols. (London, 1941–53), I, 594; (Toynbee edited vol. I and Laffan edited vols. II and III.); see also *New York Times*, Mar. 29, 1938.

74. Messersmith to Wiley, Mar. 16, 1938, *FR 1938*, I, 451–453; Diary entry for Mar. 12, 1938, Wilson, *Career Diplomat*, 63.

75. Welles, Memorandum, Mar. 14, 1938, *FR 1938*, I, 442.

Dieckhoff's outburst was uncustomary. He was a shrewd career diplomat, well acquainted with American diplomats from his tour of duty as counselor in the Washington embassy during 1922–1926, and had been a specialist on American affairs while serving in the Foreign Ministry in various capacities—including head of the Political Department and most recently acting state secretary—during 1930–1937. Apparently he had been instrumental in arranging to have Luther recalled in May 1937 in order that he might take his place, presumably to better German relations with the United States.[76] As noted earlier, Ambassador Dodd liked and got along well with him, and even Dodd's daughter Martha, who disliked Dieckhoff for his perpetual subservience to the Hitler regime, described him in 1939 as "not given to Nazi excesses," "never likely to fly off the handle," and "cultivated, somewhat constrained."[77]

What was apparently uppermost in Dieckhoff's mind in the spring of 1938 was the persistent thought that events were leading to a war in which Germany would have to face the combined power of Great Britain and the United States. At the time of Roosevelt's quarantine address he had warned that American isolation would last only so long as England was not menaced; once world conflict began, America would throw its weight into the scales on the side of the British. In December 1937 Dieckhoff properly evaluated the failure of the Brussels Conference, but believed that if the British had shown greater readiness to take action against Japan, "the United States could have changed its bark to a bite." Americans could not "pull the Chinese chestnuts out of the fire for England," but if they were "frightened out of their lethargy . . . the jump from isolationism to interventionism would not be too big for them." A few weeks later he warned that American public opinion bitterly opposed Germany and "only twenty years ago the development of unfavorable public opinion in America proved fateful for us."[78]

Dieckhoff carried his "campaign" into the new year. He continued to report on the decline in German-American relations—at this time

76. Department of Justice Note, Dec. 23, 1937, DS, 711.62/133.
77. M. Dodd, *Through Embassy Eyes*, 252–253. After his recall in November 1938, Dieckhoff served as ambassador on special assignment, 1938–1943, and ambassador to Spain, 1943–1945.
78. Dieckhoff to Foreign Ministry, Dec. 7, and Dieckhoff to Weizsäcker, Dec. 20, 1937, *DGFP*, D, I, 653–656, 658–661.

he began to muster decisive arguments against German cooperation with the Bund—and he warned that it would be "hopeless" to try to organize German-Americans for any purpose. In February, alluding again to the possibility of Anglo-American action, he said that in 1917 the United States belonged to no alliance but nevertheless joined the Allied Powers. In spite of current widespread opposition to overseas involvements, "the American Government, should it so desire, will encounter no insuperable difficulties in again pushing this country into war at the psychological moment, just as quickly as in the World War, and perhaps even more quickly."[79]

In reporting his difficult interviews with Hull and Welles at the time of the *Anschluss,* Dieckhoff noted that Hull was "reserved" and Welles spoke with "malevolent bitterness." The State Department, he said, was taking its cue from London and echoing "his master's voice."[80] A week later he referred to "fantastic" newspaper reports in America about "the Prussian wolf raging amongst the Austrian sheep," the death of *"gemütlich"* Vienna under the tramp of the German soldier and the S.A. man's whip. "I am perhaps becoming a bore," he told his friend Weizsäcker—who scrawled "certainly not" in the margin—but "we can no longer count on America's isolation, and . . . we must be prepared, in case of a world conflict, to see Americans throw their weight into the British scale." In another lengthy dispatch of the same day, which Weizsäcker circulated to every high diplomatic and military department, including the Reich Chancellery where it was apparently read to Hitler, and in another long dispatch on March 30, Dieckhoff kept insisting that American intervention, in behalf of England at the appropriate moment, was inevitable. The neutrality legislation, he said, would be amended or repealed as circumstances required.[81]

Dieckhoff never changed his mind about the inevitability of American intervention against Germany and persisted in the point in his diplomatic dispatches over the next three years and in public writings in 1941—the latter, for obvious reasons, written in more venomous

79. Dieckhoff to Foreign Ministry, Jan. 7 and Feb. 9, 1938, *ibid.,* 664–667, 689–690.

80. Dieckhoff to Foreign Ministry, Mar. 15, 1938, *ibid.,* 594–595.

81. Dieckhoff to Weizsäcker, Mar. 22, and Dieckhoff to Foreign Ministry, Mar. 22 and Mar. 30, 1938, *ibid.,* 697–698, 694–695, 699–701.

anti-American, and especially anti-Roosevelt, language.[82] In the spring of 1938, Weizsäcker encouraged Dieckhoff to persist: "Your warnings that we should have no illusions as to the American stand in the event of a world conflict are by all means valuable; it can do no harm if you point this out again and again."[83] Ribbentrop suggested "large-scale information activities" in the United States to explain the German case, but Dieckhoff, probably recognizing the heavy-handed approach his brother-in-law and other Nazis would take, put off the proposal, indefinitely as it turned out, on the ground that the time was not yet ripe, especially in an election year.[84] Aside from his general lack of interest in the United States, Hitler was of course far more interested in wooing Mussolini and thinking about Czechoslovakia.

Practically, Hitler had little to fear. Neither England nor France contested Germany's coup, save to register formal protests which were rejected. In Parliament on March 14 Chamberlain spoke harshly of Germany's assault on Austria, but confessed that "unless we and others with us had been prepared to use force to prevent it" nothing could be done.[85] Ten days later Chamberlain publicly declared that an assault on Czechoslovakia would probably involve more than just those nations—France and the Soviet Union—legally obligated to its defense, but he rejected a proposal from the Soviet Union to consider ways to implement the Franco-Soviet Pact. He insisted that

82. See, for example, Dieckhoff Note, Apr. 25, 1939, *DGFP*, D, VI, 331; Dieckhoff Memorandum, July 7, 1940, *DGFP*, D, X, 359; Dieckhoff Memorandum, Mar. 10, 1941, *DGFP*, D, XII, 258. In 1941 Dieckhoff wrote a series of vitriolic articles under the name "Silvanus" for the *Monatshefte für Auswärtige Politik* which were expanded into a book, *Zur Vorgeschichte des Roosevelt-Krieges* (Berlin, 1943). On this work see also Compton, *Swastika and Eagle*, 49–51, and Manfred Jonas, "Prophet Without Honor: Hans Heinrich Dieckhoff's Reports from Washington," *Mid-America*, XLVII (July 1965), 232–233. Dieckhoff could also appear "Naziish" privately, as when in 1941 he drew up a long memorandum circulated throughout the Foreign Ministry which listed Jews who were supposedly urging Roosevelt to go to war. Dieckhoff Report, Oct. 9, 1941, GFM, K843/E193839-E193841. In this report as in the "Silvanus" articles, however, undoubtedly one of Dieckhoff's motives was to caution against provoking the United States and thereby causing its intervention in the war.

83. Weizsäcker to Dieckhoff, Apr. 30, 1938, *DGFP*, D, I, 705–706.

84. Ribbentrop to Dieckhoff, Mar. 29, and Dieckhoff to Ribbentrop, Apr. 14, 1938, *ibid.*, 698–699, 703–704.

85. Text of Chamberlain Statement, Mar. 14, 1938, is in *DBFP*, 3d ser., I, 44–48.

move would further threaten peace by increasing the tendency toward exclusive groupings of nations.[86]

American diplomats were not unaware of the dangers German foreign policy posed. In February 1938 Messersmith told Roosevelt and Hull that it was "utterly futile" to believe anyone could make a lasting agreement with Hitler: Germany would take Austria, and in four or five months, Czechoslovakia. The Western powers would offer little resistance. "In the end," Messersmith concluded with distress, "we would have our troubles in South America" where Germany had "definite objectives."[87] From London, Ambassador Kennedy opined on March 11 to Roosevelt that Hitler and Mussolini were bluffing, but having done so well for themselves in that way "won't stop until somebody very sharply calls their bluff." But the United States, he added, could not possibly do anything at the moment; only after Chamberlain had made "the political offers necessary," could Roosevelt make a world-wide gesture based "completely on an economic stand."[88] After the *Anschluss* Americans were angry, but as Messersmith told Wiley on March 16 Roosevelt and Hull had made clear that "there will be no change in our policy no matter what may take place elsewhere."[89] At the National Press Club next day Hull reiterated this policy, declaring that although the United States needed to arm itself against rampaging international lawlessness, it had no intention of "policing the world."[90] In London, Kennedy gave his first public address on March 18 and said much the same thing. He would have gone further and said that even in event of major war the United States would not offer assistance, had not Hull struck these words from the ambassador's text.[91]

The *Anschluss* aggravated relations with Germany. The United States closed its embassy in Vienna, established a Consulate General,

86. Text of Chamberlain's remarks on the Soviet proposal are in Lewis, ed., *Documents 1938,* I, 47–48.

87. Messersmith to Hull, Feb. 18, 1938, *FR 1938,* I, 17–24.

88. Kennedy to Roosevelt, Mar. 11, 1938, Hull papers, Box 42. Kennedy sent Hull this carbon on Mar. 14.

89. Messersmith to Wiley, Mar. 16, 1938, *FR 1938,* I, 451–453.

90. *Peace and War,* 407–419.

91. Kennedy to Hull, Mar. 10, and Hull to Kennedy, Mar. 14, 1938, Roosevelt papers, Official File 3060, Joseph P. Kennedy. Text of Kennedy's address in *New York Times,* Mar. 18, 1938.

and said the German government must honor Austria's bonded debts of nearly $25 million owed the American government and business-men.[92] In April, Roosevelt instructed Secretary of the Treasury Morgenthau to remove Austria, effective in thirty days, from the list of nations enjoying most-favored-nation privileges and tariff concessions under the Reciprocal Trade Agreements Act.[93] The Germans, as earlier in the case of their own debts, insisted that an unfavorable balance of trade made them unable to meet the Austrian debts and protested the loss of most-favored-nation privileges. Roosevelt refused to rescind his order—the United States recognizing *de facto* the incorporation of Austria into Germany. The Germans refused to honor the Austrian debts, except to offer what the State Department considered an unsatisfactory arrangement, namely, to exchange the Austrian bonds, which were payable in dollars, for 4½ per cent German bonds payable in Reichsmarks.[94]

Another problem, a source of argument at the highest levels of the Roosevelt administration, and much talked about in the United States and Germany, was whether the American government would sell helium to the German government. The problem antedated the *Anschluss,* for in May 1937 Roosevelt had asked his secretaries of state, war, navy, commerce, and interior for a policy on sale and export of helium. As a committee they recommended that because the government had a virtual monopoly of helium (owning all important reserves, with the one private producer, the Girdler Corporation of Louisville, willing to sell its properties to the government), it would be both morally and militarily proper to sell helium to foreign nations for scientific, medical, experimental, and commercial purposes. Congress on September 1, 1937, passed the Helium Act which allowed licensed sale of helium to foreign nations provided the helium was not of military importance and both the National Munitions Control Board (composed of the secretaries of state, treasury, war, navy, and commerce) and the secretary of the interior approved. Provisions relating to licensing and export were put under the jurisdiction of the

92. Hull to Wilson, Apr. 5, 1938 (two cables), *FR 1938,* II, 473, 483–484.
93. *New York Times,* Apr. 7, 1938. German Embassy to Department of State, Apr. 14, and Department of State to German Embassy, Apr. 29, 1938, *FR 1938,* II, 502–505.
94. Hull to Gilbert, Nov. 23, 1938, *FR 1938,* II, 497–499.

National Munitions Control Board; those relating to sale, under the secretary of the interior.[95]

The German government wanted helium for zeppelins. Following the disastrous explosion of the *Hindenburg* at Lakehurst, New Jersey, in May 1937, the Germans had halted construction of the highly flammable hydrogen-inflated zeppelins; but when Congress passed the Helium Act, the German Zeppelin Company, through its agent the Zeppelin Company of America, ordered 17,900,000 cubic feet of helium. Hull and other members of the National Munitions Control Board approved the order on November 23, by proxy vote, and the Germans sent tankers to Houston to pick up the helium. Public protests, including ones by Senator Henry Cabot Lodge, Jr., of Massachusetts and seven other congressmen, forced delay. But after experts from the War and Navy Departments testified that it was inconceivable for lighter-than-air craft to be used for military purposes, and the clamor subsided, the State Department on January 31, 1938, granted a license for export to Germany of the first 2,600,000 cubic feet of helium.[96]

Harold Ickes, secretary of the interior, would not acquiesce in the proceedings. Though he originally approved the sale of helium, by February 1938 he had hardened his attitude toward Germany and upset both the State Department and the German government with derogatory comments about politics in the Third Reich. He balked at signing the contract for sale of helium, and without consulting other members of the cabinet convinced Roosevelt, early in March, to support three amendments to the Helium Act. The new provisions required the purchasing nation to pledge the helium would not be used for military purposes, to post a domestic surety bond of an amount to be fixed by the secretaries of the interior, navy, and war (Ickes demanded the Germans post five times the purchase price, the other officials asked only an amount equal to the purchase price), and to allow an American representative to examine the craft in which the helium would be used. Upset by this development, Hull told Roosevelt there was no reason to object to the sale on grounds of foreign policy,

95. Roosevelt to Lister Hill, May 25, 1937, and Ed. Note, *PPFDR*, VI, 223–227.

96. Hull to Roosevelt, Mar. 21, 1938, Hull papers, Box 42; Green Memorandum for Roosevelt, Apr. 1, 1938, DS, 811.659 Helium/98. (Joseph C. Green was executive secretary of the National Munitions Control Board.)

and that to refuse the helium might "irritate" Germany and give rise to "unwarranted conclusions" about American relations with Germany.[97] At the secretary of state's request, Joseph C. Green, executive secretary of the National Munitions Control Board, prepared a long memorandum for Roosevelt arguing that to deny Germany the helium would contradict the administration's liberal trade policy.[98] Further, in two reports the State Department's Office of Arms and Munitions Control said that to express distrust of Germany by placing such conditions on the sale as the secretary of the interior proposed was not in "good taste"; that he apparently was trying to enforce by his own authority a provision of the law which Congress had delegated to six cabinet officials.[99]

Ickes would not budge. As long as there was any question about the military value of helium—the navy was using some newly appropriated funds to build a zeppelin—he believed that he could not legally sell it. More to the point, he recorded in his diary, the "ruthless and wanton invasion of Austria" made him doubt that selling helium to Germany was right "under any pretext." At the same time, at a cabinet meeting on March 18, Roosevelt told Ickes to delay the decision, despite Hull's objection that the United States was morally obligated.[100] That was fine with the secretary of the interior, who by now thought the State Department was "acting a little queer" over the matter.[101]

Demand for Ickes to relent mounted in the next month. The British magazine *Aeroplane* called his behavior "a crime against humanity" and "politically silly."[102] Ambassador Wilson warned that Germany's "deep resentment" would negate efforts to protect American interests there.[103] The German government pledged that it would never use the helium for military purposes.[104] Ickes would not give in. Nor did Roosevelt try to change Ickes' mind. Late in April the President told

97. Hull to Roosevelt, Mar. 21, 1938, Hull papers, Box 42.

98. Green Memorandum for Roosevelt, Apr. 1, 1938, DS, 811.659 Helium/98⅙.

99. Price and Green Memoranda, Apr. 8 and Apr. 14, 1938, DS, 811.659 Helium/98⅔, 811.659 Helium/98⅘.

100. Entry for Mar. 19, 1938, Ickes, *Diary*, II, 344.

101. Entry for Mar. 25, 1938, *ibid.*, 346.

102. April 6, 1938.

103. Wilson to Welles, Apr. 13, 1938, *FR 1938*, II, 457–458.

104. Welles Memorandum, Apr. 14, 1938, DS, 611.6331/164.

him to "adopt a Fabian policy," and two days later characteristically remarked to Attorney General Cummings, "Homer, there is an important legal question involved, and some day I am going to have you come to my office and we will sit down and discuss that legal question."[105]

By May, German and many State Department officials had no more patience. Wilson reported from Berlin that Göring had told him with "deep emotion and bluntness" that he could not understand why the United States insisted on earning Germany's "enmity" over such a small matter. The ambassador wrote Roosevelt personally, stressing the "formidable nature" of his conversation with Göring, who now counted America as "one of the enemies of Germany."[106] The State Department mustered all its arguments to convince Roosevelt that Ickes' position was morally and legally untenable. Legal Adviser Green H. Hackworth carefully reviewed the laws and treaties binding both countries and concluded they did not prevent the United States from selling helium to Germany.[107] Secretary of War Harry Woodring testified to Hull, who relayed the information to Roosevelt, that the War Department was certain the sale posed no threat to any nation's security.[108] As a last resort Captain Hugo Eckener, Germany's aged designer of zeppelins, made a special trip to the United States to plead his case to Roosevelt.[109] The only one in the administration who supported Ickes was Messersmith, who now circulated a letter in the State Department indicating that Eckener, a man of "great honesty and courage," had told him over a year before that he might not be able to express his real convictions any longer. More important, Messersmith added, zeppelin service was of little commercial value but involved "definite military risks" for the United States. And Germany's promise not to use helium for military purposes was worthless.[110]

105. Entries for Apr. 21 and Apr. 23, 1938, Ickes, *Diary*, II, 372–373, 377.

106. Wilson to Hull, Apr. 29, 1938, *FR 1938*, II, 459–460; Wilson to Roosevelt, May 2, 1938, Wilson, *Career Diplomat*, 29–31. See also Ribbentrop Memorandum, Apr. 29, 1938, *DGFP*, D, I, 704–705.

107. Hackworth Memorandum, May 2, 1938, Hull papers, Box 42.

108. Woodring to Hull, May 6, and Hull to Roosevelt, May 9, 1938, Roosevelt papers, PSF, Germany.

109. *New York Times*, May 9–12, 1938.

110. Messersmith to Hull, Welles, Moore, Dunn, and Moffat, May 9, 1938, Messersmith papers, Box 1.

Roosevelt seemed anxious to end the debacle and, probably more out of embarrassment than desire, disposed to sell Germany the helium. At a critical meeting on May 11 with Ickes, Solicitor General Robert H. Jackson, Army Chief of Staff General Malin Craig, and Chief of Naval Operations Admiral William D. Leahy, Roosevelt argued "quite effectively," as Ickes admitted, that helium had no military importance and ought to be sold. Craig and Leahy supported that view. Ickes still would not give in—even with a guarantee of peaceful uses from Hitler whom he said he would not trust. But it was Jackson who proffered the decisive legal judgment that Roosevelt had no authority in the matter and that Ickes' negative vote was enough to block any license the National Munitions Control Board issued. "At this point the President gave up," Ickes recorded, and the White House press secretary, Stephen Early, promptly announced that because the National Munitions Control Board could not reach a unanimous decision there would be no sale.[111] Roosevelt received Eckener and Dieckhoff cordially, but insisted the law was binding.[112]

State Department officials bristled. Ambassador Wilson deplored the decision, warned it would have "serious repercussions" on many aspects of American relations with Germany, where there was "disappointment and resentment," and told the State Department not to ask him to request any favor from the German government.[113] At a cabinet meeting on May 14 Hull—"his voice was tense and his hands trembled," Ickes noted—again read all the documents that supported the sale. Roosevelt now said he would take full responsibility for the sale as commander in chief of the army and navy, thus offering Ickes a graceful way out. The "curmudgeon" secretary of the interior prevailed, despite the fact that every member of the cabinet either supported or acquiesced in the sale, including Morgenthau who had battled the State Department over imposing countervailing duties on German goods in 1936. The case closed.[114]

At least one historian, Joachim Remak, has condemned Ickes' be-

---

111. Entry for May 12, 1938, Ickes, *Diary,* II, 391–393; Early Press Statement, May 11, 1938, DS, 811.659 Helium/133.
112. Dieckhoff to Foreign Ministry, May 21, 1938, *DGFP,* D, I, 706–707.
113. Wilson to Welles, May 12, 1938, Wilson, *Career Diplomat,* 31–32; see also Wilson to Hull, May 14, 1938, *FR 1938,* II, 460–461.
114. Entry for May 15, 1938, Ickes, *Diary,* II, 396–399.

havior in this "foolish and disreputable incident."[115] Indeed, Ickes knew that his logic sprang more from his heart than his head, that the military importance of helium was nil, and this he did "confess frankly," knowing he had used the "rape of Austria" as a "good excuse" for refusing Germany the helium.[116] But to criticize Ickes' behavior and to say in the next phrase, as Remak does, that "Hitler's expansion plans remained unaffected," is perhaps to miss the point that so long as Hitler's appetite was insatiable, there was no reason to give him anything. Ickes' action, within the letter of the law as long as there remained the slightest question about the military importance of helium, was really a moral rebuff to immoral German behavior. If the "rape of Austria" did not provide sufficient reason for the secretary of the interior, events of the next months certainly would.

115. "Germany and the United States," 236.
116. Entry for July 23, 1938, Ickes, Diary, II, 428. Curiously, when Ickes was in London in June 1938 both Chamberlain and Halifax told him they approved his decision. Entry for June 26, 1938, *ibid.*, 406.

# 9.

## TO MUNICH AND WAR

From spring to autumn 1938 the developing crisis between Germany and Czechoslovakia absorbed European energies. American diplomats abroad seemed to fear most that England and France would oppose Hitler's demands and thus precipitate world war. Ambassador Wilson, sympathetic toward German aspirations, confessed limited admiration for Czechoslovakia's "gallant impulse" to resist, but doubted its wisdom if it jeopardized peace. He also suspected, as he confided to his equally suspicious colleague in Berlin, Nevile Henderson, that the Czechs were counting on French and Soviet, and eventually British, support and therefore intended to provoke a showdown with Germany rather than await negotiations.[1] Ambassador Bullitt, once the champion of the Soviet Union but after three disillusioning years in Moscow now its bitter critic, believed that the best way to thwart Soviet designs would be to encourage reconciliation between France and Germany.[2] He seemed relieved when in May French Premier Edouard Daladier snapped "With what?" when he asked if France would fight if Germany attacked Czechoslovakia.[3] Ambassador Kennedy thought that almost no price was too high to pay to avert war and that, above all, if war

1. Wilson to Hull, Apr. 28, 1938, *FR 1938*, I, 490; Henderson to Halifax, May 13, 1938, *DBFP*, 3d ser., I, 290–291.
2. William W. Kaufmann, "Two American Ambassadors: Bullitt and Kennedy," in Craig and Gilbert, eds., *The Diplomats*, 656–657; Beatrice Farnsworth, *William C. Bullitt and the Soviet Union* (Bloomington, Ind., and London, 1967), 158–159.
3. Bullitt to Hull, May 9, 1938, *FR 1938*, I, 493–494.

came the United States must stay out. In August he worriedly told Foreign Secretary Halifax that if Hitler seized Czechoslovakia "it will be hell," and that if France went in, so must Great Britain, with the United States following shortly. Perhaps, then, if Germany were allowed to control southeastern Europe, economic developments would either paralyze or pacify Germany politically.[4] Kennedy's unabashed favoring of German economic expansion and closer Anglo-German relations, and his desire to say publicly, "I can't for the life of me understand why anybody would want to go to war to save the Czechs"—the State Department struck this from the text of an address in September—implied too much for his superiors in Washington. Roosevelt concluded to Morgenthau that Kennedy "needs his wrists slapped rather hard."[5] But the American attitude toward European developments and the position the United States might take in event of a crisis, or war, remained ambiguous at best, on the side of misguided appeasement at worst.

The United States minister to Czechoslovakia, Wilbur J. Carr, signified, and knew, as little about American intentions as any diplomat. Although he had been in the State Department since 1892, he had been concerned almost wholly with administrative and personnel matters, had never served abroad, and knew nothing about the language or politics of Czechoslovakia.[6] At the time Roosevelt, for reasons best known to himself, appointed Carr in the summer of 1937, he was sixty-seven years old and thoroughly surprised at his selection, for he had intended to retire that autumn.[7] In addition to his own limitations, Carr was not well advised. At the end of March 1938, he sought to determine from a State Department officer visiting Prague what policy was. He learned only that opinion divided at home: some State Department people were hostile to German ambitions, others were

4. Halifax to Lindsay, Sept. 2, 1938, *DBFP*, 3d ser., II, 212–213. See also Kaufmann, "Two Ambassadors," in Craig and Gilbert, eds., *The Diplomats*, 658–659.

5. Morgenthau Diary, as cited in Blum, *Morgenthau Diaries*, 518.

6. Katharine Crane, *Mr. Carr of State: Forty Seven Years in the Department of State* (New York, 1960), 329.

7. Carr to Vinton Chapin, July 9, 1937, Wilbur J. Carr papers, Box 14, Manuscript Division, Library of Congress. Chapin was second secretary at the embassy in Prague.

convinced that Chamberlain was on the right path and that the United States should follow his lead. Carr inclined toward believing only a "solid front among the democracies" would halt Hitler, and he agreed with the recent barb of Jan Masaryk, minister to England, that Chamberlain had "yet to find out that Czechoslovakia was a country and not a disease." In April Carr drafted a cable expressing bleak views and dire warnings, but his aides insisted it would only alarm the State Department and persuaded him to tone it down. At the end of the month, writing Hull, Carr correctly surmised that agreement existed between Hitler and Konrad Henlein, the Nazi leader of the Sudeten Germans who had visited Berlin at the end of March, to press unreasonable demands upon Czechoslovakia to create an excuse for eventual German intervention.[8]

At Karlsbad on April 24 Henlein put forward eight demands which included so much autonomy for the Sudeten Germans that the Czech government could not accept them in entirety without destroying its political sovereignty and military defenses.[9] The British knew this but urged negotiations; in the meantime, in London on April 28–29 Chamberlain and Halifax conferred with Daladier and his foreign minister, Georges Bonnet.

In the initial talks which concerned military matters, Chamberlain emphasized that in event of war England's far-flung commitments, need to concentrate on air defense, and the fact that it was "no longer possible confidently to count upon being able to purchase munitions from the United States to the same extent as had been possible during the Great War" meant that England could contribute little to a Continental force. Naval talks were out of the question at the moment because such discussion might offend Mussolini or Hitler. Daladier countered that he had no doubt their two countries could resist aggression if they coordinated their forces. Moreover, the purchase of supplies, including airplanes, in the United States had recently proved easier than expected, and he advised approaching American industry

8. Crane, *Carr of State*, 338–343. According to Henlein's summary view, on March 28 Hitler agreed that he and the Sudeten Germans "must always demand so much that we can never be satisfied." Unsigned Report (undated), *DGFP*, D, II, 107–108. The report is from State Secretary Weizsäcker's files.

9. Henlein's Eight Demands in *DGFP*, D, II, 242. See also Andrew Rothstein, *The Munich Conspiracy* (London, 1958), 55–56.

at once and outlining the scope of British and French needs in case of war. Turning to political matters, Chamberlain insisted that the British and French had to use all their influence to get the Czech government "to make a supreme effort" to reach an agreement with its German minority, although at some time the Germans ought to be told they could not "impose any settlement they would on Czechoslovakia by force or by threat of force." Daladier argued that he thought, to judge from the Karlsbad speech, that Henlein sought not concessions but rather the destruction of the Czechoslovak state. The Beneš government had made great concessions to its minorities and there was no need to put pressure on it. More important, the real issue was not the dispute between the Czech government and the Sudeten Germans but "German policy readily translated into action, designed to tear up treaties and destroy the equilibrium of Europe." The Rhineland occupation and the *Anschluss* ought to have been opposed. Now every effort had to be made to solve matters through negotiations, but first England and France had to make clear their intention, if sufficient concessions failed to satisfy the Sudeten Germans, to preserve the independence of Czechoslovakia.

Chamberlain did not agree. To put forward a firm statement based on the "united forces of France, Great Britain, and such assistance as might be obtainable from outside forces" was what "the Americans in their card games called bluff." The odds against war were 100 to 1, he said, but even so the British and French had to consider their position carefully. It "made his blood boil to see Germany get away with it time after time" and dominate free peoples, but "sentimental considerations were dangerous." His "cool judgment" told him the time was not right to adopt Daladier's view.

Supported by Halifax, who similarly countered Bonnet's contentions, Chamberlain prevailed. In the end the diplomats decided to apply maximum pressure on Czechoslovakia for concessions. They would also inform the Germans of their effort, ask what they considered to be a fair settlement, and tell them that if they resorted to force they "must realise what the dangers were." In case of war the French were still bound by treaty to aid Czechoslovakia and the British had not said they would not come in.[10] Halifax promptly informed Theodor

10. Record of Anglo-French Conversations, Apr. 28–29, 1938, *DBFP,* 3d ser., I, 198–233.

Kordt, counselor and chargé at the German embassy, that the British had assumed no further obligations or commitments and, as Kordt reported it, "the best thing would be if the three kindred nations, Germany, Britain, and the United States, could unite in joint work for peace." Germany and Britain, it seemed, were the "protagonists whose task it was to encourage the others."[11]

Chamberlain clearly intended to take the initiative in finding a solution to the argument between the government of Czechoslovakia and the Sudeten Germans; he also determined to see that no situation would develop in which England would have to fight to defend Czechoslovakia. In the next weeks the British undertook diplomatic soundings and on May 12–14 Henlein visited London where, Kennedy reported, he made a good impression.[12] In Berlin, Weizsäcker told Ambassador Wilson that the Czechs were trying to provoke a crisis to ward off "the authentic chemical process of disintegration" of their country, while Bullitt reported that he concluded from talks with Bonnet that in event of war France would be sentencing its youth to death if it honored its commitment to Czechoslovakia.[13]

Amidst negotiations and worries a crisis erupted. The Sudeten Germans broke off negotiations with the Czech government on May 19, and reports of German troop maneuvers were mistakenly feared to portend an attack on Czechoslovakia. In the evening of May 20 the government in Prague undertook partial mobilization.[14] Bullitt grew panicky. He thought the Czechs preferred general war to giving the Sudeten Germans autonomy and worried that the French as a matter of honor would fulfill their military obligations to Czechoslovakia. He urged that if a clash seemed imminent Roosevelt should persuade the French, Germans, English, and Italians to confer at The Hague, with a United States representative sitting in. Convinced that war would lead to "an Asiatic despotism established on the fields of the dead,"

11. Kordt to Foreign Ministry, Apr. 29, 1938, *DGFP*, D, II, 246–247; see also Kordt to Foreign Ministry, Apr. 30, 1938, *ibid.*, 248–249, and Halifax to Henderson, Apr. 29, 1938, *DBFP*, 3d ser., I, 235.

12. Kennedy to Hull, May 14, 1938, *FR 1938*, I, 498–499; see also Vansittart Note, May 16, 1938, *DBFP*, 3d ser., I, 630–633.

13. Weizsäcker Memorandum, May 14, 1938, *DGFP*, D, II, 780; Bullitt to Hull, May 16, 1938, *FR 1938*, I, 501–502.

14. Gerhard L. Weinberg, "The May Crisis, 1938," *Journal of Modern History*, XXIX (Sept. 1957), 214, 217.

Bullitt figured that the assembled powers would agree on a plebiscite, which the Czechs would have to accept; if they refused it, the French would be relieved of their military obligations and there would be no war. As for future charges that America had sold out a tiny nation, the ambassador counseled the President: "I should not hesitate to take that brick on my head and I don't think you should either if thereby you could avoid a general European war."[15] In the meantime Ambassador Wilson in Germany requested that the State Department instruct both him and Carr to approach the governments in Berlin and Prague and urge them to resolve their difficulties peacefully.[16] Officials in Washington said nothing. They disregarded Bullitt's proposal and Hull told Wilson he would not advise a simultaneous approach.[17]

The Germans had not ordered an attack, and in a few days the crisis subsided. But the French, while urging restraint on the Czechs, had to reassure them of their guarantee in case of an attack, and the British had to engage in sharp exchanges while warning the Germans that "His Majesty's Government could not guarantee that they would not be forced by circumstances to become involved also."[18] Hitler was enraged, probably because the appearance was given that a united front had forced Germany to retreat. A military directive of May 20, drawn at Hitler's instruction, had stated that he did not intend to crush Czechoslovakia by force "in the immediate future" without timely provocation.[19] Hitler now reviewed his military plans and concluded on May 30 that the political leadership had to bring about the appropriate situation that would precipitate conflict because "it is my unalterable decision to smash Czechoslovakia by military action in the near future."[20]

---

15. Bullitt to Hull, May 22, 1938, *FR 1938,* I, 509–512.

16. Wilson to Hull, May 21, 1938, *ibid.,* 506–507.

17. Hull to Wilson, May 23, 1938, *ibid.,* 515.

18. Phipps to Halifax, May 22, and Halifax to Henderson, May 20, 1938, *DBFP,* 3d ser., I, 340, 331–332; Weizsäcker Minute, May 22, 1938, *DGFP,* D, II, 319–320. See also Schmidt, *Statist auf diplomatischer Bühne,* 388–389, and Weinberg, "The May Crisis," *Journal of Modern History,* 221–222.

19. Keitel to Hitler (Enclosing Revised Draft for Operation "Green"), May 20, 1938, *DGFP,* D, II, 299–303.

20. Hitler to the Commanders in Chief, May 20, 1938, *ibid.,* 357–362. See also General Strategic Directive, June 18, 1938, *ibid.,* 473–474, and Robertson, *Hitler's Pre-War Policy,* 134–135.

Diplomats in the United States had said little during the May crisis, and at its conclusion Hull announced, typically, that his government followed European events closely and considered the Kellogg Pact binding.[21] During the next months American diplomats in Europe, each in his own way, urged peace. In June Wilson told Ribbentrop that unrestrained anti-German agitation in the United States was actually having a reverse effect, and that he would do "everything in his power" to keep America out of any European conflict. Visiting Carr in Prague in early August, Wilson told President Beneš that the National Socialists had changed their attitude somewhat, that he should not be misled by the anti-German sentiment of the "Jewish-controlled press" in the eastern United States, and that the United States would not give military aid to any European country. On September 1 Wilson told Weizsäcker that he believed a peaceful solution to the crisis at hand possible; regardless, he could not conceive Germany would be willing to provoke a general war over the Sudetenland. Weizsäcker said nothing.[22]

Bullitt meanwhile told Bonnet in July that Roosevelt would not arbitrate or become otherwise involved in the Czech-German dispute, and on September 2 he told his British colleague in Paris, Sir Eric Phipps, that if war came the United States would neither fight nor offer aid. The American people had no intention of committing themselves to a struggle in which they "would get more kicks than ha'pence for their help." But the essential point, Phipps reported Bullitt told him, was that "Russia's great wish is to provoke a general conflagration in which she herself will play but little part, beyond perhaps a little bombing from a distance, but after which she will arise like a phoenix, but out of all our ashes, and bring about a world revolution."[23]

Ambassador Kennedy meanwhile was busy cultivating the confidence of not only Chamberlain and the Cliveden set, but his German colleague Herbert von Dirksen, who had been transferred from Tokyo to London during the diplomatic reorganization in February. During the spring of 1938 Kennedy apparently approached Dirksen at numerous social functions and tried to impress upon him his influence with Roo-

21. Hull Press Statement, May 28, 1938, *FR 1938*, I, 520–521.
22. Ribbentrop Memorandum, *DGFP*, D, I, 713; Carr to Hull, Aug. 6, and Wilson to Hull, Sept. 1, 1938, *FR 1938*, I, 540–544, 567.
23. Bullitt to Hull, July 13, 1938, *FR 1938*, I, 530–531; Phipps to Halifax, Sept. 2, 1938, *DBFP*, 3d ser., II, 218–219.

sevelt, his interest in improving American-German relations, and his desire to tour Germany. Dirksen, although skeptical about Kennedy's influence on the President, nevertheless believed the proposed trip would be useful.[24]

When the Foreign Ministry made no response to the overture, Kennedy evidently grew impatient. He approached Dirksen in mid-June, apologized for the conflict concerning Ickes and helium, blamed strong anti-German views in the United States on American diplomats and travelers who never said anything good about Germany—largely because they were afraid of the Jews on the East Coast. Kennedy continued that he understood Germany's Jewish policy, "repeatedly" said that Germany ought to have colonies and an economic free hand in eastern and southern Europe, and noted that he took a dim view of the Soviet Union. Kennedy reiterated similar themes in July: he would "be prepared to support Germany's demands vis-à-vis England or to do anything that might lead to pacification" (he was probably again thinking largely in economic terms), and he did not think the world had much confidence in Beneš.[25] In mid-September, while chiefly concerned that the crisis be resolved peacefully, Kennedy told other officials of the German embassy that the United States was wrongly more anti-German than ever and that Hitler had done wonders for his country. Finally, two weeks after the Munich Conference, Kennedy requested an opportunity for a conference with Hitler; in that way, he said, he could improve relations between the United States and Germany.[26]

Most German diplomats were unenthusiastic about Kennedy's proposed venture, Dirksen's encouragement notwithstanding. Since the May crisis Dieckhoff had grown deeply pessimistic about the possibility of improved relations with the United States. He believed that Roosevelt had wanted to issue a declaration of solidarity with England and France, but past setbacks such as at the time of his quarantine address and the Brussels Conference, and Hull's caution, had restrained him. Nevertheless, Roosevelt and State Department officials—including more than just Messersmith—were determined opponents of Germany,

24. Dirksen to Foreign Ministry, May 31, 1938, *DGFP*, D, II, 368–369.

25. Dirksen to Weizsäcker, June 13 and July 20, 1938, *DGFP*, D, I, 713–718, 721–723.

26. Kordt to Foreign Ministry, Sept. 12, 1938, *DGFP*, D, II, 744, and Dirksen to Weizsäcker, Oct. 13, 1938, *DGFP*, D, IV, 634–636.

and if the Czech crisis precipitated war "the United States would not permanently stand aside, but would enter the conflict against us."[27] Hence, when Kennedy was pressing Dirksen in July and saying that he would use as a pretext for his trip the fact that he was president of the International Wheat Advisory Committee which was considering meeting in Berlin, Weizsäcker wrote in the margin of Dirksen's cable that Dieckhoff thought Kennedy's judgment "poor" and that excuses would have to be made to deny the request.[28] A month later Dieckhoff insisted Kennedy's appraisal of American policy toward Germany was "too optimistic," but the embarrassed Germans concluded they would have to allow Kennedy to come under his suggested pretext.[29] September was a month of crisis, but in the aftermath of the Munich settlement the Germans agreed to arrange a meeting for Kennedy with Hitler, if Roosevelt approved, despite Dieckhoff's persistence that "small palliatives" would not improve German-American relations and that if Roosevelt was "anti-German" it was because he chose to be, not because he needed to be better informed.[30] Before formal plans were made, however, the November pogrom against the Jews and the mutual "recall" of ambassadors caused the project to be abandoned.[31]

Kennedy's visit, especially in the summer of 1938, would have served no useful purpose. Hitler intended to precipitate a crisis in Czechoslovakia to bring about the solution he wanted, and he was mainly concerned with ridding himself of those advisers, especially in the military, who opposed his policy. American intentions did not concern him. He had all the "warnings" he needed from Dieckhoff, whose reports in September 1938 were supported by Hans Thomsen, the chargé in the Washington embassy who had also served four years in the Reich Chancellery under Hitler, and by the military attaché in Washington,

27. Dieckhoff to Weizsäcker, May 31, 1938, *DGFP*, D, II, 369–372; Dieckhoff to Foreign Ministry, June 25, 1938, *DGFP*, D, I, 718–720.

28. Dirksen to Weizsäcker, July 20, 1938, *DGFP*, D, I, 723n88. Dieckhoff was in Berlin at the time and about to present to the Foreign Ministry a long list of reasons, chiefly concerning the *Anschluss*, for German disfavor in America. Dieckhoff Memorandum, July 28, 1938, *ibid.*, 724.

29. Woermann to Kordt, Aug. 16, 1938, *ibid.*, 725.

30. Dirksen to Weizsäcker, Oct. 18, and Dieckhoff to Dirksen, Nov. 2, 1938, *DGFP*, D, IV, 634n4, 637.

31. The International Wheat Advisory Committee met in London in January 1939.

Friedrich von Boetticher, who generally denigrated American power. On September 1, for example, Thomsen reported that even Boetticher agreed that in event of war involving England and France "leading political circles" in the United States would urge American entry. Two weeks later Thomsen sent a long report explaining that the administration's emphasis on the ideological confrontation between dictatorship and democracy had created a situation wherein "little is needed to change a confirmed isolationist into an equally confirmed interventionist." The government was preparing the nation for war. It would at first support England and France with economic aid and arms—British assets in America made it possible to get around the Johnson Debt Default Act and British control of the seas made the neutrality legislation's "cash and carry" provision on raw materials work in their favor—and if that proved insufficient the United States would enter the war whenever "the prospects of victory incline toward the totalitarian states."[32] Kordt, at the London embassy, expressed similar views in his reports in September. He also added that even Kennedy, who would do all he could to prevent American entry into a war, conceded that eventual American participation was inevitable.[33]

Hitler did not interest himself in such considerations, even when they came from General Ludwig Beck, chief of the army General Staff. Beginning in May, Beck undertook to convince Hitler and other military men that Germany could not go to war over Czechoslovakia. Although Beck concerned himself chiefly with the prospect of British and French intervention, he regarded the American role as significant. On May 5, for example, in a memorandum—"observations on the present military-political situation in Germany"—he argued that the United States would materially support British and French war efforts and that the basis for this development was further along than it had been in 1914. One week after the May crisis, Beck wrote that "a coalition of Czechoslovakia, France, England, and America, whose cooperation in event of war" was nearer than in 1914, opposed Germany.[34] On the

32. Thomsen to Foreign Ministry, Sept. 1, 1938, *DGFP*, D, II, 680–681; Thomsen to Foreign Ministry, Sept. 12, 1938, *DGFP*, D, I, 726–732. See also Thomsen to Foreign Ministry and Supreme Headquarters of the Wehrmacht, Sept. 24, 1938, *DGFP*, D, II, 922–923.

33. Kordt to Foreign Ministry, Sept. 12, 1938 (two cables), *DGFP*, D, II, 742–744.

34. Wolfgang Foerster, *Generaloberst Ludwig Beck, sein Kampf gegen den*

next day, May 30, Hitler signed his directive declaring his intention to crush Czechoslovakia, and a few days later Beck informed the commander in chief of the army, General von Brauchitsch, that the army General Staff regarded the plan as militarily unsound.[35]

During July and early August Beck drew up his "testament," opposing military action against Czechoslovakia. Essentially, he did not believe Germany could withstand a counterattack by England and France. Again he insisted that the United States would support the democracies with all the political, propagandistic, and then material means available. In every sense America was at least twenty times a more formidable opponent than it had been in 1914. And, he concluded, if "the United States threw its vast war potential into the scale on the side of England and France—and that unfortunately one must regard as probable—the opposition would receive an increase of power, especially in case of a long war, which Germany could not oppose."[36]

Hitler would not accept these judgments. At a conference with his younger military leaders on August 10, he insisted that it would be possible to overrun Czechoslovakia rapidly, and that even if England and France attacked, Germany could maintain its western fortifications for not only three weeks but three years. On August 18 Beck resigned his General Staff position—although the fact was not made public until after the Munich crisis—and on September 1 General Franz Halder assumed his duties.[37] At a conference on September 9–10 in Nuremberg, where the Nazi party rally was in full sway, Hitler outlined for his military leaders the probable course of military action that would have to be taken against Czechoslovakia—to be preceded by an uprising in Czechoslovakia and to take place not later than September 30.[38]

*Krieg: Aus nachgelassenen Papieren des Generalstabchefs*, 2d ed. (Munich, 1953), 101, 110.

35. Shirer, *Rise and Fall*, 367.

36. Foerster, *Generaloberst Ludwig Beck*, 132.

37. John W. Wheeler-Bennett, *The Nemesis of Power: The German Army in Politics, 1918–1945*, 2d ed. (London, 1964), 390–404; Goerlitz, *German General Staff*, 328–330.

38. Manuscript Notes by Hitler's Adjutant on Conference at Nuremberg, Sept. 9–10, 1938, *DGFP*, D, II, 727–730; Bullock, *Hitler*, 452, and Robertson, *Hitler's Pre-War Policy*, 129–135.

During the summer of 1938 diplomats in Washington watched European events through worried eyes. Reports from overseas led them to conclude that Hitler would wage war over the Sudetenland but might be dissuaded by firm statements. As Bullitt put it, clearly overoptimistically, fear of what the United States might do was a "large factor in Hitler's hesitation to start war."[39] The State Department, helping to draft a speech for Roosevelt, hoped that was the case. As Assistant Secretary Adolf A. Berle wrote, Europe was on the verge of a "blow-up" and the purpose of the speech would be "to create a certain amount of doubt as to what our intentions may be," and thus have "a moderating effect."[40]

At Queens University in Kingston, Ontario, on August 18 Roosevelt declared that the United States would not sit idly by if another empire tried to dominate Canada, and that the day had passed when controversies beyond the seas did not interest or harm the people of the Americas.[41] This meant, of course, that the United States would defend Canada, not European nations, and Roosevelt admitted privately that an American President could have made the identical statement fifty years before; he had made it then because it seemed "to fit in with the Hitler situation," and perhaps would have "some small effect in Berlin."[42]

Hitler paid no attention, at least to judge from his military preparations and dismissal of Beck's warnings. The German press ridiculed assertions, which the French were attempting to give rise to, that Roosevelt's remarks had extended the guarantee for Canada to the whole British empire and France.[43] The British, or at least Halifax, approved the address; on August 24 he told the chargé in London, Herschel Johnson, that they feared German military action in the near future, and he said that perhaps another similar statement might help

39. Bullitt to Roosevelt, Aug. 17, 1938, Roosevelt papers, PSF, France: William Bullitt.

40. Berle Memorandum for Roosevelt, Aug. 15, 1938, Roosevelt papers, PSF, State Department Files: Adolf A. Berle.

41. Text in *PPFDR*, VII, 491–494.

42. Roosevelt to Lord Tweedsmuir, Aug. 31, 1938, Roosevelt papers, President's Personal File, 3396.

43. Boris Celovsky, *Das Münchener Abkommen von 1938* (Stuttgart, 1958), 250; Heindl, *Die diplomatischen Beziehungen zwischen Deutschland und den Vereinigten Staaten*, 123–124.

to restrain Hitler.[44] Halifax also saw Kennedy a week later and apparently asked him to inquire what position the United States would assume if Germany marched but England did not.[45]

Kennedy meanwhile conferred with Chamberlain on August 30. Chamberlain made a veiled reference to the secret talks on August 18-19 between the chief diplomatic adviser for the Foreign Office, Sir Robert Vansittart, and Churchill, and the emissary who had been sent to London by the German military, Ewald von Kleist. Kleist had emphatically warned that Hitler intended war at a specific date, that the military opposed the plan, and that Hitler might be restrained if a leading British statesman warned that a German attack would lead to a "general catastrophe."[46] According to Halifax's report to Ambassador Lindsay in Washington, Chamberlain on August 30 told Kennedy that the British had heard from various sources that Hitler intended to invade Czechoslovakia and that only a firm British declaration could force him to abandon the idea. But, Chamberlain said, the British were in no position to stop Hitler, and threats would be unwise. Kennedy agreed, and added that "it will be hell" if Germany attacked Czechoslovakia, and that if France went in, and the British had to, the United States would probably follow before long. Both men concluded that repetition of Roosevelt's warning would be "bad" and Kennedy said that Roosevelt had "decided to go in with Chamberlain; whatever course Chamberlain desires to adopt he would think right." The next day Kennedy also told Halifax that although Americans would be "shocked" by German aggression, they would not feel that was sufficient reason to plunge Europe into general war.[47] Kennedy himself reported he thought that if Germany attacked Czechoslovakia Chamberlain would try to keep France out and failing that,

44. Johnson to Hull, Aug. 24, 1938, *FR 1938,* I, 551; see also Halifax to Lindsay, Aug. 24, 1938, *DBFP,* 3d ser., II, 149.

45. Kennedy to Hull, Aug. 31, 1938, *FR 1938,* I, 565–566.

46. On these talks see Note of Conversation between Vansittart and Kleist, Aug. 18, Chamberlain to Halifax, Aug. 19, Note of Conversation between Churchill and Kleist (undated), and Letter given by Churchill to Kleist, Aug. 19, 1938, *DBFP,* 3d ser., II, 683–689. See also Foreign Ministry Memorandum (undated), *DGFP,* D, II, 704–710, which includes Churchill's letter and other public and private statements concerning foreign resistance to a German assault on Czechoslovakia.

47. Halifax to Lindsay, Sept. 2, 1938, *DBFP,* 3d ser., II, 212–213.

keep England out as long as he could. Chamberlain, he concluded, looked ill but not jittery, and was the "best bet" against war.[48] To all of these questions and comments, Hull replied only that American sentiments were well known and that nothing could be said about American responses to hypothetical situations.[49]

A few days later Bullitt caused a mild sensation. At a banquet in Bordeaux attended by Bonnet on September 3, the ambassador, speaking in French and extemporaneously, allegedly declared that the United States and France were "indefectively united in war as in peace." Next day, at an unveiling commemorating American aid to France in the First World War, Bullitt declared that in event of war no one could foretell whether the United States would become involved.[50] On September 8, however, Bullitt said that his remarks on September 3 had been misinterpreted, and on September 9 Roosevelt stated at a press conference that it was "100 per cent incorrect" to interpret his policy as associating the United States with France and Great Britain in a front against Hitler.[51] Essentially this assertion was true. Nevertheless, as Lindsay told Halifax on September 12, Roosevelt was "aroused by Germany's brutal diplomacy," and officials in Washington favored England's "making a strong stand against aggression and I anticipate that any compromise with it may bring a certain let-down." This feeling did not preclude a wise accommodation, he cautioned, and Roosevelt had admitted privately that "you may count on us for everything except troops and loans." But Lindsay, who had encouraged his government to respond favorably to the American overtures in late 1937 and early 1938, believed that if war came America would enter in "far less" time than it had the first time.[52]

Chamberlain remained uninterested in American assistance and the

---

48. Kennedy to Hull, Aug. 30, 1938, *FR 1938*, I, 560–561.
49. Hull to Kennedy, Sept. 1, 1938, *ibid.*, 568.
50. *New York Times*, Sept. 4 and Sept. 5, 1938.
51. *Ibid.*, Sept. 9 and Sept. 10, 1938. The corrected version of Bullitt's Sept. 3 remarks appeared Sept. 9: "We are united by our devotion to liberty, democracy, and peace. We are united by an old friendship, by the aid each has brought the other in his hour of need." The French reporter working for the Associated Press said he had misinterpreted Bullitt's remarks. *New York Times*, Sept. 12, 1938. See also John McVickar Haight, Jr., "France, the United States, and the Munich Conference," *Journal of Modern History*, XXXII (Dec. 1960), 345–347.
52. Lindsay to Halifax, Sept. 12, 1938, *DBFP*, 3d ser., II, 301.

additional warnings that he received through Weizsäcker and Theodor Kordt during the first two weeks of September.[53] On September 4-5 Beneš agreed to virtually all of the demands Henlein had put forth at Karlsbad on April 24; the Sudeten Germans, unprepared for this, thereupon used a minor incident on September 7 to break negotiations.[54] At the same time the London *Times* on September 7 carried a lead article urging that the Czech government cede its German-speaking areas to Germany. Five days later, concluding the Nazi rally at Nuremberg, Hitler, "his words, his tone, dripping with venom," as William Shirer noted, denounced Beneš for playing a "tactical game" and making insufficient "little appeasement presents," and he warned that "the Germans in Czechoslovakia are neither defenceless nor are they deserted, and people should take note of that fact."[55] There followed uprisings by Henlein's followers, Beneš' proclamation of martial law (and restoration of order), and Henlein's announcement that the issue was no longer autonomy but return to the Reich.[56]

The French were deeply disturbed, and on September 13 let Chamberlain know they thought a conference "à trois" advisable. Chamberlain instead requested an interview with Hitler himself—much to Daladier's distress, Hitler's surprise, and the amazement of Mussolini, who thought it meant "the liquidation of English prestige"—and on September 15 flew to Berchtesgaden.[57] Bullitt reported that Bonnet told him the Czechs "had failed to play straight" and the French "would be fully justified in washing their hands of their obligations." On the day of Chamberlain's flight Bullitt concluded that the French

53. On the controversy concerning the possibility of a *putsch* in September 1938, cf. Hans Rothfels, *The German Opposition to Hitler: An Appraisal* (Hinsdale, Ill., 1948), 58–63, who blames its collapse largely on Chamberlain's failure to oppose Hitler, and Wheeler-Bennett, *Nemesis of Power*, 414–424, who sees the plot as vastly exaggerated by its conspirators, who found a scapegoat for their own irresolution and inactivity.

54. John W. Wheeler-Bennett, *Munich: Prologue to Tragedy* (London, 1948), 90–92.

55. Entry for Sept. 12, 1938, Shirer, *Berlin Diary*, 126–127; text of speech in Baynes, ed., *Hitler's Speeches*, II, 1487–1499.

56. Henlein's Statement, Sept. 15, 1938, *DGFP*, D, II, 801–802.

57. Phipps to Halifax, Sept. 13 and Sept. 14, 1938, *DBFP*, 3d ser., II, 313–314, 329; Hitler's expression of surprise, *"Ich bin vom Himmel gefallen,"* noted in Lewis B. Namier, *Diplomatic Prelude, 1938–1939* (London, 1948), 35; Mussolini's remark in entry for Sept. 14, 1938, Ciano, *Diary*, 156.

generally believed that the Treaty of Versailles was "one of the stupidest documents ever penned by the hand of man," that it would have to be revised to permit "an alteration of the Czech state," and that the French "will support any arrangement that Chamberlain may be able to make with Hitler."[58] Bullitt shared these sentiments. Nevertheless, a while later he reflected to Roosevelt: "The moral is: If you have enough airplanes you don't have to go to Berchtesgaden."[59]

Publicly Hull committed the United States only to observing proceedings with "greatest interest."[60] Roosevelt doubted the wisdom of the conference. He worried, as he wrote Ambassador Phillips (who thought the flight a "fine and courageous thing to do"), that the talks would only postpone the "inevitable conflict," and at a cabinet meeting on September 16 he lamented that Chamberlain was for "peace at any price."[61] Next day he remarked tartly to Ickes that it seemed England and France were going to abandon Czechoslovakia and "wash the blood from their Judas Iscariot hands." Roosevelt said that he thought England and France should refuse Germany's demands and, if war came, announce they would not invade Germany but would blockade its borders and bombard the Germans until they gave in.[62]

A few days after Chamberlain returned from his difficult interview, in which Hitler said he would take the Sudetenland at risk of war but agreed to give Chamberlain a chance to work out a peaceful transfer, the British and French proposed to Czechoslovakia that it cede to Germany all districts in which the German population was 50 per cent or more.[63] Kennedy telegraphed an unofficial version of the plan to Roosevelt on the afternoon of September 19. Fifteen minutes later, in a frantic cable, Bullitt elaborated on German military superiority and the destruction of Czechoslovakia and France; the stake, he said,

58. Bullitt to Hull, Sept. 14 and Sept. 15, 1938, *FR 1938*, I, 595–596, 600–601.

59. Bullitt to Roosevelt, Sept. 20, 1938, Roosevelt papers, PSF, France: William Bullitt.

60. Hull Statement in *FR 1938*, I, 605.

61. Entry for Sept. 15, 1938, Italian Diary, VIII, and Roosevelt to Phillips, Sept. 15, 1938, Phillips papers.

62. Entry for Sept. 18, 1938, Ickes, *Diary*, II, 467–469.

63. Schmidt, *Statist auf diplomatischer Bühne*, 394–399; Schmidt Memorandum, Sept. 15, 1938, *DGFP*, D, II, 786–798; text of Anglo-French plan in Lewis, ed., *Documents 1938*, II, 213–214.

was the entire youth of France and every building in the country. He pleaded that it would be wrong to allow a France misguided by the spirit of a Jacobin or Jeanne d'Arc to "march into the furnace" to keep three million Sudeten Germans under rule of seven million Czechs. Because the United States intended to remain at peace, for any American official to urge the French to resist would be dishonorable.[64]

Roosevelt was not so sure. Without a word to anyone in the State Department, he summoned Lindsay for a secret conference in the White House that night. He felt that the Anglo-French plan demanded "the most terrible remorseless sacrifice" ever demanded of a country, and that it would provoke unfavorable response in America. Nonetheless, Roosevelt remarked, he understood the difficulties confronting the governments of England and France, and if British policy succeeded he would be "the first to cheer." Further, he would not express disapproval of German aggression "lest it might encourage Czechoslovakia to vain resistance." Roosevelt said he feared that Czechoslovakia might provoke war by not giving in; yet, even if Hitler got what he wanted now, he would press demands upon Poland, Denmark, and Rumania until war came. And England, France, and Russia could not win if they fought along classical lines. There seemed to be, then, two alternatives. First, he suggested, the Western powers could call a world conference, which he said he would be willing to attend provided it met somewhere other than in Europe, to reorganize "all unsatisfactory frontiers on rational lines." Second, if the Western powers thought a conference unworkable and elected to fight, they should blockade Germany and close off the North and Mediterranean seas and the Suez Canal. America's contribution to this effort, Roosevelt explained, would be limited. He could not send troops to Europe, nor ignore the Neutrality Act's prohibition on exporting arms and munitions to belligerents. All the President could do under the Constitution and the Neutrality Act was forbid American ships to enter danger zones, except at their own risk.[65] Lindsay reported his conversation to Halifax, who thanked Roosevelt for his interest but questioned the effectiveness of a blockade.[66]

64. Kennedy to Hull, and Bullitt to Hull, Sept. 19, 1938, *FR 1938*, I, 615–619.
65. Lindsay to Halifax, Sept. 20, 1938, *DBFP*, 3d ser., VII, 627–629.
66. Halifax to Lindsay, Sept. 23, 1938, *ibid.*, 630.

Pressed by the English and French, refused their last-minute appeal for a statement from Roosevelt or Hull (on grounds that the United States could not advise a nation to fight, the Czechoslovaks agreed to Anglo-French demands.[67] Chamberlain flew to Godesberg on September 22. Hitler now pressed the demands of Poland and Hungary against Czechoslovakia and insisted that the evacuation of the Sudetenland be started by September 26 and finished by September 28. After sharp exchanges, during which time word came of Czech mobilization, Hitler agreed to extend the deadline to October 1. Chamberlain said he would present the proposal to his government and the government of Czechoslovakia.[68]

Bullitt again pleaded that Roosevelt, in event the British and French rejected Hitler's latest demand and war seemed imminent, summon the heads of state of England, France, Germany, Italy, and Poland—but absolutely not of the Soviet Union—to meet at The Hague with an American representative. But even Bullitt deemed German terms "totally unacceptable" when he learned on the morning of September 25 that in addition to immediate occupation they demanded that the Czechs not remove a single piece of military or factory equipment, not a morsel of food or anything else. Beneš too found the demands unacceptable, and that same morning summoned Carr, told him his people would rather die fighting than accept the terms, and begged him to ask Roosevelt to prevail upon England and France not to desert Czechoslovakia.[69]

Roosevelt's advisers had been conferring all day. Moffat and Assistant Secretary Berle had worked out an "appeal to the American people" in which Roosevelt was to offer his services as mediator rather than summon an international conference. As Moffat recorded, "there was a definite hint of treaty revision in the note, designed like bait to induce Germany to request the President's good offices." Hull agreed to the plan, but Norman Davis took "violent exception" to it; he in-

---

67. Moffat Memorandum, Sept. 20, 1938, *FR 1938*, I, 626–627.

68. Schmidt, *Statist auf diplomatischer Bühne*, 399–407; Schmidt Memorandum, Sept. 23, 1938, *DGFP*, D, II, 898–908; Note of Conversation between Chamberlain and Hitler, Sept. 22 and Sept. 23, 1938, *DBFP*, 3d ser., II, 463–473, 497–508.

69. Bullitt to Hull, Sept. 24 and Sept. 25, and Carr to Hull, Sept. 25, 1938, *FR 1938*, I, 641–642, 648–650.

sisted that it was not the Treaty of Versailles that was the root of all evils, but American failure to ratify. Discussion continued late into the night until Roosevelt decided to omit the offer of his services on grounds that it was implicit in the exhortation to negotiate.[70]

Roosevelt appealed for peace shortly after 1:00 A.M. on September 26, at a time when it appeared that the British and French, no matter how reluctant, would have to fight. He asked the heads of Germany, England, France, and Czechoslovakia not to break negotiations, insisting that no problem was too difficult to be resolved peacefully; at the same time he reaffirmed that the United States had "no political entanglements." Chamberlain, Daladier, and Beneš approved Roosevelt's message.[71] Roosevelt was especially pleased with Chamberlain's warm response, Welles told Kennedy; nonetheless, when the prime minister hinted that his radio address on the current situation, scheduled for the night of September 27, be broadcast directly to the United States, Roosevelt vetoed the idea on grounds that it "might be misconstrued." American stations could pick up the broadcast on their own.[72]

Hitler's reply to Roosevelt reached Washington just after 9:00 P.M. on September 26. The Chancellor agreed with the President's feelings about the unforeseeable consequences of a war, but insisted that Woodrow Wilson had proclaimed self-determination "the most important basis of national life" and that the Sudeten Germans had been deprived of this right. Everyone had agreed that the Sudetenland should join the Third Reich and now the Beneš government was delaying the proceedings. The Germans could wait no longer, Hitler warned, and the decision for war or peace rested with Czechoslovakia alone. That same night, in a near frenzy, Hitler shrieked at the *Sportpalast* in Berlin that "the Czech state began with a single lie, and the father of this lie was named Benes," and that if the Czechs did not

70. Entry for Sept. 24 and Sept. 25, 1938, Moffat Diary, II, Moffat papers. See also Joseph Alsop and Robert Kintner, *American White Paper: The Story of American Diplomacy and the Second World War* (New York, 1940), 8–9.

71. Roosevelt's message in *PPFDR*, VII, 531–532; formal replies in Lewis, ed., *Documents 1938*, II, 262–264. Apparently Phipps had to urge Chamberlain to hasten his reply. Phipps to Halifax, Sept. 26, 1938, *DBFP*, 3d ser., II, 546.

72. Memorandum Welles-Kennedy Conversation, Sept. 26, 1938, *FR 1938*, I, 660–661.

give the Sudeten Germans immediate freedom, "we will go and fetch this freedom for ourselves."[73]

On the morning of September 27 the British Foreign Office issued a statement by Chamberlain asking Europe to avoid general war over questions on which agreement already had been "largely obtained," and promising British responsibility for seeing to it that terms agreed to by discussion would be carried out.[74] Shortly after noon (Berlin time) Sir Horace Wilson saw Hitler, who insisted that unless his demands were met he would "smash" Czechoslovakia. Wilson emphasized the advantages that would accrue to England and Germany through a peaceful settlement, and said that if Germany attacked Czechoslovakia, France would be bound to its treaty obligations— although he could not say in what form this commitment would be met—and if French and German troops became "actively engaged," England would be bound to support France.[75]

That, and ensuing general war, were precisely what American diplomats wanted to prevent. Roosevelt called a special meeting of his cabinet and advisers on September 27. Welles and Berle drafted a proposal similar to Bullitt's earlier proposal: a conference at The Hague, on September 29, with the United States sending an observer and committing itself to an economic settlement parallel to a political settlement. Hull opposed the idea, and Roosevelt supported him.[76] They agreed, however, that it would be worthwhile to appeal to Hitler to find some way of preventing war, perhaps by continuing negotiations at a neutral site with the British, French, and Czechs.[77]

No sooner had the meeting ended than the State Department re-

73. Hitler to Roosevelt, Sept. 27, 1938, *ibid.*, 669–672; Baynes, ed., *Hitler's Speeches*, II, 1508–1527.

74. Text of statement in Halifax to Henderson, Sept. 27, 1938, *DBFP*, 3d ser., II, 559–560.

75. Henderson to Halifax, Sept. 27, and Notes of Hitler-Wilson Conversation, Sept. 27, 1938, *ibid.*, 563–567. See also Schmidt Memorandum of Hitler-Wilson Conversation, Sept. 27, 1938, *DGFP*, D, II, 963–965, and Schmidt, *Statist auf diplomatischer Bühne*, 407–409.

76. Alsop and Kintner, *American White Paper*, 10.

77. Entry for Sept. 30, 1938, Ickes, *Diary*, II, 478. Ickes' contention that no one seriously thought that the appeal would do any good, and that its real purpose was to establish, in event war began, "who was responsible for starting it," tells only part of the story; Roosevelt no doubt wanted to establish a "war guilt," but he desperately wanted to prevent war.

ceived a cable from Bullitt, at 2:30 P.M., the Bonnet had just "astounded" him by saying that the British and French Foreign Offices were secretly working on a plan to turn over to Germany by October 1 those regions Czechoslovakia had consented to cede. Bullitt refused to believe that Daladier would agree.[78] Chamberlain, in fact, was about to send two telegrams to Beneš that afternoon, the first warning that Germany would overrun Czechoslovakia if Hitler's demands were not met (and insisting that the British government could not assume responsibility for advising a course of action), and the second urging acceptance of Chamberlain's plan for surrender of the Sudetenland on a schedule close to Hitler's.[79] In the meanwhile, Welles instructed Bullitt and Kennedy to inform Daladier and Chamberlain of Roosevelt's planned appeal and to get their responses; Hull cabled Phillips to tell Mussolini that Roosevelt hoped the Duce would do all he could for peaceful negotiations.[80]

Reports from Europe were frightening. Ambassador Wilson reported on the afternoon of September 27 that Horace Wilson had informed him that Chamberlain was tired and uncertain of what he would say in the House of Commons next day; it appeared that even British and French guarantees that Czechoslovakia would fulfill the terms of the British proposal for ceding the Sudetenland had made no impression on the Germans. Sir Horace thought Roosevelt should urge Chamberlain to keep England out of a war over a matter agreed to in principle. Ambassador Wilson thought that Hitler had burnt his bridges and could not retreat; it was necessary that Czechoslovakia change its attitude.[81] Kennedy could not get an audience with Chamberlain until shortly after 10:30 P.M. (London time) and called Welles back at 5:45 P.M. (Washington time). By then Chamberlain, having appealed

78. Bullitt to Hull, Sept. 27, 1938, *FR 1938*, I, 680–681.

79. Wheeler-Bennett, *Munich*, 151–152, 154–155.

80. Memoranda Welles-Bullitt and Welles-Kennedy Conversations, and Hull to Phillips, Sept. 27, 1938, *FR 1938*, I, 675–679. Hull also instructed every American ambassador or minister—except those in Germany, England, France, Italy, Czechoslovakia, Hungary, and Poland—to tell the head of state to which he was accredited that the United States, without judging the points at issue between Germany and Czechoslovakia, felt it would be wise for him to urge them to peaceful settlement. Hull to Officers in Charge of American Diplomatic Missions, Sept. 27, 1938, *ibid.*, 677–678.

81. Wilson to Hull, Sept. 27, 1938, *ibid.*, 638–684.

through his emissary, Wilson, for direct German-Czech negotiations with the British present as an interested third party, had received Hitler's reply in which he defended his Godesberg demands but left it up to Chamberlain if he wished to make a last-hour appeal to the government in Prague.[82] Chamberlain, Kennedy told Welles, found little cheer in Hitler's reply, thought Germany might even march the next day, and saw little prospect for accomplishing anything. If Roosevelt wanted to try there was nothing to lose. Welles replied that Roosevelt would send Hitler a message that night "without fail."[83]

Roosevelt, smoking incessantly, Hull, swearing under his breath, and Welles and Berle, fidgeting from tension, worked in the White House study all evening; by about 9:00 P.M. they finished the draft of an appeal to Hitler, and a half-hour later Roosevelt added the final editorial touches and his signature.[84] The appeal insisted that there was agreement in principle between the German and Czech governments, and that all differences "could and should" be settled peacefully. Roosevelt urged continued negotiation, broadened if need be into a conference at a neutral European site attended by all nations directly interested. The State Department cabled the message at 10:18 P.M. (Washington time) on September 27.[85] Just thirty-two minutes before, as John McVickar Haight, Jr., has pointed out, the State Department received a message from Bullitt that Daladier was "delighted" with the proposed Roosevelt appeal and approved a conference to work out peaceful transfer of Czech territory to Germany, although deep down he did not think there was one chance in a thousand of peace. Yet Haight gives too much credit to Roosevelt and his aides, attaches too much meaning to their appeal, and makes assumptions they dared not make themselves when he says that Roosevelt, while

82. Chamberlain to Hitler, Sept. 26, and Hitler to Chamberlain, Sept. 27, 1938, *DGFP*, D, II, 944–945, 966–968. Chamberlain sent a copy of his letter to Roosevelt on September 27. *DBFP*, 3d ser., II, 541n1.

83. Memorandum Welles-Kennedy Conversation, Sept. 27, 1938, *FR 1938*, I, 679–680.

84. Alsop and Kintner, *American White Paper*, 11.

85. Roosevelt to Hitler, Sept. 27, 1938, *FR 1938*, I, 684–685. Celovsky, *Das Münchener Abkommen*, 448–449, attributes Roosevelt's appeal largely to "political" motivation: the desire during an election campaign to appear as one who had taken part in international developments. This emphasis, however, overlooks Roosevelt's dominant motive: the desire to avert war and its attendant catastrophe.

favoring the peaceful transfer of the Sudetenland, supported collective security by standing behind "the Daladier-Bullitt-Welles plan to resist rather than capitulate before the threat of force," and further, that Roosevelt "assumed Chamberlain stood with Daladier as an opponent to capitulation" and expected Chamberlain to negotiate at Munich on the basis of "reason and equity." Haight also overstates what occurred at Munich.[86]

To begin, Welles had told Kennedy that Roosevelt would appeal to Hitler even before Bullitt cabled Daladier's approval. Their appeal was written well before word came from Paris, and not in the thirty-two-minute interval between the incoming and outgoing messages. There is no evidence Roosevelt read Bullitt's message before cabling Hitler, nor is there reason to believe that Roosevelt intended to encourage the British and French to be firm, for this might have been interpreted as encouragement to fight and, as the Czechs had learned earlier, he was in no position to proffer such advice. Further, hours before (Washington time) Chamberlain had made his famous broadcast in which he said not only that it was horrible and incredible that the British should be digging trenches and trying on gas masks on account of a quarrel between people "in a far-away country of whom we know nothing," but also that war preparations did not mean war was inevitable or imminent. No matter how much one sympathized with a small country confronted by a big and powerful one "we cannot in all circumstances undertake to involve the whole British Empire in war simply on her account. If we have to fight it must be on larger issues than that."[87] Roosevelt could only have concluded that Chamberlain absolutely did not want to resist Germany, and that though under the circumstances England might have been forced to war if Germany attacked Czechoslovakia and France fought, once a conference was arranged Chamberlain would go to nearly any length to give Hitler those things even Roosevelt recognized everyone had agreed in principle to give him. Roosevelt's chief concern was to encourage further negotiation without committing the United States, and thereby arousing congressional and public wrath, to European political settlements. He also might have suspected that English and French

86. Bullitt to Hull, Sept. 27, 1938, *FR 1938*, I, 686–688; Haight, "France, the United States, and Munich," *Journal of Modern History*, 355–356.
87. Text of address in Lewis, ed., *Documents 1938*, II, 270–271.

leaders only would have sneered at the head of an uncommitted nation urging them to war.

It is also incorrect to say that there was a "sellout" at Munich, not only of the Czechs but of Roosevelt's hopes.[88] That conference, as John W. Wheeler-Bennett has stated, was only a ceremony signifying that Hitler, in advance, had won his essential demands.[89] Both Hitler's and Chamberlain's biographers agree that the terms of the Munich settlement varied only slightly from Hitler's Godesberg demands and generally favored Anglo-French demands.[90] That Hitler would violate certain arrangements, not hold a plebiscite, for instance, could not be determined in advance, even if it might have been conjectured. There is no reason to believe, however, that the settlement, or events of the the next few weeks, disappointed Roosevelt. On October 11 he wrote the prime minister of Canada, MacKenzie King, that he rejoiced that war had been averted. Explicitly and plainly he told Phillips six days later: "I want you to know that I am not one bit upset over the final result."[91] Certainly Roosevelt had misgivings; he likened Poland's demand for Teschen to a cruel kick at a small boy who was being held down by a bully.[92] But by and large Roosevelt had convinced himself that Munich opened the way to a new and better world.[93]

There is nothing in diplomatic records to indicate that the President's aides disapproved the Munich settlement—the evidence, in fact, indicates the opposite. Hull later would say that he urged Roosevelt, against Welles's pressure, to "go slow" and not, through appeals, associate himself with Chamberlain's appeasement.[94] But if Hull had mis-

88. Haight, "France, the United States, and Munich," *Journal of Modern History*, 358, suggests that the cautious nature of American diplomatic statements had an impact upon the French that was actually opposite the real wishes of American leaders. To some extent this is true, but again, Roosevelt knew how little material support he could offer, and, for example, on September 16 Welles apparently told Daladier and Bonnet that they would not get "a single soldier, nor a sou of credit." Georges Bonnet, *Défense de la Paix: De Washington au Quai d'Orsay*, 2 vols. (Geneva, 1946–48), I, 212.

89. *Munich*, 173.

90. Bullock, *Hitler*, 469; Macleod, *Neville Chamberlain*, 253.

91. Roosevelt to King, Oct. 11, and Roosevelt to Phillips, Oct. 17, 1938, *FDRL*, II, 816–819.

92. Roosevelt to Hull, Sept. 29, 1938, Roosevelt papers, PSF, State Department Files: Cordell Hull.

93. Langer and Gleason, *Challenge to Isolation*, 35.

94. *Memoirs*, I, 591–595.

givings at the time, he did not express them in council, nor seek to slacken the President's pace.[95] In his press statement on September 30, Hull said only that the results at Munich afforded "a universal sense of relief," and that the United States would not judge the dispute itself.[96] Welles was more certain. In a national broadcast on October 3 he said there was now more opportunity to establish "a new world order based upon justice and upon law" than at any time during the last twenty years.[97] Moffat, head of the European desk in the State Department, wrote Ambassadors Wilson and Kennedy that he did not sympathize with those Americans who criticized arrangements at Munich; a country that had no intention of fighting, he said, had no business criticizing decisions of other countries that were "nearer the abyss."[98]

Viewed in this light, the meaning of Roosevelt's "Good man" cable, sent through Kennedy on the afternoon of September 28 after Chamberlain had accepted Hitler's invitation to Munich, is clear.[99] Only a few hours before Chamberlain took off, the British apparently asked that Roosevelt publicly endorse the move. Hull, Moffat, and Messersmith adamantly opposed giving a "blank check"; the British, they felt, were trying to get them to share responsibility in case ultimate arrangements proved unpopular.[100] Nonetheless, Roosevelt and his aides knew Hitler's Godesberg demands, had agreed to transfer of the Sudetenland to Germany, knew that Czechoslovakia would not be at the conference to defend itself, knew that Hitler would not and could not back far off his demands, and knew that Chamberlain and Daladier could not and would not push Hitler because England and France were desperate not to fight. Nor did the Americans want them to fight. Mistakenly or not, diplomats in Washington sought, if not peace at any price, peace with honor; but above all, peace. Chamberlain claimed to stand for an honorable peace, and when he agreed to go to Munich Roosevelt told him sincerely that he was a "good man."

95. Pratt, *Hull,* I, 296–298.
96. *FR 1938,* I, 703.
97. *New York Times,* Oct. 4, 1938.
98. Moffat to Wilson, Oct. 5, and Moffat to Kennedy, Oct. 7, 1938, Moffat papers.
99. Hull to Kennedy, Sept. 28, 1938, *FR 1938,* I, 688.
100. Entry for Oct. 14, 1938, Moffat Diary, II, Moffat papers.

Bearing in mind that the European powers could discount American military intervention, what was Roosevelt's contribution to the events of September 26–28? His first message of September 26 to the heads of the German, English, French, and Czech states contributed in a general way to continuing negotiations, but was by no means decisive. On September 27 Dieckhoff sent a cable insisting that Hitler would get "practically all he is demanding" if he agreed to negotiations, and reiterating his persistent theme that in the event of war the United States would choose the appropriate time to enter on the side of England.[101] Several hours later there followed Roosevelt's second appeal to Hitler, which arrived at the Foreign Ministry at 9:45 A.M. (Berlin time) on September 28 and went unanswered.[102] Afterward, however, Captain Fritz Wiedemann, Hitler's *aide-de-camp,* did tell Ambassador Wilson that the telegram had been translated by 10:00 A.M. and that Wiedemann "supposed it had already been brought to the Chancellor" sometime between then and 11:00 A.M., when his interview with Ambassador François-Poncet began. Hitler had probably read it, then, about a half-hour before François-Poncet arrived and about an hour before the Italian ambassador, Bernardo Attolico, interrupted with Mussolini's request that mobilization be delayed twenty-four hours; Hitler had Roosevelt's message well over an hour before Ambassador Henderson arrived with Chamberlain's request for a conference.[103]

Mussolini usually has been credited with making the decisive intervention, and this assumption probably is correct.[104] The major influences on Mussolini's decision, in addition to the important facts that he neither wanted war at that time nor was prepared for it, were the two British requests to him made by the British ambassador in Rome, Lorth Perth, through Ciano. The first request reached Mussolini around 10:30 A.M.; the second, a personal message from Chamberlain,

101. Dieckhoff to Foreign Ministry, Sept. 27, 1938, *DGFP,* D, II, 981–982.
102. Printed *ibid.,* 983–985.
103. Wilson to Welles, Oct. 21, 1938, *FR 1938,* I, 727–729. On Mussolini's intervention, see Kordt, *Wahn und Wirklichkeit,* 125, and François-Poncet, *Fateful Years,* 266–267.
104. Weizsäcker, *Memoirs,* 153, attributes the "credit" for bringing about the Munich Conference to "many people," including Roosevelt. Weizsäcker also recalls that as late as August 31, 1938, he told Attolico "Mussolini was the only man in Europe who could influence Hitler." *Memoirs,* 147.

around noon.[105] Frequently overlooked is Roosevelt's message to Mussolini, transmitted via the State Department and Ambassador Phillips on the afternoon of September 27, asking him to intervene in behalf of a negotiated settlement.[106] Because of differences in time between Washington and Rome, the message did not reach the American embassy until after midnight, and Phillips did not present it to Mussolini until nearly 4:00 P.M., September 28.[107] But as Phillips reported afterward, he had learned "positively" that Mussolini and Ciano were "thoroughly aware" of the message's contents before 10:00 A.M., or about an hour before the English, through Perth, prevailed upon the Duce. The cable from Washington, Phillips said by way of explaining Mussolini's knowledge, had been sent in a "well known" code.[108] Roosevelt replied that he knew well when he ordered the message sent that it would not reach Rome until after midnight and that Phillips would not be able to get an audience with Mussolini at least until the morning of September 28. The President expressed no surprise or upset that the Italians knew of his message by 9:45 A.M., and he seemed delighted that "we actually got in about one hour ahead of Perth"; the American press was wrong in thinking that he had "missed the boat" with an appeal that reached Mussolini only after others had persuaded him to intervene.[109] One can only conclude that it was no accident that the message was sent in a well-known code.

How much the appeal influenced Mussolini is difficult to estimate; clearly he did not act until he heard from the English. Roosevelt, however, gave him one more good reason to intervene at the eleventh hour. The incident further emphasizes how strongly Roosevelt wanted negotiations, the outcome of which could not be in much doubt.

105. Entry for Sept. 28, 1938, Ciano, *Diary,* 165–166.

106. Hull to Phillips, Sept. 27, 1938, *FR 1938,* I, 677.

107. After Phillips had left, Ciano noted that Mussolini remarked: "As you can see, I am only moderately happy, because, though perhaps at a price, we could have liquidated France and Great Britain forever. We now have overwhelming proof of this." Entry for Sept. 28, 1938, Ciano, *Diary,* 166.

108. Phillips to Roosevelt, Oct. 6, 1938, DS, 760.F62/1462½. At 9:45 A.M. on September 28 the embassy counselor called the Italian Foreign Office and asked that an interview be arranged for Phillips with Mussolini. The Italians were not told the contents of Roosevelt's confidential message, but they were given "an unmistakable intimation of its purport." Phillips to Hull, Oct. 1, 1938, *FR 1938,* I, 703–704.

109. Roosevelt to Phillips, Oct. 17, 1938, *FDRL,* II, 818–819.

The events that led from Munich to war in September 1939, and to American entry in December 1941, are not the subject of this volume. The joy, really relief, which Americans shared with Europeans following the Munich Conference was short-lived. For some there was not even an interlude of hope. The day that Chamberlain flew to Munich, Messersmith wrote a long memorandum for Hull, who passed it to Roosevelt, about the difficulty of reaching an equitable and lasting settlement. Hitler's Germany, he argued, was not Stresemann's Germany; arrangements that were possible a decade ago were not possible now. Czechoslovakia was not Hitler's last territorial demand any more than Austria had been. The stronger Germany became, the more diplomats conceded to Hitler, the further he would press German territorial expansion, even into the New World.[110] The government of Czechoslovakia announced the terms of the Munich agreement on the afternoon of September 30; that night Carr walked through the streets of Prague, across the Charles Bridge spanning the Moldau. The people seemed crushed, their spirit broken; "it was as if the life of the city had died," and although it was too early to make a final assessment, it was clear he wondered if the price paid had not been too high.[111] Surely it had been, Claude Bowers raged; "the rape of the Czechs is the most shameless thing that has happened since the partition of Poland," he wrote Hull. "The Great Betrayal of Munich" only reduced France to a second-rate power and destroyed its alliance system, the League of Nations, and collective security. Chamberlain, he concluded, had brought England to its "darkest hour."[112] Less heatedly, but equally incisively, Howard Bucknell, Jr., the consul general at Geneva, wrote that statesmen had only reached a temporary detente and that recurring crises would lead to war unless the British and French stood firm.[113]

American relations with Germany worsened five weeks after Munich. Following the German pogrom against the Jews in the middle of November Roosevelt ordered Ambassador Wilson home for "consultation." At the time he did not say the recall was permanent, but despite Wilson's urgings, and those of the British, Roosevelt never permitted

110. Messersmith to Hull, Sept. 29, 1938, *FR 1938*, I, 704–707.
111. Notes for Diary, Carr papers, Box 6.
112. Bowers to Hull, Oct. 3 and Oct. 10, 1938, Hull papers, Box 43.
113. Bucknell to Hull, Oct. 12, 1938, *FR 1938*, I, 86–92.

him to return to the Berlin embassy.[114] Hitler recalled Dieckhoff a week later, permanently as the case turned out, but decided against breaking diplomatic relations so as not to provide Roosevelt with support for rearmament or economic pressure against Germany.[115]

Forbidding as was the international outlook, Roosevelt retained faint hope that German aggression could be prevented, and after the war began, that it could be contained. Following Germany's destruction of Czechoslovakia in March 1939, and Italy's invasion of Albania in early April, Roosevelt acted on a suggestion by Bullitt and on April 14 appealed to Hitler and Mussolini to pledge that for at least ten years they would not attack the thirty-one nations of Europe and the Near East.[116] Both dictators replied with scornful speeches. Mussolini on April 20 said that he would not be moved by "convivial vociferations, or Messiah-like messages."[117] Hitler particularly delighted his howling Reichstag audience on the night of April 28 with bitter and sarcastic rejoinders to Roosevelt's assumptions and proposals. The chancellor said that a poll of the governments Roosevelt had named as being menaced by Germany revealed that none felt need for the suggested guarantees; he also pointed with relish to such inconsistencies as the United States proposing international conferences while not belonging to the "largest conference in the world," the League of Nations. He noted carefully that English troops, not German, oppressed Ireland and Palestine.[118] In May Germany and Italy concluded their Pact of Steel.

When it became apparent in late summer that Poland probably would not give in to German demands, Roosevelt appealed on August 24 to both Hitler and the president of Poland, Ignacy Moscicki, to refrain from hostilities and to solve differences by direct negotiation,

114. Memorandum Welles-Lindsay Conversation, Nov. 18, 1938, *FR 1938*, II, 402–403. Wilson, hoping to return, allowed his wife to remain in Berlin until the end of March 1939. But the State Department, counseled by Messersmith, would not allow the ambassador to go back. He resigned his position on August 31, 1939, and no successor was named. Messersmith to Hull, Feb. 15, 1939, DS, 123W693/601, and Wilson to Mrs. Wilson, Mar. 20, 1939, 123W693/603.

115. Woermann Memorandum, Nov. 22, 1938, *DGFP*, D, IV, 644–648; see also Hull Memorandum, Nov. 23, 1938, *FR 1938*, II, 405.

116. Hull, *Memoirs*, I, 620; Roosevelt to Hitler, Apr. 14, 1939, *FR 1939*, I, 130–133.

117. *New York Times*, Apr. 21, 1939.

118. Baynes, ed., *Hitler's Speeches*, II, 1605–1657.

arbitration, or conciliation. Next day Moscicki agreed to direct negotiation or conciliation; Hitler said nothing. Roosevelt forwarded Moscicki's reply to Hitler and asked him to accept one of the two methods.[119] The chancellor replied through diplomatic channels on August 31 that he had "left no stone unturned" in his effort to settle the German-Polish dispute peaceably.[120] Next day German troops entered Poland.

Following the brief but decisive Polish campaign, in February 1940 Roosevelt sent Welles on a mission to Europe's major capitals (Rome, Berlin, Paris, London, and back to Rome) to determine whether a just peace was negotiable. Immediately before Welles reached Berlin, Hitler on February 29 issued a directive to all German officials that in the forthcoming talks they were to argue that England and France had made the war and rejected peace, and that nothing was to be said that indicated Germany had any interest in peace talks; rather, Germany was "determined to conclude this war victoriously."[121] Welles, who had persisted in his belief throughout the thirties that it would be possible to negotiate with Nazi Germany, found no encouragement in Berlin. Ribbentrop, who received him first, was at his most arrogant; Hitler was more composed but no less inflexible. Weizsäcker, who informed Welles of the directive of February 29, also hinted that perhaps Hitler might be willing to negotiate a peace settlement if the suggestion came from Mussolini. After his return to Rome on March 16, Welles pursued this idea cautiously, and Mussolini asked him to delay his departure for a day while he and Ciano met with Hitler and Ribbentrop at the Brenner on March 18. But the hope for a favorable development was vain. The Americans had nothing concrete to offer. Hitler, who did not tell Mussolini of his plans, was determined on his spring offensive; and Mussolini, after their meeting, was perhaps more convinced than ever that Germany would triumph and more determined to have his share of the spoils.[122]

119. Roosevelt to Hitler and Moscicki, Aug. 24, Moscicki to Roosevelt, and Roosevelt to Hitler, Aug. 25, 1939, *FR 1939,* I, 360–362, 368–369.

120. Ribbentrop to German embassy, Aug. 31, 1939, *DGFP,* D, VII, 473, and Thomsen to Hull, Aug. 31, 1939, *FR 1939,* I, 396. See also Hull, *Memoirs,* I, 662–665.

121. Directive for the Conversations with Mr. Sumner Welles, Feb. 29, 1940, *DGFP,* D, VIII, 817–819.

122. Welles's account of his mission is in *Time for Decision,* 73–147. See

Germany attacked Denmark and Norway on April 9 and Belgium, the Netherlands, and Luxembourg on May 10. By June 22 Hitler had his revenge as France surrendered. The United States procrastinated in its own curious way, as it would for another year and a half. After war had begun in September 1939 Roosevelt said he could ask the American people to be neutral in action, if not in thought.[123] American action from then to December 1941, however, was not neutral. The administration did not intend neutrality in November 1939 when it secured replacement of the arms embargo with "cash and carry" provisions; nor did it intend neutrality in the summer of 1940 by shipping war supplies to England and exchanging fifty destroyers for leases on military bases. In 1941 the lend-lease law (H.R. 1776), the defense of Greenland arrangement, movement of American troops into Iceland, Roosevelt's meeting with Churchill in August, and finally the convoying of British ships and "shoot on sight" orders given to the navy in the autumn, were all partisan acts to help the Allies defeat Germany, and perhaps to keep the United States out of war if others truly could be given materials to finish the job.

Whether the Second World War originated in 1919 at Versailles, or in 1933 when Hitler became chancellor, or in 1939 when Germany invaded Poland, no longer mattered once shots had been fired. England, the Free French, and then the Soviet Union after June 1941, were fighting a total war that was as much America's as it was Europe's even if Americans recognized this fact only slowly and grudgingly and never themselves resolved their international commitment. Japan resolved it for them at Pearl Harbor on December 7, 1941. Next day the United States declared war on Japan, and three days later Germany and Italy declared war on the United States. At 3:05 P.M. that same day Roosevelt affixed his signature to America's declaration of war against Germany and Italy.

The thought that somehow, somewhere along the line, the war that Churchill branded "unnecessary" might have been prevented will probably haunt men forever. Many people have argued that there were

also Langer and Gleason, *Challenge to Isolation,* 361–375, and Elizabeth Wiskemann, *The Rome-Berlin Axis: A Study of the Relations Between Hitler and Mussolini,* rev. ed. (London, 1966), 229–246.
123. Text of Fireside Chat, Sept. 3, 1939, in *PPFDR,* VIII, 460–463.

at least three or four critical situations when England and France could have halted Germany, called Hitler's "bluff," and perhaps caused the Nazi regime to collapse. Such speculation must take account of the disillusioning aftermath of the First World War and the gripping fear of repeating mistakes that had led to it, the effect of the Great Depression, the popular desire to resolve difficulties peacefully and the faith that this could be done, the widespread legitimate revulsion in the face of warfare's horrors, and belief that at least some of Germany's grievances were real and demands just. These factors affected Americans as profoundly as they did Europeans. Under the circumstances the especial lure and challenge of appeasement—defined by Chamberlain's biographer as neither a foolish nor ignoble hope but a moral imperative not to accept war until every effort had been made to redress legitimate grievances peacefully—is readily understood.[124] But American diplomats, as surely as their British and French colleagues, committed mistakes that went beyond justifiable appeasement, and kept them from achieving the ends they sought.

Perhaps it was natural in 1933 to regard Hitler, as Davis did, as a relative moderate among radicals making legitimate, if overstated, claims, or to assume, as did even Messersmith for about a year, that Hitler's regime could not last if it did not follow traditional economic and diplomatic guidelines. But America's policy makers and analysts, especially the President, were wrong to throw away almost carelessly their opportunity to place their nation in position to cooperate in a system of collective security, and were wrong to be more sympathetic toward German demands for equality of armaments than the French need for security. The implications of Germany's abandonment of the Disarmament Conference and the League of Nations (the latter of course was an embarrassing issue for the United States) were not entirely clear in autumn 1933. But American diplomats might have urged a more cautious if not firmer policy on the British and French instead of immediately retreating behind a public declaration of lack of involvement in European political affairs and almost wistfully hoping that Germany's action would have a "sobering" effect and make the French less rather than more recalcitrant.

American diplomats disapproved of Germany's unilateral decision

124. Macleod, *Neville Chamberlain*, 209.

to rearm, but they also questioned the wisdom or effectiveness in 1935 of the restriction of the Treaty of Versailles. They wished neither to protest Germany's action nor to encourage the Stresa conferees— whom they suspected of meeting only to "blow off steam," as Bingham had put it—to take serious action. It was wrong, however, to approve the Anglo-German Naval Agreement a few months later, thus condoning both German rearmament and British revisionist policy, the latter so politically ill conceived at that juncture. Even more mistaken was the failure to take a more aggressive position during Italy's assault on Ethiopia. The President and the State Department made various diplomatic efforts and invoked their moral embargo, but they counted too heavily on British and French pressure, and would not risk a political fight over an oil embargo which, if successful, might have forced others to follow suit and probably would have ended the drive of Mussolini's forces. As noted before, Erich Kordt's claim that the outcome of the Italian-Ethiopian conflict determined whether Europe would have war or peace is overstatement, but Italy's unchecked aggression contributed significantly to setting the stage first for the reoccupation of the Rhineland, then for the march into Austria and the confrontation, as Hassell noted even in 1935, between the "static" and "dynamic" powers.

During the Spanish civil war, and the attendant German and Italian assault, the United States exhibited incredible political blindness. The British and French did not play their proper roles, but the United States went beyond even the legal requirements of its neutrality legislation. Had aid been forthcoming from the United States and from England and France, considering that Hitler's position on aid to Franco was not firm at least until November 1936, the Spanish Republicans could well have triumphed. Instead, Germany gained every advantage from the Spanish civil war: fascism triumphed over democracy, France was ringed with a third hostile neighbor, and the groundwork was more securely laid for the Rome-Berlin-Tokyo alliance. The United States succeeded only in making itself increasingly vulnerable to war in Europe and Asia.

The American government in 1937 and early 1938 tried to make up for time and opportunity lost by achieving a joint policy with England that might appease or curb Germany. The Americans and English had failed to agree in major areas of economics and disarmament. The State Department and Foreign Office in 1933 had failed to agree on a joint policy for the sale of airplanes to Germany. The British in 1934 secured a bilateral debt settlement with Germany without considering how it would affect Germany's other creditors. By the spring of 1937 Chamberlain was in power, and for several years before that time his attitude toward an American contribution to the search for peace had been derisive. His response to Roosevelt's first overture in 1937 was standoffish. But the State Department's pious response to his request for changes in American trade and neutrality policies, and assistance in the Far East, was no better. Significantly, when Japan went to war against China in July 1937, both the United States and Great Britain felt their vital interests were threatened, but neither knew how to cope with the problem. Roosevelt wanted to "quarantine" the aggressor, but was afraid of sanctions and feared having American policy appear to be a "tail to the British kite." Hull scotched Welles's Armistice Day scheme. Chamberlain opposed sanctions against Japan, the French would do nothing unless assured of military support in Indochina, and the Brussels Conference, which might have served as a useful example for European developments, collapsed.

Chamberlain next threw a deadly damper on Roosevelt's conference proposal in January 1938, although its formal burial did not occur until after Eden's resignation—which the proposal ironically hastened —and the *Anschluss*. What Roosevelt might have accomplished had he taken advantage of his slim opportunity to summon an international conference is questionable. The Welles-Lindsay exchange in February and March 1938 demonstrated that the United States was uncertain about recognizing Italy's conquest of Ethiopia. Recognition was central to Chamberlain's appeasement policy. Even Welles admitted that once the nations had gathered around the conference table and agreed to a code of international ethics—a noble undertaking— he did not know what would come next. If it was to be concessions to Germany, and the evidence indicates he intended that, there is little reason to think those concessions would have contained German aggression any more than the ones England and France were about to make.

In the matter of Czechoslovakia and the Munich Conference, American diplomats displayed no more insight or foresight than anyone else. They did not see that the stake was more than commitment to a nation's life; it was the entire system of French, if not European, security and the opening of eastern Europe to German economic and political domination, to say nothing of the forcing of the Soviet Union to alter its foreign policy. A. J. P. Taylor is correct: Americans, whatever misgivings they might have had at the time, only later condemned the British and French for doing what they would have done in their place.[125]

Some Americans quickly perceived the threat of Nazi Germany to the United States and the world: Dodd especially, and Bowers and Morgenthau. In a year's time Messersmith became perhaps his country's most astute diplomatic analyst, and by the middle of the decade Davis had become a strong proponent of collective security. Others did not see so well or quickly. Hull, of course, loathed every form of German brutality and international aggression, but failed to recognize that his economic liberalism and moral persuasion were insufficient to combat Germany's new order. His responses to the crises and chaos of his era were excessively cautious. Roosevelt was able, shrewd, and farsighted, but expended most of his energy on domestic problems and belatedly and without daring or dash turned to foreign policy. Early and often he talked about blockade, boycott, and economic sanctions to bring pressure on Germany, but there is little reason to believe he took these schemes seriously. If he did, he demonstrated his naïveté about the Third Reich and international problems. In addition, as he remarked to Phillips in mid-September of 1938, he felt that the United States could do nothing except wait for Europe to blow itself up and then have America "pick up the pieces of European civilization and help them to save what remains of the wreck—not a cheerful prospect."[126] That idea, tragically, was a popular one. Further, to a shocking degree those responsible for planning and executing their nation's foreign policy did not heed Messersmith's charge that they were responsible for informing and guiding the public in its own interest.

It is impossible to know precisely in what way bolder policy might have caused Hitler to revise his distorted assessment of the United States or to alter his foreign policy; as it was, he disregarded the more

---

125. *Origins of the Second World War,* 191.
126. Roosevelt to Phillips, Sept. 15, 1938, Roosevelt papers, PSF, Italy: William Phillips.

realistic, if sometimes exaggerated, assessment of German diplomats, and American behavior during 1933–1938 tended to reinforce his ill-founded conclusions. Other studies have shown that even as the United States pursued a more belligerent policy during 1939–1941 Hitler remained largely unable or unwilling to grasp the implication of the American balance of power. Nevertheless, it is clear that whatever Hitler's larger designs, during 1933–1938 he improvised according to the opportunities he saw, and he was frequently fearful of foreign response and prepared to alter immediate policy. Bolder American policy might not only have encouraged others to greater daring and resistance, but could have changed, in a way highly advantageous to the democracies, the critical political circumstances in which German, and European, policy developed.

Underlying these failures is the inescapable conclusion that from Roosevelt, through Hull and Welles, and down through the ranks of the State Department, in the Congress, and in all walks of life, with too few exceptions, there persisted a belief that Europe's problems were Europe's, that an ocean three thousand miles wide separated the New World from the Old. As a rule Americans cared about Europe's troubles only within their limited framework; they would render what assistance they could by disarmament talks or reciprocal trade programs. When the great crises came, Americans, as Chamberlain had said of his countrymen, regarded them as being in a faraway country between people they did not know. Indeed, when war began in Europe Americans naïvely declared their independence.

# BIBLIOGRAPHICAL ESSAY, INDEX

# BIBLIOGRAPHICAL ESSAY

Historians of the peacetime diplomacy of Franklin D. Roosevelt's administration generally have concentrated on the two or three years preceding American entry into the Second World War, focusing on the Far East. Some reasons for so doing appear, along with indication of areas in need of further study, in the able compilation by Wayne S. Cole, "American Entry into World War II: A Historiographical Appraisal," *Mississippi Valley Historical Review,* XLVII (Mar. 1957). In the decade since Cole's article numerous scholars have dealt with disarmament, neutrality, Latin American policy, the Italian-Ethiopian War, the Spanish civil war, and the Sino-Japanese conflict. My own work covers American foreign policy with respect to Germany and the threat that nation's regime offered to American and European security during 1933–1938. The following essay includes sources pertinent to this study.

## SOURCE MATERIALS

*Government Records, Unpublished and Published*

Indispensable for any study of American foreign policy are the diplomatic records of the United States. Records of the Department of State for 1933–1938 are on deposit in the National Archives, Washington, D.C., and classified "limited access"; they are open to researchers who are United States citizens with permission from the Historical Office of the Department of State. The review policy is extremely liberal; virtually none of my notes was edited. The Department of State records, organized in decimal files, contain information on nearly every aspect of diplomacy. The Department publishes annually, on an approximate twenty-year-time-lag basis, *Foreign Relations of the United States,* which beginning with volumes for the year 1932 consists of at least five annual volumes. (A short history of this series is in Richard W. Leopold, "The *Foreign Relations* Series: A Centennial Estimate," *Mississippi Valley Historical Review,* XLIV [Mar. 1963].) Supplementary volumes are *Peace and War: United States Foreign Policy, 1931– 1941* (Washington, D.C., 1943); *The Soviet Union, 1933–1939* (Washington, D.C., 1952); and *Japan, 1931–1941,* 2 vols. (Washington, D.C., 1943). As Leopold points out, the latter was a poorly conceived and executed white paper, not properly labeled as such. *Foreign Relations* is an excellent documentary account of American foreign policy—although documents tend to show the final decision rather than how it was reached and the alternatives—and offers a great deal of information about activities of diplomats of other countries.

After the Second World War the governments of the United States, Great Britain, and France undertook to publish *Documents on German Foreign Policy, 1918–1945* (Washington, D.C., 1949———), using the captured German Foreign Ministry and Reich Chancellery records. Series C, for 1933–1937, lacks the sixth and final volume. Series D, originally intended to cover 1937–1945, was concluded at December 11, 1941, in the thirteenth volume. Series A and B, for the Weimar period, and Series E, for 1941–1945, will be published in German only. Copies of the unpublished records of the German Foreign Ministry for 1933–1938 are available on microfilm from the National Archives (Microcopy T-120). The files that have been filmed have been assigned a serial number and each page of a document given a frame number. An indispensable guide for these microfilm records is George O. Kent, comp. and ed., *A Catalog of Files and Microfilms of the German Foreign Ministry Archives, 1920–1945,* 3 vols. (Stanford, 1962 ———). A planned fourth volume has not yet appeared. The Department of State has also published *Nazi Conspiracy and Aggression,* 8 vols. plus Supps. A and B (Washington, D.C., 1946–48). Available too is *The Trial of the Major War Criminals Before the International Military Tribunal,* 42 vols. (Nuremberg, 1947–49).

The British government has made part of its diplomatic record available in E. L. Woodward and Rohan Butler, eds., *Documents on British Foreign Policy, 1919–1939,* three series, 32 vols. (London, 1946 ———); archives for the period 1933–1937 opened after this study was completed. France's Ministère des Affaires Etrangères has begun publishing *Documents Diplomatiques Français, 1932–1939* (Paris, 1963———). Three volumes of the second series (1936–1939) have appeared, covering part of 1936. French archives are not open. The Royal Institute of International Affairs has published for this decade, as well as for others, its annual *Documents on International Affairs,* which contain the text of each year's major public speeches, treaties, and agreements. The annual volumes in the Institute's *Survey of International Affairs* are contemporary as well as retrospective history.

Domestic debate over foreign policy is readily available in the *Congressional Record.* Some effects of German policy on American life appear in U.S. Congress, *Investigation of Nazi Propaganda Activities and Investigation of Certain Other Propaganda Activities,* Hearings before the House Special Committee on Un-American Activities, 73d Cong., 2d sess., on H. Res. 198 (Washington, D. C., 1934–35), and U.S. Department of Labor, *Annual Report of the Commissioner of Immigration,* especially persecution of Jewish and other minorities.

*Personal Papers and Organization Records*

The Franklin D. Roosevelt papers, at the Franklin D. Roosevelt Library, Hyde Park, New York, are an important collection. They include the President's correspondence with his ambassadors, and many letters, memoranda, and notes exchanged with American and European diplomats. At this library too are the R. Walton Moore papers, which include several boxes of important correspondence with William E. Dodd.

There are several valuable collections in the Manuscript Division of the Library of Congress. The Cordell Hull papers are a large collection; materials from 1933–1938 are available with permission of the Historical Office. Ten boxes of correspondence pertain to European affairs, German in particular. Hull quoted many of these documents in his *Memoirs,* but did not cite them; close reading of them, along with materials in other files, leads to the conclusion that the secretary of state was not as farsighted as he would have had his readers believe. The Norman H. Davis papers are an interesting collection. Davis was not a decision-maker but he was a frequent emissary for Roosevelt and as adviser and friend of Hull he was abreast of developments in the State Department. There are ten boxes of correspondence with important officials, including Roosevelt, Hull, Welles, and Moffat. The William E. Dodd papers, available for use with permission of his daughter Martha Dodd, span his career as scholar and diplomat. Included are highly interesting exchanges with Roosevelt, House, and Moore.

Two less important collections are the Breckinridge Long papers and Wilbur J. Carr papers. Long's papers include many letters to Roosevelt and State Department officials, and a detailed diary in which he recorded his increasingly desperate feelings about European politics. Carr's papers too include a detailed diary for 1896–1943, with interesting comments on politics in Czechoslovakia in 1938.

The Jay Pierrepont Moffat papers (available for use with permission of his widow, Mrs. Albert Lévitt) and William Phillips papers are at the Houghton Library at Harvard University. Both men kept highly detailed diaries which afford valuable insight to State Department activities: Moffat was head of the European desk, 1933–1935 and 1937–1940, and Phillips was under secretary, 1933–1936, and ambassador to Italy, 1936–1941. They corresponded at length with a great many diplomatic officials. Both collections are important reading.

Equally important are the George S. Messersmith papers in the Manuscript Division of the University of Delaware Library. Messersmith was probably the most knowledgeable American diplomatic observer, as his extraordinarily long letters and reports testify. He left no formal memoir, but in 1955, at age seventy-one, shortly before his death, he dictated a massive series of discerning, although random, memoranda on many subjects and colleagues.

The Theodore J. Marriner papers at Columbia University include two boxes of correspondence and a diary for 1918–1937. But the amount of political information is disappointingly thin. Three diplomats who contributed to The Oral History Collection of Columbia University are Claude Bowers, William Phillips, and John C. White. There is little in the Bowers and Phillips statements not available elsewhere; White, counselor of the Berlin embassy, 1933–1935, has made a few comments on Dodd's good analyses of Nazi Germany and his aloofness from diplomatic life.

The Jacob Gould Schurman papers at Cornell University contain only a few interesting exchanges with public figures of the 1920's and 1930's.

The Jewish refugee problem was a major one. Disappointingly thin on this subject are the Baruch Charney Vladeck papers at the New York University Libraries, Tamiment Library. Vladeck, general manager of the *Jewish Daily Forward,* was also cochairman of the Joint Boycott Council of the American Jewish Congress and the Jewish Labor Committee. There are a few letters to other interested persons and government officials concerning boycotts and Jewish refugees. The papers of the Joint Boycott Council are in the Manuscript Division of the New York Public Library. The large collection—thousands of letters from outraged citizens, transcripts of speeches, reports from merchants who discontinued German goods, and others who had not, pamphlets, broadsides—is a sad reminder of a futile effort to arouse consciences and halt Nazi terror.

Another good source is the *Annual Report* of the American Jewish Committee, a record of efforts to organize boycotts and rallies and to enlist government assistance for refugees; that organization's *American Jewish Yearbook* summarizes events of each year. Finally, contemporary journals created to attack the purchase of German goods are the monthly *Anti-Nazi Economic Bulletin* (1934–1940), published by the Non-Sectarian Anti-Nazi League to Champion Human Rights, and the Joint Boycott Council's *Boycott: Nazi Goods and Services* (1937–1939).

*Published Diaries, Letters, Memoirs, and Speeches*

Samuel I. Rosenman, comp., *The Public Papers and Addresses of Franklin D. Roosevelt,* 13 vols. (New York, 1938–50), is highly useful; so too is Elliott Roosevelt, ed., *F.D.R.: His Personal Letters, 1928–1945,* 2 vols. (New York, 1950). Many State Department officials, cabinet officers, and ambassadors have published informative records. *The Memoirs of Cordell Hull,* 2 vols. (New York, 1948) is essentially accurate, although the hard-working secretary emerges more the embattled prophet than he was. Sumner Welles, close friend of Roosevelt, frequently at odds with Hull, has written two accounts: *The Time for Decision* (New York, 1944) and *Seven Decisions That*

*Shaped History* (New York, 1950). In the first, written shortly after he had to resign as under secretary, Welles is especially critical of Hull for spoiling his proposed 1937 Armistice Day conference, that "Last Frail Chance . . ." Welles's work, like Hull's is both argument and defense, and although accurate must be measured carefully against the documentary record. Raymond Moley, assistant secretary of state in 1933, has some caustic comments about early New Deal economic and diplomatic policies in *After Seven Years* (New York, 1939). Herbert Feis, *1933: Characters in Crisis* (Boston and Toronto, 1966), is an excellent memoir-narrative.

Views of two other State Department officials are available in Nancy Harvison Hooker, ed., *The Moffat Papers: Selections from the Diplomatic Journals of Jay Pierrepont Moffat, 1919–1943* (Cambridge, Mass., 1956), which is good reading, and William Phillips, *Ventures in Diplomacy* (Boston, 1952), spare on activities during the thirties. Two of Roosevelt's more vociferous cabinet members were Harold Ickes (Interior) and Henry Morgenthau, Jr. (Treasury). *The Secret Diary of Harold L. Ickes,* 3 vols. (New York, 1953–55) includes *The First Thousand Days, 1933–1936* and *The Inside Struggle, 1936–1939;* the latter is helpful particularly on the helium argument. Morgenthau kept a minutely detailed record of activities and conversations, which John Morton Blum has been using as the basis of a multivolume study. Morgenthau serialized part of his recollections in "The Morgenthau Diaries—III—How FDR Fought The Axis," *Colliers,* CXX (Oct. 11, 1947), which overstates the case. Daniel C. Roper, secretary of commerce, 1933–1939, in *Fifty Years of Public Life* (Durham, N.C., 1941), explains how he helped Dodd get the Berlin appointment.

William E. Dodd, Jr., and Martha Dodd have edited their father's controversial and valuable *Ambassador Dodd's Diary, 1933–1938* (New York, 1941). His successor in Berlin, Hugh R. Wilson, has left two volumes that treat the relevant years: *Diplomat Between Wars* (New York, 1941) and *A Career Diplomat, The Third Chapter: The Third Reich* (New York, 1960). The latter volume, published by Hugh R. Wilson, Jr., after his father's death, contains numerous letters that demonstrate both the ambassador's genuine desire to see peace secured through appeasement and his frequently too sympathetic attitude toward Nazi Germany. The commercial attaché in Berlin during the thirties, Douglas Miller, in *Via Diplomatic Pouch* (New York, 1944), has put together some of his better reports on economic and political developments to the Bureau of Foreign and Domestic Commerce.

Although it does not deal directly with experiences in Germany, Claude Bowers, *My Mission to Spain: Watching the Rehearsal for World War II* (New York, 1954) is a sad review of democratic impotence in the face of fascist aggression by a historian-diplomat whose views and warnings were much like Dodd's. Joseph E. Davies, once intended as Dodd's successor, has put together some interesting contemporary commentary of his own on the Soviet Union and European problems generally in *Mission to Moscow* (New York, 1941).

William L. Shirer, the American newspaperman deeply involved in events of the 1930's, has published *Berlin Diary: The Journal of a Foreign Correspondent, 1934–1941* (New York, 1941). Martha Dodd, an interesting woman in her own right, accompanied her father to Germany; her *Through Embassy Eyes* (New York, 1939) contains some lucid sketches of events and personalities. Lillian T. Mowrer, *Journalist's Wife* (New York, 1937), comments on developments as she saw them while accompanying her newspaperman husband Edgar Ansel Mowrer; his *Germany Puts the Clock Back* (New York, 1933), combined with his daily reports, caused him to be expelled. Edward J. Flynn, *You're the Boss* (New York, 1947) contains a wholly erroneous story of Dodd's appointment, which he retracted in the *New York Times,* Nov. 2, 1947. *The Autobiography of Sol Bloom* (New York, 1948), by the man who headed the House Committee on Foreign Affairs in the late 1930's, says little.

Hitler's words appear in many sources. *Mein Kampf* is available in numerous editions; I have used the John Chamberlain, Sidney B. Fay, and others edition published by Reynal and Hitchcock (New York, 1939). Some lengthy comments on the United States are in Gerhard L. Weinberg, ed., *Hitlers Zweites Buch: Ein Dokument aus dem Jahr 1928* (Stuttgart, 1961), translated by Salvator Attanasio as *Hitler's Secret Book* (New York, 1961). Major speeches are in Norman H. Baynes, ed., *The Speeches of Adolf Hitler, April 1922–August 1939,* 2 vols. (London, 1942). Wartime reflections, arranged according to subject, appear in Henry Picker, ed., *Hitlers Tischegespräche im Führerhauptquartier, 1941–42* (Bonn, 1951); more nearly complete and chronologically organized is H. R. Trevor-Roper, ed., *Hitler's Secret Conversations, 1941–1944* (New York, 1953). And finally, François

Genoud, ed., *The Testament of Adolf Hitler: The Hitler-Bormann Documents, February-April 1945,* translated by R. H. Stevens (London, 1961).

Various of Hitler's conversations with foreign diplomats are in the useful Paul Schmidt, *Statist auf diplomatischer Bühne, 1923-1945: Erlebnisse des Chefdolmetschers im Aüswartigen Amt mit den Staatsmännern Europas,* 2d ed. (Frankfurt am Main-Bonn, 1964); unrevealing is Otto Meissner, *Staatssekretär unter Ebert-Hindenburg-Hitler: Der Schicksalsweg des deutschen Volkes von 1918-1945, wie ich ihn erlebte* (Hamburg, 1950). More informal accounts of conversations, and of personal relations, are in Ernst Hanfstaengl, *Unheard Witness* (Philadelphia, 1957), Hermann Rauschning, *The Voice of Destruction* (New York, 1940), and *My First Seventy Six Years: The Autobiography of Hjalmar Schacht,* translated by Diana Pyke (London, 1955).

German diplomatic memoirs are useful, although there is little material concerned specifically with the United States. Friedrich W. von Prittwitz und Gaffron, a popular ambassador during the Hoover administration, kept no formal record but reflects pleasantly on his stay in *Zwischen Petersburg und Washington—ein Diplomatenleben* (Munich, 1952). Hans Luther died before writing an account of his ambassadorship; his *Politiker Ohne Partei: Errinerungen* (Stuttgart, 1950) remarks briefly on his appointment and image as the "man of Locarno." Hans Dieckhoff did not write a memoir. Herbert von Dirksen in *Moscow, Tokyo, London: Twenty Years of German Foreign Policy* (Norman, Okla., 1952) does not mention his talks with Joseph Kennedy in 1938. Critical of Nazi diplomats and diplomacy are Erich Kordt, *Wahn und Wirklichkeit: Die Aussenpolitik des Dritten Reiches, Versuch einer Darstellung* (Stuttgart, 1948) and *Nicht aus den Akten* . . . (Stuttgart, 1950). Rudolf Nadolny, *Mein Beitrag* (Wiesbaden, 1955) recalls cooperation with Americans in Geneva and the disarmament debacle. Franz von Papen, *Memoirs,* translated by Brian Connell (New York, 1955), records his agreement with quitting the disarmament talks but not the League of Nations. *The Ribbentrop Memoirs,* translated by Oliver Watson (London, 1954), is brief, caustic, and inaccurate about American foreign policy. *Memoirs of Ernst von Weizsäcker,* translated by John Andrews (Chicago, 1951), has an excuse for everything.

Military matters are discussed in the valuable Friedrich Hossbach,

*Zwischen Wehrmacht und Hitler, 1934–1938* (Wolfenbüttel and Hanover, 1949), and Grand Admiral Erich Raeder, *My Life,* translated by Henry W. Drexel (Annapolis, 1960). Opposition to Hitler's military tactics and strategy is recorded in Wolfgang Foerster, *Generaloberst Ludwig Beck, sein Kampf gegen den Krieg: Aus nachgelassenen Papieren des Generalstabchefs,* 2d ed. (Munich, 1953).

Many English memoirs provide insights. Most important is *The Memoirs of Anthony Eden, Earl of Avon: Facing the Dictators* (Boston, 1962), the second volume of his trilogy, which points to the failure of the United States and Great Britain to achieve a working relationship in Europe and the Far East as having disastrous consequences on world developments. Eden indicates that his departure from the Foreign Office was hastened by Chamberlain's unenthusiastic response to Roosevelt's overture in January 1938. Another cabinet official who resigned, after Munich, was the first lord of the Admiralty, Alfred Duff Cooper. He supports some of Eden's contentions in *Old Men Forget: The Autobiography of Duff Cooper* (New York, 1954). Two of Eden's predecessors have explained their own, and British, policy: Viscount Simon, *Retrospect* (London, 1952), and Viscount Templewood (Sir Samuel Hoare), *Nine Troubled Years* (London, 1954). Both Templewood and Eden's successor, Lord Halifax, *Fullness of Days* (New York, 1957), express skepticism about American efforts. *The Mist Procession: The Autobiography of Lord Vansittart* (London, 1958), by the permanent under secretary for foreign affairs, 1930–1938, is bitter about American policy, and about matters generally. Nevile Henderson, Chamberlain's emissary, has recorded his *Failure of a Mission: Berlin 1937–1939* (New York, 1940).

Relevant French reviews include Pierre-Etienne Flandin, *Politique Française, 1919–1940* (Paris, 1947), which explains French unwillingness and unpreparedness to drive German forces from the Rhineland when he was foreign minister in 1936, and Georges Bonnet, *Défense de la Paix,* 2 vols. (Geneva, 1946–1948), which emphasizes American, especially William Bullitt's, agreement with French policy over Czechoslovakia in 1938 in the first volume, *De Washington au Quai d'Orsay.* André François-Poncet, *The Fateful Years: Memoirs of a French Ambassador in Berlin, 1931–1938,* translated by Jacques LeClercq (New York, 1949), is a good account by a skillful diplomat, but makes him appear more prescient than he was. Also helpful are Malcolm Muggeridge, ed., *Ciano's Diary, 1937-1938,* translated by Andreas Mayor (London, 1952), which is quite uninhibited, and the more reserved Malcolm Muggeridge, ed., *Ciano's Diplomatic Papers,* translated by Stuart Hood (London, 1948).

## SECONDARY MATERIALS

*Background: The 1920's*

Many volumes deal in whole or in part with American diplomacy between the world wars; following are only the volumes I have used. For background on the 1920's, Selig Adler, *The Isolationist Impulse: Its Twentieth Century Reaction* (New York, 1957) is a fine study of a perplexing problem; his *The Uncertain Giant: 1921–1941, American Foreign Policy Between the Wars* (New York, 1965) is an able synthesis. Foster Rhea Dulles, *America's Rise to World Power, 1898–1954* (New York, 1954), in Richard B. Morris and Henry Steele Commager, eds., *The New American Nation Series,* is a good survey. In the same series is John D. Hicks, *Republican Ascendancy, 1921–1933* (New York, 1960), which contains several fine chapters on foreign policy. The same is true of William E. Leuchtenburg, *The Perils of Prosperity, 1914–1932* (Chicago, 1958), in Daniel J. Boorstin, ed., *Chicago History of American Civilization Series,* and Arthur M. Schlesinger, Jr., *The Crisis of the Old Order, 1919–1933* (Boston, 1957), the first volume in his *The Age of Roosevelt* series. The paralyzing effect of economic collapse on diplomacy is treated in Robert H. Ferrell, *American Diplomacy in the Great Depression: Hoover-Stimson Foreign Policy, 1929–1933* (New Haven, 1957). Useful but outdated is William Starr Myers and Walter H. Newton, *The Hoover Administration: A Documented Narrative* (New York, 1936).

A number of works concentrate on individuals or special problems. Gordon A. Craig and Felix Gilbert, eds., *The Diplomats: 1919–1939* (Princeton, 1953) is an outstanding collection of essays on American and European diplomats of the interwar period. Included is a sharp analysis by Dexter Perkins, "The Department of State and American Public Opinion." Judicious is Robert H. Ferrell, *Frank B. Kellogg—Henry L. Stimson* (New York, 1963), vol. XI in Samuel Flagg Bemis and Robert H. Ferrell, eds., *The American Secretaries of State and*

*Their Diplomacy* series. Norman A. Graebner, ed., *An Uncertain Tradition: American Secretaries of State in the Twentieth Century* (New York, 1961) includes essays on Charles Evans Hughes by John Chalmers Vinson, Frank B. Kellogg by L. Ethan Ellis, and Henry L. Stimson by Richard N. Current. Merlo J. Pusey, *Charles Evans Hughes,* 2 vols. (New York, 1951) is uncritical. Bascom N. Timmons, *Portrait of an American: Charles G. Dawes* (New York, 1953) is a flattering study of a shallow figure.

The rapid change in American attitude toward German responsibility for causing war in 1914 is shrewdly analyzed in Selig Adler, "The War-Guilt Question and American Disillusionment, 1918–1928," *Journal of Modern History,* XXIII (Mar. 1951). Louis A. R. Yates, *The United States and French Security, 1917–1921* (New York, 1957) is interesting on the position American diplomats took with respect to their obligations and privileges arising out of the peace settlement. Robert H. Ferrell, *Peace in Their Time: The Origins of the Kellogg-Briand Pact* (New Haven, 1952) details the American conversion of a French effort at a bilateral treaty into a meaningless world pact. Harold G. Moulton, *The Reparation Plan* (New York, 1924) and Harold G. Moulton and Leo Pasvolsky, *World War Debt Settlements* (New York, 1926) discuss the intricate arrangements in these sticky matters. The American contribution to this money muddle is analyzed in part, and labeled with respect to Germany as "financing . . . in a political fog," in Herbert Feis, *The Diplomacy of the Dollar: First Phase, 1919–1932* (Baltimore, 1950). Important on the American effort to reconstruct Germany and achieve a world "community of interest" through finance is William Appleman Williams, "The Legend of Isolationism in the 1920's," *Science and Society,* XVIII (Winter 1954).

Concerning German affairs during the 1920's, Günter Schubert, *Anfänge nationalsozialistischer Aussenpolitik* (Cologne, 1963) points to the persistent narrowness of Hitler's views and the antidemocratic strain of Nazi rhetoric. Edward W. Bennett, *Germany and the Diplomacy of the Financial Crisis, 1931* (Cambridge, Mass., 1962), an excellent and extremely fair assessment of American and European efforts to resolve difficulties, also criticizes the aggressiveness of German diplomacy. Even more critical, especially of the Brüning government's economic policies and efforts to achieve domestic control through dramatic success in foreign policy, is Wolfgang J. Helbich, "Between Stresemann and Hitler: The Foreign Policy of the Brüning Government," *World Politics,* XII (Oct. 1959), and the same author's *Die Reparationen in der Ära Brüning: Zur Bedeutung des Young-Plans für die deutsche Politik, 1930 bis 1932* (Berlin-Dahlem, 1962). Andreas Dorpalen, *Hindenburg and the Weimar Republic* (Princeton, 1964) is fair but critical of its subject.

Relations between the United States and Germany during the Weimar period are dealt with in Edward Joseph Berbusse, "Diplomatic Relations Between the United States and Weimar Germany: 1919–1929" (Ph.D. dissertation, Georgetown University, 1951), a poor study which virtually blames the collapse of Weimar democracy on American policy. Far superior and more accurate is Robert Gottwald, *Die deutsch-amerikanischen Beziehungen in der Ära Stresemann* (Berlin-Dahlem, 1965), which emphasizes the close cooperation between American and German diplomats and Stresemann's interest in cultivating American intervention in European affairs in Germany's behalf. John R. Ban, "The United States Government and the Rise of Hitler to Power in Germany" (Master's thesis, Indiana University, 1956) analyzes State Department reports up to March 1933.

### American and European Diplomacy

There is no adequate scholarly volume covering the whole of American foreign relations between 1933 and 1941, although Robert A. Divine, *The Reluctant Belligerent: American Entry into World War II* (New York, 1965) is a helpful survey. Useful too are the volumes by Selig Adler and Foster Rhea Dulles, to which may be added the thought-provoking book by George F. Kennan, *American Diplomacy, 1900–1950* (New York, 1951). William E. Leuchtenburg, *Franklin D. Roosevelt and the New Deal, 1932–1940* (New York, 1960), in *The New American Nation Series* contains three fine chapters on foreign affairs. Allan Nevins, *The New Deal and World Affairs: A Chronicle of International Affairs, 1933–1945* (New Haven, 1945), in the *Chronicles of America* series is superficial. Arthur M. Schlesinger, Jr., focuses on national politics in vol. II of his *The Age of Roosevelt* series, *The Coming of the New Deal* (Boston, 1959), but there are two important chapters on the London Economic Conference. Roland

N. Stromberg, *Collective Security and American Foreign Policy: From the League of Nations to NATO* (New York, 1963) provocatively assesses past and present possibilities in preventing war by collective security. Donald F. Whitehead, "The Making of Foreign Policy During President Roosevelt's First Term, 1933–1937" (Ph.D. dissertation, University of Chicago, 1951) is thin.

On the period 1937–1941, Joseph Alsop and Robert Kintner, *American White Paper: The Story of American Diplomacy and the Second World War* (New York, 1940) is a brief, informal account with useful insights. Donald F. Drummond, *The Passing of American Neutrality, 1937–1941* (Ann Arbor, Mich., 1955) is excellent. The most comprehensive and thoughtful volumes, William L. Langer and S. Everett Gleason, *The Challenge to Isolation, 1937–1940* (New York, 1952) and *The Undeclared War, 1940–1941* (New York, 1953) show some commitment to the Roosevelt administration; nonetheless, they are wholly honest and reliable and superior to anything the administration's most bitter assailants have produced. Basil Rauch, *Roosevelt: From Munich to Pearl Harbor* (New York, 1950) is too uncritical and too much devoted to rebutting Charles A. Beard's *American Foreign Policy in the Making, 1932–1940* (New Haven, 1946) and *President Roosevelt and the Coming of the War, 1941* (New Haven, 1948). Beard, an early leader of the "revisionist" historians, sees a far more deceptive design in Roosevelt's pronouncements measured against his actions than there ever was. Similarly, Harry Elmer Barnes, ed., *Perpetual War for Perpetual Peace: A Critical Examination of the Foreign Policy of Franklin Delano Roosevelt and Its Aftermath* (Caldwell, Idaho, 1953) contains essays by nearly all the revisionist historians, who have generally misunderstood and misinterpreted what Roosevelt did and did not do. Charles Callan Tansill, *Back Door to War: The Roosevelt Foreign Policy, 1933–1941* (Chicago, 1952) distorts documents and events.

European diplomacy between the wars is surveyed generally, with hindsight but not without special claim to prescience and involvement, by Winston Churchill, *The Gathering Storm* (Boston, 1948), the first of six volumes in his *The Second World War*. Arthur H. Furnia, *The Diplomacy of Appeasement: Anglo-French Relations and the Prelude to World War II, 1931–1938* (Washington, D.C., 1960) is highly detailed and critical. Perhaps most controversial of all books about

European interwar diplomacy is A. J. P. Taylor, *The Origins of the Second World War* (London, 1961). Taylor merits serious attention: he shows how Hitler achieved traditional German demands through diplomatic improvisation at critical moments, and how British leaders concurred in Hitler's efforts to realize greater German ambitions. Taylor has caused many historians to look more closely at the way in which events actually developed. The book makes interesting reading contrasted with Taylor's earlier *The Course of German History: A Survey of the Development of German History Since 1815* (London, 1945).

In addition to analysis afforded in Taylor's works, German foreign and domestic policy are surveyed in Thomas L. Jarman, *The Rise and Fall of Nazi Germany* (New York, 1956) and William L. Shirer, *The Rise and Fall of the Third Reich: A History of Nazi Germany* (New York, 1960). Karl Dietrich Bracher, Wolfgang Sauer, and Gerhard Schulz, *Die nationalsozialistischer Machtergreifung: Studien zur Errichtung des totalitären Herrschaftssystems in Deutschland, 1933/34* (Cologne and Opladen, 1960) contains an excellent section by Bracher on the totalitarian tactics of Hitler's foreign policy in the first years of the Nazi regime and the implications of that policy for the future. Also helpful is Gordon A. Craig, "Totalitarian Approaches to Diplomatic Negotiation," in A. O. Sarkissian, ed., *Studies in Diplomatic History and Historiography in Honour of G. P. Gooch, C.H.* (London, 1961).

British foreign policy in the 1930's has been roundly criticized, oftentimes more because of the distorted political, economic, and social perspectives of the policy-makers than because of any ability or inability to wage "preventive" war. Martin Gilbert and Richard Gott, *The Appeasers* (Boston, 1963) contends that military and general war considerations did not dictate Chamberlain's policy at Munich; rather, appeasement was "an attempt to move closer to Germany, despite German domestic brutality and eastward expansion." Similarly, Margaret George, *The Warped Vision: British Foreign Policy, 1933–38* (Pittsburgh, 1965) scores the attitudes and assumptions of the Conservative appeasers, and the spendidly written memoir by A. L. Rowse, *Appeasement: A Study in Political Decline, 1933–39* (New York, 1961) is angry and caustic about conceit and stupidity among public figures in Britain. Equally unsparing of British foreign policy, and its makers, including Eden, is A. J. P. Taylor's *English History, 1914–1945* (New York and Oxford, 1965), vol. XV in Sir George Clark, ed., *The Oxford History of England.*

### United States–German Relations

Diplomatic relations between the United States and Germany before the outbreak of war in Europe have been examined in Joseph Engelbert Heindl, *Die diplomatischen Beziehungen zwischen Deutschland und den Vereinigten Staaten von Amerika, von 1933 bis 1939* (Ph.D. dissertation, University of Wurzburg, 1963 [privately printed, 1964?]), which treats the increasing hardening of attitudes between the two countries as German efforts at revision of the Versailles Treaty, and various domestic policies, became more brutal; and Joachim Remak, "Germany and the United States, 1933–1939" (Ph.D. dissertation, Stanford University, 1956) which is critical of German policy but also frequently peevish toward American resistance. Remak's study did not have benefit of the Department of State files, nor personal paper collections, nor *Foreign Relations* after the publication for the year 1935. In "Two German Views of the United States: Hitler and His Diplomats," *World Affairs Quarterly,* XXVIII (Apr. 1957), Remak contrasts the traditional German diplomatic assessment of the United States with the Nazi view. Gerhard Weinberg, "Hitler's Image of the United States," *American Historical Review,* LXIX (July 1964) surveys Hitler's incredible and contradictory racial perspective from 1919 to 1945.

The United States as a factor in German diplomacy and military strategy from the start of the war in Europe until its enlargement into world war in December 1941 is thoroughly analyzed in the excellent study by James W. Compton, *The Swastika and the Eagle: Hitler, the United States, and the Origins of World War II* (Boston, 1967). Compton concludes that Hitler was wholly unwilling or unable to comprehend the relation between war in the Atlantic and war in the Pacific, and did not know how to cope with the implications of American power. Saul Friedländer, *Hitler et les Etats-Unis (1939–1941)* (Geneva, 1963) reaches similar conclusions about Hitler's miscalculations concerning British and Soviet resistance and the meaning of American intervention. Still useful although superseded is H. L.

298 | BIBLIOGRAPHICAL ESSAY

Trefousse, *Germany and American Neutrality, 1939–1941* (New York, 1951). Trefousse's "Failure of German Intelligence in the United States, 1935–1945," *Mississippi Valley Historical Review,* XLII (June 1955) focuses on the wartime years and concludes that secret service reports were "singularly ineffective."

Two works concerned with Nazi propaganda are Alton Frye, *Nazi Germany and the American Hemisphere, 1933–1941* (New Haven and London, 1967) and O. John Rogge, *The Official German Report: Nazi Penetration, 1924–1942, Pan-Arabism, 1939–Today* (New York, 1961). The question of the effectiveness or real purport of Nazi propaganda remains moot. Probably it did the German cause more harm than good, as Joachim Remak concludes in his " 'Friends of the New Germany': The Bund and German-American Relations," *Journal of Modern History,* XXIX (Mar. 1957).

*Special Studies*

On the problem of collective security, there is the general work by Stromberg; critical developments in the first year of the New Deal are keenly analyzed in Robert A. Divine, "Franklin D. Roosevelt and Collective Security, 1933," *Mississippi Valley Historical Review,* XLVIII (June 1961), which concludes that Roosevelt carelessly opened the way to later, greater consequences by failing to fight against an impartial embargo.

American disarmament policy, with emphasis on naval conferences, is surveyed in Merze Tate, *The United States and Armaments* (Cambridge, Mass., 1948), while John W. Wheeler-Bennett, *The Pipe Dream of Peace: The Story of the Collapse of Disarmament* (New York, 1935) blames the United States for failing to take stronger initiative and greater responsibility at the Geneva conferences.

From the German point of view, Gerhard Meinck, *Hitler und die deutsche Aufrüstung, 1933–1937* (Wiesbaden, 1959) sees Hitler pressing for "equality of rights" to justify rearmament, the ultimate purpose of which was not the sovereign right of self-defense but aggression and territorial expansion. German military matters and politics are also examined at length in Walter Goerlitz, *History of the German General Staff, 1657–1945,* translated by Brian Battershaw (New York, 1953) and John W. Wheeler-Bennett, *The Nemesis of Power:*

*The German Army in Politics, 1918–1945,* rev. ed. (New York, 1964), which is highly critical of the military leaders for allegedly wishing to act against Hitler before war began but failing to do so. A highly sympathetic attitude toward the military "opposition" is put forward in the early and sketchy work by Hans Rothfels. *The German Opposition to Hitler: An Appraisal* (Hinsdale, Ill., 1948).

Concerning the matter of preventive war against Germany in 1933, Alexander Bregmann, "German Fears of Preventive War in 1933," *Poland and Germany,* II (Mar. 1958) feels it would have been possible to end Hitler's regime; Zygmunt J. Gasiorowski, "Did Pilsudski Attempt to Initiate a Preventive War in 1933?" *Journal of Modern History,* XXVII (June 1951) thinks Poland sought to use threats only to induce Germany to follow a peaceful path; and Wacław Jędrzejewicz, "The Polish Plan for a 'Preventive War' Against Germany in 1933," *Polish Review,* XI (Winter 1966) concludes that the French discouraged Pilsudski from undertaking the effort.

William Kamman, "The United States and the London Economic Conference of 1933" (Master's thesis, Indiana University, 1956) is adequate. Briefer published accounts are Jeannette P. Nichols, "Roosevelt's Monetary Diplomacy in 1933," *American Historical Review,* LVI (Jan. 1951), the chapters in Arthur M. Schlesinger, Jr.'s *The Coming of the New Deal,* and the recent sprightly account by Herbert Feis in his memoir-narrative, *1933.*

The economic ideas and policies of Hull appear in two essays by William R. Allen, "International Trade Philosophy of Cordell Hull, 1907–1933," *American Economic Review,* XLIII (Mar. 1953) and "Cordell Hull and the Defense of Trade Agreements Program, 1934–1940," in Alexander De Conde, ed., *Isolation and Security: Ideas and Interests in Twentieth Century American Foreign Policy* (Durham, N.C., 1957). More comprehensive are Grace Beckett, *The Reciprocal Trade Agreements Program* (New York, 1951) and Lloyd G. Gardner, *Economic Aspects of New Deal Diplomacy* (Madison, Wisc., 1964), the latter emphasizing the influence of older principles and traditions on New Deal foreign policy.

American financial involvements, some of which were illegal, with the Third Reich are discussed in Gabriel Kolko, "American Business and Germany, 1930–1941," *Western Political Quarterly,* XV (Dec. 1962). Roland N. Stromberg, "American Business and the Approach of War, 1935–1941," *Journal of Economic History,* XIII (Winter 1953) discusses the businessman's ambivalence: fear of war but refusal to surrender profits. Joseph Tenenbaum, *American Investments and Business Interest in Germany* (New York, [1939]), is a contemporary listing by a person who was outspoken and active in organizing boycotts of German goods. A good statistical compilation is United States Tariff Commission, *Foreign Trade and Export Controls in Germany* (Washington, D.C., 1942), which tabulates American trade with Germany. John Morton Blum, *From the Morgenthau Diaries: Years of Crisis, 1928–1938* (Boston, 1959), based largely on the meticulous Morgenthau diaries at the Roosevelt Library, gives a good account of Morgenthau's efforts—and struggles with the State Department—to retaliate against Germany by countervailing duties. Gilbert C. Fite, *George N. Peek and the Fight for Farm Parity* (Norman, Okla., 1954) recounts another of those interdepartment struggles, this time between Peek and the State Department over Peek's aborted barter scheme.

Germany's foreign trade and currency practices are in Allen Thomas Bonnell, *German Control over International Economic Relations* (Urbana, Ill., 1940), vol. XXVI in the Illinois Studies in the Social Sciences, and Edward Tenenbaum, *National Socialism vs. International Capitalism* (New Haven, 1942), which is a good analysis although the author's wartime spirit exudes. Special emphasis upon Schacht's role in the economic rehabilitation of Nazi Germany is given in Norbert Muhlen, *Schacht: Hitler's Magician, The Life and Loans of Dr. Hjalmar Schacht* (New York, 1939) and in the more thoroughly documented though poorly written work by Edward Norman Peterson, *Hjalmar Schacht: For and Against Hitler, A Political-Economic Study of Germany, 1923–1945* (Boston, 1954). Gerhard Weinberg, "Schachts Besuch in den USA im Jahre 1933," *Vierteljahrshefte für Zeitgeschichte,* XI (Apr. 1963) concludes Schacht neither made a good impression nor lessened the growing estrangement between the United States and Germany.

Robert A. Divine, *The Illusion of Neutrality* (Chicago, 1962) is a perceptive and comprehensive study of the making of American neutrality legislation and is critical of Roosevelt and his administration for failing to lead effectively against isolationist politicians. Wayne S. Cole, "Senator Key Pittman and American Neutrality Policies, 1933–

1940," *Mississippi Valley Historical Review,* XLVI (Mar. 1960) concludes that this chairman of the Senate Foreign Relations Committee,
in attitude and influence, personified American wavering between
"isolationism" and "internationalism." Isolationism in its intellectual
context is carefully explored in Manfred Jonas, *Isolationism in America, 1935–1941* (Ithaca, N.Y., 1966), and the problem of war, muni-
tions-makers, and neutrality is treated in two studies by John E. Wiltz:
"The Nye Committee Revisited," *The Historian,* XXIII (Feb. 1961)
and *In Search of Peace: The Senate Munitions Inquiry, 1934–36*
(Baton Rouge, La., 1963). Wiltz concludes that Nye's views were
more temperate than historians have contended and that his committee's work on the whole did the country more good than harm.

The problem of aid to persecuted minorities has always been difficult for the United States, especially during the 1930's. Cyrus Adler
and Aaron M. Margalith, *American Intercession in Behalf of Jews in
the Diplomatic Correspondence of the United States, 1840–1938* (New
York, 1943) is a documented narrative, chiefly press releases by the
State Department. Adler and Margalith revised this work under the
title *With Firmness in the Right: American Diplomatic Action Affecting the Jews, 1840–1945* (New York, 1946). Reviewing this edition
in the *Journal of Modern History,* XXII (Mar. 1950), 48–52, Leo L.
Honor has taken the authors to task for being far too polite and for
crediting the American government with doing a great deal, when in
fact it did little, even less than it could have. This contention is borne
out in an excellent study, Sheldon Spear, "The United States and the
Persecution of the Jews in Germany, 1933–1939" (Master's thesis,
Syracuse University, 1965). Wartime policy was no better, says
Dwight MacDonald, "Old Judge Hull and the Refugees," in his
*Memoirs of a Revolutionist: Essays in Political Criticism* (New York,
1957), and the recent work by Arthur D. Morse, *While Six Million
Died: A Chronicle of American Apathy* (New York, 1968).

German policy toward Jewish persons is covered in all its statistical
horror in the comprehensive work by Raul Hilberg, *The Destruction
of the European Jews,* rev. ed. (Chicago, 1967). Information on Jewish refugees is given in Kurt Grossman and Arieh Tartakower, *The
Jewish Refugee* (New York, 1960) and Donald Peterson Kent, *The
Refugee Intellectual: The Americanization of the Immigrants of 1933–
1941* (New York, 1953). For further primary and secondary ma-

terial, consult Philip Friedman and Jacob Robinson, *Guide to Jewish History under Nazi Impact* (New York, 1960).

Latin American policy appears in Edward O. Guerrant, *Roosevelt's Good Neighbor Policy* (Albuquerque, N.M., 1950) and Bryce Wood, *The Making of the Good Neighbor Policy* (New York, 1961), but more needs to be done, especially for the later thirties and forties, in economics and politics. Aspects of Nazi efforts are discussed in two chapters in Frye's *Nazi Germany and the Western Hemisphere.*

D. C. Watt, "The Anglo-German Naval Agreement of 1935: An Interim Judgment," *Journal of Modern History,* XXVIII (June 1956) concludes that the British gained neither political nor military advantage from the arrangement that condoned German rearmament. Brice Harris, Jr., *The United States and the Italo-Ethiopian Crisis* (Stanford, 1964) concludes that the American officials, although exceedingly cautious and limited by their neutrality legislation, tried to prod the British and French into being more resolute. Helpful too are Henderson Braddick, "A New Look at American Policy during the Italo-Ethiopian Crisis, 1935–1936," *Journal of Modern History,* XXXIV (Mar. 1962), which contends that Hull hoped to win British support in the Pacific by following their lead in this affair and thought that Mussolini eventually would give in to British pressure, and Robert A. Friedlander, "New Light on the Anglo-American Reaction to the Ethiopian War, 1935–1936," *Mid-America,* XLV (Apr. 1963). The attitude of Italian-Americans toward neutrality in this conflict is treated in John Norman, "Influence of Pro-Fascist Propaganda on American Neutrality, 1935–1936," in Dwight E. Lee and George E. McReynolds, eds., *Essays in History and International Relations in Honor of George Hubbard Blakeslee* (Worcester, Mass., 1949), and the problem of the embargo is discussed by the State Department's former adviser on international economic affairs, Herbert Feis, in his *Seen From E.A.: Three International Episodes* (New York, 1947). French complicity by way of giving Mussolini a "free hand" is suggested in William C. Askew, "The Secret Agreement Between France and Italy on Ethiopia, January 1935," *Journal of Modern History,* XXV (Mar. 1953) and D. C. Watt, "The Secret Laval–Mussolini Agreement on Ethiopia," *Middle East Journal,* XV (Winter 1961). Finally, Eden's unsuccessful effort to resolve the conflict in the summer of 1935 is discussed in Mario Toscano, "Eden's Mission to Rome on the Eve of the Italo-Ethiopian Conflict," in Sarkissian, ed., *Studies in Diplomatic History*.

The Spanish civil war has been examined from many points of view. In the context of Spanish politics, see Gabriel Jackson, *The Spanish Republic and the Civil War, 1931–1939* (Princeton, 1965). Hugh Thomas, *The Spanish Civil War* (New York, 1961) is an emotional yet objective account of the war. Dante A. Puzzo, *Spain and the Great Powers, 1936–1941* (New York, 1962) blames lack of French, and then British and American, aid for the destruction of the Republican regime. The shortcomings of American policy are set out in F. Jay Taylor, *The United States and the Spanish Civil War* (New York, 1956), and Allen Guttmann, *The Wound in the Heart: America and the Spanish Civil War* (New York, 1962) examines its impact and tensions—ideological, emotional, social. J. David Valaik, "Catholics, Neutrality, and the Spanish Embargo, 1937–1939," *Journal of American History*, LIV (June 1967) suggests that the Roosevelt administration may have overestimated Catholic support for Franco's cause. England's false hope that it might halt future German expansion by "localizing" the war, at the expense of the Spanish Republicans, is analyzed in Wm. Laird Kleine-Ahlbrandt, *The Policy of Simmering: A Study of British Policy During the Spanish Civil War, 1936–1939* (The Hague, 1962). David T. Cattell, *Soviet Diplomacy and the Spanish Civil War* (Berkeley, 1957) explains that the Soviet Union intervened after Germany did and with the hope of bringing about a coalition against future German expansion. Manfred Merkes, *Die deutsche Politik gegenüber dem spanischen Bürgerkrieg, 1936–1939* (Bonn, 1961) shows that Hitler did not conspire to bring about the civil war, committed himself firmly to aiding Franco only in November 1936, and continually found that the war was costing more men, money, and matériel than he cared to give.

Developments in the Far East, especially as the thirties wore on, were bound to have world-wide effects. Several full studies, of American and of German diplomacy, are extremely valuable. Dorothy Borg, *The United States and the Far Eastern Crisis, 1933–1938: From the Manchurian Incident Through the Initial Stage of the Undeclared Sino-Japanese War* (Cambridge, Mass., 1964), vol. XIV in Harvard East Asian Series, emphasizes American appeasement of Japan. Herbert Feis, *The Road to Pearl Harbor: The Coming of the War Between the United States and Japan* (Princeton, 1950) emphasizes patience in American policy, while Paul Schroeder, *The Axis Alliance and Japanese-American Relations, 1941* (Ithaca, N.Y., 1958) criticizes rigidity in American policy. Frank William Iklé, *German-Japanese Relations, 1936–1940* (New York, 1956), which is better on the Japanese side than the German, emphasizes the pursuit of power—real and imagined—in the Axis relationship; Ernst L. Presseisen, *Germany and Japan: A Study in Totalitarian Diplomacy, 1933–1941* (The Hague, 1958) is a balanced and detailed analysis which concludes that Germany lost a great deal and gained virtually nothing by reversing its traditional policy in Asia. The most masterful account of this alliance that had ironic and drastic consequences for both countries is Theo Sommer, *Deutschland und Japan zwischen den Mächten, 1935–1940: Vom Antikominternpakt zum Dreimächtepakt. Eine Studie zur diplomatischen Vorgeschichte des Zweiten Weltkriegs* (Tübingen, 1962). Gerhard L. Weinberg, "German Recognition of Manchuokuo," *World Affairs Quarterly,* XXVIII (July 1957) points to that decision of January 1938 as indicative of the aggressive direction in which German policy had been moving and would continue to move.

Roosevelt's "quarantine the aggressor" speech in October 1937 has been the subject of considerable evaluation. Dorothy Borg, "Notes on Roosevelt's 'Quarantine' Speech," *Political Science Quarterly,* LXXII (Sept. 1957) sees it as one of several "nebulous," ill-defined schemes of 1937–38 aimed at peacemaking without knowing how. John McV. Haight, Jr., "Roosevelt and the Aftermath of the Quarantine Speech," *Review of Politics,* XXIV (Apr. 1962) contends that the President backed off his proposal because neither Hull nor Congress supported it, the Nine Power Conference at Brussels was seeking to push the United States too far into the lead to halt Japanese expansion, and economic recession at home complicated matters. Nonetheless, Travis Beal Jacobs, "Roosevelt's Quarantine Speech," *The Historian,* XXIV (Aug. 1962) contends that public reception of the address was as much favorable as unfavorable, but that Roosevelt did not know what to do next.

The United States was not directly involved in the *Anschluss,* although Germany's brutal diplomacy served to further harden the American attitude. The European politics of that event are studied in

Gordon Brook-Shepherd, *The Anschluss* (Philadelphia, 1963) and Ulrich Eichstädt, *Von Dollfuss zu Hitler: Geschichte des Anschlusses Österreichs, 1933–1938* (Wiesbaden, 1955). Gerhard L. Weinberg, "The May Crisis, 1938," *Journal of Modern History,* XXIX (Sept. 1957) attributes part of the fear that Germany was about to attack Czechoslovakia to the recent crisis over Austria. A similar view is expressed in William V. Wallace, "The Making of the May Crisis of 1938," *Slavonic and East European Review,* XLI (June 1963).

The Munich Conference remains probably the single most controversial diplomatic event of the thirties. John W. Wheeler-Bennett, *Munich: Prologue to Tragedy* (London, 1948) remains a classic study of the misapplication of a policy of appeasement. Boris Celovsky, *Das Münchener Abkommen von 1938* (Stuttgart, 1958) concludes that Hitler ultimately intended aggression and that an essential cause of the Second World War was Chamberlain's failure to encourage Roosevelt's participation throughout 1938. Keith Eubank, *Munich* (Norman, Okla., 1963) contends that Chamberlain and Daladier lacked sufficient will, men, and armaments to fight. Lewis B. Namier, *Diplomatic Prelude, 1938–1939* (London, 1948) is extremely critical of Chamberlain for capitulating to Hitler. Andrew Rothstein, *The Munich Conspiracy* (London, 1958) argues vigorously that the British and French conspired to turn Hitler eastward against the Soviet Union; in a brief examination of American statements—chiefly those of Kennedy, Bullitt, and Hugh Wilson—Rothstein concludes that the United States made itself party to this policy. Bernadotte E. Schmitt, "Munich," *Journal of Modern History,* XXV (June 1953) concludes that both Chamberlain and Bonnet waged a similar policy to pay almost any price to Hitler in order not to have to fight; and Charles Webster, "Munich Reconsidered: A Survey of British Policy," *International Affairs,* XXXVII (Apr. 1961) determines that although no conclusion can be certain, England would have been better off fighting for the issues "so clearly revealed in 1938." William V. Wallace, "The Foreign Policy of President Benes in the Approach to Munich," *Slavonic and East European Review,* XXXIX (Dec. 1960) says that Beneš chose not to fight, and perhaps provoke general war, because he had determined to stick with the Western powers and hoped they would come to abandon their appeasement.

Two articles weigh the American contribution to this fateful conference. John McVickar Haight, Jr., "France, the United States, and the Munich Conference," *Journal of Modern History,* XXXII (Dec. 1960) says that Roosevelt moved Daladier further along the road to appeasement while meaning to encourage him to resist Hitler. M. Baturin, "The United States and Munich," *International Affairs* [Moscow], V (Apr. 1959) is a "cold war" approach to the subject; he insists that the United States participated in an Anglo-French deal to turn the fascist aggressors against the Soviet Union. His perception of United States intention and policy is as unsophisticated and conspiracy-oriented as has been that of some American revisionists.

*Biographies and Studies of Individual Statecraft*

Many leading international figures of this period have found biographers, though there are important gaps. The longest work on Roosevelt is Frank Freidel's projected nine-volume *Franklin D. Roosevelt*; the three volumes published to date, *Apprenticeship* (Boston, 1952), *Ordeal* (Boston, 1954), and *Triumph* (Boston, 1956), carry the story only to March 1933. The best single volume is James MacGregor Burns, *Roosevelt: The Lion and the Fox* (New York, 1956), critical of Roosevelt's failure to lead early in foreign affairs. Also good is Rexford Guy Tugwell, *The Democratic Roosevelt: A Biography of Franklin D. Roosevelt* (New York, 1957). John Gunther, *Roosevelt in Retrospect: A Profile in History* (New York, 1950) is adulatory and devotes only a few pages to foreign policy before 1940. Willard Range, *Franklin D. Roosevelt's World Order* (Athens, Ga., 1959) is not biography but an effort to systematize Roosevelt's thoughts. Arthur M. Schlesinger, Jr., devotes about a third of *The Coming of the New Deal* to biography of Roosevelt. Robert E. Sherwood, *Roosevelt and Hopkins: An Intimate History* (New York, 1948) has a few random comments on foreign policy before 1940.

Hitler and Chamberlain figure largely in all works dealing with the coming of war in Europe. Konrad Heiden, *Der Fuehrer: Hitler's Rise to Power,* translated by Ralph Manheim (Boston, 1944) is a fine analysis of Hitler's career and his relation to conditions in Germany through the Blood Purge in 1934. Alan Bullock, *Hitler: A Study in Tyranny,* rev. ed. (New York, 1962) remains the most incisive full-length biography. Taking into account the enormous outpouring of literature since his first edition (1952), Bullock argues that Hitler, improvising with uncanny ability, proceeded in terms of the objectives he set in *Mein Kampf*. E. M. Robertson, *Hitler's Pre-War Policy and Military Plans, 1933–1939* (London, 1963) pinpoints Hitler's aggressive intentions and improvisations. Elizabeth Wiskemann, *The Rome-Berlin Axis: A Study of the Relations Between Hitler and Mussolini*, rev. ed. (London, 1966) and D. C. Watt, "The Rome-Berlin Axis, 1936–1940: Myth and Reality," *Review of Politics* (Oct. 1960) probe the tensions and contradictions in the diplomacy of the dictators which determined their own and Europe's fate quite differently from their intentions or conceptions.

The two best works devoted solely to the British prime minister are the semiofficial, friendly but mildly critical Keith Feiling, *The Life of Neville Chamberlain* (London, 1946), and the touchingly written Iain Macleod, *Neville Chamberlain* (New York, 1961). Macleod plays up Chamberlain's progressive views on domestic matters and defends his diplomacy as a noble if unsuccessful effort to avert the general horror that war had to bring.

For introduction to many who helped determine American diplomacy in the thirties, see the informal and good book by Robert Bendiner, *The Riddle of the State Department* (New York, 1942) and Graham H. Stuart, *The Department of State: A History of Its Organization, Procedure, and Personnel* (New York, 1949). Donald F. Drummond, "Cordell Hull," in Graebner, ed., *An Uncertain Tradition* is incisive. Julius W. Pratt, *Cordell Hull*, 2 vols. (New York, 1964), vols. XII and XIII in *The American Secretaries of State* series, is favorable and mildly critical, but a thorough biography remains to be done. Richard Dean Burns, "Cordell Hull: A Study in Diplomacy, 1933–1941" (Ph.D. dissertation, University of Illinois, 1960), written without reference to the Hull papers, is critical of him for clinging too long to inapplicable precepts. Thomas C. Irvin, "Norman H. Davis and the Quest for Arms Control, 1927–1937" (Ph.D. dissertation, Ohio State University, 1963), praises Davis' persistent and high-minded efforts. There is no study of Phillips or Welles; the latter's papers unfortunately are unavailable.

Two views, slightly conflicting, are Franklin L. Ford, "Three Observers in Berlin: Rumbold, Dodd, and François-Poncet," in Craig and Gilbert, eds., *The Diplomats*, and Arnold A. Offner, "William E.

Dodd: Romantic Historian and Diplomatic Cassandra," *The Historian,* XXIV (Aug. 1962). Ford finds Dodd an even more ineffective diplomat, and poorer reporter, than his European colleagues. I believe Dodd was nearly as effective as he could have been under the conditions, and a more astute reporter than his ambassadorial colleagues, European and American. (See, for comparison, William W. Kaufmann, "Two American Ambassadors: Bullitt and Kennedy," in the same volume as Ford's essay.) Robert Dallek, "Roosevelt's Ambassador: The Public Career of William E. Dodd" (Ph.D. dissertation, Columbia University, 1964) is a favorable biographical view which praises Dodd's consistent progressivism when so many others despaired; favorable too is the same author's "Beyond Tradition: The Diplomatic Careers of William E. Dodd and George S. Messersmith, 1933–1938," *South Atlantic Quarterly,* LXVI (Spring 1967). Brief but useful is L. F. Gittler, "Ambassador Extraordinary," *Survey Graphic,* XXVII (July 1939); good historical perspective on Dodd as a "Historian of Democracy" is in Wendell Holmes Stephenson, *The South Lives in History: Southern Historians and Their Legacy* (Baton Rouge, La., 1955). Katharine Crane, *Mr. Carr of State: Forty-Seven Years in the Department of State* (New York, 1960) is an affectionate account of a man whose career was long but who had little influence on foreign policy. Beatrice Farnsworth, *William C. Bullitt and the Soviet Union* (Bloomington, Ind., and London, 1967), says that Bullitt's hatred of the Soviet Union and the Versailles Treaty blinded his judgment in 1938.

Several congressmen who influenced foreign policy have been studied at length. Wayne S. Cole, *Senator Gerald P. Nye and American Foreign Relations* (Minneapolis, 1962) emphasizes the decline of agricultural society as a major factor in the isolationist view. Fred L. Israel, *Nevada's Key Pittman* (Lincoln, Neb., 1963) underscores the special dangers in the congressional seniority system which could place a mediocre man totally unsuited for the job—who drank himself into frequent stupors—at the head of the Senate Foreign Relations Committee. Marian McKenna, *Borah* (Ann Arbor, Mich., 1961) is a sympathetic account of that steadfast isolationist.

The inglorious decline of Germany's professional diplomats under Hitler's dictatorial procedures and Ribbentrop's incursions has been surveyed in Paul Seabury, *The Wilhelmstrasse: A Study of German*

*Diplomats Under the Nazi Regime* (Berkeley, 1954). Briefer analyses are DeWitt C. Poole, "New Light on Nazi Foreign Policy," *Foreign Affairs,* XXV (Oct. 1946) and Gordon A. Craig, "The German Foreign Office from Neurath to Ribbentrop," in Craig and Gilbert, eds., *The Diplomats.* A critique of Craig's approach, which raises interesting questions about the real—or constitutionally desirable—independence of the Foreign Ministry, is offered in D. C. Watt, "The German Diplomats and the Nazi Leaders, 1933–1939," *Journal of Central European Affairs,* XV (July 1955). Two analyses praising the reports of the German ambassador to the United States are Manfred Jonas, "Prophet Without Honor: Hans Heinrich Dieckhoff's Reports from Washington," *Mid-America,* XLVII (July 1965) and Warren F. Kimball, "Dieckhoff and America: A German's View of German-American Relations, 1937–1941," *The Historian,* XXVII (Feb. 1965). Finally, a balanced reassessment of various diplomats and other German officials is offered in Eugene Davidson, *The Trial of the Germans: An Account of the Twenty-Two Defendants Before the International Military Tribunal at Nuremberg* (New York, 1966).

# INDEX

Adam Opel, 102
Adler, Cyrus, 60, 61; book by, 301
Adler, Selig: books by, 292; article by, 293
*Aeroplane,* 241
Airplanes, 72–73, 278
Allen, William R.: articles by, 299
Alsop, Joseph: book by, 295
American business: and Germany, 4, 5, 7n23, 66–67, 102–103, 147, 152; and Italian-Ethiopian war, 127–128. *See also* Aski marks; Countervailing duties
American Federation of Labor, 82
American Jewish Committee, 60; publications of, 287
American Jewish Congress, 60
Anglo-French talks, 247–248
Anglo-German Naval Agreement, 117–122, 132, 173, 277; bibliography on, 302
Anglo-Italian Agreement, 233
*Anschluss,* 88, 215, 229, 232, 236, 248; Germany and, 226–229; Great Britain and, 227–229; United States and, 234, 236, 238–239; bibliography on, 304–305. *See also* Austria
Anti-Comintern Pact, 170, 179, 186, 187, 195, 198; origins and significance, 163–165; and Brussels Conference, 198
Appeasement, 216, 277; Hull and, 115, 268; definitions of, 123, 276; and Hugh Wilson, 215; Chamberlain and, 220, 222, 225; Roosevelt and, 221, 233; Halifax and, 228–229, 230, 233; Hitler on, 259
Argentina, 168–169, 170
Arms embargo (1933), 36. *See also* Italian-Ethiopian war; Spanish civil war

Aschmann, Gottfried, 139
Askew, William C.: article by, 302
Aski marks, 147, 149, 151. *See also* Countervailing duties; Germany
Association of the Friends of the New Germany (German-American Bund), 85
Atherton, Ray, 33, 113, 142, 144
Attolico, Bernardo, 138, 270
*Auslandsorganisation,* 154
Austria, 92, 214, 277; and Dollfuss assassination, 98; Hitler and, 118, 186, 227, 229, 238; Mussolini and, 129, 176, 228; *Anschluss* with Germany, 226–227, 229; United States and, 226–227; Great Britain and, 227–229; Ickes and, 244
Avon, Earl of, *see* Eden, Anthony

Baker, Newton D., 55
Ban, John R.: thesis by, 294
Bankhead, William B., 217
Barnes, Harry E.: books by, 3, 295
Baturin, M.: article by, 306
Baynes, Norman H.: books by, 289
Beard, Charles A.: books by, 295
Beck, Josef, 113
Beck, Ludwig, 254–255, 291
Beckett, Grace: book by, 299
Bell, Golden W., 150
Beneš, Eduard: on Blood Purge, 97; on German rearmament and League of Nations, 113, 130–131; Daladier on government of, 248; Hugh Wilson visits, 251; Kennedy on, 252; Hitler on, 259, 263; rejects German demands, 262; and Roosevelt appeal (September 26, 1938), 263
Bennett, Edward W.: book by, 293
Berbusse, Edward J.: dissertation by, 294
Berchtesgaden, 226, 259–260

322 | INDEX

appointed foreign minister, 12; and Davis, 24n18; background, 30; and World Disarmament Conference negotiations, 30, 31, 32, 44, 45, 46, 47, 48, 51; and World Economic Conference, 41–42; and Jewish problems, 61; and Dodd, 74, 83, 204, 206; and trade negotiations, 94; and Simon, 110, 111; and Italian-Ethiopian war, 128; and Rhineland occupation, 137, 139; talk with Bullitt, 146; and Spanish civil war, 161; and German-Italian protocols, 162; sees Mussolini, 176; at November 5, 1937, cabinet meeting, 186; and Anti-Comintern Pact, 198; dismissed, 224; British view of, 225

Neutrality
And American policy: proposals (1933), 34–36; in Italian-Ethiopian war, 126–128; Roosevelt on, 132, 133, 134, 155–156; Hull on, 141; and Spanish civil war, 155–159; and Buenos Aires Conference, 169; and Panama Conference, 170; British proposals on, 179; after September 1939, 275; bibliography on, 300–301
And German policy: in Italian-Ethiopian war, 128–129; in Spanish civil war, 155; in Sino-Japanese war, 198

Neutrality Act: (August 1935), 126, 127; (February 1936), 130, 135, 141, 155, 158; (January 1936), 157; (May 1937), 180; (September 1939), 275

Nevins, Allan: book by, 294
New Burroughs Adding Machine Company, 64
"New Plan," 98
Newton, Walter H.: book by, 292
Nichols, Jeannette P.: article by, 299
Nine Power Treaty, 194, 199, 218. See also Brussels Conference
Nock, Albert Jay, 3
Nonrecognition, 163. See also Manchukuo
Non-Sectarian Anti-Nazi League, 61–62
Norman, John: article by, 302
NSDAP, see Nazi party
Nuremberg, 45; Nazi rallies at, 70, 71, 206, 207, 211–212, 255

Nuremberg Laws, 84
Nye, Gerald P.: and munitions investigation, 131; and embargo in Spanish civil war, 157, 158–159; attacks Dodd, 204; bibliography on, 301, 308
Nye Committee, see Nye, Gerald P.

O'Brien, John P., 60
Oil, 102, 127–128. See also Italian-Ethiopian war
Oliphant, Herman, 148
Oshima, Hiroshi, 163
Owen, Robert, 3

Pact of Steel, 202, 273
Panama, Declaration of, 170
Panay, 212. See also Sino-Japanese war
Papen, Franz von, 30, 47, 51, 224; memoir of, 290
Paris Peace Conference, 3, 6. See also Versailles, Treaty of
Pasvolsky, Leo: book by, 293
Paul-Boncour, Joseph, 30–31, 42
Pearl Harbor, 203
Peek, George N., 99–102; bibliography on, 300
Pell, Robert, 93
Perkins, Dexter: article by, 292
Permanent Court of International Justice, see World Court
Perth (Eric Drummond), Lord, 270, 271
Peterson, Edward N., 80; book by, 300
Philip of Hesse, Prince, 227
Phillips, William, 129, 174, 191, 265, 279; on Davis, 21; and disarmament negotiations, 31; and boycott movement, 61; on J. T. Robinson speech, 64; and Nuremberg rallies, 70–71; on Roosevelt speech (December 1933), 75; on German debt settlement, 77; and Dickstein resolution, 81; and Messersmith, 96; and Peek proposals, 101; and Roosevelt's boycott proposals, 105, 106; and German rearmament, 114; and Rhineland occupation, 144; and Ciano, 184, 185, 224; and Italian-Ethiopian war, 187, 191n61; on Berchtesgaden Conference, 260; and Roosevelt appeal to Mussolini,